LONG NARRATIVE SONGS FROM NORTHEAST TIBET

Long Narrative Songs from the Mongghul of Northeast Tibet

Texts in Mongghul, Chinese, and English

Translated by Limusishiden
Edited and with an Introduction by Gerald Roche

https://www.openbookpublishers.com

The University of Melbourne supported this Open Access publication.

World Oral Literature Series, vol. 8 | ISSN: 2050-7933 (Print); 2054-362X (Online)

ISBN Paperback: 978-1-78374-383-4
ISBN Hardback: 978-1-78374-384-1
ISBN Digital (PDF): 978-1-78374-385-8
ISBN Digital ebook (epub): 978-1-78374-386-5
ISBN Digital ebook (mobi): 978-1-78374-387-2
DOI: 10.11647/OBP.0124

Cover image: Golden Field (Nyingchi, Tibet, 2013) by Momo, CC BY 2.0, Flickr, http://bit.ly/2sPkbnr. Cover design: Anna Gatti

All paper used by Open Book Publishers is SFI (Sustainable Forestry Initiative), PEFC (Programme for the Endorsement of Forest Certification Schemes) and Forest Stewardship Council(r)(FSC(r) certified.

Printed in the United Kingdom, United States, and Australia
by Lightning Source for Open Book Publishers (Cambridge, UK)

Contents

Acknowledgements

Limusishiden would like to thank Jugui for her invaluable assistance in preparing the manuscript by typing the Chinese and Mongghul texts.

Gerald Roche acknowledges the financial support of the Australian Research Council for the Discovery Early Career Research Award project DE150100388 (Ethnicity and Assimilation in China: The Case of the Monguor in Tibet), which supported him while writing the introduction and editing this book. He also thanks Timothy Thurston for reading and commenting on a draft of the Introduction.

Authors' Biographies

Li Dechun (李得春, Limusishiden) is a native Mongghul from Huzhu Tu (Mongghul) Nationality Autonomous County. He currently works in Qinghai University Affiliated Hospital, Qinghai Province, as a chief surgeon. He has been researching and writing about Mongghul traditional culture since 1989.

Gerald Roche is currently a Discovery Early Career Research Award Fellow at the University of Melbourne's Asia Institute. He is an anthropologist, and researches linguistic and cultural diversity in Tibet. Gerald's publications include Introduction: The Transformation of Tibet's Language Ecology in the Twenty-first Century. *International Journal of the Sociology of Language,* 245 (2017): 1–35. The Mangghuer Nadun: Village Ritual and Frontier History on the Northeast Tibetan Plateau, in *The Silk Road*: *Interwoven History*, Vol. 1: *Long-distance Trade, Culture, and Society*, ed. by M. N. Walter and J. P. Ito-Adler (Cambridge: Cambridge Institutes Press, 2015), pp. 310–47.

Preface

Mark Turin

The World Oral Literature Series was established to serve two primary goals. First, by publishing original research through a range of innovative digital platforms, the series is changing the shape, format and reach of academic publishing in the fast-growing disciplines of anthropology and linguistics, and connecting this important scholarship with a distributed global readership. Launched in 2012 with a new edition of Ruth Finnegan's remarkable *Oral Literature in Africa*,[1] and celebrating its eighth volume with this publication, the breadth and quality of the scholarship in this series has made the study of oral literature more accessible. Second, a welcome consequence of the approach to knowledge distribution taken by the World Oral Literature Series and our partners at Open Book is the amplification of collaborative publishing partnerships between Indigenous intellectuals and outside scholars that more traditional academic imprints have been less able to support. The cooperation between Dr. Li Dechun—a Mongghul surgeon and established scholar—and anthropologist Gerald Roche is a case in point; and these trilingual texts in Mongghul, Chinese, and English, in the form of *Long Narrative Songs from the Mongghul of Northeast Tibet*, offer a rich lesson in the lasting value of respectful collaboration.

Through Limusishiden and Roche's partnership, the reader is treated to a selection of songs collected on the northeast Tibetan Plateau

---

1   Freely available at https://doi.org/10.11647/OBP.0025

of western China, among the Mongghul of the Seven Valleys. Each one of the seven long songs is a cultural accomplishment of the highest order in the Mongghul oral tradition, full of insights into the aspirations of a community and the challenges that its members face. Alongside tales of love, valor and kin relations, the songs also bear witness to the impressive plurilingual repertoire of Mongghul singers, Marshaling Tibetan, Mongghul and Chinese in one breath with agility and dexterity.

> *Mongghul khan's descendants,*
> *Singing special Mongghul songs,*
> *This is our Mongghul custom,*
> *We joyfully make our lives,*
> *Mongghul lives will be prosperous,*
> *We keep our Mongghul customs,*
> *And keep speaking our Mongghul language.*

In his introduction, Roche situates these Mongghul texts in their traditional social context, and provides helpful insights into the practices of multilingualism that have reinforced linguistic diversity in Tibet. The Tibetan Plateau has long been a site of great linguistic variation and intense language contact, and Roche is careful to introduce the reader to key concepts such as translanguaging, superdiversity, and a more nuanced reading of plurilingualism (in marriage, monasteries, and music) to help us to better make sense of contemporary language use in Tibet. Roche argues that it is through oral literature, and particularly through song, that language contact takes place, and that 'languages were interwoven in the praxis of individuals' in ways that helped constitute the emergence of the Amdo linguistic area.

Theory and ethnography are not always happy bedfellows. Struggles between emic and etic perspectives, particularly in collaborative undertakings such as this publication, can destabilize and even derail a carefully constructed cooperation. Roche addresses this tension head on, noting that

> the translator of the materials collected in this volume, Limusishiden, clearly views Mongghul as an independent language, and the endeavor to work towards its differentiation and elaboration is clearly an important motive for him; to speak of Mongghul as something other than a differentiated language would be to undermine the translator's intentions in making these materials available.

While not entirely defusing these representational and political challenges, Roche mitigates them by proposing an approach to plurilingualism and translanguaging that positions the linguistic area of northeast Tibet as 'super-diverse': not only were many languages spoken, but the region was home to a variety of social groups each of whom had different plurilingual repertoires and distinct translanguaging praxis.

Given Tibet's rich linguistic tapestry and cultural complexity, it is particularly fitting that *Long Narrative Songs from the Mongghul of Northeast Tibet* offers the reader three distinct points of linguistic entry: through Mongghul, Chinese and English. These three discrete pathways to knowledge help to generate the very access and connection to which our colleagues at Open Book Publishers are so committed: facilitating, for example, an American reader to order a hardback print copy to read on a train, a Chinese student to engage with the text through the web, or a Mongghul scholar to download the entire volume as a PDF. In short, the linguistic plurality of these beautiful narrative songs is matched by a diversity of access points and platforms by which the reader can discover the content. This synergy is what makes this wonderful volume an open book.

> *Heaven's gate was closed,*
> *This year's smoke from burning juniper twigs was rising into the sky,*
> *The smoke burst Heaven's gates open,*
> *And the gatekeeper found that the gate was opened.*

Traditional, ancestral and unceded Musqueam Territory,
Vancouver, BC, Canada.
August 2017.

Introduction

Translanguaging in Song: Orature and Plurilingualism in Northeast Tibet

Gerald Roche

The present work contains a selection of songs collected amongst the Mongghul of the Seven Valleys, on the northeast Tibetan Plateau, in western China. In this introduction, I examine how this collection of texts, and an understanding of their traditional social context, provides insights into the practices of multilingualism that supported linguistic diversity in Tibet (Roche 2014, 2017; Roche and Suzuki 2017). In particular, I feel that these songs may provide fresh insight into the ways in which orature,[1] specifically music, provided a forum for language contact, and may have contributed to the formation of a local linguistic area.

---

1   Thiong'o (2007:4) defines orature as 'the use of utterance as an aesthetic means of expression', and traces the term's origin to the Ugandan linguist, Pio Zirimu. Finnegan (2010) provides background on the debate surrounding the term 'orature' as an alternative to 'oral literature'.

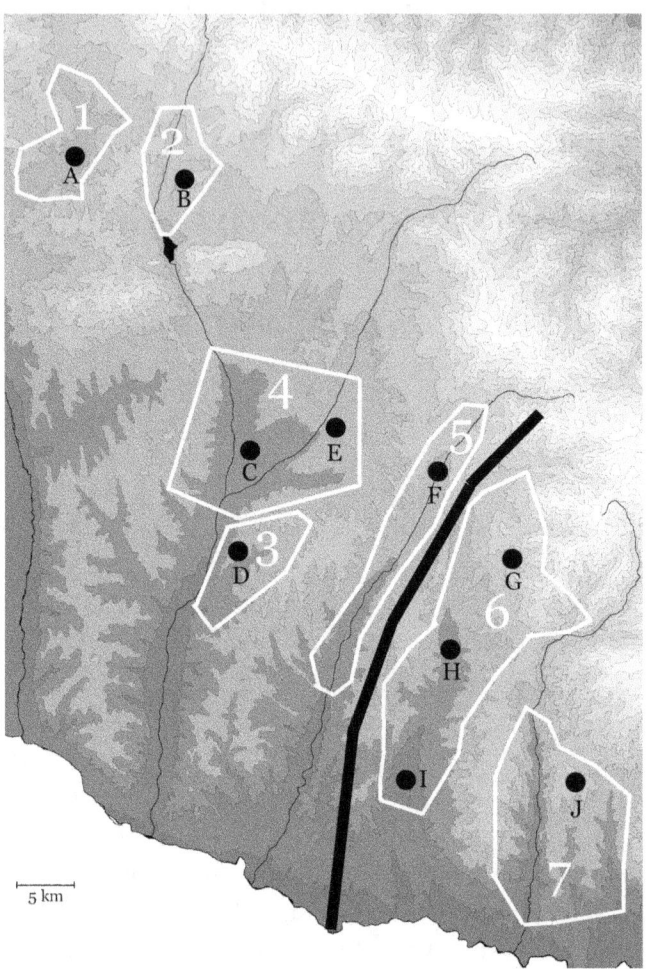

The Seven Valleys: 1. Saishigu valley; 2. Shde Qurizang valley; 3. Naringhuali valley; 4. Tangraa and Shgeayili valleys; 5. Darimaa valley; 6. Wuxi valley; 7. Shdazi valley. Letters show modern towns, all in Huzhu County, except A, in Datong County, and J, in Ledu County: A. Dongxia Township; B. Nanmengxia Town; C. Weiyuan Town, the capital of Huzhu County; D. Donghsan Township; E. Donggou Township; F. Danma Town; G. Dgon lung Monastery; H. Wuxi Town; I. Hongyazigou Township; J. Dala Township. The thick black line separates the two regions of the Duluun Lunkuang: Fulaan Nara (right) and Haliqi (left). Altitude ranges from 2200m (darkest) to 4200m, with each shade representing a change of 200m in altitude. The southern border of the shaded area is the Huang River. Map by Gerald Roche, CC BY 4.0.

The existence of a linguistic area on the northeast Tibetan Plateau is well documented (Tas 1966; Nugteren and Roos 1996; Nugteren and Roos 1998; Dede 2003; Slater 2003; Faehndrich 2007; Janhunen *et al.* 2007; Sandman 2012; Dwyer 2013; Simon 2015; Sandman and Simon 2016). Within this area, languages of numerous, divergent genetic stock, including Tibetic, Mongolic, Turkic, and Sinitic, have been in intense contact over a relatively long period of time. This contact has resulted in the exchange of linguistic features — lexical, syntactic, and phonetic — as well as other forms of contact-induced change. The Tibetic Amdo language functioned as a 'model' language in this context, meaning that it had greater and more unidirectional influence on the region's other languages (Sandman and Simon 2016). This suggests that a constellation of languages (Calveat 2006) existed within the region, with Amdo serving as a central language, and other languages occupying more peripheral positions in the language ecology, meaning that their interactions with each other were likely to be less intense than their interactions with Amdo (though interactions amongst these languages did occur, see, for example, Sandman 2012). Research by Janhunen (2005) and Dede (2003) has also given a temporal dimension to our understanding of the Amdo linguistic area, suggesting that Turkic forms the oldest language stratum, followed by Tibetic, Mongolic, and Sinitic.[2]

This view of Amdo as a linguistic area, currently the predominant stance amongst Anglophone scholars, relies on a model that treats languages as discrete entities which, whilst capable of exchange and interaction, are nonetheless clearly differentiated linguistically, spatially, and demographically. In this perspective, individual bilingualism or multilingualism exists as command of basically equivalent communicative codes, typically considered to be both written and spoken. Individuals are considered to have a componential linguistic repertoire consisting of multiple languages, each of which is clearly separable from the others and can essentially be used interchangeably to the same ends, depending on context. We might think of, for example, a bilingual resident of Delhi who speaks, reads, and writes Hindi in Delhi, but uses English when doing business in Utah, or an Italian of Arabic descent who speaks Arabic at home and Italian at work, and watches

---

2   A more accurate sequence would be Turkic, Tibetic, Mongolic (Shirongolic), Turkic, Sinitic, Mongolic (Oirat).

Arabic TV at home with her family whilst watching Italian movies in the cinema with her friends. In this framework, societal bilingualism and multilingualism are thought to equate to the maintenance of multiple, distinct languages in a sociopolitical space. In this case, we might think about Switzerland as a multilingual country where French, Italian, German, and Romanch are spoken, or marvel at the 251 languages spoken in Melbourne. Diversity, in this perspective, is considered as the sum total of languages in a place. These views of individual and social multilingualism are then extended into the past, providing a model of linguistic history as essentially the interaction between languages over time, typically in terms of distinct populations that are considered either monolingual or dominant in a particular language. We might, for example, consider the history of the English language according to the various influences of Celtic-, Latin-, and French-speaking populations, or the history of minority and regional languages in France as being gradually replaced by French.

Sociolinguists are increasingly critical of such perspectives on language, multilingualism, and (to a lesser extent) historical linguistics. Over the past thirty years, they have assembled a toolkit of alternative concepts for thinking about languages, individual and social multilingualism, and linguistic history. Makoni and Pennycook (2007), for example, advocate an approach of 'disinventing languages', encouraging us to see languages as non-natural, institutional constructs that have been created to meet specific ideological goals in particular regimes of power. What constitutes a language is therefore context-bound and subject to change—a 'convenient fiction' in Haugen's words (1972). Authors such as Garcia and Kleyn (2016) have extended such perspectives into the study of individual multilingualism, advocating a focus on 'translanguaging'—the process by which individuals assemble unique repertoires of linguistic resources, which form a non-componential whole. This perspective encourages us to transcend 'the two named languages of bilinguals... and to think of bilinguals/ multilinguals as individuals with a single linguistic system... that society... calls two or more named languages' (Garcia and Kleyn 2016:10). In amplifying this perspective on language to the macrosocial level, sociolinguists such as Arnaut, Blommaert, Rampton, and Spotti

(2011) have begun characterizing social contexts as linguistically 'superdiverse'—characterized by an unprecedented 'level and kind of complexity' (Vertovec 2007:1024), which cannot be described simply in terms of the number of languages, but must be examined in terms of the numerous ways of 'languaging' employed by people in a given context. Meanwhile, Canagarajah and Liyanage (2012) have projected these critical, post-structural sociolinguistic perspectives into the past, to explore 'pre-colonial multilingualism'. They see 'pre-colonial' contexts as being not only more diverse, but diverse in fundamentally different ways. They contrast this view with traditional multilingualism by referring to 'pre-colonial' situations as 'plurilingual', a term which 'allows for the interaction and mutual influence of... languages in a more dynamic way' than multilingualism, which 'keeps languages distinct' (Canagarajah and Liyange (2012:50). Critical, post-structural sociolinguistics therefore offers insights into our view of languages as entities, of individual and social multilingualism, as well as the nature of linguistic history, all of which are united by a common focus on the praxis of individuals rather than demographic patterns formed by social collectives.

I will use the concepts of translanguaging, superdiversity, and plurilingualism to provide a new perspective on language use in Tibet, which might help us to understand the practices that not only maintained the diversity of the region, but also gave rise to the structuring of this diversity into linguistic areas. I argue that the Amdo linguistic area emerged not as a result of long-standing interactions between basically monolingual populations but through the ways that languages were interwoven in the praxis of individuals. This collection of Mongghul orature provides a unique opportunity to undertake such a task, because, as I argue below, orature, particularly song, was one of the key venues through which language contact took place. Temporally, my discussion of these issues focuses on the recent 'pre-colonial' past, prior to the establishment of the People's Republic of China. My sources for this discussion include ethnographic accounts from the early twenty-first century (Schram 2006 [1954, 1957, 1961]), contemporary ethnographic accounts (Limusishiden 2008, 2015), and a piece of creative non-fiction, *Passions and Colored Sleeves: Mongghul Lives in Northeastern Tibet* (Limusishiden and Jugui 2012).[3] Finally, videos of Mongghul orature performances, filmed primarily in the early twenty-first century and available online, were also consulted (see Appendix 1).

My exploration of Mongghul languaging practices and orature through the concepts of translanguaging, superdiversity, and plurilingualism comes with one caveat. Namely, I employ these terms whilst avoiding the incitement to 'disinvent' languages as distinct, differentiated objects, and will thus seek a rapprochement across the theoretical divide between multilingualism and its post-structuralist critics, for two reasons. First, in examining the texts presented in the volume, we find ample evidence that languages were considered, or at least spoken about, as if they were discrete, independent, and stable. The fluid, mutable, fuzzy logic of post-structuralism might, in some ways, more accurately describe linguistic realities; however, in this case, it also does ontological violence to the worldview expressed by these texts, which not only posits discrete languages, but also assigns social significance to these differentiated codes. A second reason, which I return to in the Conclusion, is that the translator of the materials collected in this volume, Limusishiden, clearly views Mongghul as an independent language, and the endeavor to work towards its differentiation and elaboration is clearly an important motive for him; to speak of Mongghul as something other than a differentiated language would be to undermine the translator's intentions in making these materials available.

Recent work by Singer and Harris (2016) has employed a similar approach, seeking to acknowledge Indigenous views of languages as discrete and differentiated, while also examining individual and social multilingualism beyond traditional sociolinguistic frameworks. Specifically, they engage with literature on 'small-scale', 'traditional', or 'egalitarian' multilingualism—the maintenance of multiple languages in social contexts where functional specificity of different codes is not maintained (as in classical models of diglossic multilingualism). They describe such contexts as being defined by the following features: 1)

---

3   This narrative, based on interviews with residents of the Seven Valleys, follows the fortune of a single family over the course of the twentieth century, and contains rich details of daily life in the area, including details of languaging practices, as well as numerous, contextualized examples of orature.

multiple languages with small numbers of speakers; 1) universal or widespread individual multilingualism; 3) obligatory or preferential linguistic exogamy; and 4) multilingualism within households. This suite of features, they argue, make classical notions of the maintenance of multilingualism through diglossia and 'domain specificity' inapplicable. And whilst the case of the Mongghul, and the context of the Amdo linguistic area more broadly, do not fit Singer and Harris's criteria for 'small-scale' multilingualism, nonetheless their work is relevant in that it highlights the extent to which classical models of multilingualism, derived primarily from European nation-state contexts, need to be iterated to fit other social, political, and historical contexts. With this in mind, I turn to the question of how the Mongghul practiced plurilingualism, and the unique role that orature and oracy[4] played therein.

Classically conceived social multilingualism, where individuals have full communicative command of multiple codes, did exist in some Mongghul communities. For example, the Mongghul singer Lamuzhaxi states (Limusishiden 2015:84-85) that:

> Mongghul, Tibetan, and Chinese people live mixed together in my village… In my childhood, I spoke Mongghul with Mongghul children and Tibetan with Tibetan children when we played together in village lanes or herded on the high slopes. By doing this, I learned Tibetan. I rarely played with Chinese children, so my Chinese language, including my reading and writing, was mostly learned in school…

Far more common, however, was plurilingualism that was largely restricted to three contexts — marriage, monasteries, and music — only one of which (marriage) involved what we might consider 'communicative command' of a language, and even then, only the spoken form. Examining these three contexts will show how language contact in the Seven Valleys, and the formation of a larger linguistic area in northeast Tibet, was primarily constituted through gendered translanguaging practices and the construction of individual plurilingual repertoires.

Marriage amongst the Mongghul, as with most groups in northeast Tibet, appears to have been preferentially endogenous. Marriage

---

4   The term 'oracy' refers to competence in oral media, in the same way that literacy refers to competence in written media (Wilkinson 1970).

between linguistic groups did occur, but was generally considered hypogamous—a form of downward social mobility—and was therefore uncommon, while strong proscriptions existed regarding marriage between Muslims and non-Muslims. Women who married into a household that spoke another language typically shifted to the household language, and although they might have spoken their natal language to their children, offspring typically obtained only passive fluency, and so such women's opportunities to use their natal tongue *in conversation* were limited after marriage. Women who married outside their language group can be said to have experienced 'life-cycle bilingualism', speaking one language in their childhood, and another in their adulthood. For these individuals, opportunities to speak their natal tongue were limited to occasional, typically annual, visits to their parents' home, their birthplace. Participation in this life-cycle bilingualism was gendered, since although men did marry out, they did so far less frequently than women: linguistically exogenous marriage of men was perhaps the least desired form of marriage for most groups in northeast Tibet.

Limusishiden and Jugui's *Passions and Colored Sleeves* provides some insights into women's inter-language marriages in the early twentieth century. They relate the story of Zhualimaxji, a Mongghul woman who, after disputes with her husband's family, returns to her natal home, only to encounter further conflicts, this time with her brother's wife. She therefore goes into self-imposed exile, wandering to distant villages, begging, looking for somewhere to make a new life. She eventually comes to a village where Chinese is spoken, a language she cannot speak or understand. She meets a villager as he is cooking dinner at a mill which he operates, and tries to beg some food from him, speaking Mongghul, but he cannot understand her. The two nonetheless manage to communicate via gestures, and Zhualimaxji then stays with the man for several days, before wandering off to beg again. Zhualimaxji then learns some Chinese during her travels, and when she later returns to the miller's home she is able to communicate with him. She moves in and they 'become a family'. At the book's conclusion, the authors of the novel go to visit the real-life Zhualimaxji, and find that although she has lived in a Chinese-speaking village for most of her life (they meet her at the age of 87), she is still able to communicate in Mongghul.

When asked how it is that she could still speak her natal tongue, she replies, 'How could I forget? I would not forget it if I lived another sixty years' (Limusishiden and Jugui 2012:269). Nonetheless, it is made clear that her children speak Chinese. Although Zhualimaxji's experience of flight and exile are by no means typical, they do capture the nature of the life cycle bilingualism that some Mongghul women experienced, switching language, more or less permanently, when they married into their husband's home.

Beyond marriage, a second significant venue of plurilingualism was the monastery. This context primarily involved males and, for the most part, did not involve alternating languages according to different stages in the life cycle.[5] Mongghul participation in formal institutions of Tibetan Buddhism was significant. Rgulang Monastery was a large and politically significant institution at the heart of the Seven Valleys and, at its peak, probably housed around 2,000 monks, mostly from the Seven Valleys (Sullivan 2013, 2015).

Rgulang Monastery (2010). Photo by Brenton Sullivan, CC BY 4.0.

---

5   To the best of my knowledge, there were no nunneries in the Seven Valleys, though there are likely to have been some Mongghul nuns in nunneries elsewhere.

Several other monasteries were scattered throughout the Seven Valleys, and Mongghul monks also travelled to live in other monasteries, for example in Hgunbin Monastery near Xining, and Yonghe Monastery in Beijing. Every Mongghul household strove to have at least one monk amongst its members, if possible. Therefore, although no statistics exist, it seems fair to say that a large proportion of the male Mongghul population was involved in monasticism; Samuel's (1993:582) estimate that the population of monks in Tibet 'would seem to have been in the region of 10 percent to 12 percent' is perhaps the closest we can get to an estimate of the monastic population of the Seven Valleys.

We know very little about the languaging practices within Tibetan Buddhist monasteries. In monasteries like Hgunbin, where monks spoke numerous languages (at least Amdo, Mongghul, Mangghuer, Oirat, and Halh), some form of Tibetan was likely to have been used as a lingua franca. In monasteries like Rgulang, however, where the majority of monks were Mongghul speakers, anecdotal evidence seems to suggest that Mongghul was used in monks' everyday life. As Limusishiden and Jugui (2011:60-61) report, 'Of the several hundred mostly Mongghul monks in the monastery, few could speak Tibetan well. They used Mongghul in their daily lives, and only used Tibetan when chanting scriptures.'

Regardless of which language was used for daily communication, monks in all monasteries spent large amounts of time reading and reciting scriptures in written Tibetan. Memorization of a text, and its correct enunciation through chanting, were the focus of such exercises, rather than comprehension. This is because rather than being primarily considered vessels for meaning, scriptures were predominantly props for the transformation of reality via sonic means (Ekvall 1964, Thurston 2012). Accurate and melodious recitation of a text was considered efficacious, having the capacity to create prosperity, remove obstacles to fortune, and even improve one's karmic storage, future births, and progression towards enlightenment. Foley (2002:72), drawing on the work of Klein (1994), describes the role of texts in this situation as 'vehicles for creating a holistic acoustic experience, not visual keys to revelatory thought'. Mongghul monks in monasteries therefore would have chiefly focused on memorizing and chanting texts in order to maximize their efficacy, which primarily required a fluid, sonorous delivery, rather than intimate understanding of content.

In addition to chanting, monks in certain monasteries, such as Rgulang, also participated in debates in Tibetan.[6] As with scriptural recitation, however, participation in debates largely relied on the memorization rather than comprehension or analysis of text (Lempert 2012). A debater's skill lay primarily in knowing which piece of memorized text to deploy at which moment in the debate, rather than synthesizing a novel answer to an opponent's questions, based on an analytical understanding of scripture.[7]

For most Mongghul monks, at least those who stayed in monasteries in the Seven Valleys, bilingualism appears to have taken the form of translanguaging that involved the memorization of chunks of Tibetan language, encoded in text, and their deployment in specific ritual and performative contexts, rather than command of a spoken language that was used for communication. The written language, moreover, was used primarily as an aid to memory—a prop for recitation—and there was probably little to no expectation that monks would attain any significant competency in producing the written language beyond writing words and copying texts (as opposed to composing original texts). The translanguaging of Mongghul monks was essentially a form of text-mediated oracy which provided them with a plurilingual repertoire that included elements of spoken Mongghul and recited written Tibetan.

This phenomenon of text-mediated plurilingual oracy extended to the lay population to some extent, with recitation of Tibetan and Sanskrit mantra being one of the most common aspects of Mongghul lay religious practice. The extent to which this saturated daily life in the Seven Valleys can be seen in the following passage from the missionary Louis Schram, whose discussion of the use of the mantra *Om mani padme*

---

6   Brenton Sullivan (personal communication) notes that within the vicinity of the Seven Valleys, the following monasteries had philosophical colleges, and therefore probably also held debates: Gser khog, Chu bzang, Stong shags bkra shis chos gling, Mchod rten thang, The thung dgon chen, The thung brag, The thung rdo rje 'brag, The thung dgon chung, Se rtsud chu lung, and Sems nyid.

7   An interesting parallel to this is the nature of improvisation in the singing of Tibetan songs, particularly *layi* (*la gzhas*), 'love songs'. Skal bzang nor bu (2015:4) describes how singers needed to have 'a rich database of memorized lyrics' which they would 'improvise for a given situation by modifying the lyrics, using similar patterns or elements'. As with debate, we see here a form of improvisation by the reorganization of components, rather than through spontaneous creation.

hum was based on observations of Mongghul life in the early twentieth century (Schram 2006:286-87):

> *Om Mani Padme H'um...* is repeated by old and young, both men and women, hundreds of times a day, under all circumstances. The mind of the Monguor appears to be fixed on religion in a most unusual way. Mothers, kissing and cuddling their babies, like to say happily, over and over, 'Om Mani', 'Om Mani', as if thanking Buddha (Avalokita) for the baby. The sick... find relief in sighing *Om Mani* the whole day, hoping to be cured. When hailstorms threaten crops, *Om Mani* will be said hundreds of times by every terrified farm family, in the hope that Buddha will make the wind change the course of the clouds. When someone in the village dies, all the villagers gather at night in the courtyard of the deceased, where they sit for many hours saying the *Om Mani* for the deceased... A farmer becoming angry at the lazy oxen, while plowing his fields, will beat them and swear furiously with a well-articulated *Om Mani*; gamblers, on losing the game, their patience wearing thin, will say *Om Mani* in a blasphemous tone. While weeding fields, if a lascivious song is enjoyed, farmers say *Om Mani*, meaning the song is well sung. When a smutty joke is told, listeners will say *Om Mani*, laughing, to indicate it is a good joke. It is said that thieves and robbers say *Om Mani* as an aid to their practice of larceny. Foreign travelers jest that, if robbers kill their victim, he will have the consolation, when dying, of hearing the killer saying *Om Mani*. *Om Mani* can be and is offered under all circumstances: riding horseback, working in the fields or at home, while laughing, gambling, singing, conducting business, and even sleeping.

Not only was this short Sanskritic formula an integral part of daily life, but much longer texts were recited in Tibetan on a daily basis by Mongghul people, sometimes with the use of manuscripts as aids, but often not. To some extent, there was a life-cycle element to this praxis, with elders spending more time chanting than adults and youths. Lamuzhaxi highlights the extent to which chanting can basically become a fulltime occupation for Mongghul elders (Limusishiden 2015:86):

> I get up at seven o'clock in the morning... After washing my face, I sit down on the bed and chant Buddhist scriptures while I drink my morning tea. After I eat bread for my breakfast, I continue chanting Buddhist scriptures while other family members go to work in the fields... After lunch, I chant Buddhist scriptures until I go to bed at about nine o'clock in the evening... From early morning to late night, I can chant *Zhualima* more than twenty times. In a word, my daily work is to chant Buddhist scripture.

Every single Mongghul person, therefore, translanguaged at least to this extent, of being able to recite scriptures. This aspect of lay religious translanguaging varied throughout the lifespan, with chanting often taking up more and more time as people grew older.

By far the most widespread platform for plurilingual practices in Mongghul society, however, was music. Music involved both lay and monastic populations, and although it was to some extent gendered, with differential participation in genres and contexts, music, with lyrics in Mongghul, Tibetan, and Chinese (or, as reported by Qi and Levy 2015, in both Chinese and Mongghul), was performed by both men and women of all ages. Music saturated daily life, accompanying agricultural work and domestic tasks. It also permeated longer time-cycles, including the annual cycle and its ritual punctuation, and the sequence of life-cycle rituals, including weddings and funerals. The ubiquity of song, and near universal participation of lay people in it, meant that most Mongghul people, to the extent that they encountered other languages, did so through the medium of song and the translanguaging practices associated with it. This was not only the case of the Mongghul, but also for speakers of numerous other languages throughout Tibet, including Salar, Mangghuer, Manegacha, Ngandegua, Khroskyabs, Rta'u, Choyu (Queyu), Gochang (Guiqiong), Nyarong Minyag, and Darmdo Minyag. As with the monastic context, translanguaging in song was primarily achieved through memorization, which could occur either with or without the aid of texts. Plurilingual repertoires throughout Tibet therefore consisted primarily of a combination of spoken languages and sung memorized texts, rather than spoken and written communicative command of languages.

Two case studies from the writing of Limusishiden are instructive regarding not only how songs were learned and performed, but also their relationship to individual and communal identities, as well as broader linguistic repertoires. In a 2015 paper, Limusishiden introduces Lamuzhaxi, 'the last outstanding Mongghul folk song singer'. Lamuzhaxi, born in 1932, grew up in a community where both Mongghul and Tibetan were spoken, and is thus bilingual in the traditional sense of the term. He was one of the first Mongghul to study written Chinese at school, a skill he later used in learning songs. Although his song repertoire is entirely in Tibetan, he compiled it by listening to singers and transcribing what they sang in Chinese characters. Lamuzhaxi took every opportunity to learn songs from a wide range of teachers, both laymen and religious practitioners. The most important of his teachers was a monk, named Losiza, in Mantuu Monastery, within the Seven Valleys, who taught him the important songs *Szii* and *Rdang* from Tibetan texts (which Lamuzhaxi transcribed in Chinese). In assembling his repertoire, Lamuzhaxi strove for scale, both in the number of songs he performed and in their length, as a large repertoire was not only a source of personal pride, but also the foundation of a singer's public reputation, whilst command of longer songs enabled one to defeat singing opponents more easily. For Lamuzhaxi, the relationship between singing and reputation is paramount, as he states in Limusishiden's (2015:88) article: 'One learns folksongs in order to show one's ability in public gatherings, such as weddings, family affairs, or village or household celebrations.' Lamuzhaxi describes his singing abilities as peaking in his 50s, at which time his reputation ensured that he was frequently invited to sing at various communities' events throughout the Seven Valleys. The capacity to master a large song repertoire, and the translanguaging that undergird it, therefore served as a vehicle for both physical and social mobility in the area. Moreover, the importance of written Tibetan in this repertoire highlights its status as a local prestige language.

Passions and Colored Sleeves also provides insights into the music-plurilingualism nexus in Mongghul communities. Much of the narrative focuses on the life of a man called Sixty-Nine, who, as a youth, is given the responsibility of representing his family at communal events such as weddings. He therefore needs to learn to sing in order to maintain the family's reputation and protect its honor, an aspiration that once again lay bare the connection between song, reputation, and social mobility. Sixty-Nine studies under a locally renowned singer, Xoshidosirang, who sends him to learn written Tibetan from a Mongol living in Rgulang Monastery, as all of the most important Mongghul folk songs are in Tibetan. Throughout his life, Sixty-Nine sings at love song festivals in the summer[8] and weddings in the winter. He hears funeral laments sung by women following the death of loved ones. On one occasion,

---

8   On these festivals, see Tuohy (1988) and Mu (1994).

he engages in a song competition that lasts several days, and which he manages to win by playing a linguistic wild card, singing in Mongghul in a forum where the more prestigious Tibetan language was expected. In this case, it is Sixty-Nine's capacity to draw on the full range of his plurilingual repertoire, rather than his command of any particular language, that affords his prestige and social mobility.

These brief biographies demonstrate how singers in the Seven Valleys drew on both musical and linguistic repertoires as a means to bolster prestige and attain both social and physical mobility. They also show the ways in which deft translanguaging and a broad plurilingual repertoire were socially valued. Taken together with the efficacious, sonorous translanguaging that was fostered in monasteries, but also widely practiced in lay life, as well as the life-cycle plurilingualism of hypogamously married women, translanguaging in song forms the third, and perhaps most significant arena in which Mongghul of the Seven Valleys developed their plurilingual repertoire and practiced translanguaging.

This focus on plurilingualism and translanguaging enables us to imagine the linguistic area of northeast Tibet as 'super-diverse'. It was not simply an area of 'diversity', where many languages were spoken, and where the population could be demographically sorted into distinct linguistic clusters. It was also 'super-diverse', consisting of a variety of social groups with different plurilingual repertoires and distinct translanguaging praxis. The most obvious divide was gendered, with women more likely to experience life-cycle bilingualism and men more likely to engage in sonorous translanguaging. These profiles were also tied to age, with sonorous translanguaging increasing over time. They were also tied to personality, with devoted singers being motivated to accumulate more complex plurilingual repertoires and engage more frequently in translanguaging. In this volume, Limusishiden also shows that plurilingual repertoires in the Seven Valleys were localized, with use of Chinese more common in some areas, Tibetan in others.

Taking into account this 'super-diverse' view of language practices, linguistic history can be viewed as more than simply the interactions between different populations speaking different languages, stemming from their relations through trade, conquest, and other forms of contact. It suggests that we also need to consider the ways in which language contact comes about through the practices of individuals, including, in this instance, the ways that mothers spoke to their children, the way that monks chanted, and the way that singers sang. In attempting to understand how a linguistic area was formed on the northeast Tibetan Plateau, we therefore need both top-down and bottom-up approaches. A top-down approach would look at long-term historical processes of migration, trade, warfare, and rule. It would examine broad-scale patterns of how linguistic diversity was spatially organized. From this perspective, language contact is both demographic and spatial. A bottom-up approach, meanwhile, would, first of all, ground its analysis in local perceptions of what constituted a distinct language, and how these differentiated languages were valued, and therefore likely to be acquired and used. It would look ethnographically at the daily lives of speakers and how daily rhythms were embedded in annual and life-cycle patterns. It would examine how individuals engaged in translanguaging, and assembled plurililingual repertoires that varied with gender, age, location, and other social positions. From this perspective, language contact is intensely intimate. It takes place in the mouths and minds of individuals, and in moments of symbolically loaded exchange, between mothers and children, monks and patrons, and singers and their audiences.

A focus on translanguaging, plurilingualism, and super-diversity is particularly revealing in considering the ways in which the song texts in this volume have been presented, and what this tells us about the contemporary language regime on the northeast Tibetan Plateau. The songs presented here were originally in Chinese, Tibetan, or Mongghul, or sometimes in both Chinese and Mongghul. As presented here, however, each of the songs is given in three versions: Mongghul, Chinese, and English, with no 'mixing of languages'. I argue that what we see in Limusishiden's presentation of these texts are processes of elaboration, purification, and standardization. These processes enable Limusishiden to speak to distinct audiences, namely, a Mongghul audience, a national Chinese audience, and an international audience, and thus work towards respective projects of nativization, nationalization, and globalization, each of which I examine below, before turning to look at the broader political implications of these projects.

The project of nativization, or vernacularization, is aimed at a Mongghul audience, and has several goals. First is the transferal of what is perceived as Mongghul patrimony firmly into the realm of the

Mongghul language, via the translation of song lyrics from Tibetan and Chinese into Mongghul. The nativization project therefore seeks to reinforce exclusive relations between ethnic identity and language, based in Romantic ideologies of nationalism, filtered through the lens of the Chinese state's *minzu* paradigm. The process of nativization seen in the presentation of these texts also works towards the elaboration of the Mongghul language. The texts provide a forum in which the language not only continues its expansion into the written domain,[9] but also expands its lexical breadth in order to articulate concepts previously expressed through borrowing. This is closely linked to purification, which not only refers to lexical purification, but also to the clear separation of linguistic codes in discourse. None of the texts presents any examples of 'mixed languages'. For example, the original use of both Chinese and Mongghul in *the Ballad of Marshal Qi*, with alternating lines in the two languages, is purified by translation, with the three texts of the song—Mongghul, Chinese, and English—all containing only a single, differentiated linguistic code. This is achieved in part through standardization, not of the language, but of the presentation of the texts, with every text presented in the same order of Mongghul, Chinese, and English. This standardization also entails a certain amount of erasure, as texts that were originally in Tibetan are now presented only in Mongghul, Chinese, and English.

Inherent in the project of nativization is a parallel one of nationalization—of placing the Mongghul people, and Mongghul linguistic and cultural patrimony, in the context of the Chinese state. In erasing the presence of the Tibetan language, the translation strategy used here suggests a realignment of the language ecology of northeast Tibet. Amdo is replaced as the central language, its place taken by Modern Standard Chinese. The elaborated Mongghul language and reclaimed Mongghul patrimony are viewed *vis-à-vis* a state identity that is essentially Han, and a linguistic context that is 'Chinese'. Although the standardizing of the translations as elaborated, purified texts consisting of simplified characters to some extent represents the subordination of

---

9   The Mongghul texts are presented in Mongghul Latin orthography. See Limusishiden and Dede (2012), Shoji (2003), and Hugejiltu (1987) for details on the development, teaching, and use of this writing system. For a selection of materials published in the Mongghul orthography from 2008 to 2011 in the magazine *Chileb*, see https://archive.org/details/ChilebMagazinehuzhuMongghultuAutonomousCounty

Mongghul within a new language hierarchy, it can also be viewed as a strategic maneuver aimed at presenting the language as functionally equivalent to the nationally dominant script, and Mongghul people therefore as equals of the Han.

This interpretation is further strengthened if we look at the third translation strategy, that of internationalizing Mongghul identity and patrimony through English. Presenting the texts in this globally dominant medium of communication is, to me, suggestive not only of an attempt to locate Mongghul people, language, and tradition within a universal forum of peoples that transcends state boundaries, but also to gain prestige for Mongghul as rightful members of this international community. So, in this light, I would interpret the translation processes of elaboration, purification, and standardization, and the projects of nativization, nationalization, and internationalization, as being part of a broader endeavor towards 'language emancipation'—'the process through which the dominated language is brought into use in various sectors of public life... while the status of the language is enhanced' (Huss and Lindgren 2011:2).

The strategies used to present these texts and the broader goals these represent are indicative of the ways in which the language ecology and language culture of northeast Tibet have changed drastically since its origins as a linguistic area. Instead of translanguaging and plurilingual repertoires, we see instead the emergence of multingualism as the establishment of fully elaborated, interchangeable, distinct linguistic codes. This will inevitably change the languages in question, not only disentangling them from their complex mutual engagement, but also reembedding them in a new, centralized national language constellation in which all languages interact primarily with the national standard language—Modern Standard Chinese—and in which horizontal interactions are minimized. It also signals a change in the language praxis of individuals in which the text-mediated translanguaging performed in orature, both chanting and song, are likely to be stigmatized as imperfect command or impure mixing, rather than celebrated as a prestigious achievement leading to mobility. The effects of these changes on languages like Mongghul remain to be seen. Whilst the elaboration of the Mongghul language is probably necessary to its survival in this new linguistic regime, the attitudes of purism that accompany this process will probably be inimical to the practices of translanguaging that once played such an important role in plurilingual practices, and the maintenance of relatively small languages such as Mongghul.

Coda: The Corpus

The songs transcribed in this book represent the apogee of Mongghul orature. All of the seven songs are long songs, defined in terms of their length rather than their coherence as an emic genre (i.e., in contrast to the Mongolian genre of long song, *urtiin duu*—see Pegg 2001). Most of the songs are narratives, relating stories of romance, bravery, or family relations. Two of the songs deal with the nature and structure of the world, as well as the origin of certain cultural practices. All of these texts provide, to varying extents, insights into the internal lifeworlds of Mongghul people—their hopes, dreams, and concerns. They also bear testimony to the impressive plurilingual repertoire commanded by some Mongghul singers.

The first two songs presented here are ballads of martial heroism. *The Ballad of Taipinggoor* (sung in a mixture of Mongghul and Chinese) relates how a virgin-born hero appears in the Seven Valleys. He travels to Beijing to suppress a rebellion, acquiring both technical and magical assistance along the way. After successfully quelling the rebellion in Beijing, he returns to the Seven Valleys to live with his mother. Meanwhile, *The Ballad of Marshal Qi* describes the exploits of a Mongghul 'chieftain' (*tusi*) who is summoned by imperial edict to battle 'rebels' (actually soldiers of the Later Jin) to break the siege of Luoyang. Marshal Qi travels from the Seven Valleys to Luoyang with his Mongghul army, meeting difficulties along the way, but eventually arrives in Luoyang and retakes the city. He and his soldiers then travel home, once again overcoming challenges to reach their destination.

The third song in the collection, *Laarimbu and Qiimunso* (in Mongghul), tells the story of two star-crossed lovers. Laarimbu is a herder from a poor family, whilst Qiimunso cares for the livestock of her wealthy family. They meet while out herding and fall in love, but their plans to unite as a couple are thwarted by Qiimunso's brother. Finding Qiimunso's choice of a lover unacceptable, he murders Laarimbu. Qiimunso thereafter commits suicide by throwing herself on

Laarimbu's funeral pyre. Reunited in the afterlife, the two lovers take their revenge on Qiimunso's brother.

The next two songs, *The Song of the Dildima Bird* and *The Song of the Calf*, each deal with family relations, especially between parents and children, themes that also appear in other songs presented in this book. *The Song of the Dildima Bird* is a lament, sung by a woman after marrying into her husband's home. She describes her miserable existence—her decrepit appearance and the poor treatment she is receiving—to a bird, the eponymous *dildima*, asking the bird to carry her message back to her parents in her natal home. *The Song of the Calf*, meanwhile, tells the story of a calf and her mother. The two animals live as domestic livestock in a valley, and the calf dreams of escaping to freedom in the mountains. The mother discourages the calf, but she nonetheless escapes to the mountains, where she is surrounded by wolves. The mother appears to rescue the calf, who flees and, returning one week later, finds her mother's remains. She then meditates on death, impermanence, and filial piety before returning to the valley to continue her life there.

The final two songs, *The Crop-Planting Song* and *The Song of the Sheep*, are as much maps as they are narratives. They provide descriptions of space, place, and culturally important objects and procedures. *The Crop-Planting Song* describes the origins of agriculture amongst the Mongghul. It begins with humanity living in cold, hungry darkness, and then describes how the Buddha created the sun and moon, bestowed crops upon people, and taught them how to farm. In doing so, it also provides a map of the cosmos—the heavens and celestial bodies, Mount Sumeru, the Earth and its regions, and so on. *The Song of the Sheep*, meanwhile, is a musical omnibus depicting various aspects of life on the northeast Tibetan Plateau, and in the same way as *The Crop-Planting Song* it spends considerable time mapping space at various levels: the cosmos and its bodies, the earth and its social and political organization, as well as individual landscapes and their inhabitants.

References

Arnaut, Karel. 2011. Jan Blommaert, Ben Rampton and Massimiliano Spotti (eds). *Language and Superdiversity*. London: Routledge.

Calvet, Louis-Jean (translated by Andrew Brown). 2006. *Toward an Ecology of World Languages*. Cambridge: Polity.

Canagarajah, Suresh, and Indika Jananda Liyanage. 2012. Lessons from Pre-colonial Multilingualism. In Marilyn Martin-Jones, Adrian Blackledge and Angela Creese (eds). *The Routledge Handbook of Multilingualism*. London: Routledge, 49–65.

Dede, Keith. 2003. The Chinese language in Qinghai. *Studia Orientalia* 95:321–46.

Dwyer, Arienne. 2013. Tibetan as a Dominant Sprachbund Language: Its Interactions with Neighboring Languages. In Gray Tuttle, Kunsang Gya, Karma Dare and Jonathan Wilber (eds). *The Third International Conference on Tibetan Language (volume 1): Proceedings of the Panels on Domains of Use and Linguistic Interaction*. New York: Trace Foundation, 259–302.

Ekvall, Robert. 1964. *Religious Observances in Tibet: Patterns and Function*. Chicago: Chicago University Press.

Faehndrich, Burgel R.M. 2007. *Sketch Grammar of the Karlong Variety of Mongghul, and Dialectal Survey of Mongghul*. PhD dissertation, University of Hawaii.

Finnegan, Ruth. 2010. Rewards and Issues in Studying Oral Literature: Some Personal Reflections. In Imogen Gunn and Mark Turin (eds). *Oral Literature and Language Endangerment. Language Documentation and Description* 8:13–26. http://www.elpublishing.org/PID/092

Foley, John Miles. 2002. *How to Read an Oral Poem*. Champaign: University of Illinois Press.

García, Ofelia, and Tatyana Kleyn (eds). 2016. *Translanguaging with Multilingual Students: Learning from Classroom Moments*. London: Routledge.

Haugen, Einar. 1972. The Ecology of Language. In Anwar Dil (ed.). *The Ecology of Language: Essays by Einar Haugen*. Stanford: Stanford University Press, 325–39.

Hugejiltu. 1987. Fonnu Muxi Jarim Fondu Mongghul Pujigla Pujig Sghurguisghagu Baudal (The Achievement of Teaching the Mongghul Written System in the First Six Months of 1987). *Chileb* 3:38–40.

Huss, Leena, and Anna-Riitta Lindgren. 2011. Introduction: Defining Language Emancipation. *International Journal of the Sociology of Language* 209:1–15.

Janhunen, Juha, Lionel Ha Mingzong and Joseph Tshe dpag rnam rgyal. 2007. On the Language of the Shaowa Tuzu in the Context of the Ethnic Taxonomy of Amdo Qinghai. *Central Asiatic Journal* 51.2:177–95.

Janhunen, Juha. 2005. The Role of the Turkic Languages in the Amdo Sprachbund. *Studia Turcologica Cracoviensia* 10:113–22.

Klein, Anne C. 2003. Orality in Tibet. *Oral Tradition* 18.1:98–100.

Lempert, Michael. 2012. *Discipline and Debate: The Language of Violence in a Tibetan Buddhist Monastery*. Berkeley: The University of California Press.

Limusishiden. 2008. *Mongghul Memories and Lives — Asian Highlands Perspectives* 8:1–119.

Limusishiden. 2015. The Last Outstanding Mongghul Folksong Singer. In Gerald Roche, Keith Dede, Fernanda Pirie and Benedict Copps (eds). *Centering the Local, A Festschrift for Dr. Charles Kevin Stuart on the Occasion of his Sixtieth Birthday. Asian Highlands Perspectives* 37:79–98.

Limusishiden and Keith Dede. 2012. The Mongghul Experience: Consequences of Language Policy Shortcomings. *The International Journal of the Sociology of Language* 215:101–24.

Limusishiden and Jugui. 2012. Passions and Colored Sleeves: Mongghul Lives in Eastern Tibet. *Asian Highlands Perspectives* 7:1–322.

Makoni, Sinfree, and Alastair Pennycook (eds). 2007. *Disinventing and Reconstituting Languages*. Clevedon: Multilingual Matters.

Mu, Yang. 1994. On the Hua'er Songs of North-western China. *Yearbook for Traditional Music* 26:100–116.

Nugteren, Hans and Marti Roos. 1996. Common Vocabulary of the Western and Eastern Yugur Languages: The Turkic and Mongolic Loanwords. *Acta Orientalia* 49.1:25–91.

Nugteren, Hans, and Marti Roos. 1998. Common Vocabulary of the Western and Eastern Yugur Languages: The Tibetan Loanwords. *Studia Etymologica Cracoviensia* 3:45–92.

Pegg, Carole. 2001. *Mongolian Music, Dance, and Oral Narrative: Performing Diverse Identities*. Seattle: University of Washington Press.

Qi Huimin and Burgel Levy. 2015. Bilingualism in Song: The Rabbit Song of the Fulaan Nara Huzhu Mongghul. In Gerald Roche and Charles Stuart (eds). *Mapping the Monguor. Asian Highlands Perspectives* 36:106–13.

Roche, Gerald. 2014. The Vitality of Tibet's Minority Languages in the Twenty-first Century: Preliminary Remarks. *Multiethnica* 35:24–30.

Roche, Gerald. 2017. The Transformation of Tibet's Language Ecology in the Twenty-first Century. *The International Journal of the Sociology of Language* 245:1–35.

Roche, Gerald, and Hiroyuki Suzuki. 2017 (forthcoming). Tibet's Minority Languages: Diversity and Endangerment. *Modern Asian Studies*.

Samuel, Geoffrey. 1993. *Civilised Shamans: Buddhism in Tibetan Societies*. Washington and London: Smithsonian Institute Press.

Sandman, Erika. 2012. Bonan Grammatical Features in Wutun. *Mémoires de la Société Finno-Ougrienne* 264: 375–87.

Sandman, Erika, and Camille Simon. 2016. Tibetan as a 'Model Language' in the Amdo Sprachbund: Evidence from Salar and Wutun. *Journal of South Asian Languages and Linguistics* 3.1:85–122.

Schram, Louis M. J. 2006 (1954, 1957, 1961). Reprint of *The Monguors of the Kansu-Tibetan Frontier, Parts I-III*, http://hdl.handle.net/1811/24312

Schram, Louis M. J. 1954. The Monguors of the Kansu-Tibetan Frontier. Their Origin, History, and Social Organization. *Transactions of the American Philosophical Society* 44.1:1–138.

Schram, Louis M. J. 1957. *The Monguors of the Kansu-Tibetan Frontier: Part II. Their Religious Life*. Philadelphia: American Philosophical Society.

Schram, Louis M. J. 1961. *The Monguors of the Kansu-Tibetan Frontier: Part III. Records of the Monguor Clans. History of the Monguors in Huangchung and the Chronicles of the Lu Family*. Philadelphia: American Philosophical Society.

Shoji, Hiroshi. 2003. Mother Tongue Education for Revitalising a Vigorous Language? The Case of Monguor, a Minority Language of China. In Leena Huss, Antoinette Camilleri Grima and Kendall King (eds). *Transcending Monolingualism: Linguistic Revitalization in Education*. Netherlands: Swets and Zeitlinger, 277–92.

Simon, Camille. 2015. Linguistic Evidence of Salar-Tibetan Contacts in Amdo. In Marie Paule Hille, Bianca Horlemann and Paul Nietupski (eds). *Muslims in Amdo Tibetan Society: Multidisciplinary Approaches*. New York: Lexington Books, 87–107.

Singer, Ruth, and Salome Harris. 2016. What Practices and Ideologies Support Small-scale Multilingualism? A Case Study of Warruwi Community, Northern Australia. *International Journal of the Sociology of Language* 241:163–208.

Skal bzang nor bu. 2015. An Introduction to Amdo Tibetan Love Songs or *La gzhas*. In Gerald Roche, Keith Dede, Fernarda Pirie and Benedict Copps (eds). *Centering the Local: A Festschrift for Dr. Charles Kevin Stuart on his Sixtieth Birthday. Asian Highlands Perspectives* 37:1–36.

Slater, Keith. 2003. *Mangghuer: A Mongolic Language of China's Qinghai-Gansu Sprachbund*. London and New York: Routledge.

Sullivan, Brenton. 2013. *The Mother of All Monasteries: Gönlung Jampa Ling and the Rise of Mega Monasteries in Northeast Tibet*. PhD dissertation, University of Virginia.

Sullivan, Brenton. 2015. Monastic Customaries and the Promotion of Dge lugs pa Scholasticism in Amdo and Beyond. In Gerald Roche and Charles Stuart (eds). *Mapping the Monguor. Asian Highlands Perspectives* 36:84–105.

Tas, A. Rona. 1996. *Tibeto-Mongolica: The Tibetan Loanwords of Monguor and the Development of the Archaic Tibetan Dialects*. The Hague: Mouton.

Thiong'o, Ngũgĩ Wa. 2007. Notes towards a Performance Theory of Orature. *Performance Research* 12.3:4–7.

Thurston, Timothy. 2012. An Introduction to Tibetan sa bstod Speeches in A mdo. *Asian Ethnology* 71.1:49–73.

Tuohy, Sue. 1988. *Imagining the Chinese Tradition: The Case of Hua'er songs, Festivals and Scholarship.* PhD dissertation, Indiana University.

Vertovec, Steven. 2007. Super-diversity and its Implications. *Ethnic and Racial Studies* 30.6:1024–54.

Wilkinson, Andrew. 1970. The Concept of Oracy. *The English Journal* 59.1:71–77.

Appendix: Mongghul Orature Online

Mongghul Funeral Lamentations:
https://archive.org/details/MongghulFuneralLamentations

Mongghul Weeding and Love Songs:
https://archive.org/details/MongghulWeedingAndLoveSongs

Mongghul Singing and Dancing:
https://archive.org/details/HuzhuMongghultuDancingAndSinging1997

Mongghul Love Song Meeting:
https://archive.org/details/HuzhuMongghultuLoveSongMeeting

Mongghul Drinking Songs:
https://archive.org/details/HuzhuMongghultuDrinkingSongs2002

Mongghul Women Sing Drinking Songs:
https://archive.org/details/
FourHuzhuMongghultuWomenSingADrinkingSong

Shgeayili Village Mongghul Wedding:
https://archive.org/details/ShgeayiliMongghultuVillageWeddingIn2004

Huzhu Mongghul Wedding:
https://archive.org/details/HuzhuMongghulWedding

Mongghul Bo Ritual:
https://archive.org/details/
MongghulBospiritMediumRitualInHuzhuCountyQinghaiProvince

Mongghul Love Songs:
https://archive.org/details/HuzhuMongghultuMonguorLoveSongs

A Mongghul Love Tragedy, Wedding Lamentation, and Funeral Lamentation:
https://archive.org/details/AMongghulLoveTragedylarinbogAndQiminsuu
FuneralLamentationsAnd

Xeojinhua and Jiuyahua Sing Mongghul Drinking Songs:
https://archive.org/details/
XeojinhuaAndJiuyahuaSingAMongghultuMonguorDrinkingSongIn2004

Mongghul Weddings in Wushi and Danma:
https://archive.org/details/MongghultuWedding2005InWushiAndDanma

Mongghul Women Sing in Tibetan:
https://archive.org/details/MongghultuMonguorWomenFromHuzhuSing
InTibetanIn2004

Qijia Yanxi:
https://archive.org/details/QijiaYanxiAMongghulNarrativePoemSungIn
QinghaiChineseDialect

1. The Ballad of Taipinggoor

Historically, the traditional Mongghul homeland, the Seven Valleys (Duluun Lunkuang), was divided into two parts: Fulaan Nara (literally, Red Sun) and Haliqi. The Fulaan Nara region includes the present Wushi Town and Songduo, Hongyazigou and Shdara[1] Townships. The Haliqi region includes Danma and Weiyuan Town, as well as Donggou, Taizi, and Dongshan Townships. This folksong was mostly sung in Haliqi, in Donggou, Taizi, and Donghe Townships and Weiyuan Town, where Mongghul people also sang *The Ballad of Marshal Qi* and *Tangdarihgiima*. In Fulaan Nara, Mongghul almost never sing *The Ballad of Taipingoor*, but sing several genres of song in Tibetan, because historically they were much influenced by Tibetans.

The Ballad of Taipinggoor relates how once Beijing was under siege by an imams' rebellion. The Emperor and all the common people were suffering greatly. When the Jade Emperor in Heaven learned of he dispatched a man to Putuo Mountain in the South Sea, from where he invited Avalokitśvara to his palace in Heaven. The Jade Emperor then asked Avalokitśvara to go to the Earth to rescue all the suffering common people, and Avalokitśvara transformed into a magpie and came to the human world.

She flew to Nanjing City and to Lhasa, but was not satisfied with them as places to incarnate in a human body. Finally, she came to a remote valley in the Seven Valleys, where she found a Mongghul woman. The woman, named Lenjii, was in her forties, but was still unmarried. Avalokitśvara decided that Lenjii would be her mother, and that she

---

1   In the Ledu Region.

© 2017 Li Dechun (李得春, Limusishiden) and Gerald Roche, CC BY 4.0
https://doi.org/10.11647/OBP.0124.01

would reincarnate in her new human body as Lenjii's child. Lenjii then fell pregnant. One day served as one month, and so nine days later a baby was born, and took the name Taipinggoor. Then Taipinggoor told his mother he wanted to buy weapons and planned to go to Beijing to save the common people from their suffering.

Taipinggoor bought his weapons and left his mother. He arrived in Lanzhou City, where he found a fine red-maned horse. Finally, he arrived in Beijing and rescued the Emperor and saved all the common people in Beijing City. The Emperor wanted to make him a high official, but he declined. He returned home to the Seven Valleys and lived with his mother.

The Ballad of Taipinggoor is a long folksong, and is sung mostly by men during drinking parties. In Mongghul communties, only a few good singers can sing this song. They mostly learned it from others at drinking parties by imitation and repetition. When singing at such parties, people typically sang excerpts from the song rather than the whole song.

Although Taipiingoor was an important figure in Mongghul culture, today he only appears in this song, which is sung by fewer and fewer people as time goes by. The song is performed without musical instruments. The voice sound in the song is soft, high, slow and gentle. This tune is unique amongst Mongghul folksongs.

The song was traditionally sung in both Chinese and Mongghul. For example, in the following verse the first and last lines are in Chinese:

我的好阿妈你就听着 (wode hao ama ni jiu tingzhao),
Bu saihan moringe hgilegunii,
Malang buda ghuila mori awula yau,
没有好马阿么出大兵 (meiyou hao ma amen chu dabing)?

Mother, please listen:
I need a fine horse.
Tomorrow, we will go buy a fine horse.
How could I go to battle without a fine horse?

Taipinggoor

太平歌

The Ballad of Taipinggoor

 Listen to the audio recording of this song:
https://archive.org/details/Taipinggoor

1. Jawaa Awu

1. 下界

1. Incarnation

Tingerenu ude zongda neeji gui,
Nonggu fondu szang fune ghariji ireja,
Tingerenu idenii turgua neewaaxja,
Udenu sgijin Yiizi tenu mudeexja.

千年万年的天门没开,
今年藏烟冲上九霄天,
藏烟上来者天门冲开,
天门冲开羿子知道了。[2]

Heaven's gate was closed,
This year's smoke from burning juniper twigs was rising into the sky,
The smoke burst Heaven's gates open,
And the gatekeeper found that the gate was opened.

---

2   羿子: 据唱述人说是守天门的天神。(It is said that Yiizi is Heaven's gatekeeper).

Udenu neewaa Yiizi mangdaaxja,
Maalii maalii tingerdu kilela yau,
Tingere haandu xiilala yau,
Simqandu shge dundog gharija.

天门冲开者羿子忙了,
羿子忙了者天宫里走,
玉皇爷哈赶紧报给走,
凡间里出了大事情了。

The gatekeeper was alarmed,
And went straight to the Heavenly Palace
To report to the Jade Emperor,
Something significant must have happened on Earth.

Tingere haanjeen qi sau juu?
Tingere haanjeen qi sainiisa?
Munu Yiizi qi nige kuri wuu?
Haadan boodandu qi yama ginii?

玉皇万岁爷你坐着吗?
玉皇万岁爷你好着啥?
我的小羿子你到来了?
你忙死忙活的咋来了?

Are you sitting comfortably, Jade Emperor?
How are you, Jade Emperor?
My gatekeeper, why have you come?
Why have you come so breathlessly?

Tingerenu ude zongda neeji gui,
Nong szang fune udenu neewaaxja,
Udenu neewaanu bu mangdaxja,
Bu haadan boodandu xilala irewa.

千年万年的天门没开,
今年藏烟冲上九霄天,
藏烟上来者我就忙了,
忙死忙活的我报来了。

Heaven's gate was closed,
But this year's smoke from burning juniper twigs has burst it open,
I was alarmed by this,
And rushed here to report to you.

Munu Yiizi qi diixinge sunusi,
Sajaghaingedu xjeelee simqandu xji,
Sajaghaingedu xjeelee qi ujela xji,
Yaan dundog gharijiiha qi kilela ire.

我的小羿子你听详细，
你变上个喜鹊下凡间，
变上个喜鹊看一回去，
出了啥事哈你就报来。

My dear gatekeeper, please listen carefully,
Please change into a magpie and go down to Earth,
Change into a magpie and take a look,
Then come back and report what has happened.

Munu sain Tingere haanjeen,
Hara kireedu bu lii xjeelem,
Qighaan ngusgedu bu xjeelegunii,
Ngusgedu xjeelee bu ujela xjigunii.

好我的玉皇万岁爷哩，
长嘴巴黑乌鸦我不变，
我要变上个白鸽子哩，
变上鸽子了看一回去。

My great Jade Emperor,
I do not want to change into a black crow,[3]
I want to become a white dove,
And go take a look as a white dove.

Munu Yiizi qi diixinge sunusi,
Ngusgenge xjeeleenu simqandu xjisa,
Ghadaadu bausa mughui qimii norlom,
Kun jirgendu bausa kun qimii norlom.

好我的小羿子你听着，
变上个鸽子了下凡间，
大山里到了哈蛇伤哩，
人间里到了哈人抓哩。

My gatekeeper, please listen carefully,
If you change into a white dove and go to Earth,
Snakes will hurt you if you land on the mountains,
People will hurt you if you go where they live.

---

3   Although it should be a magpie, the original text says 'black crow'.

Sajighaidu xjeelee simqandu xjisa,
Ghadaadu bausa moghui lii norlom,
Kun jiregendu bausa kun lii norlom,
Tingerdu nesisa saar lii norlom.

变上个喜鹊了下凡间，
蛇山里到了哈蛇躲哩，
人间里到了哈人躲哩，
半空里飞来哈鹰躲哩。

If you change into a magpie and go to Earth,
Snakes won't hurt you if you land on the mountains,
People won't hurt you if you go where they live,
Eagles won't hurt you if you fly in the sky.

Tingere haanjeennu szang saina,
Sajighaidu xjeelee bu ujela xjiya.
Alag sajighaingedu xjeeleenu,
Tingere furongsa nesiji simqandu bauya.

玉皇爷话儿我听上，
变上个喜鹊了看一回。
变来变去变了个喜鹊，
离开了天宫者下凡间。

The Jade Emperor's suggestion is good,
I will change into a magpie and go take a look.
He changed into a magpie,
Left the Heavenly Palace, and came to Earth.

Nesaanu Gansin ghajardu kurija,
Xiiniin bazardu ujela xjija,
Xiiniin bazardu ndang naamawa,
Lanzhou bazardu ujela xjija.

一飞飞到甘省地方里，
西宁的城里看一回走，
西宁的城里没有啥事情，
兰州的城里看一趟走。

He flew to the Gansin[4] area,
Had a look at Xining City,
But nothing had happened in Xining City,
So he went to look at Lanzhou City.

---

4   This location is unclear; it may be today's Gansu Province.

Lanzhou bazardu haannu pujignii naalghaja,
Pujignu naalghaa harwan fon dawaaja,
Rjanag bazaar jublongdu unaaja,
Hara tiruududa jublongdu unaaja.

兰州城里皇榜挂着哩,
皇榜挂给了整十年了,
北京城里反贼造反了,
万民百姓遇难遭殃了。

An announcement of state affairs was posted in Lanzhou City;
Ten years had already passed since the announcement was posted,
A rebellion had happened in Beijing City,
Common people were suffering greatly because of the rebellion.

Nigedu nesaa Rjanag kurija,
Bazar tolghuindu pusaa ujesa,
Zhonla naasan bazaar aldaja,
Tensa turogu bazarda aldaja.

一飞飞到了北京的城,
北京城头上站哈了看,
北京的砖包城失掉了,
北京的里摞城失掉了。

He flew quickly to Beijing,
And looked inside Beijing City, while perching on the city wall:
He found that the city's brick walls had collapsed,
And the buildings of the inner city had been damaged.

Zijin bazaar xjighaar lailaja,
Jong menhange qirig hujija,
Ghuraan aahunye qirignu durija,
Smu jiidaa turoji nesina.

只有那紫禁城还没失,
千军万马把城围着哩,
三个阿訇爷领兵着哩,
强弓硬箭往里射着哩。

Only the Forbidden City had not fallen into the enemy's hands.
Hundreds and thousands of soldiers encircled the city,
They were led by three imams,
Arrows were shot into the city.

Nudu ujesaar Rjanag bazaar buraana,
Haanjeen hudunge nanqudu uroja,
Uladu ghariji szang gharghaja,
Szang fune tingere udenu needija.

北京城眼看着攻下了，
皇上爷到了难处了，
上去高山者煨了个藏，
藏烟上来天门冲开了。

Beijing City soon fell into the enemy's hands,
The Emperor was in danger.
He went atop a high mountain and burned juniper twigs,
And the smoke of the juniper twigs burst open Heaven's gates.

Caalan caalandu isge mudewa,
Ghurdin ghurdin tingerdu yau,
Tingere haandu xiilala yau,
Dii udaasa Rjanag bazaar buraaguna.

查来查去才说查到了，
快快价回到天宫里走，
玉皇爷哈赶紧报给走，
再迟哈北京城就完了。

He had finally discovered the situation on Earth,
And needed to return to Heaven as quickly as possible
To report to the Jade Emperor.
Beijing City would be destroyed if he returned late.

Munu Yiizi qi isgi kuri uu,
Simqandu yaan dundog gharija?
Bu simqandu bauji caalala xjiwa,
Sghaunge uliji isgi mudewa.

我的小羿子你到来了，
凡间里出了啥事情了？
我下到凡间里查事情，
查来查去才说查到了。

My gatekeeper, you are back,
What has happened on Earth?
I went to Earth to investigate,
And finally discovered the situation.

Ghuraan aahunye fanlaadija,
Rjanag bazarnu hujisan ni batiwa,
Zhonla naasan bazaar aldaadija,
Tensa turogu bazarda aldaadija.

三个阿訇爷哈造反了，
千军万马围了北京城，
北京的砖包城失掉了，
北京的里擦城失掉了。

Three imams have rebelled,
Beijing City has been tightly encircled,
I found Beijing's brick walls had collapsed,
And the buildings of the inner city had been damaged.

Zijin bazar xjighaar lailaja,
Jong menhange qirig hujija,
Haanjeen uladu szang gharghaja,
Szang fune tigerenu udenu neewaaxja.

剩下个紫禁城还没丢，
千军万马城外围着哩，
皇上上山着煨了个藏，
藏烟上来天门冲开了。

Only the Forbidden City has not fallen into the enemy's hands,
Hundreds and thousands of soldiers have encircled the city,
The Emperor went atop a high mountain and burned juniper twigs,
And the smoke of the juniper twigs burst the Heavenly gate open.

Munu Yiizi qi diixiinge sunusi,
Ulongla nesaa ghurdi nanhaidu xji,
Nanhai putoo ulare qi nige xji,
Xjariizignu qi ghurdi urila xji.

我的小羿子你听着，
你快驾云到南海里去，
南海的普陀山走一趟，
观世音普萨哈你快请去。

My dear gatekeeper, please listen carefully:
Please fly to the South Sea quickly,
Go to Putuo Mountain in the South Sea,
And invite Avalokitśvara here.

Nigedu nesaa nanhai kurija,
Munu xjariizig qi sau juu?
Oola munu Yiizi qi kuri uu?
Haadan boodandu yama ginii?

一飞飞到南海普陀山，
观世音菩萨你坐着吗？
阿来我的羿子到来了？
忙死忙活的你咋来了？

He flew to Putuo Mountain in the South Sea.
How are you Avalokitśvara?
Have you come, my dear gatekeeper?
Why have you come here in such a rush?

Tingere haanjeen qimii urina,
Qi maali ndaa daghaawaa yau.
Qi muxi haanjeendu kilela xji,
Bu rzaama xoordana kuriya.

玉皇大帝把你邀着哩，
你快快跟上我去一趟。
你前走一步了报玉皇，
我后行一步了就到来。

You have been invited by the Jade Emperor,
Please come with me quickly.
You go ahead,
I will come soon.

Tingerenu haanjeen qi sau juu?
Oola munu xjariizig kuri uu?
Simqandu gharisan dundog shgewa,
Rjanag bazarnu hujaa harwan fon ulija.

玉皇大帝爷你坐着吗？
阿来观世音菩萨到了吗？
凡间里出了大事情了，
北京城围给了十年了。

How are you, Jade Emperor?
Have you come, my dear Avalokitśvara?
There has been a big event on Earth,
Beijing City has been under siege for ten years.

Ghuraan aahunye falaadija,
Rjanag bazarnu hujisan ni batiwa,
Qi simqandu nige xjigu kurija,
Hara tiruudu amun torlaguxja.

三个阿訇爷造反了，
千军万马围了北京城，
你快到凡间里去一趟，
快去解救万民百姓去。

Three imams have been rebelling,
Beijing City has been tightly encircled.
You are needed on Earth,
You are needed to save common people's lives there.

Munu tingere haanjeen qi sunusi,
Simqan tamqandu bu lii xjim,
Xira deel mosisa huiqaa moxiguxja,
Hara deel mosisa sgil haradim.

好我的玉皇爷你听着，
凡间里我万万去不成，
黄衣裳穿上哈念经哩，
黑衣裳穿上哈心黑哩。

Jade Emperor, please listen,
I won't go to Earth,
I need to chant Buddhist scriptures and wear yellow robes—
My heart would become black if I wore black robes.[5]

Munu xjariizig qi diixi sunusi,
Hara tiruudu jublongdu unaaja,
Qi lii xjisa bu bauji xjiya,
Munu urondu qi saula ire.

我的观世音你细听着，
凡间里老百姓遭了难，
你不发慈悲了我下凡，
玉皇的宝座上你来坐。

Dear Avalokitśvara, please listen,
Common people on Earth have suffered,
I will go myself if you don't want to,
But please take my position while I am away.

---

5   That is, do harmful things, like killing rebels.

Tin giji jilaji uligudii gua,
Qinu urondu bu sau adan,
Do bu simqandu ujela xjiya,
Hara tiruududu amun torlalghaya.

我的玉皇爷可使不得,
玉皇宝座上我坐不了,
我还是凡间里走一趟,
我万民百姓哈解救去。

Please don't do that,
I cannot replace you,
Let me go to Earth,
And save the common people's lives.

Bu simqandu bauji xigundu,
Purghaan buyenaa kendu geegunii?
Yerdu kurisa fuuwaa xjim,
Rguldu kurisa koraa xjim.

我下凡到人间里救百姓,
我的佛身子靠给谁哩?
夏天里到了哈坏掉哩,
冬天里到了哈冻掉哩。

When I go to Earth,
Who will take care of my celestial body?
My celestial body will rot in summer
And freeze in winter.

Qi sgilnaa geewaa simqandu xji,
Qinu buyenu bu saihan daglaya,
Yerdu tirgela qimu furooya,
Rguldu mianhuala qimu hujiya.

你放心到凡间去一回,
你的佛身子哈我管上,
夏天里到了绸缎俩裹,
冬天里到了棉花俩包。

Please go to Earth,
I will take care of your celestial body,
I will wrap it in silk and satin in summer,
And wrap it in cotton in winter.

Qi sajaghaingedu xjeelee nige xji,
Qinu buyenaa sgil bii tida.
Sajaghai du bu lii xjeelem,
Qighaan ngusgenge xjeelegunii.

你变上个喜鹊去一趟，
你的佛身子哈甭扯心，
长嘴巴喜鹊我不变，
我变个鸽子者下凡哩。

Please go to Earth in the form of a magpie,
I will take care of your celestial body.
I don't want to change into a magpie,
I would like to change into a white dove.

Ngusgedu xjeelesa haazhangwa,
Hara ghadaadu kurisa mughui norlom,
Tebxin tangdu kurisa kun norlom,
Undur tingeredu nesisa saar norlom.

变上个鸽子哈坏事哩，
蛇山里到了哈蛇伤哩，
平川里到了哈人抓哩，
半空里飞着哈鹰撵哩。

It isn't good to change into a dove:
Snakes will hurt you if you land in the mountains,
People will hurt you if you go to the plains,
Eagles will hurt you if you fly high in the sky.

Sajaghaidu xjeelee simqandu xjisa,
Ghadaadu kurisa mughui lii norlom,
Kun jirgendu kurisa kun lii norlom,
Tingeredu nesisa saar lii norlom.

变上个喜鹊了下凡间，
蛇山里到了哈蛇避哩，
人间里到了哈人不抓，
半空里飞着哈鹰躲哩。

Go to Earth in the form of a magpie:
Snakes won't hurt you if you land on the mountains,
People won't hurt you if you go where they live,
Eagles won't hurt you if you fly in the sky.

Haanjeennu szangnii bu sunusiya,
Sajaghaidu xjeele bauji xjiya,
Kun tiruudunu jiula shdasamba,
Bu yaandu xjeelesada uliguna.

玉皇爷的好话我听上，
我变个喜鹊了下凡间，
只要万民百姓能得救，
我变成个啥都成者哩。

I will follow your instructions
And go to Earth in the form of a magpie;
As long as I can save common people's lives
I'd be happy to change into anything.

Alag sajaghaingedu xjeeleja,
Nesaanu Rjanag bazardu kurija,
Rjanag bazardu debxjir gua,
Xjawaa awugu saihan ghajar gua.

变来变去变个花喜鹊，
飞来飞去飞到北京城，
北京城到了哈乱哄哄，
没有个投生的好地方。

She changed into a magpie
And flew to Beijing City.
Beijing City was in noisy chaos,
So she couldn't find a suitable place to assume human form.

Nigedu nesaa Nanjin kurija,
Nanjin bazardu sain kun gua,
Arin xirin kudunge gua,
Buye xjeelegu logge gua.

回过头飞到了南京城，
南京城到了哈没好人，
没有个干净的好人家，
我阿么投生者活人哩。

Then she flew to Nanjing City:
There were no kind-hearted people there,
There were no pure households in the city,
So she couldn't find a suitable place to assume human form.

Nigedu nesa Ghuisang kurija,
Saihanhaan kudunge yeriya,
Yerin yerindu yeriji ulin gua,
Buye xjeelegu kudunge gua.

一下飞到了西藏拉萨城，
拉萨城里有个好人家，
找来找去还是找不到，
没有个投生的好人家。

Then she flew to Lhasa City
And went looking for a nice household.
In the end, she couldn't find one that was suitable for her,
So she couldn't find a suitable place to assume human form.

Nigedu nesaa Gansindu kurija,
Nesaa ghulgenu hgendu kurisa,
Hgendu Mongghul ayilge waina,
Sain szu sain ula sain ghajarwa.

一下飞到甘省地方里，
飞到了脑山的沟脑里，
沟脑里有一个土民庄，
山清水秀是个好地方。

She flew to the Gansin area,
And arrived in a deep, remote valley.
A Mongghul village was located in the valley,
It was a picturesque scenic area.

Xjunge waisa Lenjii daudana,
Xjighaar sauji tijin deeren fon ulija,
Nenu buyenii pudoglaji gua,
Munu xjeelegu aama nimbaa.

有一个老丫头叫连吉，
单身过了四十又四年，
连吉丫头身子没有脏，
她是我投生的好阿妈。

There was a woman named Lenjii,
Who had been living alone for forty-four years,
Her body had not been stained.
She will be my mother so I can take human form.

Tingerenu furaaji tolghuinge murguya,
Bu mongghul ayildu buye xjeelewa,
Shge tingere munu aamanu furongla,
Shdehaan ndaa turoji baulghaguxja.

回头拜谢过了老天爷，
我今日投生在土民庄，
老天爷保佑我好阿妈，
早日把我哈生下来。

She kowtowed to Heaven,
I have decided to take human form in this Mongghul village,
May Heaven protect my mother
So that she will give birth to me early and safely.

Lenjii aamanu arin buye ni,
Tijin nasire bulainge rguja,
Niguudur nige saranu diinkina,
Szin udur ulisa turogu bulenna.

连吉老阿妈的好身子，
四十上怀了个娃娃了，
一天里能顶它一个月，
九天里到了哈要养哩。

Lenjii mother's pure body,
Became pregnant with a baby while in her forties,
One day served as one month,
She would give birth after nine days.

Munu shge tingere qi sunusi,
Hurin hujinre bulainge rguji gua,
Tijinre yama gaa bulai rguaxja?
Kidiudurdu turogu bulenna.

我的个老天爷你听着，
二十三十上没怀个娃，
四十者阿么价怀了娃?
几天肚子大者要养哩。

Great Heaven, please listen,
I didn't fall pregnant in my twenties or thirties,
So how did I fall pregnant in my forties?
I will give give birth in several days.

Lenjii aamanu keele ni udaaxja,
Nogxjil dongghudaa hamburaan gua,
Hara kii tauwaa zhuulaji gua,
Deeren rogdu tingere fuleexja.

连吉阿妈肚子痛开了，
天狗么喊者个不停了，
大黄风刮给了一天了，
四面的蓝天哈烧红了。

Mother Lenjii's belly began aching,
Lightning was accompanied by continuous thunder,
Fierce winds blew continuously,
Flaming clouds covered the sky in all directions.

Darmaa naama kuunge turoja,
Lenjii aama beesaa ulaawaaxja,
Munu aama qi bii ulaa joo,
Qi ndaa yaan nirenge fuyaagunii?

阿妈养哈了个胖儿子，
连吉阿妈高兴者哭了，
我的好阿妈你不要哭，
你给我起个啥名字哩?

Soon, Mother Lenjii gave birth to a son.
She was so happy that her tears rolled down,
Dear Mother please don't cry,
What name do you want to give me?

Shge tingere qi sunisi,
Bu turosan bulai goorjiwa,
Saranu bulai ama nghaina,
Saranu bulai ugo gulena.

我的老天爷你听着，
我养哈的娃娃怪不怪，
月子里的娃娃开口哩，
月子里的娃娃说话哩。

Great Heaven, please listen,
My new baby boy is so strange,
This new baby boy opens his mouth and speaks,
This new baby boy speaks words.

Mongghul kudugu nemqong bulaiwa,
Yaan baisan nirege fuyaa joo.
Munu hairgha aama qi sunisi,
Munu nire Taipinggoor wai.

穷土民家里的穷娃娃，
是啥名字起上就对了。
我的个好阿妈你听着，
我的名字就是太平哥。

You, a poor boy in a Mongghul family,
I will give you a name at random.
Dear Mother, please listen,
My name is Taipinggoor.

Lenjii aama beesaa duulina,
Munu bulai ziliu gua nuu!
Njeedunaa nire fuyaa shdaja,
Qimii jubda Taipinggoor daudaya.

连吉阿妈高兴者跳了，
我的个好娃娃多机灵！
给个家起了个好名字，
那我就把你叫太平哥。

Mother Lenjii jumped with joy,
How intelligent my son is!
He named himself,
I'll call you Taipinggoor from now on.

2. Qirig Ghari

2.出征

2. Expedition

Taipinggoor oosisa ghurdinwa,
Nige sara nige fonnu diinkina,
Nige fondu haran ghoor nasilaja,
Bunkog shge kujida shgewa.

太平哥儿实话长着快,
一个月顶它十二个月,
一年就长者像十二岁,
个子又大者力气又大。

Taipinggoor grew up quickly,
One month was equivalent to twelve months,
And after one year he acted like a twelve-year old,
A man with a powerful figure and great strength.

Munu aama qi sunisi,
Rjanagnu hara tiruudu jublong ujena,
Taipinggoor piinnannu baulaguxja,
Qinaada bu qirig gharigunii.

我的好阿妈你就听着,
北京城里万民遭了难,
太平哥就是要保平安,
我后天就出兵去打仗。

Mother, please listen,
Common people have been suffering in Beijing City,
Taipinggoor wants to go there and make peace,
I'm going out to battle the day after tomorrow.

Lenjii aama sunusaa honglaaxja,
Qi darang tigii mulaa bulaingewa,
Yama giji qirig duriji baghaldula xjigui?
Ndaa hgalaa geesa bu yama gigunii?

连吉阿妈听者心慌了,
你是个娃娃还这么小,
阿么价出大兵去打仗?
丢下我一个人阿么过?

Mother Lenjii was shocked:
You are such a little boy,
How will you go out to battle leading soldiers?
How will I make a living after you leave?

Munu aama qi nige sunisi,
Hara tiruudu jublong ujena,
Bu lii jiulala xjisa ken xjigui?
Ghoor ghuraan fondu bu hariji ireye.

我的好阿妈你就听着,
万民百姓遭了大难了,
我不救去哈谁就去哩?
两三年回来了养你哩。

Mother, please listen,
Common people have been suffering,
Who will go to save them except me?
I will be back to visit you in two or three years.

Qimu rguji yama tigii jublong ujeja,
Qimu tijeesa yama tigii loosowa,
Niudur qi ndaa geewaa yauguna,
Bu qimu yama giji muulaguna.

我怀你者受了多少苦,
我养你者费了多少心,
你今日抛下我要走哩,
我以后阿么价想你哩。

I suffered from being pregnant with you,
I suffered feeding you,
Today you will leave me,
I will miss you so much in the future.

Aamanu shge hajinnu bu modem,
Nenge sasiire yama gisada harliya,
Kun tiruudu shge jublong ujena,
Lii jiulala xjisa bu Piinnangoor puxa.

阿妈的恩德哈我知道，
这辈子我一定报答你，
万民百姓遭了大难了，
见死不救不是太平哥。

I understand your kindness,
I will repay you in my life,
Common people have been suffering,
I'm not Taipinggoor if I do nothing to save them.

Nige saradu ugo nige kuriya,
Nige fondu ujela irelghaya,
Ghuraan fondu qimu tijeela ireya,
Qimuu xjirbuu aadalge ulaalghaya.

我去了一月带一句话，
一年叫人来看一回你，
三年后来养我好阿妈，
把阿妈伺候者很舒坦。

I will send you word monthly,
I will ask people to visit you annually,
I will come back to visit you three years later,
I will look after you nicely.

Yama giji kilesada kileji adaguna,
Taipinggoor yama gisada yauguna,
Aama xeele adasa ama faar gua,
Ulaan ulaandu uliguna gija.

说来说去还是说不过，
太平哥还是要出大兵，
阿妈舍不得哈没办法，
哭里喊里的就答应了。

There was no way to persuade him not to go to battle.
Taipinggoor decided to go to battle.
Mother does not want you to leave, but there's no way to stop you—
Crying, she allowed him to leave.

Munu aama qi nige sunisi,
Bu saihan moringe hgilegunii,
Malang buda ghuila mori awula yau,
Moringe guise yama giji qirig durigui?

我的好阿妈你就听着，
我要一个好的骏马哩，
明天我俩街上买马走，
没有好马阿么出大兵？

Mother, please listen,
I need a fine horse.
Tomorrow we will go buy a fine horse,
How could I go to battle without a fine horse?

Munu aam qi nige sunisi,
Bu shdaghudii imelge hgilegunii,
Malang buda ghuila imel awula yau,
Imelge guise yama giji qirig durigui?

我的好阿妈你就听着，
我要一个桦木的鞍子，
明天我俩街上买鞍走，
没有好鞍阿么出大兵？

Mother, please listen,
I want a birch saddle.
Tomorrow we will go buy a saddle,
How could I go to battle without a saddle?

Munu aama qi nige sunusi,
Bu toorghunu simbeenge hgilegunii,
Malang buda ghuila simbee awula yau,
Simbeenge guise yama giji qirig durigui?

我的好阿妈你就听着，
我要件织锦的盘袄哩，
明天我俩人买盘袄走，
没有盘袄阿么出大兵？

Mother, please listen,
I want a brocade robe.
Tomorrow we will go buy a robe,
How could I go to battle without a robe?

Munu aama qi nige sunisi,
Bu aasi arasidii hamge hgeilegunii,
Malang buda ghuila ham awula yau,
Hamge guise yama giji qirig durigui?

我的好阿妈你就听着，
我要双牛皮的马靴哩，
明天我俩人买马靴走，
没有马靴阿么出大兵？

Mother, please listen,
I want a pair of cowhide shoes.
Tomorrow we will go buy a pair of cowhide shoes,
How could I go to battle without a pair of shoes?

Munu aama qi sunisi,
Bu fulaan funige malghange hgeilegunii,
Malang buda ghuila malgha awula yau,
Malghange guise yama giji qirig durigui?

我的好阿妈你听着，
我要顶红狐的狐帽哩，
明天我俩买红狐帽走，
没有狐帽阿么出大兵？

Mother, please listen,
I want a red fox-fur hat.
Tomorrow we will go buy a hat,
How could I go to battle without a hat?

Munu aama qi nige sunisi,
Bu haladan guaisan uldinge hgeilegunii,
Malang buda ghuila uldi awula yau,
Uldinge guise yama giji qirig durigui?

我的好阿妈你就听着，
我要把镶金的大刀哩，
明天我俩人买大刀走，
没有好刀怎么出大兵？

Mother, please listen,
I want a sword inlaid with gold.
Tomorrow we will go buy a sword,
How could I go to battle without a sword?

Munu aama qi nige sunisi,
Bu mengu baldagdii jiida hgilegunii,
Malang buda ghuila jiida awula yau,
Jiida guise yama giji qirig durigui?

我的好阿妈你就听着，
我要杆银把的钢枪哩，
明天我俩人买钢枪走，
没有钢枪阿么出大兵？

Mother, please listen,
I want a silver-handled spear.
Tomorrow we will go buy a spear,
How could I go to battle without a spear?

Hara kidi hainagnu daaldaadiija,
Haran kidi huniu daaldaadiija,
Saihan morinu kudulaa ireja,
Shdaghunu imelnu awuji ireja.

十几头牦牛哈卖掉了，
十几只绵羊哈卖掉了，
善走的骏马儿拉来了，
桦木的好鞍子买来了。

They sold more than ten of the family's yaks,
They sold more than ten of the family's sheep,
They bought a fine horse,
And bought a birch saddle.

Haldan guaisan uldinu awuji ireja,
Mengu baldagdii jiidaanu awuji ireja,
Toorgu simbeenu awuji ireja,
Fulaan funige malghanu awuji ireja.

镶金的好大刀买来了，
银把的好钢枪买来了，
织锦的好盘袄买来了，
红狐的好帽子买来了。

They bought a sword inlaid with gold,
They bought a silver-handled spear,
They bought a brocade robe,
And bought a red fox-fur hat.

Aasi arasidii hamnu awuji ireja,
Samba yambanu awuji ncoglalghaja,
Hairghannu aama hgerli giya joo,
Malang bu qirigsgenu duraa yaugunii.

牛皮的好马靴买来了，
值来值去东西值全了，
我的好阿妈哈多谢了，
明天我就要出大兵了。

They bought a pair of cowhide shoes,
And all the necessary materials were collected.
Thank you my dear mother,
Tomorrow I will go to battle, leading my soldiers.

Aamanu jirgere qudughula shdughuna,
Tijinre yasidu dahunge gharija,
Malang ulisa hulo moor ghariguna,
Munu yasidu ken dahu saugunii?

连吉阿妈的心刀搅了，
我四十上有了骨主了，
没知道明日里出大兵，
我的老骨头谁作主哩？

Mother Lenjii felt as if a knife were being twisted in her heart.
I gave birth to a son in my forties,
But tomorrow he will go to do battle far away,
Who will take care of me?

Muni aama qi nige sunusi,
Qinu yasidu dahu bu sau shdam,
Qi xjighaar ghoor ghuraan fonge sau,
Bu iregu dii qimu tijeeye.

我的老阿妈你就听着，
你的老骨头我作主哩，
你一个人过上两三年，
回来了养我的好阿妈。

Mother, please listen,
I will take care of you,
You will live alone for two or three years,
And I will take care of you when I come back.

Munu Taipinggoor qi sunisi,
Hulo moordu gharis qi simjongla,
Moor yausa mau kunnu simjongla,
Den sausa mau dennu simjongla.

我的太平哥儿你听着，
远路上你去了要小心，
走路了要防着坏人跟，
住店了要防着黑店害。

My Taipinggoor, please listen,
Be careful on the long way,
Be careful of bad men,
Be careful not to live in thieves' dens.

Nige moor sain njilagunaa bii mardaa,
Mau njilagu bii sana,
Saihan dundognu ulonge njila,
Nin gisa aama isge beesiguna.

一路上你行善要干好，
害人的事儿你不要干，
帮人的事儿你要多干，
这样阿妈我就高兴。

Be good on the way to the battlefield,
Do not do evil things on purpose,
Do good things for others,
Only in this way will your mother be happy.

Nige saradu ugonge kurilgha,
Nige fondu ujela irelgha,
Bu durdundu manee moxiji ughua giya,
Qimu debxjirege hariji ire giya.

一月里不要忘带句话，
一年里不要忘看回我，
天每日我念经求佛爷，
保佑你平安地回家来。

Please send word to me monthly,
Please ask people to visit me annually,
I will chant Buddhist scriptures for you daily,
To protect you and bring you safely back home.

Lenjii aama niguu soni kileja,
Taipinggoor sgodaa sunusina,
Nudu ujesaar nara gharaa irewa,
Taipinggoor yaugu qag ni kurija.

连吉阿妈说了一晚夕,
太平哥儿跪下听详细,
眼看着天气儿上来了,
太平哥儿就要出征了。

Mother Lenjii spoke to her son the whole night,
Taipinggoor listened, kneeling down on the ground.
The sun soon rose,
It was time for Taipinggoor to set off.

Aama mengunaa awuji gharghaya,
Mengu qimu jarigunge waina,
Puseere furoowaa yoowaa ughuya,
Idexi ideji den sausa qi jariguxja.

拿出我积攒的银子来,
全部数给了三十六两,[6]
腰带上裹给者缝好了,
住店吃饭走路你去用。

Lenjii took out her silver.
This silver will be sufficient for you.
She wrapped the silver in his belt and sewed it tightly and safely.
Spend it on meals and accommodation on the road.

Ugo guleji gui sgildunaa sanaja,
Munu aama qimu hgerli giwa joo,
Sgodaa ulaaji ghuraan tolghui ujeja,
Shdoogu aamanu hajinnii hariligu rgom.

说不出话来者心里想,
多谢了我的个好阿妈,
跪下了哭着叩三个头,
老人家的恩德定要报。

Taipinggoor thought in his heart
Many thanks, my mother.
He kowtowed thrice to his mother, weeping sadly.
I must repay my mother's kindness.

---

6   Here it is mistakenly said that the total amount of silver is thirty-six *liang* (one *liang* is five grams). No amount is specified in the Mongghul version.

Saihannu morinu bu laakiya,
Shdaghudi imelnu bu tughuya,
Toorghu simbeenu bu mosiya,
Fulaan funige malghanu bu jooya.

善走的骏马哈我牵上，
桦木的好鞍子我备上，
织锦的好盘袄我穿上，
红狐的好帽子我戴上。

Leading my fine horse,
Putting a birch saddle on the horse's back,
Wearing my brocade robe,
Wearing my red fox-fur hat.

Aasi arasidii hamnu mosaanu,
Haldan guisan uldinu joowaanu,
Mengu balfagdii jiidaanu urguadiisa,
Anamana tingernu huawuqi bau ireja.

牛皮的好马靴穿上了，
镶金的好大刀挎上了，
银把的好钢枪提上了，
就像天兵天将下凡了。

Wearing the cowhide shoes,
Carrying the sword inlaid with gold,
Holding the silver-handled spear,
As if divine troops were descending to Earth from Heaven.

Munu aama qi sau joo,
Taipinggoor xoorda yaugunii,
Morinaa harilaa furiji yau,
Nimpusi bulag szu tigii urosina.

我的个好阿妈你坐着，
太平哥儿就要出发了，
马缰绳一拉着转了头，
眼泪花就像是泉水流。

Goodbye Mother,
Taipinggoor will set off soon.
Holding the rein, he turned and walked away,
His tears flowed like a bubbling spring.

Saihan mori haulaa hulodija,
Lenjii aama shgedu ulaawaadija,
Nimpusi ghajarnu noorghoodija,
Hger ni ghadaanu sirgeedija.

善走的骏马儿跑远了，
连吉阿妈大声哭开了，
眼泪把大片地淌湿了，
喊声把大石山吵醒了。

The fine horse was galloping away.
Mother Lenjii cried loudly,
Her tears wetted the soil,
Her crying woke up the rocky mountain.

Nige tangzidu hulodaaxja,
Furaaji munu aamanaange ujesa,
Nimpusi tangghurloo lii sgeni,
Morinaa harilaa nige ujeya.

一趟子跑给了十里路，
回过头看我的老阿妈，
清眼泪挡住者看不见，
回转马再看看老阿妈。

After a while, Taipinggoor had already reached a fair distance,
He turned around and saw his mother;
His vision was blocked by tears from his eyes.
Once again, he turned his horse back to watch his mother.

Aama shge moore harlaa xjija,
Ghajar purghaan kadaa gija ireja,
Qi maali qirignaa durila xji,
Aamanu ndaa digeelghagu laghu wai.

老阿妈昏倒在大路上，
土地爷过来者劝来了，
你快快出你的大兵去，
我有办法救活你阿妈。

His mother fainted on the road.
The God of the Earth quickly came to advise him,
Please go on your expedition,
Let me revive your mother.

Morinaa harlaa durnaji yau,
Nigedu haulaa lanzhuu kurija,
Sargunu shge denre kun duurija,
Gerilnu mulaa denre sauwaadiya.

再回转马头了往东走，
一趟子跑到了兰州城，
北门的大店里人满了，
南门的小店里住下了。

He turned his horse and galloped in an easterly direction,
And quickly arrived in Lanzhou City,
The inns in the northern city gate were full,
So he stayed at an inn at the city's southern gate.

Oorqiiwaa bazaar gaixangdu hargisa,
Walghasire haanuu pujignu naalghaja,
Naalghaanu harwan fon dawaaja,
Niudurgu udurdu bu huuli awuya.

天亮了起来街道里转，
城墙上皇榜哈挂着哩，
皇榜哈挂给者十年了，
今天我把皇榜揭掉了。

Morning broke, so he strolled in the streets,
There was an announcement of state affairs on the city walls,
It had been posted there for ten years,
Today I will open it.

Sgijin qirigsge sgeexja,
Zunduusangdu jilaji kilela yau.
Bulainge waisa buye shge gua,
Te haannu pujignu haulaaxja.

守榜的衙役们看见了，
总督大人哈快报给走。
有一个尕娃娃身不大，
他去把皇榜哈揭掉了。

The guards who deal with state affairs
Quickly went to report to the governor-general.
A boy of short stature
Has opened the announcement of state affairs.

Nenge bulainu jirge ni shgewa,
Deelgela tenu qogloo ire.
Zunduu sangnu szangnii sunusiya,
Deelgela buda ghuila qoglala xjiya.

这一个尕娃娃胆子大,
猪毛绳俩绑上见我来。
听从总督大人说的话,
我俩猪毛绳俩就绑去。

How brave this boy must be,
Tie him up with a rope and bring him to see me.
Obeying the governor-general's order,
They went to tie up Taipinggoor with a rope.

Qirig ghuila jilaji harija,
Jarin moordu jii gilduna,
Buda ghuilanu guailghaa alaw,
Xjigula guailghasan seer hgileya.

两个衙役赶紧往回走,
半路上到了者细商量,
我俩跑来跑去跑坏了,
去了我俩人脚钱点要。

The two guards hurried back
And conferred on the way:
We have walked a lot because of this matter,
We will ask the boy for money when we get back.

Gerilgu mulaa dendu kuraanu,
Deelgenu awuji qoglagunii gina.
Xira nghasidii bulai qi sunusi,
Zunduu furongdu nige yauguxja.

来到了南门的小店里,
拿出了猪毛绳要绑哩。
毛头尕娃娃你就听着,
快点总督府里走一趟。

The two arrived at the inn at the southern city gate,
And began to tie up Taipinggoor with a rope.
Little boy please listen,
You must go to the governor-general.

Haannu pujignii haulaa sain ireji gua,
Zunduu sang jiilaanu duulina,
Buda ghuilanu daabulaji irelghawa,
Deelgela qimii qoglala irewa.

皇榜揭掉者你闯了祸，
总督爷爷气者跳者了，
我俩哈打发者来给了，
猪毛绳俩把你绑来了。

You were wrong to open the announcement of state affairs,
The governor-general was furious,
We two have been sent here
To tie you up with a rope.

Buda ghuilani guailghaa alawa,
Ghoor daa serge hgilegunii,
Lii ughusa qogloo alagunii,
Qimu qogloo alasa ken mudena.

我俩跑来跑去的跑坏了，
脚钱多少你要给点哩，
不给了往死里绑你哩，
把你哈绑死哈谁管哩。

We two ran here because of you,
So we want to get some money from you:
You will be sorry if you don't give us money,
No one would know if you died here.

Nohui qirig ghoorla sunusi,
Lanzhuu zunduu sai nuyoonge puxa,
Ndaa kunsge kamada jaaji gua,
Yaandu ni ndaa yaamundu warinii?

两个狗衙役你们俩听，
兰州总督是个大赃官，
我没有告人人没告我，
阿么者把我往衙门绑？

You two dogs, please listen,
The Lanzhou governor-general is a corrupt official,
I have not been accused,
So why am I being sent to his palace?

Uldinaa waraa ghoor hargulsa,
Qigi szaardu kii xjolaaxja,
Buda ghuila maali kilela yau,
Dii udasaa amunnu hgileguna.

手拿上大刀半空里抡，
耳朵里刮开了大黄风，
我俩人赶紧把话回走，
再慢了尕命哈要掉哩。

Taipinggoor immediately brandished his sword,
And thunder roared in the two guards' ears.
We must go report this as soon as possible,
We will be killed if we are late.

Nige ni ayaa ngurooxja,
Tolghuinaa teeraa ulaawaaxja,
Nige ni jilaji pusilghana,
Lauxi mauxinu sgesan maduwa.

一个人门槛上绊倒了，
两只手抱头者喊开了，
另一个赶紧扶起来了，
就像老鼠见了猫儿了。

One guard was so scared he fell to the ground,
They cried in each other's arms,
One guard quickly helped the other to stand up,
The two of them looked like mice that had seen a cat.

Munu zunduu sang uligudii gua,
Tenge bulaixag qiidagnungewa,
Uldinaa hargulsa kii xjolina,
Nigiijiha tolghuinu awaa daglawa.

好我的总督爷不得了，
那一个尕娃娃了不起，
把大刀抡开哈刮风哩，
差一点把我俩头砍下。

Dear governor-general, the boy is terrible,
The boy is amazing,
He brandished his sword and thunder roared,
We were almost slaughtered by him.

Te qimu bamunjamun nayoonge gina,
Rgennu kemada jaaji gua,
Rgenda kemanu jaaji gua,
Yama gaa rgennu goglanii?

他说你是个糊涂的官,
他没把人告到衙门里,
也没人告他到衙门里,
为啥把他猪毛绳俩绑?

He scolded you as a stupid official:
He has not been accused,
And he has never accused other people,
So why was he tied up?

Zunduu sang ayisange jirge diulina,
Niur ni xira laa tigiinge ulija,
Ghoor huawuqidu urila xjilghaja,
Udaasa rgennu qinji ni ghariguna.

总督大人听者心慌了,
脸色哈变成个黄蜡了,
派两个将爷快请他去,
再慢哈把人家惹急哩。

Hearing this, the governor-general was scared,
His face turned yellow,
He sent his generals to go invite the boy,
As he was afraid of offending Taipinggoor.

Huawuqi ghuila mulaa dendu ire,
Zooyenge baghaa kilegu ni,
Mulaa aawu qi daghaawaa yau,
Lanzhuu zunduu qimu urina.

二将爷来到了小店里,
作了个揖着说了声谢,
尕哥哥请跟上我俩走,
兰州总督爷请你着哩。

The two generals arrived at the inn,
They bowed with clasped hands and said
Little brother, please follow us,
You have been invited by the Lanzhou governor-general.

Urigu pujignu ghoor gharla ughuna,
Sgil unaasange nige rogdu pusija.
Tanu zunduu zhiblog ni nimbaa,
Nin gisa isge saihan nuyoonwa.

大红的请柬双手俩呈，
恭恭敬敬地旁边里站。
你们的总督爷做对了，
这样才算是个清贤官。

Taipinggoor submitted the announcement of state affairs,
Then he stood aside.
Taipinggoor said that the governor-general was doing the right thing,
And praised him as a worthy officer.

Den dahunu daudaji qi ndeexi ire,
Munu morinu tijeeji sulaa,
Imel da xjaunu buletilgha,
Bu huawuqinu daghaawaa nige yauya.

叫一声店家到跟前来，
把我的马喂饱饮足水，
备好鞍子和那马鞭子，
我要跟将爷们走一趟。

Then Taipinggoor asked the inn-keeper,
Please feed and water my horse,
Saddle the horse and prepare a horsewhip,
And I will go to the governor-general's.

Ndaa hujin jirghoon xjir mengu wai,
Munu aama ughusan moor seer wai,
Moor dire bu mengunu jariji gui,
Niudur bu qimu arindu ughuya.

我有三十六两碎银子，
老阿妈给我的盘缠钱，
在路上没舍得把它花，
今日里我把它全给你。

I have thirty-six taels
Which were given to me by my mother to be used on the way,
I haven't used them on the way,
Today I will give all of them to you.

Puseenaa adalghaji mengu awuja,
Den dahu beesaa tolghui murguna,
Joroti morinu tijeeji qadilghaja,
Mulaa aajanu kurgeeji gharghana.

解开腰带者把银子取，
店主爷高兴着磕头哩，
善走的骏马给喂饱了，
送我的尕哥儿上路了。

He loosened his belt and took out his silver,
The innkeeper was very glad, and kowtowed,
The fine horse was fed until full.
I will see you off, my little brother.

Taipinggoor morinaa funaanu,
Zunduu furongnu udendu kurija,
Zunduu udendu ghariji zeelena,
Taipinggoor jilaji sgodaadiija.

太平哥儿骑上骁骏马，
来到了总督的府门外，
总督爷出门者来迎接，
太平哥儿忙着跪倒地。

Taipinggoor mounted his horse,
And when he arrived at the front gate of the governor-general's palace
The governor-general came out and greeted him.
Taipinggoor dismounted and knelt down before the governor-general.

Zunduu furong turo kuraanu,
Zunduu Taipinggoordu qaa warina,
Sain idexi xireere duurija,
Harghaadu xulaajin xjun duurija.

来到了总督的府里头，
总督请太平哥吃宴席，
山珍海味眼前摆满了，
侍女丫鬟跟前站满了。

He entered the palace of the governor-general,
A party was held for Taipinggoor,
A feast of fatty food was offered on the table,
And beautiful girls served him.

Zunduu sang qi mau bii kile,
Taipinggoor turoo lii modem,
Idexinu sgesa idegunaange modem,
Lisgenu sgesa warigunaange modem.

总督爷你不要见我怪，
太平哥儿不懂啥礼行，
见饭菜就知往饱里吃，
见活了就知往死里干。

Governor-general please forgive me,
I, Taipinggoor, do not know much about etiquette,
I eat a lot if I see food,
And I work hard if I labour.

Xuurnu wara tawangnu duloja,
Sbai duraasinu uqaa sogdooja,
Idee uqaa qadisa ntiraana,
Zunduu yaan kilegunu golan gua.

拿上筷子端起了盘子，
青稞酒喝了个醉烂泥，
吃饱喝足了找炕着睡，
不管总督爷笑不笑话。

I'd like to eat by holding chopsticks and carrying a tray,
Drink highland barley liquor until drunk,
And go to bed after eating and drinking my fill.
I don't care what the governor-general thinks of me.

Nara baugu qagdu pusija,
Lanzhuu bazardu rdomlana,
Timur udengenu muxi kurisa,
Fulaan ngogmaadii moringe sgeja.

天气儿上来着起来了，
兰州的大街里转一转，
来到了一扇铁闸门前，
看见了里头的红鬃马。

Morning broke, and he got up,
Then he strolled in the streets of Lanzhou,
He saw a metal cage,
With a red-maned horse inside.

Fulaan ngogmaadii sain moriwa!
Mori jirgeregu sain moriwa,
Timur xirgii turo jublong ujena,
Tigii jublong anjiisa ireja?

好一匹红鬃的大野马!
你是马伙里的甩稍子,
圈着铁闸门里受滥气,
这么价可惜的阿门了?

What a fine red-maned horse this is!
It is the best horse among horses,
It is suffering, penned inside an iron cage,
Why is this horse being treated like this?

Munu xjariizig qi ire uu,
Bu qimu sgiji alawa,
Bu simqandu ireenu ghoor fon uliwa,
Qi yama gaa isge simqandu irewa?

我的观音菩萨到来了,
把我在这等着急死了,
我下凡着等了两年了,
你为啥才来到凡间里?

My Avalokitśvara, you have come,
I have waited here for you for a such long time,
I came to Earth and waited for you for two years,
Why did you come to Earth so late?

Bu baasi xeesire kideenii,
Kiduudurha baasi ndaa bulaaguna,
Ujesan jublongnu kileji buraagunu gua,
Qi ndaa ghurdi telgeji ghargha.

我粪堆尿窝里卧着哩,
在几天粪堆里埋掉哩,
你受哈的孽障说不成,
你快快价把我放出去。

I have lain on the dunghill,
I will surely be buried by dung after a few more days,
I have suffered so much,
Please quickly let me out of this cage.

Fulaan ngogmaadi mori qi sunusi,
Qi yaandu fog dire kideenii?
Yaandu timur xirgiire huriwa?
Qi ndaa diixidu kileji ughu.

我的红鬃野马你听着，
你为啥粪堆里卧着哩?
阿门着把你哈圈着哩?
你给我详细地说一说。

Red-maned horse, please listen,
Why did you lie on the dunghill?
Why are you penned in an iron cage?
Please tell me in detail.

Munu sain xjariizig qi sunusi,
Bu tingere furongnu mori wai,
Tingere haanjeen ndaa irelghawa,
Qimu nukorqileji baghaldula irewa.

好我的观世音你听着，
我是天宫里的神战马，
玉皇大帝派我下凡了，
帮你出兵者打仗来了。

My Avalokitśvara, please listen,
I'm a horse from the Heavenly Palace,
I have been dispatched here by the Jade Emperor
Who sent me to go into battle with you.

Usi hoolonu bu iden gui,
Kun maha kun qisi te saina,
Ghuraan buliqinnu bu idewa,
Hanala mudeenu ndaa huraaxja.

麦草豆料哈我不想吃，
要吃个人肉着喝血哩，
吃了个强盗着人见了，
人把我抓住着圈哈了。

I don't like to eat grass,
I like to eat human flesh and blood,
And because I ate three robbers' flesh
I have been penned inside this iron cage.

Taipinggoor zunduu furongdu hariji,
Zunduunu sgee ghuirlagu ni,
Fulaan ngogmaadii morinu hurisa hairghanna,
Munu joroti morila raaljiji ughu.

太平哥儿回到总督府，
见了总督着下了个话，
红鬃马圈下着太可惜，
你我的尕马俩换给吧。

Taipinggoor returned to the palace of the governor-general,
And beseeched him:
It's too bad that the red-maned horse has been caged,
Please exchange that horse for mine.

Zunduu sunurdoo beesaaxja,
Bulaixagnu hgugu ni ghurdilaja,
Ne mori kun ideji qisi uquna,
Bulaixag qi yama giji jarigunii.

总督爷听了着高兴了，
尕娃娃的死期到来了，
红鬃野马吃人喝血哩，
我看你阿么价制服哩。

Hearing this, the governor-general was glad.
The boy will soon die,
This red-maned horse eats human flesh and blood,
Let's see how he will subdue it.

Qi qugudur ndaa zaaliu ughuwa,
Niudur qimu xinjiidu xjilghaya,
Amun lai sainiisa kundu rghang gua,
Amun lai mauniisa purghaandu rghang gua.

你把我昨天整了个扎，
我叫你今日里见阎王，
运气好了哈由不得人，
运气坏了哈由不得神。

You played tricks on me yesterday,
Today I will send you to the King of Hell.
If he is lucky, nothing will happen to him,
But if he isn't, even the deities won't be able to help him.

Munu Taipinggoor qi sunusi,
Fulaan ngogmaadii mori munu haulig wai,
Haannu niurdu ujeenu qimu ughuya,
Qi funaanu shge nire awula xji.

我的太平哥儿你听着，
红鬃马是我的好宝马，
为了皇上的面子给你，
你骑上它了争大功去。

My Taipinggoor, please listen,
The red-maned horse is my precious horse,
For the sake of the Emperor's face, I will give it to you,
Please mount it and go to battle.

Lanzhuu zunduu ugo bauja,
Qirigsge deeren udenu batila,
Hara tiruudu udendu bii ghari,
Nuyoonsge walghasire gharaa ujeldu.

兰州总督爷传下了话，
衙役把四城门顶死了，
叫百姓家里不出门，
叫百官上城墙看阵势。

The Lanzhou governor-general ordered:
Gatekeepers, please bolt the gates tightly,
Ask the common people not to go out of the city,
Ask all officials to climb the city walls to see.

Ghoor huawu ger dire gharija,
Xirgiinu neeji morinu gharghaja,
Timur xirgiinu suulaa neewaaxja,
Fulaan ngogmaadii mori gharaa ireja.

两个小将爷上了房顶，
抽开个闸栏把野马放，
铁闸栏的门哈抽开了，
红鬃的野马就出来了。

Two generals went on to the roof,
Ready to open the gate and let the horse out of the cage.
They opened it,
And the red-maned horse came out of the iron cage.

Amanaa nghaiwa nige hailasa,
Amangu ghal kile tingeredu pujirina,
Taipinggoornu taada ni haulaa ireja,
Beesaanu diuliji hailagu gina.

张大嘴巴了长叫一声，
喷出的火焰有三丈三，
来到太平哥儿的跟前，
奔来跳去实在太高兴。

The horse opened its mouth and roared,
A flame leapt into the air,
The horse ran toward Taipinggoor,
And happily ran around him.

Taipinggoor nige halgha taiji xjilghasa,
Morini mangliire baghaa ughuja,
Mangliire ghar halgha bauwaaxja,
Fulaan ngogmaadii mori sgodaaxja.

太平哥儿抬起小巴掌，
打在红鬃野马额头上，
马额上留下了白掌印，
红鬃野马赶紧跪下了。

Taipinggoor used his palm
To pat the horse's forehead.
His white palm-print was left on the horse's forehead,
And the red-maned horse knelt down immediately.

Fulaan ngogmaadii mori munu sunusi,
Niudurgunsa huino qi munu nukorqiwa,
Sain kunnu kuu xjunnu qi bii ide,
Fulaan mori tolghuinaa dinsilina.

我的红鬃野马你听着，
从今后你成了我伴儿，
再不要吃人家好儿女，
红鬃野马起来点了头。

My red-maned horse, please listen,
From now, you will be my companion,
Please don't eat kind people's flesh and blood.
The red-maned horse nodded its head.

Taipinggoor moridu imelnu tughuja,
Funaanu bazaar turo nige haulija,
Fulaan morinu kol dooro ulong oosija,
Haulisa nesiniigu tigii ghurdinna.

太平哥儿给马备上鞍，
骑上着城里头跑一圈，
紅鬃野马四蹄生云了，
看起来就像是飞着哩。

Taipinggoor saddled the horse,
He mounted it and galloped a lap inside the city,
Clouds arose around its hooves,
It galloped as if flying.

Morinu hger ni noxjil tigiingewa,
Zunduu sunurdoo ayaa harlaaxja,
Nuyoon huawuqisge ayaa hargidina,
Taipinggoornu ughua giji digeelghana.

紅鬃野马叫声震天哩，
总督爷听见着吓晕了，
文官武将们也吓坏了，
求太平哥想法救总督。

The horse's roaring sounded like thunder,
The governor-general was shocked and fainted,
All the officials were frightened,
They begged Taipinggoor to save the governor-general.

Gaixangdu szang gharghaji guji dilena,
Sbai talghanu funirnii awulghana,
Nuyoosge gharghasan szangnu saidu ni,
Zunduu sang isge digeeji ireja.

大街上煨个藏上个香，
再用那炒面俩熏给个，
文官们煨藏武馆们熏，
总督爷慢慢地活来了。

They burned juniper twigs in the street,
And added roasted highland barley flour.
Thanks to the officials burning juniper twigs,
The governor-general slowly woke up.

Huiji udur ni sain tingerewa,
Zunduu sang Taipinggoornu urija,
Niudur bu qinu huawunu ujegunii,
Huawu sainiisa qirig gharila xji.

第二天到了哈天气好，
总督请太平哥上衙门，
我今天把你的武艺试，
你武艺好了就出大兵。

The weather was good the next day,
The governor-general invited Taipinggoor
To have a test of martial skills:
You'll be allowed to go to battle if your martial skills are good.

Taipinggoor nigedu daayinlaja,
Undur uladu szang garghaja,
Ulon purghaan furonglaji ughu,
Huawu szarlasa kuji gharghaji ughu.

太平哥儿很快答应了，
上去高山着煨了个藏，
叫声山神土地爷们听，
我今天比武你们出力。

Taipinggoor agreed immediately,
He offered juniper twigs atop the mountain,
And asked all the deities:
I'm going to take part in a test of martial skills today, so please help me.

Ulon purghaasge jilaji daayinlana,
Munu xjariizig sgil ndangla,
Qi huawunaa ghurdi gharghala xji,
Budangula qimu kuji gharghaya.

山神爷土地爷忙答应，
叫一声观世音你放心，
你去了显你的武艺去，
有我们给你哈出力气。

All the deities agreed immediately,
Avalokitśvara, please be reassured,
Go ahead and take part in the test of martial skills,
We will help you.

Zunduu timur tulghange pusilghaja,
Taipinggoor harwannu moorsa smudana,
Harwannu moor nigiiji taadadaaxja,
Hurinnu moorsa bu nige smudaya.

总督爷立了个铁柱子,
叫太平哥十里射柱子,
十里的路儿哈太近了,
二十里路上我射准里。

The governor-general inserted an iron pillar in the ground
And asked Taipinggoor to spear it from ten miles away.
Ten miles away is too near,
Let me spear it from twenty miles away.

Mengu baldagdii jiidaanaa waraanu,
Kujinaa gharghaji nige tardasa,
Jiidaa hurinnu moordu nesija,
Timur tulghanu xjiidu ni nauja.

拿上我的银把好钢枪,
往远处铁柱子用力抛,
钢枪飞给了二十里整,
正插在铁柱子当中心。

He held his silver-handled spear,
And threw it toward the iron post,
The spear flew twenty miles,
And landed at the center of the iron pillar.

Nuyoonsge ayaa qiree aldaaxja,
Zunduu sang ayaa harlaaxja,
Szang gharghaji xagdir taisandu,
Isge zunduu sangnu digeelghaja.

文武官员们哈吓坏了,
总督爷见了着吓晕了,
又煨藏上香炒面俩熏,
才算把总督爷救活了。

All the officials were surprised,
The governor-general fainted.
They burned juniper twigs immediately,
And the governor-general woke up.

Munu Taipinggoor qi sunusi,
Tigii shge huawunu qi surija,
Yaandu qi simbeenge musijii?
Yaandu qi funige malghange joojii?

我的太平哥儿你听着,
这么好的武艺学下了,
为什么你穿的是盘袄?
为什么你戴的是狐帽?

My dear Taipinggoor, please listen,
You have such great martial skills,
Why do you wear a robe?
Why do you wear a fox-fur hat?

Munu zunduu szaliunge sunusi,
Jang iresa qi ndaa nudundu jooji gui,
Shdima hgilejin bulaidu ulilghawa,
Hghai nghuasinu deelgela qoglaji irewa.

我的总督你详细听着,
刚来时把我没当个人,
当成了过路的要馍馍,
猪毛绳俩把我绑来了。

My dear governor-general, please listen,
You did not treat me kindly when I first came here,
You regarded me as a beggar,
And also sent people to tie me up with a pig-hair rope.

Fulaan ngogmaadii moridu idelghaya giwa,
Timur tulgha pusilghaji nanqidu baghawa,
Muxigudire bu qimu ranglawa,
Niudur bu qimu nige shdaya ginii.

既想让红鬃马把我吃,
还立了铁柱子为难我,
前几回我没算你的账,
今日里我就要清算哩。

You wanted to let the red-maned horse eat me,
And you inserted the iron pillar in the ground to embarrass me,
But I forgive you,
Today I'm going to take revenge on you.

Uldinaa sulaa gujire ni taija,
Zunduu ayaa xeesi ni gharaa ireja.
Munu Taipinggoor qi sunusi,
Qi munu nohui amunnu nige gee joo.

大刀抽出来脖子上放，
吓死了兰州狗总督爷。
我的太平哥儿你听着，
你把我的狗命先留下。

He drew out his sword and held it to the governor-general's throat.
The governor-general was so frightened he pissed his pants.
My Taipinggoor, please listen,
Please let me live.

Moorregu seernu bu arindu gharghaya,
Bu qimu xini deel raaljiji ughuya,
Qirig da morinu hgilegulaa ughuya,
Taraa da usinu hgilegulaa kurilghaya.

路上的盘缠我全管上，
你穿的衣裳我全换给，
你要的兵马我全借给，
你用的粮草我全带给。

I will pay all your expenses on your journey,
I will give you new clothes,
I will give you soldiers and horses,
I will give your army provisions.

Qinu nige seernuda lii hgilem,
Qinu nige deelnuda lii hgilem,
Qinu nige qirignuda lii hgilem,
Qinu nige taraanuda lii hgilem.

我不要你的一两银钱，
我不要你的一件衣裳，
我不要你的一个兵娃，
我不要你的一颗粮食。

I don't want your money,
I don't want your new clothes,
I don't want even one of your soldiers,
I don't want even one seed of your grain.

Qi hara tiruudunu sgilge udi,
Qi sain nuyoonge uliji su,
Nensa huino dii qi hau bii njila,
Bu hariji iresa qimu szagunii.

要你为官清廉爱百姓，
要你公正无私勤断案，
从今后你要是再胡来，
太平我回来时在算账。

Please treat the common people kindly,
Please make yourself a righteous official,
Please don't fool around anymore,
I will settle accounts with you when I come back.

Fulaan ngogmaadii morinaa funaanu,
Tirge turghu simbeenaa mosaanu,
Hujadu jiidaa da uldinaa waraanu,
Lanzhuusa haajaji durna rogdu yau.

骑上我的红鬃大野马，
穿上我的织锦长盘袄，
带上我的钢枪镶金刀，
离开了兰州城向东走。

He mounted his red-maned horse,
Wearing his brocade robe,
Holding his sword and spear,
And left Lanzhou City in an easterly direction.

Nigedu yauwaa Yanmungon kurija,
Yanmungonnu dire sgijin waina,
Gaasi aahunnu shge kuu niwa,
Menhannu moorsa qudughu nesilghana.

一直走到了那雁门关，
雁门关有人把守着哩，
是尕四阿訇的大儿子，
千里的路儿上放飞刀。

He arrived at Yanmenguan.[7]
Yanmenguan was guarded by men,
The head of the guard was the eldest son of Gaasi, an imam,
The guards threw knives at Taipinggoor.

---

7   In today's Shanxi Province.

Gaasinu kuu ni bazaar diresa ujesa,
Menhange qirig mori haaji irena,
Ixi taadadisa qirig ixi qoondina,
Taada kurisa nigehaan bulaiwa.

尔四的儿子城头上看，
千军万马涌向雁门关，
越近时人马就越少了，
到跟前时只剩一个娃。

Gaasi's son climbed atop the city wall,
Hundreds of thousands of soldiers and horses were seen rushing towards
    Yanmenguan,
But there seemed to be fewer the closer they came.
Finally, only a boy arrived at the city.

Gaasinu kuu ni ujee hadanglaja,
Qudughuanaa nesilghagunu mardaaxja,
Nenge bulainu qiree morgo zanjinna!
Fulaan ngogmaadii moringe funija.

尔四的儿子看着出神，
忘了千里路上放飞刀，
这一个娃娃长哈的俊！
骑的是高头红鬃野马。

Gaasi's son was shocked,
He forgot to throw his knife.
What a handsome boy he was!
Mounted on a red-maned horse.

Mori funisan bulai qi sunusi,
Bu qimu qudughu nesilghaji alaji gui,
Qi aamanaa dii ghoor fon kugola xji,
Hariji iregu ndaala baghaldula ire.

骑马的尔哥儿你听着，
我没有放飞刀打死你，
你快快回去吃两年奶，
再来了我俩人干一仗。

You, boy on a horse,
I didn't throw my knife at you,
Please go back and drink your mother's milk for another two years,
Then please return and fight me.

Munu qudughu nesilghajin shge huawuqi,
Menhange qirig qinu huinosa dawaana,
Qi yaandu qudughunaa nesilghan gui?
Daagu ndaala tangxaalaji yama ginii?

好我的飞刀大将军呀，
千军万马从你后头过，
你为啥不放飞刀杀人？
倒把我看着扯闲话哩？

Great knife-throwing general,
You have hundreds and thousands of soldiers,
Why don't you throw your knife?
Why do you waste your time chatting with me?

Qudughuqi huawu huinoji ujeniisa,
Nuri xjiidu ni jiidaa qoogaaxja,
Hgergeda ghari adaa nguurooxja,
Taipinggoor tenu alaaxja.

飞刀将军看了回头看，
一把钢刀扎在他背上，
他没喊一声就倒下了，
原来是太平哥开杀戒。

As Gaasi's son was looking back
A knife plunged into his back,
He fell down silently.
Taipinggoor had slaughtered him.

Iredulaa aama ndaa kidinge kilena,
Kunnu duraala hau bii ala gina,
Rjanagda kuri shdaji gui kun alaaxja,
Hariji xjisa aamadu yama giji kilem?

来时阿妈说了千百遍，
叫我千万不要乱杀人，
还没到北京就开杀戒，
回去给阿妈阿么说哩？

My mother told me repeatedly when I was leaving her,
Don't kill people deliberately,
Now I've already killed one person before arriving at Beijing City,
How will I explain this to my mother?

Fulaan ngogmaadii mori ugo guleexja,
Qi darang xjariizignu joolon sgiwa,
Rgen menhannu moordu qudughu nesilghana,
Qi lii alasa yama giji rjanag kurigunii.

红鬃野马见者开口了，
你还是观世音菩萨心，
人家千里路上放飞刀，
不开杀戒阿么到北京。

The red-maned horse spoke,
You still have Avalokitśvara's mercy,
He threw a knife from a distance of 1,000 *li*.
How will you reach Beijing without killing?

Nigehaan kun alasa uladija,
Rjanag bazarnu yama giji tarlaghagunii?
Ghurdi ghurdi Yanmungonnu dawaa yau,
Kun turuudunu amun tarlaghala yau.

才杀了一个着哭下了，
北京城阿么价解围哩？
快快价过那个雁门关，
北京城救万民百姓走。

You cried after slaughtering only one person,
If you're like this, how will you raise the siege of Beijing City?
Please quickly pass Yanmenguan,
Then go on to save the common people's lives in Beijing.

Taipinggoor laagunaa geewaaxja,
Morinaa funaa Yanmungon dawaaja,
Ghurdin ghurdinge Rjanagji yauna,
Nudu ujesaar Rjanag kuriji irena.

太平哥儿听着不哭了，
骑上那红鬃马过了关，
紧赶慢赶的往北京走，
眼看着离北京不远了。

Taipinggoor stopped crying,
Mounted his horse, and passed Yanmenguan,
Going as quickly as possible in the direction of Beijing,
He would soon arrive in Beijing City.

Jongge moorha Rjanag kurija,
Jangjasang zeelela kurija.
Munu xjariizig qi kuri uu,
Kun turuudunu ntarlaghala ire uu.

离北京不到一百里路,
章家活佛迎面走来了。
好我的观世音你来了,
快快到北京城解围去。

When he arrived one hundred *li* away from Beijing City
He was greeted by Zhangjia Living Buddha.[8]
You have come, my dear Avalokitśvara,
Please quickly save the common people's lives here.

Bu Rjanagsa jangge tudaaji irewa,
Nigiijiha amunnaa kurgeediwa,
Bu huiqaa moxji foronglaya,
Qi jilaji kun turuudunu jiulala xji.

我才从北京城逃出来,
差一点送掉了老命儿,
我念经求佛者保平安,
你大发慈悲去救百姓。

I excaped here from Beijing City,
I was almost killed,
I have chanted Buddhist scriptures for security and peace,
Please have compassion and save the common people.

---

8   Zhangjia was one of seven *hutukhtu* in Qinghai, and later was granted the title State
     Master (*guoshi*, meaning 'most knowledgeable man'). He often stayed in Dolonnor
     Lamasery in Inner Mongolia, Songzhu Lamasery in Beijing, and at Wutai Mountain
     in Shanxi. The first Zhangjia Living Buddha was Zhabaesseer. He was of the Huzhu
     Zhang family. See Stuart and Limusishiden (1994) for more.

3. Rjaala

3. 告捷

3. Victory

Nige aurdu Rjanag bazaar kurija,
Tolghuinaa gidaiji nige ujesa,
Bazar tolghuindu jiidaa uldila duurija,
Bazar jiida da uldinu dangraawa.

一口气来到北京城外，
抬起头来往城头上看，
城墙上反贼们站满了，
砖包城成了那刀枪城。

Soon, Taipinggoor arrived at Beijing City,
He looked up at the city walls
Which were full of rebel soldiers,
Full of knives and spears.

Munu xjariizig qi ghurdinla,
Munu imelnu baulghaadii,
Bu xjaa tesgenu idée buraaya,
Qi jiidaa da uldinaa ghudulghagu murgoom.

我的观世音你快一点，
我身上的鞍子全卸下，
我去了把反贼吃干净，
不费你砍一刀动一枪。

My dear Avalokitśvara, please listen,
Please unsaddle me,
I will eat them up,
You needn't use your weapons.

Taipinggoor imelnu baulghaja,
Mori nige hailaa bazaar urooxja,
Shghaila sgoldasa shdila jauna,
Maha ideji qisi uquji kurija.

太平哥把马鞍卸下了,
红鬃马嘶鸣着进了城,
蹄子俩踢来用嘴俩咬,
吃够了人肉喝够了血。

Taipinggoor removed the saddle,
The red-maned horse whinnied and galloped into the city,
It kicked with its forehooves and bit with its mouth,
Which filled with flesh and blood.

Mau kunnu uroo ni ula maduwa,
Mau kunnu qisi ni muroon maduwa,
Ghuraan aahunye ayaa suneesi aldaja,
Turo bazardu uroji xjaa ghariji iren gua.

反贼的尸体堆成了山,
反贼的黑血淌成了河,
三个阿訇爷哈吓坏了,
跑到了里摞城不出来。

Rebel corpses were piled in mounds,
Rebel blood flowed like a river,
The three imams stood numb with fear,
And ran into the inner city, not daring to come out.

Fulaan ngogmaadii mori hariji ireja,
Bur buye qisila budaa fulaangewa.
Bu mau kunsgenu ala buraawa,
Ghuraan aahun bazaar turo tudaaxja.

红鬃马从城里回来了,
浑身子鲜血俩染红了。
我把反贼们全杀完了,
三个阿訇爷就逃跑了。

The red-maned horse came back,
Its whole body was covered with red blood.
I have killed all the rebels,
And the three imams have run away.

Ghuraan aahunnu qimu geejii joo,
Qi xjigu yama gisada bii hairla,
Munu diregu qisinu nghua arilgha,
Ndaa funaanu bazarnu turo ni yau.

阿訇爷全给你留下了，
你去了把他们不要留，
把我身上的血洗干净，
再骑上我了进里摞城。

The three imams are left to you,
When you go, please do not have mercy on them,
Please wash the blood from my body,
Then mount me and go to the inner city.

Taipinggoor bazaar udendu kurija,
Deeren udenu haasan ni batiwa,
Fulaan ngogmaadii mori nige hailasa,
Bazar ude sajiraaji walghasi niuraana.

太平哥来到里摞城下，
四城门关严着开不下，
红鬃马开口着大喊了，
城门破了着城墙到了。

Taipinggoor arrived in front of the inner city gates,
The four gates were bolted,
The red-maned horse whinnied,
And the gates opened and the walls collapsed.

Bazarnu zhon waar hau nesina,
Aahunyenu yagha tughoonii hghalija,
Ghuraan aahunye ayaa xeesinu aldaja,
Sgodisa gula Taipinggoornu zeelena.

城里头破砖瓦满天飞，
砸烂了阿訇的锅和碗，
阿訇爷们吓着尿淌了，
双膝俩跪着接太平哥。

The city wall's bricks and tiles flew everywhere,
Smashing the imams' bowls and pots to pieces.
The imams were so frightened they pissed their pants,
They knelt on the ground and greeted Taipinggoor.

Budasge turong ni sain kunnii,
Falagu tigiinu muulaji gui,
Janchinnu sgil ni muriiwa,
Mauniunu kuunii hailaa alaaxja.

我们原是守本分的人，
没想造反着把祸害造，
都怪奸臣贼子坏心肠，
害死了牦牛的大儿子。

Originally, we were honest men,
We didn't think of rebellion,
But the hearts of treacherous ministers were ill-disposed,
And they murdered Maoniu's[9] son.

Shinjanu ghuraan aghadiu ni muriiwa,
Haannu muxi ni mau ama jauja,
Mauniunu kuu ni deeren piindii nuyoonwa,
Kuigaa buraawaa duko rgulghaja.

申家弟兄心肠坏透了，
皇上爷跟前把坏话说，
牦牛的儿子是四品官，
受尽了冤枉着判了罪。

The Shen family's three brothers were bad men,
And said something bad to the Emperor.
Maoniu's son was an official with a rank higher than the fourth level.
He was treated unjustly and convicted.

Bazar udere ghadaji alaja,
Narandu duluudur heelghaja,
Budangulu mudee jiilaa alawa,
Qinjire qirig ghudilghaji falawa.

四合的城门上钉给了，
大天气里晒了七天整，
我们知道着都气坏了，
气头上起兵着造反了。

Maoniu's son was nailed to the front gate,
He was baked in the sun for seven days,
We were angry to see this,
So then we rebelled.

---

9   We do not know who Maoniu is.

Shinjanu aghadiusgenii wariya giwa,
Kuigisan kundu kamaa awuya giwa,
Kunsgedu debxjir lii iregunu ken modem,
Njeenaadunaa duko rgugunu ken modem.

本想抓住申家三弟兄，
给受冤的人们报仇哩，
没想到害百姓不平安，
没想到害自家成罪人。

We wanted to arrest the Shen family's sons
And avenge those innocent people,
We didn't expect to harm the common people,
We didn't expect to become offenders.

Yama giji kilesada budasgenu puxa,
Taipinggoor aadee qi sain sgilge sana,
Buda ghuraanlanu amunnunge gee,
Nensa huino kun lii alam ndangge sauya.

千错万错是我们的错，
央及太平爷打发慈悲，
留下我们的三条狗命，
从此后再不敢害人了。

We are responsible for a thousand mistakes.
Please Grandpa Taipinggoor have mercy on us,
Do not kill the three of us,
We won't harm people in the future.

Taipinggoornu sgil ni joolonwa,
Ghuraan aahunyenu alaji gua.
Bu tasgenu amunnu liukiya,
Nensa huino mau uile bii njila.

太平哥怀慈悲心肠软，
留下了三个阿訇的命。
我把你们的尕命留下，
以后了再不要干坏事。

Taipinggoor forgave them,
And did not kill the three imams.
I do not want to kill you,
Do not do evil things from now on.

Kui giji alasan ni nige kunwa,
Tasge kidinge kunnu alaja,
Maalii kudunaa taraa tarila xji,
Debxjir aadalnaa ulaala xji.

受了冤枉的是一个人，
你们可错杀了不少人，
快快价回去了种庄稼，
平平安安地活一回人。

Only one person was treated unjustly,
But you have killed so many people—
Go back to your homes and become farmers,
And live your lives peacefully.

Ghuraan aahunye beesaa hghui taija,
Tolghuinge murguanu yauldaaxja,
Bazarnu hujisannu sajilija,
Rjanagnu kun turuudu amun torloja.

三个阿訇爷高兴坏了，
叩头谢恩赶紧离开了，
紫禁城的兵围解开了，
北京城的万民得救了。

The three imams were so happy,
They kowtowed to Taipinggoor and left quickly.
Beijing was rescued,
And the people in Beijing were saved.

4. Hari

4. 凯旋

4. Triumph

Haan furongsanaa bauji zeelela ireja,
Naiman kun tailajin jauzila tailaja,
Ndughong turo Taipinggoordu qaa warina,
Shge nuyoon hanala duraasi ujena sauduja.

皇上爷下殿着接来了，
八抬大轿把太平哥抬，
大殿上摆宴席庆大功，
文武百官全来陪功臣。

The Emperor came out of his palace to receive Taipinggoor,
Taipinggoor was carried in a sedan chair borne by eight men,
He was entertained with fancy food,
And all the officials offered him liquor.

Haan szong bauji nuyoon fungina,
Taipinggoornu gunlau ni shgewa,
Xiinan furongdu dargha saula xji,
Fulaan jauzinge qimu nanglaya.

皇上爷传旨着风封功臣，
太平哥儿平贼功劳大，
封你当西安府大知府，
大红的轿子赐给你坐。

The Emperor wanted to reward Taipinggoor:
Taipinggoor had done a great deed in suppressing the rebellion,
So he appointed him as the first magistrate of the government of Xi'an
    Prefecture.
Taipinggoor was presented with a big red sedan chair.

Daamoo gunzhunu qimii beeridu ughuya,
Tendu nughoon jauzinge nanglaya,
Zhangja sangdu gunlauda shgewa,
Xire jauzinge ughuji lus baghaxi lulaja.

达摩公主哈慈配给你，
公主哈赐给个绿轿子，
章家佛爷念经有功劳，
赐给个黄轿子当国师。

Princess Damao was betrothed to Taipinggoor,
Princess Damao was given a green sedan chair,
Zhangjia Living Buddha chanted Buddhist scripture,
He was given the title of State Master and given a yellow sedan chair.

Qi yaan hgilesa maalii kile,
Yaan hgilesa qimu yaan ughuya,
Taipinggoor jilaji sgodaaxja,
Tolghuinge murgua kilena.

你要啥东西了赶紧说，
要啥了我给你答应啥，
太平哥儿上前忙跪倒，
三拜九叩罢了把话说。

Please tell me at once what you want,
I'd like to give you whatever you want,
Taipinggoor immediately knelt before the Emperor,
And said after kowtowing—

Bu dongxi seer yamada lii hgilem,
Xiinan furongnu darghada lii danglam,
Ndaanu kudu darang shdoogu aama wai,
Rgen daagu yoodongre aadal ulaana.

我不要东西我不要钱，
西安府的知府我不当，
我家里还有个老阿妈，
她还在窑洞里过日子。

I don't want any things or money,
I don't want to be the first magistrate of Xi'an Prefecture,
My mother is in my hometown,
She lives in a cave.

Kilesan ni ghuraan fondu hariya giwa,
Munu aama sgiji sghau udaaja,
Bu jilaji aamanaa ujela xjigunii,
Aamanaa xulaaji aadal ulaala xjigunii.

说下的三年了回家哩，
老人家在家里等坏了，
我要赶紧回家看阿妈，
伺候我老阿妈过日子。

I promised her that I would return home after three years.
My mother must miss me very much,
I want to go back and visit her as soon as possible,
And to live together with my mother.

Qinu aama qimu turosa gunlau shgewa,
Qi aamanaa sgil tidasa shge xauziwa,
Yeelan jaozinge tanu aamadu ughuya,
Piinan lautaijun gijin nire nanglaya.

你阿妈养你着功劳大，
你心牵老阿妈是孝子，
再赐顶蓝轿你阿妈坐，
赐封她为平安老太君。

Your mother has also made a great contribution,
And you are a filial son,
I would like to give your mother a blue sedan chair,
And give her the respected title of Empress Dowager.

Haanjeennu hgerli ginii joo,
Bu daagu gulegu ugonge wai,
Shinjanu aghaduu ghuraanla ni,
Qinu ghar doorogu shge janchinna.

多谢了我的好万岁爷，
我还有话儿给你老说，
申龙申虎申豹三兄弟，
朝廷里他们是大奸臣。

Thank you so much,
I have more to tell you:
The three Shen brothers are treacherous ministers,
They are traitors in the government.

Maoniunu kuunii kuigaa alaja,
Shinjanu aghaduusge hailasanna,
Janchinnu ghurdi lii buraalghasa,
Kun turuudu da lusdu debxjir gua.

牦牛的儿子受冤枉死，
全是申家弟兄搞的鬼，
不除掉奸臣哈民不安，
万民不安哈国阿么保。

Maoniu's son was wrongly convicted,
He was harmed by the Shen brothers,
Please quickly do away with the treacherous ministers.
State and people will not have peace until you do away with them.

Munu Taipinggoor qi sgil ndangla,
Janchinnu bu kujaa buraalghawa,
Shinjanu ghuraan aghaduunu alawa,
Tolghuini gaixang kunsgedu ujelghana.

我的太平哥儿你听着，
奸臣贼子我已除掉了，
申龙申虎申豹三弟兄，
砍了头大街上示了众。

Taipinggoor, please don't worry,
I have already done away with the treacherous ministers,
I have beheaded the three Shen brothers,
And their heads were displayed in public.

Bu nensa huino saihan njilaya,
Janchinsgedu dii bii shdughulghaya,
Qi sgilnaa geewaa kudunaa xji,
Aamanaa saihange xulaala xji.

从今我好好的理朝政，
再不让奸臣们乱朝纲，
你就放下心了回家去，
给你的老阿妈尽孝去。

From now on, I will govern the state well.
Do not ask those traitors to make trouble again,
Go back to your home,
And treat your mother with filial piety.

Taipinggoor kudunaa hariji xjina,
Haanjeen kurgeeji bazaar ghada gharghaja,
Hujin ghuraan huawuqi daghaaja,
Ghuraan menhen qirig huino yauna.

太平哥坐红轿回家去，
万岁爷送出了北京城，
三十三个将军护他走，
三千三百兵马随他行。

Taipinggoor began his journey home,
The Emperor escorted him out of the city gate,
Thirty-three generals escorted him,
Three thousand soldiers followed behind him.

Daamoo gunzhu nughoon jauzire sauja,
Kurgeennaa daghaawaa kudunaa xjina,
Daghaasan kun ulon gula ujuur gua,
Kol sger ni nogxjil tigii dautiwa.

达摩公主坐着绿轿子，
跟着夫君去看老阿妈，
跟的人多着看不到尾，
脚步声就像雷响哩。

Princess Damao sat in the green sedan chair,
Following her husband back home.
So many people followed Taipinggoor that it was difficult to see the end of
    the procession,
Their footfalls were as loud as thunder.

Gansin ghajardu kuriji ireja,
Aama ndaa turosan sain ghajarwa,
Taipinggoor huawuqinge daudaji,
Bayar gesinennu aamadunaa kurgeeja.

飞马快步来到甘省地，
是阿妈生我的好地方，
太平哥叫上个小将爷，
一道帖给阿妈报喜讯。

Taipinggoor arrived in the Gansin area.
It's the excellent place where my mother gave birth to me.
Taipinggoor dispatched a general ahead of him
To inform his mother that he was coming.

Lenjii aama xjighaar aadal ulaana,
Durdundu kuunaa sanaji ulaana,
Jirge da helge nige sajiraaja,
Nudu ni sughuroowaa sgen gua.

连吉阿妈单个过日子，
天每日盼的是太平哥，
痛烂了肝花想烂了心，
哭瞎了一对儿明眼睛。

Mother Lenjii was living alone,
She missed her son and wept daily,
She missed her son greatly,
She had cried so much that she had gone blind.

Murge wangxir tasiraawaa shdaasiwa,
Shdaasire boosi tagxi nagxi haulina,
Shdaasire qiirsi sauwaanu duurija,
Raawa ni boosi foor tigiigewa.

褐褃烂着剩了几根线，
虱子褐线上来回价走，
虮子在褐线上爬满了，
头发成了虱子的窝了。

Her garments were in rags,
Lice infested her garments,
And their eggs covered her garments.
Her hair had become a nest of lice.

Turongdar bayar gesnen kurija,
Lenjii aama qi nige sunusi,
Bulai gunlau zinlaji ireja,
Ghuruudurnu huino kuriguna.

头一道喜帖子到来了，
连吉老阿妈你详细听，
你儿子立功着回来了，
三天日子里就能到了。

The first report reached Mother Lenjii:
Dear Mother Lenjii, please listen carefully,
Your son has achieved distinction,
He will arrive here three days later.

Bayaan kudu bayar kilela xji?
Munu yoodongre yama gila irenii?
Munu kuu yauwa ghuraan fon ulija,
Fugujuu digeejiiha lii mudeni.

你不去富人家报喜讯?
来我的破洞里做啥哩?
我儿子走掉着三年了,
死着吗活着的谁知道。

Why don't you go make this announcement at a rich man's home?
Why do you want to come to my poor cave?
My son has been gone for three years,
I don't know whether he's dead or alive.

Ghoordar bayar gesnen kurija,
Lenjii aama qi diixi sunusi,
Qimu Piinnan Lautaijun funkija,
Qinu bulai malang kuriguna.

第二道喜帖子报来了,
连吉老阿妈你详细听,
你今日里封了老太君,
你儿子明日里就到哩。

The second report reached Mother Lenjii:
Dear Mother Lenjii, please listen carefully,
You have been granted the title of Empress Dowager,
You son will arrive tomorrow.

Ghuraandar bayar gesnen kurija,
Piinnan Lautaijun qi sunusi,
Qinu bulai beerinaa duriji irena,
Niudur tanu kudu kuriguna.

第三道喜帖子报来了,
平安老太君你详细听,
你儿子带来了尕媳妇,
今日里就要到你家里。

The third report reached Mother Lenjii:
Dear Empress Dowager, please listen carefully,
Your son is coming with your daughter-in-law,
They will arrive today.

Shdoogu aama beesaa diulaaxja,
Munu Taipinggoornaa zeelela yau,
Tendilin mandilin yoodongsa gharija,
Suuraan muuraandu muxiji yauna.

老阿妈高兴着跳开了，
我快去接我的太平哥，
摸哩揣哩地出了洞口，
溜哩爬哩地直往前走。

Mother Lenjii jumped with joy,
I will go to receive my Taipinggoor.
Guiding herself out of the cave with her hands,
She walked forward unsteadily.

Taipinggoor aamanaa sgeexja,
Sgodaa shgedu ulaawaaxja,
Piinnan Lautaijun kuunaa shdirina,
Ulaawaa sghur nudunu sgelgheexja.

太平哥儿见了老阿妈，
跪在那地上着放声哭，
平安太君摸着好儿子，
清眼泪洗亮了瞎眼睛。

Taipinggoor arrived and was greeted by his mother,
Kneeling down on the ground and crying.
The Empress Dowager touched her son's head,
And cried; her tears restored her sight.

Munu aama shge jublong ujeja,
Murge wangxir shdaasidu furaaxja,
Bur buye boosi foordu furaaxja,
Qi yama giji nailaji saunii!

老阿妈你受了大苦了，
褐褂子变成了褐线了，
满身满头成了虱子窝，
你阿么价挨着坐着哩!

My mother has suffered so much,
Her garments are in rags,
Lice are creeping all over her body,
How have you borne it!

Xjeelesan nemqong amundii kunna,
Jublongge ujesa yiixi xjon gua,
Munu Taipinggoornaa sanaa alawa,
Niudurgu udurdu isgenee sgewa.

生来的穷人苦命的根，
受一点寒苦哈没有啥，
想坏了我的太平哥儿，
今日里才把你盼来了。

I have had a sad fate since I was born,
Suffering doesn't matter,
I missed Taipinggoor so much,
I have finally seen you today.

Murgongxirnu tailaa xini deel raaljija,
Qirig bulaisgedu boosi warilghana,
Nige boosi warisa nige xjir menguwa,
Nige qiirsi warisa jamtag xjir menguwa.

脱下褐褂换上新衣裳，
叫兵娃们过来抓虱子，
抓一个虱子赏一两银，
抓一个虮子赏半两银。

Take off your garments and put on new clothes,
Ask some soldiers to kill the lice,
Offer each soldier a *liang*[10] of silver for each louse he catches,
And half a *liang* of silver for each egg he finds.

Ghuraan shge yagha boosi warija,
Ghuraan mulaa yagha qiirsi warija,
Mau murge wangxirnu awuji ireenu,
Boosi qiirsinu furoo ughuja.

虱子抓给了三大碗半，
虮子抓给了三尕碗半，
破烂的褐褂子拿上来，
虱子虮子包在褐褂里。

They collected three large bowls of lice,
And three small bowls of eggs,
Took her old garment,
And wrapped the lice and eggs up in it.

---

10   One *liang* is five grams.

Daamoo gunzhunu daudaji ireja,
Geril uladu xjaa xiraawaanu kile,
Bayaanjasa hanala bayaanjaya,
Nemqongraasa hanala nemqongraaya.

叫来达摩公主尕媳妇，
你拿到南山上放火烧，
说一声富了哈大家富，
再说声穷了哈大家穷。

Princess Damao requested,
Burn the old garment on South Mountain, and said,
Regardless of poverty or wealth,
Let's work together.

Daamoo gunzhu geril uladu gharaanu,
Nige ghaldu murgongxirnu xiraaxja,
Bayaan kun ixida bayaanjaldu,
Nemqong kun ixida nemqongraadu.

达摩公主来到南山上，
一把火烧掉了破褐褂，
富人家富了哈越要富，
穷人家穷了哈越要穷。

Princess Damao came to the South Mountain
And burned the old garment in the fire.
Regardless of poverty or wealth,
Let's work together.

Daamoo gunzhu ugonu gulee nqiglaja,
Simqnnu nemqong kunnu alaja,
Bayaan kun bayaan ghula toosi urosina,
Nemqong kun nenqong ghula nghusi nerdena.

达摩公主说错两句话，
害苦了天下的穷苦人，
富人家富着淌油着哩，
穷人家穷着没法活哩。

Princess Damao said something is wrong,
The poor people of the world are suffering,
Rich people are so rich they are dripping with oil,
And poor people are too poor to survive.

Lautaijun nige jong ghuraan nasilaja,
Daamoo gunzhu tijin nasilaja,
Shdoogu aamanaa tailaji gharghaanu,
Bu nanhai putu ularenaa xjigunii.

老太君活了一百零三,
达摩公主活了四十岁,
抬送了养我的老阿妈,
再回我南海普陀山走。

The Empress Dowager lived for 103 years,
Princess Damao lived to be 40 years old.
I finished performing my mother's funeral,
I returned to Putuo Mountain in the South Sea.

2. The Ballad of Marshal Qi

When I was a child, some guests visited my home. My parents feted them with warm liquor and delicious food as they sat on a heated platform in the main room of our house. After drinking for a while, they began singing the Mongghul folksong, *The Ballad of Marshal Qi,* using the local Han Chinese dialect. In total, I guess I heard this song sung around three times during my childhood. At that time I only understood a little of the local Han language, so I did not understand what they were singing about. Those guests came from south of my hometown (Danma Town), from Donggou, Taizi and Donghe Townships and Weiyuan Town, where Mongghul people often sing *The Ballad of Marshal Qi* and *Tangdarihgiima,* another very popular Mongghul folksong.

Danma Town is located at the center of the traditional Mongghul homeland, the Duluun Lunkuang or Seven Valleys. Behind my village is a mountain that historically marked the division between the Haliqi area, where my village is, and the Fulaan Nara region to the east. Within Haliqi, *The Ballad of Marshal Qi* is mostly sung in Weiyuan Town, and Taizi and Donghe townships, where there are many people with the Qi surname who are believed to be the descendants of the Qi *tusi* (chieftain).

The song describes Qi *tusi,* Qi Bingzhong who, at eighty years of age, was sent to suppress a rebellion. The song is sung in the local Han dialect during gatherings when liquor is consumed.

The *tusi* system was abolished in 1939 in Huzhu County. In 2014 Mongghul people under the age of forty had almost no idea about *tusi.* Even those who still sing *The Ballad of Marshal Qi* do not know that it is related to the Qi *tusi.* Thus the system that was practiced for several hundred years among Mongghul people has come to an end in their minds. In fact, the system once played a negative role in Mongghul society (Limusishiden and Stuart 2006: 66):

> The *tusi* generally did not speak Monguor—instead they spoke only Chinese. In fact, Kevin Stuart was told that the reason many Minhe Mangghuer wedding songs are sung in Chinese is that the *tusi* did not understand Mangghuer. When *tusi* did attend weddings, they were the honored guests and songs were sung in Chinese so that they would understand. The *tusi*, as described by Schram, ensured that their children learned Chinese, they did not wear Monguor clothes, they married Chinese, and their daughters mostly married Chinese.

So this folksong is another piece of evidence regarding the influence of the Chinese language among the Mongghul. Nonetheless, *The Ballad of Marshal Qi* is still very much a Mongghul folksong and is a living treasure that reflects their history.

In order to provide some background on the Qi *tusi*, I have translated an article by Qi (2012):[1]

Exploring *The Ballad of Marshal Qi* and Its Place of Origin

I was born in a small mountain village in one of the Upper Thirteen Villages[2] that were historically governed by the East Qi *tusi* in Mongghul areas. When I was very young, I began listening to the heroic folk songs *The Ballad of Marshal Qi* and *The Ballad of Taipinggoor*[3] from people in my parents' generation. In 2012, when I went to work in Baiya Village, Weiyuan Town, I surprisingly found the birthplace of the long heroic folksong, *The Ballad of Marshal Qi*. I looked over the ancient citadel that was built and inhabited by Marshal Qi and his descendants, which is still relatively well preserved. I located their military camp, trenches, stables, wooden boxes, cornerstones, seals, sacred spring, and many other relics. I was so happy to see them and regarded them as treasures. Later, when I finished my official work in the countryside, I again went

---

1 Many thanks to Qi Wenru, who kindly gave permission for his article to be translated here.
2 Tangba Big Household, Changshou Big Household, Yatou Household, Yongan Household, Xiaosi Household, Bulong Household (Dasi Village), Erxiangbu Household, Tieling Household (Jijiawan Village), Gongta Household (Baiya Village), Dacaizi Household and Yaomu Household (etc.)
3 See above.

to Baiya, Yatou, Tangba, Xiaozhuang, Dasi, and Qiaka villages, among others. In the Tangba Thirteen Villages[4] formerly governed by the East Qi *tusi*, I visited some elderly people, searched for relics, and consulted historical materials. Finally, I conclude that Baiya Village is the source of the *The Ballad of Marshal Qi*, which has been sung in various versions throughout the Huzhu area. The elderly singers I visited all agreed that songs should be sung in different versions, as nobody would listen to it if everybody sang it the same way. Therefore each Mongghul singer improvised and added elements when singing *The Ballad of Marshal Qi*.

Visiting the Baiya Old Citadel

Baiya was a wilderness area.
Marshal Qi came here and did a geomantic survey.
In front of the wilderness was Kuixin Mountain.
The mountain behind the wilderness was a holy mountain.[5]
They camped along the riverside.
My 7,600 subjects, please listen.
This golden basin[6] is an abundant farmland;
We will build a citadel in Baiya in the shape of a red square.

These are the opening sentences of the Baiya version of *The Ballad of Marshal Qi*. The citadel, located southeast of today's Baiya Village, consists of an inner citadel and an outer citadel. The west gate of the inner citadel has been replaced by a road stretching from east to west. On the whole, its outer wall is still well preserved, but it has become lower and thinner than before. Local people are said to have used some of the soil from the wall in their fields. A drainpipe made from red stone can still be seen protruding from the citadel and stretching into the south lane. Eight households reside within the northern and southern sections of the inner citadel: Chang, Gong, Wen, Liu, and Li. About forty meters from the inner citadel's south and west sides, the base of the walls of the outer citadel can be seen. The walls in this part were low inside and high outside.

---

4   This is an alternative name for the Upper Thirteen Villages.
5   Mongghul: Hudu Kuji.
6   That is, the Baiya area.

The inner citadel was registered in the Record of Cultural Relics in Huzhu and Ping'an County:

> The Baiya Citadel is oblong; the length from south to north is eighty meters and from east to west is eighty-two meters. The walls are eleven meters high, and four meters wide at the base. The thickness of the levee to make the wall is 0.16 meter. The gate was built in the western wall and had a width of 4.2 meters. It was constructed in Qing Dynasty and the city wall is preserved well.

Chang Zenghua (b. 1932), an elderly resident from inside the inner citadel, said:

> I still remember clearly that a front gate was built in the west side of the inner citadel and the north side of the outer citadel. The area between the two citadels was Master Qi's garden and vegetable plot. When the *tusi* system was abolished in August 1939, grain was confiscated from the Qi chieftain and made the property of the county's residents, and then Master Qi's family began to decline. In 1946, Master Qi, Qi Huan, divided his inner citadel into six parts. We three households bought three parts, located in the south of the citadel, each paying 300 taels of silver. Master Qi and Disabled Master Qi Yinsi[7] lived in their eastern courtyard, located in the northern side of the citadel. The middle yard was left to their third brother, Qi Bing, who lived in the Shaba area of Nianbo, Ledu Region. When Master Qi died in 1954, the Disabled Master was taken to Ledu by Third Master Qi Bing. The government confiscated all of Master Qi's houses and fields, and distributed them to some people who had no houses or fields. The current eight households that live inside the inner citadel moved in after the Land Reform Movement in 1951.

Li Honglin (b. 1941), who lives in Baiya Village, said:

> Before the Land Reform Movement in 1951, there were three graveyards for Qi *tusi* in front of the households surnamed Bai in the fourth natural village, Yatou Administrative Village. We call it 'Nayanhe.'[8] There were six large trees in front of the graveyards. One of them was used to make Master Qi's coffin. His funeral was held by the Qi family. In the past, all the sons in the family of the Qi *tusi* in Baiya Village were buried at the Qi family's graveyards in Ashiji area, governed by Tangba Village. According to village elders, there were eighty ridges of hills behind the

---

7   Qi Huan's younger brother, a disabled man.
8   In Mongghul, this refers to official graveyards and the official families in Yatou Village called 'Laoye Fentan' (referring to the Master's graveyards).

graveyards, and the location of the graveyards was supposed to have an influence on the fortune of Master Qi's family.

Two residents of Yatou Village, Qi Mingsi, a retired teacher from Huzhu Number One Middle School, and his cousin, Qi Huisi, are two descendants of the East Qi *tusi* family. They said:

> Master Qi was living in Baiya Village and already in his sixties around the time the People's Republic of China was founded. Disabled Master's right arm and left leg were deformed. They were poor, so we supported them, but they also had to go begging to support themselves. When Qi Master died, Disabled Master was taken to live in Nianbo by Third Master, and after that, we never heard from them again.

When I asked them where Marshal Qi was buried, they replied:

> Our ancestors told us that Marshal Qi was buried in Xining when he died. Master Qi was from the old Baiya citadel. All *tusi* after Marshal Qi were buried in Qijia graveyards in Ashiji, including Qi Guiyu, the last *tusi*. When he died, his corpse was put in a cart and drawn by a horse to the Qijia graveyard from the valley opening of Hongyazigou Township by people from our Upper Thirteen Villages. In order to prevent the graveyard being trampled by livestock, a wooden fence was built to enclose the graveyard and a gate was put in the fence.

Today, Xie Lianji (b. 1932), a Tibetan from Qiaka Village (which was historically part of Ashiji) in Taizi Township, told me:

> Before I went to Yushu to suppress bandits in 1958, there were twenty or thirty tombs of the Nianbo Qi *tusi*[9] at the Xiaoquzhang and Kegan places inside the Qijia graveyards which are located in our village's shady side. Before liberation, on Mourning Day on the fourth or fifth day of April each year, many descendants and relatives of the *tusi* came to the family graveyard with their horse carts from Ledu County. The biggest graveyard occupied about 0.4 acres, and had a stele as tall as two people. Later, during China's big steel-making drive in 1958, the stele was smashed and used to build a steel furnace, the tombs were leveled, and the graveyards became cultivated land. Now all the *tusi*'s graveyards have become either farming fields or local villagers' graveyards.

From historical data and the East Qi *tusi*'s *Qi Family Genealogy* we learn that at least thirteen East Qi *tusi* lived in Baiya, Yatou and Ashiji villages

---

9   The Nianbo Qi *tusi* is also the East Qi *tusi*.

in Weiyuan Town within the boundary of Huzhu County. Historically, many talented people were produced in each generation among the Chang *bazong*[10] and Tong *bazong*'s descendants under the Qi *tusi*: for example, Chang Yuzhang was a descendant of Chang *bazong* in Baiya Village who had graduated from the seventeenth grade of the Huangpu (Whampoa) Military Academy and later became the director of the political department of the military academy. After liberation in 1949, Tong *bazong*'s descendants included senior colonels and officers.

Having explained the matter of the graveyard in the old citadel in Baiya Village, how can we explain the names of places that surround the citadel: Jiaomu 角木 Trench, Camp Field, Under the Ditch, and Qianjiu that surround the old citadel? I was told by old men from Baiya Village that when Marshal Qi finished building the inner and outer citadels in one and a half years, he ordered Eighth Master Tong[11] to channel water from a miraculous spring, by digging a ditch from Dacaizigou Plain to the inner citadel, in order to water the garden. The water was also used to create a moat. Today, the Jiaomu Trench is located to the east of the old citadel, with a depth of between forty and fifty meters and a length of from five to six kilometers. Northwest of Baiya Village, a kilometer away from the old citadel, there is still a ditch ten to twenty meters wide and one kilometer long, which villagers call Under the Ditch. Today, traces of human construction can still be seen in the soil on both sides of the ditch. Marshal Qi's descendants drank from a so-called Hidden Spring located in the Jiaomu Trench.

West of the ditch, there are several hundred *mu* (equivalent to 0.165 acres) of fields and villagers' households. Local villagers Li Honglin and Li Yande said that historically that area was Marshal Qi's camp and drill ground. South of the ditch there is a ridge stretching from east to west. This was the place where Marshal Qi's cavalry tied their horses up. Stories of the shining spears and armored horses have been buried in the dust of history, but in tracing back the source of the place name Qianjiu, which means 1,900, and is located northeast of the village, Qi Youren, who currently lives in Shaba Village,[12] said that the name dates from when Qi Guobing had gone out to battle in the Hexi area. At that

---

10   *Bazong* is a military rank, below that of commanding officer.
11   That is, Tong *bazong*.
12   Nianbo Town, Ledu Region.

time, alien bandits arrived and killed 1,900 unarmed common people of the Thirteen Villages. The Baiya Citadel was seriously damaged, and some families of the East Qi *tusi* had to move to live in neighboring Yatou Village, where their descendants still live today. Later, with the Emperor's kind approval, Qi Bozhi constructed a Qi *tusi yamen* in Nianbo. The old citadel in today's Baiya Village was built by Qi Baozhi's younger brother, Qi Zhongzhi, when he took office in Weiyuan Camp Garrison. Before he built the citadel there was a *yamen* for *tusi* at the location where the citadel was later built.

Singing *The Ballad of Marshal Qi*

This heroic epic was created and sung by folk artisans, the beloved generals and common people of the Qi *tusi*, within a certain social environment and under certain historical conditions. *The Ballad of Marshal Qi (Qijia Yanxi)* was sung widely in Huzhu and the surrounding area. *Yanxi* is probably a sound change from *yuanshuai*, marshal, in the same way that Jieguanting 'Take Over Guanting' is mistakenly pronounced as Jingguantian, literally well-observe-sky. Tu nationality people regarded any military officer who went out to battle as a marshal. The others under Marshal Qi—Chang *bazong*, Tong *bazong*, lŭ *bazong* and Li *bazong*—were generals at his command.

In order to safeguard national unity and territorial integrity, Qi Bingzhong (childless), his nephew Qi Guobing, and his greatnephews Qi Bozhi and Qi Zhongzhi went to battle despite Qi Bingzhong's advanced age. The opening sentence of the song is:

> Rebels arise in Luoyang Citadel (actually it is Liaoyang Citadel or Lŭyangyi 'Lŭyang Station'), bully and oppress the common people.

Commanding Officer Chai received the order and went out to battle, but returned home to receive treatment for an illness. He dared not report to the government of the Ming Dynasty, so he made several false decrees and military proclamations in succession to the Gansu commanding officer, Qi Bingzhong (that is, Marshal Qi), forcing him to go out to battle. On the way to the battle, he unluckily encountered over forty days of autumn rain. The grain became mildewed. Lü *bazong*, who was in charge of the grain, went back to take more grain, but Commanding

Officer Chai's soldiers stole his grain on the way. At last, Marshal Qi's horse was startled, and its hoof dug potatoes from the ground. This helped his soldiers deal with their hunger. Next, they artfully crossed over the Black River, across the Shaliu Bridge, outwitted the rebels at Luoyang Citadel, and saved the suffering common people.

On the way back, Qiija Yanxi was again betrayed by Commanding Officer Chai and was shot with an arrow by one of Commanding Officer Chai's soldiers. He adopted an infant son on his way home. When he arrived home, he introduced the baby boy to his family, explained his funeral arrangements and other things to his family, and then pulled the arrow out of his body and died.

From the details of the story, we know that they were very troubled times at the end of the Ming Dynasty and the beginning of the Qing Dynasty. Such times make heroes, and so at just this time, such famous generals as Chai Guozhu and Qi Bingzhong emerged in the Hehuang area.

Chai Guozhu was born in December in the second year of Longqing Ming Emperor Muzong (1568) in Qingshuibu in Xining prefecture.[13] He was a famous general in the Ming Dynasty. In the summer of the forty-sixth year of the Wanli reign (1618), Chai Guozhu, the commanding officer of Gansu, was ordered to garrison in Shanhaiguan[14] by the Ming government, where he personally fought against the Later Jin invasion with his soldiers. When the Ming soldiers were utterly defeated in the battle of Saeryou,[15] Chai Guozhu was ordered to garrison in Shenyang 沈阳 by the central Ming government. Later, he had several fierce battles with soldiers of the Later Jin of Nurhaci and Huang Taiji. There were many dead and injured on both sides. In July of the forty-eighth year of the Wanli reign (1620) he fell ill and was allowed to return home for treatment. Not long after Chai Guozhu left, the Later Jin invaded Shenyang and Liaoyang, overwhelming the Ming soldiers. During this period, the central Ming government gave Chai Guozhu the power of *youjun*, 'Military of the Right', and *zhongjun*, 'Military of the Center', and

---

13   Today's Jingyang Town, Datong Hui and Mongghul Autonomous County.
14   In today's Qinhuangdao City, Hebei Province.
15   The battle of Saeryou occurred in today's Fushun City, Liaoning Province, between the soldiers of the Later Jin and Ming, in 1619.

ordered him to go to the battlefront at Liaodong[16] as soon as possible. He left home immediately, but when he arrived at Gaolan in Gansu, his disease deteriorated and he had to return to Xining. Finally, he died in May of the fifth year of the Tianqi reign (1625), at the age of fifty-six.

Qi Bingzhong was born in April of the first year of the Wanli reign (1573). He was the East Qi *tusi* and marshal. In the spring of the first year of the Tianqi reign (1621), led by Chai Guozhu and following the recommendation of the central Ming government's civil and military ministers, the Emperor made an imperial order to Commander Qi in Gansu, who was made assistant commissioner-in-chief, and asked him to lead his own soldiers, as well as some soldiers stationed in Gansu, to Liaodong to defend Puhe.[17]

Liaoyang and Puhe had already been occupied by soldiers of the Later Jin before Qi Bingzhong arrived. Mingxizong made Qi Bingzhong Official Commanding Officer and ordered him to garrison in Lüyangyi[18] with ten thousand soldiers. The following year, on the twenty-second day of the first lunar month, Qi Bingzhong went to help Xiping. The Ming soldiers encountered the Later Jin soldiers at Pingyang Bridge (southeast of today's Heihe, Liaoning Province). Initially, Sun Degong and Zu Dashou were ordered to be the vanguard army of Ming soldiers. However, the two ran away as they met Later Jin soldiers face to face. This forced Qi Bingzhong and Liu Qu's[19] soldiers to fight with the Later Jin's soldiers. Qi Bingzhong himself fought in spite of his illness, and his generals, Tong *bazong* and Lü *bazong*, fought bravely against the Later Jin soldiers. Both sides fought for about half a day, but no clear outcome was reached.

At this crucial juncture, the cunning Sun Degong and other vanguard soldiers turned back and fled. Seeing soldiers turning back and fleeing, all the other soldiers thought they were being defeated and ran for their lives. Qi Bingzhong shouted at them to stop, but was unsuccessful, and the Ming army was defeated. Liu Qu was killed. Qi Bingzhong's left arm was cut off and he was shot with three arrows, but he still managed to

---

16 Liaodong refers to the southern and eastern areas of today's Liaoning Province and the southeastern area of Jilin Province.
17 Northeast of today's Shenyang.
18 Northeast of today's Jingxian, Liaoning Province.
19 A commanding officer in the Ming Dynasty.

fight while retreating, until he finally fell from his horse due to loss of blood. He was supported by his brave hometown soldiers to fight and open a way forward to Lüyang. However after walking for only a short while Qi Bingzhong died, aged forty-nine.

When Emperor Xizong learned this, he awarded Qi Bingzhong the titles of State Junior Guardian, Grand Master of Glorious Happiness, and Left Commissioner-in-Chief, and also paid the funeral expenses and built a stele for him. Qi Bingzhong's corpse was buried by his family at their graveyard south of Xining. Emperor Qianlong of the Qing Dynasty posthumously awarded him the title of martyr.

Qi Bingzhong had no son, so his nephew, Qi Guoping, inherited his *tusi* position. In the eighth year of the Chongzhen reign (1635), due to his merits, he was awarded the title of *xanjiang*, 'Chief of Staff', in Zhuanglang (today's Zhuanglang County, Gansu Province). In the sixteenth year of the Chongzhen reign (1643) a rebellion arose in Xining, so he returned from Zhuanglang to suppress the rebellion. He led his people to submit to the new Qing Dynasty in the second year of the Shunzhi reign (1645). In the fifth year of the Shunzhi reign (1648), Ganzhou, Liangzhou and Suzhou fell into rebels' hands, and so he went and recaptured Ganzhou and Suzhou. In the ninth year of the Shunzhi reign (1652) he was awarded the title of Deputy Commander of the Xining Military Region and presented with an official seal. He retired at an advanced age.

Qi Bozhi inherited the *tusi* position. In the fourteenth year of the Kangxi reign (1675) Wu Sangui rebelled, assisted by Wang Fucheng, the chief of public security in Pingliang. The rebels stormed Gongchang, Lingtao, and Lanzhou. Qi Bozhi guided all *tusi* around Xining and accompanied the Xining Commanding Officer, Wang Jinbao, to go east and suppress the rebellion. When he and others arrived at Zhangjiahewan[20] they crossed over the Yellow River at night on skin rafts, and then defeated the rebels at Xincheng and Longwei Mountains. They then went to Lanzhou, guarded the city and managed its affairs. Due to his achievements, Qi Bozhi was promoted to the position of Regimental Commander. He was considered a hero, and was well known for his skills at riding horses and shooting arrows. In the twenty-eighth year of the Kangxi reign (1689) the Emperor invited him for an audience. The Emperor personally

---

20   This might be today's Hekouxiang, Xigu District, Lanzhou City, Gansu Province, http://www.tcmap.com.cn/gansusheng/xiguqu_hekouxiang.html

examined Qi Bozhi's wounds, and promoted him to the position of Lieutenant in Gansu. Later, he was promoted to the position of Deputy Commanding Officer in Jingyongchang and later to Commanding Officer in Jingxiangyang. He soon retired from his position and went back to Nianbo, where he built his *tusi yamen*. He had no descendant to inherit his position. He helped people in need. He died in his home.

Qi Zhongzhi was Qi Bozhi's younger brother. In the eighth year of the Kangxi reign (1669) he took part in a martial exam and in the ninth year he passed the highest imperial exam. In the fourteenth year (1675), he followed Commanding Officer Wang Jinbao to recapture Lingtao, Gongchang, and Qinzhou and was then promoted to Regimental Commander in Weiyuan Camp in Xining. Later, he was ordered to defend Qinzhou. He recaptured Xihe and Lixian, and was then promoted to the position of Xining Deputy Commander. Later, his successor was promoted to the position of Deputy Commander in Zhangjiakou. In the thirty-fourth year (1695), he went on an expedition in Geerdan and reached Kundulu, where he fought despite poor health. In the thirty-fifth year (1696), he went to fight against Galdan with the Emperor. In the thirty-sixth year (1697), he went to the frontier with the Emperor, arrived at Eerduosi,[21] and transported rice to the frontier at Shashatu.[22] Based on his achievements, he was promoted to the position of Lieutenant in Hebao Camp in Shanxi. Later, he was moved to Zhumaluo. Finally, he returned home to Baiya. In the fifty-second year (1713) he was still *tusi* and was much loved by locals. He died in his fifty-seventh year (1718).

From the above, we know that both Chai Guozhu and Qi Bingzhong, the two well known generals, lived in turbulent times in the Hehuang area. Chai Guozhu was five years older than Qi Bingzhong. The two generals participated in the Huangzhong battles[23] to defeat Mongol invaders. The two were both promoted to Regimental Commanders, Assistant Commanders, and Hongshui Camp Deputy Commanders in Gansu (later changed to Zhenhai Deputy Commanders in Xining).

---

21 In today's Inner Mongolian Autonomous Region.
22 We cannot establish where this is today.
23 In 1595, the Ming government soldiers repelled three Mongol invasions: in Nanchuan (South Plain), Huangyuan, and Huangzhong areas of today's Xining Municipality.

Later, both Chai Guozhu and Qi Bingzhong became officers in the Hexi Corridor, though Chai Guozhu's position was higher than Qi Bingzhong. In 1604, Chai Guozhu was promoted to the position of Assistant Commander, Commanding Officer in Shaanxi, and in the spring of the following year he was moved to become Commanding Officer in Gansu, where he joined the battle of Yongchang. From 1609 to 1617 he stayed at home and looked after his mother. In 1618 he became Gansu Commanding Officer, but he no longer went to fight at the frontier.

Qi Bingzhong was promoted to the position of Yongchang Deputy Chief of General Staff in Gansu in 1616. In August 1618 he was promoted to the position of Vice-Commanding Officer in Liangzhou. Later, Qi Bingzhong Qi Bingzhong took over the Gansu commanding officer position. His promotion was perhaps recommended by Chai Guozhu. Therefore, there may not have been any resentment between the two well-known Ming Dynasty generals, Chai and Qi. While Chai Guozhu was receiving treatment for an illness, there were no qualified people to take his position. However, he could not reject the central government's requests, and therefore he may have recommended that Qi Bingzhong go instead. After Qi Bingzhong died in battle, his family and descendants hated Commanding Officer Chai for 'forcing' Qi Bingzhong to go to battle, and therefore when they sing *The Ballad of Marshal Qi* they defame Commanding Officer Chai in the song.

Qi Bingzhong died in battle when he was forty-nine, but in *The Ballad of Marshal Qi*, it is sung that he was almost eighty when he went to battle. Probably his descendants and other people have purposefully exaggerated his heroic deeds. Qi Guobing and Qi Zhongzhi died of natural causes in their old age in their sixties or seventies. Qi Zhongzhi's official position was Regimental Commander of Weiyuan Camp, and he was known to have treated common people kindly, so he was greatly respected by his people.

In the Huzhu Tu People's Investigative Records it states:

Jinhua Vice-commanding Officer, Qi Zhongzhi's tomb is in Tangba Fort[24] The *Xining Prefecture New Record: Geography* shows that *The Ballad*

---

24   Tangba Fort is located northeast of Xining, about one hundred *li* away in Ashiji graveyard. Father and son were buried in the same graveyard.

of Marshal Qi contains elements of the story of Qi Bingzhong, mixed with elements of the stories of their first ancestor, Duoerzhishi, as well as their descendants Qi Guobing, Qi Baozhi, and Qi Zhongzhi's construction of cities, going to battle, and so on. Such brilliant stories were merged together in one song, and Marshal Qi became a hero. He was dedicated to the service of the country and loved his people very much. So those folk song singers sung his merits and praised his virtues.

In the *Xining Continued Annals: Archaeology* it is recorded that:

> The Nianbo hereditary *tusi* commander, Qi Guobing, was buried about 120 *li* northeast of Xining. His descendants Zhaoyan, Zhaofan, Shoushan, and Chenggao were all buried with him in the same graveyard... Qi Chenggao, in the sixth year of the Tongzhi reign (1867) was ordered to defend Weiyuan Fortress (that is, Baiya Camp), but died from disease. He had no successor.

In the *Qi Family History* of the East Qi *tusi* it was recorded that Duanzhu, Duoerzhishi's brother, was buried on the sunny side of East Mountain of Baiya in Weiyuan Fortress in 1399.

In 1534, the thirteenth year of the Jiaqing reign, when the seventh-generation ancestor, Qi Lin died, his tomb was moved to the southern outskirts of Xining from Shatangchuan, where five generations of *tusi* are buried, finishing with Qi Bingzhong. Starting from Qi Bozhi, the East Qi *tusi*'s households were located both in Ledu and Huzhu. The graveyards were mostly located in Qiaka and Qijiafengwan in Huzhu. The two big graveyards were selected in the two areas that had created a distance between the *tusi* and his subjects, and the distance produced a sense of beauty. So this resulted in Marshal Qi's story being sung more and more vividly.

From the above, we can see that the Upper Thirteen Villages governed by Baiya Citadel are the home and origin of the *The Ballad of Marshal Qi*. Weiyuan Camp, located at the old location of Baiya ancient citadel, is where the first ancestor of East Qi *tusi*, Shizuduoer, constructed a *yamen* for his regime in Weiyuan. The existing Baiya citadel was built by Qi Zhongzhi and its location coincides with that mentioned in the records in the *Huzhu County Cultural Relics and Records*.

Qiija Yanxii

祁家延西

The Ballad of Marshal Qi

Qiijanu Yanxii ni Qiizunbiinna,
Xiinin ghajarnu darijinna,
Dalan da nayannu nasiwa,
Nasindu gharisan Qiizunbiinna.

祁家延西祁总兵，
保境安民镇西宁，
七十龄来奔八十，
祁家延西高龄人。

The marshal of the Qi family, Marshal Qi,
Who defended the country and ensured a peaceful life for the people of
    Xining City,
Was close to the age of eighty.
The marshal of the Qi family was an elderly man.

Lusdu debxjirge iren gua,
Looyang bazardu falana,
Haanjeennu szongsog ni bau ireja,
Szongsognu Caizunbiin zeeleja.

东头不乱西头乱,
耳听洛阳贼寇反,
皇上的圣旨下来了,
圣旨下到柴总兵前。

The country had not always been peaceful.
It was heard that there was a rebel uprising in Luoyang City.
The Emperor's edict arrived,
The edict came to Commanding Officer Chai's hands.

Qiijanu Yanxii ni Qiizunbiinna,
Sausan ni mulaahaan nuyoongewa,
Szongsognu Caizunbiin zeeleja,
Muxiji nindaa gharilghana.

祁家延西祁总兵,
官里做的小小官,
圣旨下到榜柴总前,
上前线要我祁老汉。

The Marshal of the Qi family, Marshal Qi,
The Marshal of the Qi family was a minor official.
The edict was received by Commanding Officer Chai,
But, I, the elderly man Qi, was pushed to the battlefront.

Turonggu jarilig bauwaa ireja,
Turonggu jarilignu zeeleji gui,
Ghuidarnu jarilig bau ireja,
Ghuidarnu jarilignu harilidiiwa.

头道帖子下来了,
头道帖子打回了,
二道帖子又到了,
二道帖子打回了。

The first note came,
But I did not receive the first note,
The second note came,
But I did not receive the second note.

Ghuraandar jarilig bau ireja,
Xongnu gharlanaa zeelewa,
Aliwan ujesa qirwalge gua,
Ghuraan udaanu dawaalghan gua.

三道帖子又到了，
三道帖子双手接，
猪怕杀来人怕打，
官怕三签不留情。

The third note came,
And I received the third note with two hands.
Swine are scared of being slaughtered and people are scared of being
    beaten up,
But I had to accept the third note.

Qanzun da Baazun ghoyurlawa,
Ta ghuila szaliunge sunusi joo,
Looyangnu bazardu loloodiija,
Budasge Looyangdu yaulduguxja.

千总把总听分明，
贼寇反在洛阳城，
为救洛阳众百姓，
我们要走洛阳城。

All commanding officers, please listen carefully:
A rebellion has arisen in Luoyang City,
To protect and save civilians there,
We must go to Luoyang City.

Qiija Yanxii ni shdoolaadiija,
Nayannu qigi szaardu gharaadiija,
Fuzu da sghal qiiwaadiija,
Buye da ghar kol hadaadiija.

祁家延西实老了，
老了老了实老了，
头发胡子发白了，
腰腿手脚不利了。

The marshal of the Qi family was very old,
Too old,
His hair and beard had turned white,
He was not healthy.

Ghar kolnaa rjanglasa loosowa,
Morire gharisa loosowa,
Uldinu hargulsa loosowa,
Numunu rjanglasa loosowa.

挥不起拳头踢不起腿，
骑不上马来踩不住镫，
拿不起刀来抬不起枪，
拉不开弓来射不出箭。

He had difficulty walking,
He had difficulty mounting a horse,
He had difficulty wielding a sword,
He had difficulty drawing a bow.

Qanzun da Baazun ghuila sunusi joo,
Mununge nasida gharaadiija,
Looyangnu bazardu yauldusamba,
Te ghuilanu suuderdu yaulduguxja.

千总把总听分明，
年事已高的祁总兵，
这回要走个洛阳城，
靠住你们把功劳争。

All commanding officers, please listen carefully:
Though, I, Marshal Qi, am of advanced age,
This time, I have decided to go to Luoyang City,
My success may depend on you.

Qanzun da Baazun ghuila sunusi joo,
Looyangnu kunsgedu uligundu,
Qirig da morinu huraaguxja,
Jiidaa da uldunu janqiguxja.

千总把总听分明，
为救洛阳的众百姓，
我们要买马和招兵，
打造好刀矛和弓箭。

All commanding officers, please listen carefully:
To protect and save civilians in Luoyang City
We will recruit men and buy horses,
And make swords, spears, bows, and arrows.

Kun dire yaanhannu laghaaguna,
Kun dire baatirnu laghaaguna,
Morire yaahannu laghaaguna,
Morire jorotunu laghaaguna.

人伙里挑了多挑上，
人伙里挑上十七八，
马伙里挑了多挑上，
马伙里挑四六口马。

Choose many among the men,
Choose seventeen- and eighteen-year-old warriors among them,
Choose many among the horses,
Choose four-, five-, and six-year-old warhorses among them.

Imelre yaanhannu laghaaguna,
Fulaan imelnu laghaaguna,
Tughumre yaanhannu laghaaguna,
Honghu tughumnu laghaaguna.

鞍伙里挑了多挑上，
鞍伙里挑上大红鞍，
鞯伙里挑了多挑上，
鞍伙里挑上水红鞯。

Choose many among the saddles,
Choose bright red saddles among them,
Choose many among the saddlecloths,
Choose bright saddlecloths among them.

Yobjolre yaanhannu laghaaguna,
Yobjolre jasnu laghaaguna,
Olore yaanhannu laghaaguna,
Shdaasila gurisannu laghaaguna.

镫伙里挑了多挑上，
镫伙里挑上梅花镫，
肚带里挑了多挑上，
肚带里挑上编肚带。

Choose many among the stirrups,
Choose plum flower stirrups among them,
Choose many among the girths,
Choose knitted girths among them.

Ghadarre yaanhannu laghaaguna,
Munqogdii ghadarnu laghaaguna,
Snerre yaanhannu laghaaguna,
Arasila gurisannu laghaaguna.

辔头里挑了多挑上,
辔头里挑上穗辔头,
鞴伙里挑了多挑上,
鞴伙里挑上牛皮鞴。

Choose many among the bridles,
Choose tasseled bridles among them,
Choose many among the hip belts,
Choose cow-hide leather straps among them.

Uldire yaanhannu laghaaguna,
Szu qirghaa shdajinnu laghaaguna,
Jiidaare yaanhannu laghaaguna,
Xuuge tigii jiidaanu laghaaguna.

刀伙里挑了多挑上,
刀伙里挑上褶花刀,
矛伙里挑了多挑上,
矛伙里挑上马耳矛。

Choose many among the swords,
Choose many precise blades among them,
Choose many among the spears,
Choose sharp spears among them.

Numure yaanhannu laghaaguna,
Aasi werla furuusannu laghaaguna,
Smure yaanhannu laghaaguna,
Borghul foodidii smunu laghaaguna.

弓伙里挑了多挑上,
弓伙里挑上牛角弓,
箭伙里挑了多挑上,
箭伙里挑上雕翎箭。

Choose many among the bows,
Choose ox-horn bows among them,
Choose many among the arrows,
Choose eagle-feather-plumed arrows among them.

Qanzun da Baazun ghuila xiilana,
Munu dargha qi nige sunusi joo,
Qinu sanaa shdaar laghaalduwa,
Kilesan hananu nzomlalghawa.

千总把总叩头秉，
总兵大人您细听，
照您的想法挑全了，
照您的吩咐挑全了。

Commanding officers reported while kneeling down:
Marshal Qi, please listen carefully,
We have chosen everything according to your orders,
Everything is ready now.

Qirig da morinu kuijelghawa,
Ghuraan jong jirannu kuijelghawa,
Jiidaa da uldinu kuijelghawa,
Numu da smunu kuijelghawa.

祁家兵马挑齐了，
三百六十名挑齐了，
大刀长矛挑齐了，
硬弓长箭挑齐了。

Soldiers and horses were ready,
Three hundred and sixty soldiers were ready,
Swords and spears were ready,
Bows and arrows were ready.

Qiijanu Yanxii ni jarilig bauya,
Qanzun da Baazun ghuila sunusi,
Qabsarnu soni ni nire daudaya,
Xini nigedu qirig ghariya.

祁家宴席传将令，
千总把总听分明，
三十晚夕点大兵，
初一早上开拨行。

Marshal Qi commanded:
All commanding officers, please listen carefully,
We will gather men for a roll call on the night of the thirtieth,
And march the army to battle on the next day.[25]

---

25   That is, the first day of the next lunar month.

Qiijani Yanxii ni jarilig bauya,
Idexi zungon sunusi joo,
Qirig da morinu idexiwa,
Muxileji idexinu yaulghaguxja.

祁家宴席传将令，
催粮总管听分明，
兵马粮草托靠你，
兵马未动粮草行。

Marshal Qi commanded:
Grain officers please listen carefully,
You are in charge of soldiers' and horses' food,
You should set off first.

Qiijanu Yanxii ni jarilig bauya,
Qirigsge szaliunge sunusi joo,
Alinge jariligun lii sunusisa,
Jongge tegdaji gulegunii.

祁家宴席传将令，
兵将哥哥听分明，
哪个不听我的令，
一百军棍法难容。

Marshal Qi commanded:
All soldiers please listen carefully,
If anybody disobeys my orders,
They will be punished with 100 lashes.

Qiijanu Yanxii ni jarilig bauya,
Qirigsge szaliunge sunusi joo,
Alinge biixindu mau galasa,
Alagunu puxiisa yamada gui.

祁家宴席传将令，
兵将哥哥听分明，
哪个糟蹋好百姓，
定斩不饶绑出营。

Marshal Qi commanded:
All soldiers please listen carefully,
If anybody hurts ordinary people,
They will be killed.

Kudunaa xjaanunge kilegu ni,
Shgenqin mulaaqin sunusi joo,
Nuyoon sausan ni mulaawa,
Looyang bazardu xjigu kurija.

布置停当回后房，
大妇小妻你细听，
官里做的小小官，
要走一回洛阳城。

Then he returned to his home and said,
My dear wives, please listen carefully,
I'm a small official,
This time, I must go to Luoyang City.

Tangula manenaa bii tasili,
Szang da lamarnaa bii tasili,
Shde uruinu tolghuinaa bii tasili,
Sgildunaa tidaji bii tasili.

嘛呢佛语嘴里念，
早煨桑来晚点灯，
早晚长头要常磕，
祈祷我平安回家门。

All of you should chant Buddhist scriptures often,
Keep burning incense and lighting butter lamps every day,
Make prostrations in the morning and night,
And pray for me to come back home safely.

Mugesnu nimpusi nguroona,
Sgilnu ugonaa gulena,
Nigelaa nasindu gharaaxja,
Ghoyurlaa bulangeda ireji gua.

大妇小妻泪水涌，
叫声官人你细听，
一来你的年纪老，
二来无嗣更难行。

His wives' tears rolled down,
And they spoke from their hearts:
On the one hand, you are man of advanced age,
On the other hand, you have no children.

Shgeqin mulaaqin sunusi joo,
Turonggu pujiunu harlaadiiwa,
Ghuidarnu pujignu harlaadiiwa,
Ghuraandar pujigda kuraadiija.

叫声妻妾你细听,
头一回帖子打回了,
第二回帖子打回了,
第三回帖子又到了。

My dear wives, please listen carefully,
I refused to receive the first note,
I refused to receive the second note,
But the third note has come quickly.

Ghuraan udaa pujigda kii maduwa,
Looyangdu lii xjigu log ni gua,
Nigelaa biixindu uliguxja,
Ghoyurlaa mau kunnu buraalghaya.

三道帖子快如风,
不走洛阳实不行,
一来为了众百姓,
二来我要除贼根。

The three notes came one after another.
I cannot refuse to go to Luoyang City—
On the one hand, I must go for the sake of all ordinary people,
On the other hand, I must go in order to eliminate rebels.

Mugesnu sgilnii shdughuna,
Xongnu nimpusi nguroona,
Nasindu gharaanu qirig gharisa,
Jirge da oosgunu tidaji xjina.

妻妾心里如刀捅,
成双的眼泪豆儿滚,
七十龄来奔八十,
老了着出征实难心。

His wives felt as if their hearts had been stabbed with knives,
Tears were rolling down,
He was almost eighty years old,
It was as painful as one's heart and lungs being torn out.

Morire gharisa qirwalge gua,
Uldinu hargulsa qirwalge gua,
Numunu tidasa qirwalge gua,
Baghaldula xjisa qirwalge gua.

你骑不住马来踩不住镫，
你抡不起刀来举不起矛，
你拉不开弓来瞄不准箭，
你去了妻妾们难放心。

You can hardly mount a horse,
You can hardly brandish a sword,
You can hardly shoot an arrow from a bow,
Your wives really do not want you to leave.

Shgeqin mulaaqin sunusi joo,
Munu sgil hadaaji gua,
Nasindu gharji yama gigunii,
Munu yesi szu hadaaji gua.

再叫妻妾你细听，
我延西不服年轻人，
七十龄来奔八十，
浑身的筋骨比铁硬。

My dear wives, please listen carefully again,
My heart is still not old,
Although I'm almost eighty years old
My muscles and bones are still harder than iron.

Morinu dire ni naaldaa saum joo,
Uldila buyenaa haawaa saum joo,
Smula smudaji nesilgham joo,
Saigunu qoloonu xjilghaadim joo.

骑上马儿踩牢镫，
大刀长矛护我身，
牛角弓拉开似满月，
雕翎箭射贼嗓骨门。

I will be safe on horseback,
My sword and spear will protect my body,
I will use the ox-horn bow powerfully,
Eagle-feathered arrows will puncture my enemies' throats.

Mugensge ghuraan tolghui murguya,
Shge tingerda furongla joo,
Ulon purghaanda furongla joo,
Qar njeennaa hudunge simjongla joo.

妻妾下跪拜三拜,
一拜苍天保佑我夫君,
二拜诸佛保佑我夫君,
三拜夫君你多保重。

All wives kowtowed to their husband,
First, we kowtow to Heaven, to protect our husband,
Second, we kowtow to all deities, to protect our husband,
Third, we kowtow to our husband, to take good care of himself.

Szang da lamarnu bii tasiliya,
Lamu sang qimu furonglam joo,
Baghar sang qimu furonglam joo,
Niidag sang qimu furonglam joo.

早煨桑来晚点灯,
骡子天王保佑你,
五台护法保佑你,
山神土地保佑你。

We will burn incense and light butter lamps for you every day,
Lamusang[26] will protect you,
Bagharisang[27] will protect you,
Niidosang[28] will protect you.

---

26 Lamusang is an important protector deity in the Duluun Lunkuang. Luozi Tianwang 骡子天王 (Heavenly Mule Riding King) in Chinese.

27 Bagharisang (King Foorigisigari), a well-known deity worshipped by Mongghul. He was a rival of King Gesar.

28 Niidosang (Guo'erduo, Gelete, Aodan, Aolute Danbajiacuo, Aolute, Aoluchi) was a general under Genghis Khan, and is now an important protecting deity in the Huzhu Mongghul area. For more detail, see Limusishiden, Ha and Stuart (2013).

Xini nigedu kuraadiija,
Qirig mori xarlaadiija,
Kengerge shgedu dongghudina,
Morilagu sghau kuraadiija.

初一早晨已来临，
兵马排列齐整整，
催人战鼓响叮咚，
祁家延西出府门。

The first day of the lunar month arrived,
Soldiers and horses lined up neatly,
Drummers encouraged people to go to battle,
The marshal of the Qi family walked out of his mansion.

Solghuinu ghardu ramdawa joo,
Warang ghardu mugenwa joo,
Halghunu taisada loosawa joo,
Hajiraagu taadada loosawa joo.

左手牵着马缰绳，
右手领着妻子行，
走一步来停一停，
生离死别实难心。

He held his reins in his left hand,
He held his wives's hands in his right hand,
He paused often while walking,
They were reluctant to part from each other.

Morinu ghuraandaa harliwa joo,
Kudunaa ghuraandaa nauwa joo,
Sgilnaa ixinge bii tida joo,
Budasge muxiji yaugunii joo.

拨转马头返三次，
深情往家看三次，
妻妾不要太难心，
好男儿今天要成行。

He turned his horse to his mansion thrice,
And looked at his mansion thrice affectionately.
You wives, please do not be sad,
I, a man, am starting off today.

Mugensge ramdasa waraadiija,
Sgilnu ugodu buraagunu gua,
Uldinu hoyiisa suulaadiija,
Ramdanu shdolaanu tasilaadiija.

妻妾抓住了马缰绳,
劝官人一定多保重,
腰间的宝刀出了鞘,
一刀割断了马缰绳。

His wives held his horse's reins,
And told him to take good care of himself,
He took his sword out of its sheath,
And cut the reins.

Qiijanu Yanxii ni jarilig bauya,
Qanzun da Baazun sunusi joo,
Niudurgu udurdu qirig ghariya,
Qirignu duraanu muxiji yau.

祁家延西传将令,
千总把总听分明,
今日祁家兵要出征,
催动人马往前行。

Marshal Qi gave the order:
All commanding officers, please listen carefully,
Today, the Qi family's soldiers will set off,
Please set off now.

Bazarnu Dungonsa moor ghariwa,
Dungonsa gharisa Loojawana,
Dii muxiji yausamba Yinhuntanna,
Yinhuntan dawaasa Hiihoo muroonna.

炮响三声出东关,
东关出去是罗家湾,
罗家湾过去是映红滩,
映红滩过去是黑河边。

When the cannons had resounded thrice, the soldiers had already left
    Dongguan;[29]
After walking out of Dongguan, they arrived at Luojiawan,[30]
Then they walked farther and arrived at the Yinghong Plain;[31]
After passing the Yinghong Plain, they arrived at the bank of the Black
    River.[32]

Hiihoo muroonre kurgo gua,
Qirig mori yama giji dawaagunii?
Qiijanu Yanxii ni jarilig bauya,
Muroonnu qireedu xirgiilaya.

黑河上没有一座桥,
兵将人马阿门价过?
祁家延西传将令,
黑河边上安营坐。

There was no bridge over the Black River:
How could soldiers and horses cross it?
The Marshal of the Qi family ordered,
Camp at the riverside.

Caizunbiinnu jarilig kuraadiija,
Ghuruundurdu muroonsa dawaadii,
Ghuruudurdu dawaa adasa,
Tolghuinaa awaanu sgela ire.

---

29   The eastern district of today's Xining City.
30   Today's Luojiawan area, Pingan Region, Haidong Municipality.
31   Unknown location.
32   Unknown location.

柴总兵将令到来了，
限你三日过黑河，
三日里黑河过不了，
三天后提头来见我。

The order issued by Commanding Officer Chai has arrived:
You must cross the Black River within three days,
If you are not over within three days,
Report to me without your head.

Jarilig tingerla nigewa,
Qiijanu Yanxii ni jiisuuraaxja,
Turongge ghadange jorolana,
Ghuruudurdu yama giji dawaagunii?

将令一到如山倒，
祁家延西急死了，
里外三进坐不稳，
三天里黑河怎么过?

The order was like a landslide.
Yanxi of the Qi family was getting very anxious,
He went in and out of his tent nervously:
How can we cross the river within three days?

Qanzun da Baazun sunusi joo,
Molsi kurgonu ujela xji,
Molsi korijiisa dawaaya,
Koriji guisada dawaaya.

千总把总听分明，
明天黑河上看冰桥，
有了冰桥过冰桥，
没有冰桥也要过。

All commanding officers please listen carefully:
Tomorrow, please go see if the river has frozen or not;
We will cross the river if it has frozen,
We will have to cross over it.

Qanzun da Baazun jariji,
Tanmaaqi kurgo ujela xjija,
Muroonnu szuda rdemxina,
Ghayardu korigu log ni gua?

千总把总传命令，
派两个探马看冰桥，
河里的波浪三尺高，
六月天阿门价坐冰桥？

All the commanding officers gave orders,
Two scouts were sent to see if the river was frozen or not.
They saw waves on the river almost one meter high,
How could the river freeze over in summer?

Tanmaaqi haraanu kilena,
Muroonre molsi koriji gua,
Jarlig bauji yang ujela xjija,
Muroonre molsi mu koriji gua.

探马回来叩头禀，
黑河里没有坐冰桥，
传下将令再去探，
黑河里还是没冰桥。

The two scouts came back and reported that
The Black River was not frozen.
They were sent again to see if the river was frozen or not,
But the Black River was still not frozen.

Ghuraandar ujelada lii xjisamba,
Caizunbiin jarilig yang kurija,
Ghuruudur kuraanu daglaja,
Dii dawaa adasa alagunii.

第三回还没去探冰桥，
柴总兵的将令由来到，
三天的日子两天半，
再不过黑河把头割。

On the third day there was no time to send soldiers to see if the river was
    frozen or not.
An order from Commanding Officer Chai had arrived:
The three days are almost up,
You will be beheaded if you do not cross the river.

Qiija Yanxii jisuuraxja,
Jiila huu duulixja,
Tanmaaqi ghrdinhaan ujela xji,
Kurgo guisamba alagunii.

祁家延西急死了，
一蹦跳得五尺高，
传令探马再去探，
再没有冰桥脑袋掉。

The marshal of the Qi family was really getting nervous,
He jumped with anger,
And ordered the scouts to go check again,
Saying that if the scouts didn't see a frozen river, they would be beheaded.

Tanmaaqi muroondu kuraadiisa,
Muroon szu undurdu rdemxina,
Hariji xjaa yama giji kilegunii,
Ne yang do amunnaa kurgeediija.

探马来到河边上，
河里的波浪三尺高，
俩人在河边哭一场，
回去定把命送掉。

The scouts arrived at the riverside.
Seeing the waves on the river almost one meter high,
The two cried at the riverside:
We will be beheaded if we go to back.

Tanmaaqi ghuilada ndang baghana,
Hariji xjisa amunnaa kurgeeguna,
Muroondu diuliyada nanjinna,
Gujire uldila lii qabjiguna.

两个探马穷思量，
回去一定见阎王，
不如跳河喂鱼去，
免得血在脖子上淌。

The two scouts considered:
We will lose our lives if we go back.
It would be good to jump in the river and give our bodies to the fish,
That would be better than having our necks cut.

Tanmaaqi ghuila yang ndang baghasa,
Qiizunbiinnu sgil ni sain sgilwa,
Hariji xjildaanu nige kileya,
Buda ghuilanu yamada lii gimba.

两个探马由思量,
总兵大人好心肠,
我俩回去求个情,
看他把我俩怎么样。

The two scouts thought again:
Marshal Qi is a kind-hearted man,
We will appeal to his mercy when we return,
And see how he treats us.

Tanmaaqi ghuila dii ndang baghasa,
Uldinu gujire tai ughugula,
Jilaji ghudalge tegdaya,
Muroonre kurgo sauja giya.

两个探马再思量,
等把钢刀脖子上放,
我俩就给他扯个谎,
就说冰桥坐在黑河上。

The two scouts considered again:
If they put a knife to our necks
We will immediately lie to them
That the river has frozen over.

Nigere taiwaanu hariji ireja,
Qiizunbiinnu gurdu uroji xjaanu,
Ghoor udignaa ghajardu sgodaanu,
Ujesan waidalnaa xiilaya gina.

注意已定回营房,
急忙来到总兵帐,
两个探马跪地上,
要给大人秉情况。

They considered and returned to the camp,
And went into Marshal Qi's camp.
The two scouts knelt down on the ground,
And reported to Marshal Qi.

Qiizunbiinnu sgildu ghal ngureena,
Tog baghagu madu szaghasamba,
Tanmaaqi ghuila ayildaanu,
Kurgo sauja giji szaraa ireja.

祁家延西急如焚，
大吼一声问军情，
两个探马慌了神，
就说黑河上坐了冰。

The heart of the marshal of the Qi family was torn with anxiety,
He asked for the facts with a roar.
The two scouts were so scared,
A lie burst out, that the river had frozen.

Qiijanu Yanxii ni beesaadiija,
Ta ghuila ghurdu pusildaadii,
Bu ta ghuilanu alaya giji gui,
Qirig mori ghurdulaji yaulduya gi.

祁家延西真高兴，
叫声小哥哥快起来，
我哪里舍得杀你们，
传令人马快起营。

The marshal of the Qi family was glad.
You two get up quickly,
I don't want to kill you two.
He ordered the soldiers and horses to set off immediately.

Paunu ghuraan dau gharghaanu,
Qirig mori ghudilildaadiija,
Tanmaaqi ayaanu qagla shdaji gua,
Ghudal kileenu do yama gim?

炮响三声起了营，
却又难坏了探马兵，
大人好心不杀我们，
我俩为啥哄大人？

When the cannons had resounded thrice, the soldiers and horses started off,
The two scouts were so scared.
Superior, is this kind man who wouldn't kill us,
But why did we lie to him?

Qirig da morisge yaulduna,
Tanmaaqinu jirge ni diulina,
Molsi kurgonu sarin nida gua,
Qiizunbiindu kilegu logda gua?

大兵征程匆匆行,
两个探马心蹦蹦,
黑河里明明没冰桥,
到河边阿门价见大人?

Soldiers and horses moved in a hurry,
The two scouts' hearts were beating,
The river was not frozen,
How would they face Marshal Qi when they arrived at the river?

Hiihoo muroon rdemxina,
Molsinu kurgonge gergeljana,
Tanmaaqi ghuila juudinduwa,
Ghayardu jubda korin nuu.

黑河里河水波浪滚,
有一座冰桥亮晶晶,
两个探马好像坐睡梦,
六月天河水里真坐冰。

Waves were rolling on the Black River,
But an ice bridge glittered:
The two scouts thought they must be dreaming,
It really was frozen on a summer's day.

Qiijanu Yanxii ni jarilig bauja,
Qanzun da Baazun sunusi joo,
Qirigghula saighan sunusi joo,
Kurgo dawaadulaa simjonglaldu.

祁家延西传将令,
千总把总点好兵,
兵将哥哥听分明,
过冰桥一定要小心。

The marshal of the Qi family gave the order:
All commanding officers, please order the men to cross the bridge,
Every soldier, please listen carefully,
Take great care of yourself as you cross the ice bridge.

Qiijanu Yanxii ni jarilig bauja,
Turong ni bu njeennaa dawaaya,
Molsi kurgo lii tabdaasa,
Hanala daghaaji dawaaldu joo.

祁家延西传将令，
头一个过的是祁总兵，
倘若冰桥不塌了，
再过的就是当兵的人。

The marshal of the Qi family gave the order:
I will walk over the ice bridge first,
If the ice bridge doesn't collapse,
All soldiers and horses follow me over.

Qirig da morisge dawaa xjija,
Huino harijinge nausamba,
Jaghasi ghoyurlada diulilduna,
Purghan budasgenu furonglaja.

祁家兵马过了桥，
再回过头来仔细瞧，
两条大鱼蹦蹦跳，
神佛保佑我过了桥。

The Qi family's soldiers and horses passed over the bridge,
They turned back and looked at the river carefully:
Two big fish were jumping,
Deities and Buddhas have helped us to cross the river.

Shge szangnu gharghaji,
Ghuraan tolghuinu murguji,
Sgilnu turosa haxiliji,
Ulon purghaannu hgebli giya.

祁家延西老泪落，
三拜九磕谢神佛，
三百六十个兵哥哥，
谢天谢地恸哭豪。

The tears of the marshal of the Qi family rolled down,
He made nine prostrations to all the deities and Buddhas,
Three hundred and sixty soldiers
Thanked all the deities and cried together.

Hiifii muroonsa dawaawaanu,
Saaliu kurgore kuraadiija,
Tanmaaqi hariji iree kilena,
Kurgonu kaagaanu dawaagu log gua.

兵马过了黑水河，
再往前就是沙柳桥，
探马兵探马回来了，
贼寇卡定了沙柳桥。

After they crossed the Black River,
They arrived near Shaliu Bridge.[33]
Scouts returned and reported:
Bandits occupy the Shaliu Bridge.

Kurgosa mundee moor ni gua,
Yama gisada dawaagu kurija,
Qiijanu Yanxii ni ndang baghana,
Niguu soni noor kuriji gua.

沙柳桥以外没有道，
拼死也过个沙柳桥，
祁家延西夜苦熬，
不知不觉天亮了。

There is no way except the Shaliu Bridge,
We must cross the Shaliu Bridge.
The marshal of the Qi family was carefully considering
Until daybreak.

Qiijanu Yanxiidu laghu ulon,
Mori baasinu tungulghaja,
Mori baasi ula maduwa,
Yaandu jarigunu muden gua.

祁家延西善谋算，
不攻桥来不造船，
下令军兵拾马粪，
拾的马粪堆成山。

The marshal of the Qi family was a clever man.
We'll neither attack the bridge nor make ships.
He ordered his soldiers to pick up horse dung,
So horse dung was piled up.

33　Unknown location.

Baasinu muroondu sajaadiija,
Muroon szu xirandog ulaadiija,
Kurgonu sgijin sgeediija,
Sgilnu turosa ayaadiija.

堆堆马粪推入河,
清清河水变黄色,
守桥贼寇看见了,
疑是祁家兵已渡河。

All the horse dung was pushed into the river,
And the river turned yellow.
The bandits who were guarding the bridge saw it,
And thought the soldiers had already crossed the river.

Qiijanu qirig ni dawaaxja gaa,
Kurgonu dire ni loloodiija,
Qiijanu Yanxiidu laghu ulija,
Qirignaa duraanu muxiqilena.

守桥贼寇慌了神,
沙柳桥上乱纷纷,
祁家延西计得逞,
率领军兵往前冲。

The bandits guarding the bridge were flustered,
There was a scene of chaos on the bridge,
The marshal of the Qi family succeeded:
He led his soldiers, rushing forward.

Qiijanu Yanxii ni baatirwa,
Qirigsge amunnaa hgilen gua,
Saaliu kurgosa dawaa xjija,
Qirigsge nigeda sheeleji gua.

祁家延西逞神勇,
祁家兵个个不要命,
一口气冲过沙柳桥,
贼寇逃得无踪影。

The marshal of the Qi family was so brave,
His soldiers were not worried about their lives,
They quickly pushed across the bridge,
And the bandits all ran away.

Yaujinge yaujinge yauniisamba,
Tingere uroonu arilgunu gua,
Huraadu yausamba jublongwa,
Lii sausa yaugu log ni gua.

征程遇了个秋甲子，
连阴带下的四十天，
雨天里行军实难心，
把营盘扎在黄草滩。

On the journey autumn began,
It was cloudy and rainy for forty days;
It was very hard to walk on the rainy days,
So they camped on Huangcao Plain.[34]

Qighaan gurnu pusilghawa,
Jas loogoonu diuzilewa,
Qirignu idexi buraadiija,
Morinu hoolo buraadiija.

白布的账房扎下了，
三岔锣鼓支下了，
兵马的粮草吃完了，
没有粮草着害下了。

They pitched white cloth tents
And put three-legged pots on the ground.
Soldiers and horses had no food to eat,
They suffered from hunger.

Qirig da moridu qasga gua,
Qasga kurgeejin kurigunu gua,
Morinu hoolonii kun idena,
Amunnu hgilegu bulenna.

人没有粮来马没有料，
押粮的总管还不到，
马料鞍鞴人吃了，
兵困荒滩没救了。

Soldiers and horses were lacking food,
The grain officers had not arrived,
Soldiers were eating horses' fodder,
Facing starvation in the wilderness.

---

34   Unknown location.

Qiijanu Yanxii ni Qiizunbiinna,
Soni ni juudinge juudilesa,
Bagha rjawu szong bauna,
Bughu amunnu ntarlalghana.

祁家延西祁总兵，
晚夕里作了个好睡梦，
五台护法托了个梦，
梅花鹿儿能救人。

The marshal of the Qi family, Marshal Qi,
Had a dream in the evening:
Bagharisang told him,
Spotted deer can save your lives.

Qiijanu Yanxii ni jarilig bauna,
Tangula szaliunge sunusi joo,
Bughu amunnu ntarlalghana,
Mahanii qinaasa funirduwa.

祁家延西传将令，
兵将哥哥们听分明，
梅花鹿儿能救人，
锣锅里煮肉香喷喷。

The marshal of the Qi family gave the order:
All soldiers, please listen carefully,
Spotted deer can save our lives,
Boiled meat in the pot is very appetizing.

Bughunu baghaanu buraaguna,
Qasgaqi zungondu kurigunu gua,
Alinge udurdu kurisamba,
Qasgaqi zungondu amun gua.

眼看着鹿儿打完了，
押粮的总管还不到，
哪一日粮草押到了，
押粮的总管定不饶。

When almost all the deer had been killed,
The grain officers had still not arrived.
If the grain arrived any later,
It would be necessary to punish the grain officers.

Kii huraa qudughu madungewa,
Keele losaa naaldigu madungewa,
Qirig mori nqaadagu madungewa,
Sgil turo shdughugu madungewa.

黄草滩上风如刀,
人没有粮来马没有料,
兵马困在黄草滩,
祁总兵心里如刀绞。

The wind on Huangcao Plain was like a knife,
Soldiers and horses had no food,
Soldiers and horses were trapped on Huangcao Plain.
Marshal Qi was grief-stricken.

Agha diungula sunusi joo,
Qirig ulijin baatirwa joo,
Shge tingere furonglam joo,
Nenge purgesa dawaa xjim joo.

兵将哥哥们听分明,
吃粮当兵的是好汉,
苍天神佛保佑我,
众人一心度难关。

All soldiers please listen carefully:
All you soldiers are great men,
Great Heaven and all the deities will protect us,
All people unite to overcome this difficulty.

Shdeleji sajaghai hailana,
Qasgaqi zungon kuraadiija,
Qiizunbiin aurlaanu xirgudina,
Yama gaanu isgenge kuriwa.

黄草滩上喜鹊叫,
押粮的总管来报到,
祁总兵怒发直冲关,
粮草阿门价才运到。

Magpies were chirping on Huangcao Plain,
The grain officer came to report,
Marshal Qi's hair bristled with anger,
He asked why the grain had been delayed.

Qiijanu Yanxii ni jarilig bauja,
Zungonnu gur ghada qogloodii,
Silimnaa suulaanu gharghaadiisa,
Tolghuinu awusa gulegunu gui.

祁家延西传将令，
把总管绑在营门外，
三尺宝剑出了鞘，
斩你的首级不能怪。

The marshal of the Qi family gave the order:
Tie the grain officer up outside the gates of the camp.
He unsheathed his long sword—
I should behead him.

Tamainge udur sara ulisamba,
Taraa da hoolodu kurigunu gua,
Ntoglaja ntoglaja jub ntoglaja,
Dii yama gulegu ugo wai yiu gui.

出征到了今日了，
连一回粮草运不到，
延误征期法难容，
叫你到阴间去报到。

At a critical time in our expedition
You failed to transport grain and fodder,
You delayed the expedition and broke the law,
Now, go to Hell.

Qasgaqi zungon ughua gina,
Ndaa daagu gulegu ugonge wai,
Munu dargha qi sunusi joo,
Bu qimu szaliunge kileya joo.

押粮总管哭求饶，
斩我的首级说不过，
总兵大人你细听，
把我的冤枉说一说。

The grain officer cried and begged for mercy:
You shouldn't behead me,
Commanding Officer, please listen carefully,
I'll explain to you my innocence.

Turongdar qasganu kurgee iresa,
Turongdar qasganu bulaa xjiwa,
Hara moridii bulijinna,
Hara xadardii bulijinna.

头一回粮草发上来，
头一回粮草被抢了，
头一回抢粮的是黑贼，
黑人黑马黑旗号。

The first time we transported the grain
The grain was stolen on the way.
The robbers were clad in black clothes,
Robbers clad in black clothes with black horses and black flags.

Ghuidar qasganu kurgee iresa,
Ghuidar qasganu bulaa xjiwa,
Qighaan moridii bulijinna,
Qighaan xadardii bulijinna.

第二回粮草发上来，
第二回粮草又抢了，
第二回抢粮的是白贼，
白人白马白旗号。

The second time we transported the grain
The grain was stolen again.
This time the robbers were clad in white clothes,
Robbers clad in white clothes with white horses and white flags.

Ghuraadar qasganu kurilghawa,
Tingere uroonu kurigunge gua,
Niudurgu udurdu kuriwajida,
Qasgare nughoon turuu rguadiija.

第三回粮草发到了，
偏偏遇上秋甲子了，
连阴带下的路难行，
发来的粮草发霉了。

The third time, we finally transported the grain here.
Autumn had begun, so we met rainy and cloudy days,
The road was very difficult to walk on,
The grain became moldy.

Qiijanu Yanxii ni jarilig bauja,
Agha diusge szaliunge sunusi joo,
Qasganu kurgeewaa kuraadiija,
Sgilnu ncaraa buraadiiwa.

祁家延西传将令,
兵将哥哥们听分明,
兵马的粮草运到了,
心里的黑血塌下了。

The marshal of the Qi family gave the order:
All soldiers please listen carefully,
Grain and fodder have arrived,
I feel at ease now.

Moor dire bulijinnu xjuraadiija,
Moor dire huraanu xjuraadiija,
Qasgaqi zungonnu telgeedii,
Ghardugu uldinaa huyiilaadii.

偏偏遇上个强盗了,
偏偏遇上秋甲子了,
押粮的总管怪不得,
三尺宝剑进鞘了。

They just encountered robbers,
Just met rainy and cloudy days as autumn began—
Release the grain officer now.
He sheathed his sword again.

Zunbiinnu qinji ni buraadiija,
Qirignu aghasge beesaadiija,
Qasgaqi zungonnu telgeediija,
Hananu sgilda ndanglaadiija.

祁家延西怒气消,
兵将哥哥们高兴了,
押粮总管立放掉,
众兵将心里平静了。

The anger of the marshal of the Qi family was soothed,
All the soldiers were happy,
The grain officer was freed,
All soldiers felt at peace.

Qiijanu Yanxii ni jarilig bauja,
Qanzun da Baazun sunusi joo,
Qirig da morinu qadilighaanu,
Ghurdin ghurdin ghudiliya joo.

祁家延西传将令，
千总把总听分明，
人烙干粮马喂料，
炮响三声起征程。

The marshal of the Qi family gave the order:
All commanding officers, please listen carefully,
Fill soldiers' stomachs and feed the horses;
After the cannon has resounded thrice, we will set off on our expedition.

Qirig mori yausan ni ghurdinna,
Looyang bazardu kuraadiija,
Qiijanu Yanxii ni jarilig bauja,
Bazarnu ghadaxi gurnu pusilgha.

大兵来到洛阳城，
洛阳里贼寇众，
祁家延西传将令，
洛阳城外扎下营。

The soldiers arrived at Luoyang City wall,
Many rebels were inside.
The marshal of the Qi family gave the order:
Encamp outside the Luoyang City wall.

Looyangnu bazarda batiwa,
Bazar turogu kun ulonna,
Hadongla baghasa moordu gua,
Laghunu gharghaji awuguxja.

叫声千把总你细听，
洛阳城是砖包城，
强攻硬打万不成，
多想计谋要智胜。

All commanding officers, please listen carefully:
Luoyang City wall is made of bricks—
Attacking by force will not succeed,
We should use strategy.

Qiijanu Yanxiidu laghu ulon,
Qanzun da Baazundu qigiqilem,
Ghuraan menhan jirghoon jong imaawa,
Duloon menhen ghoor jong dangliurwa.

祁家延西智策大，
密叫千总把总把话发，
三千六百山羊紧着抓，
七千二百灯笼抓紧扎。

The marshal of the Qi family was wise,
Secretly telling every commanding officer,
Please get 3,600 goats,
And make 7,200 lanterns.

Imaanu waraanu kuijeediija,
Dangliurnu zaakaanu kuijeediija,
Looyang bazarnu awusamba,
Awugu sghau ni niusoniwa.

如数的山羊抓来了，
如数的灯笼扎成了，
羊角挂上灯笼了，
攻城的万事俱备了。

The assigned goats were caught,
The assigned lanterns were made,
Hang the lanterns on the goats' horns,
Ready to attack the city wall.

Harangghu soninu dundadu,
Imaanu wer dire dangliurwa,
Qiijanu Yanxii ni murgenna,
Baatir hanala narjaawa.

日落夜深黑沉沉，
山羊角上挂灯笼，
祁家延西密传令，
兵将哥们抖精神。

In the middle of the deep dark night,
Hang the lanterns on the goats' horns,
The marshal of the Qi family gave the order secretly,
And all the soldiers became energetic.

Ula tang guinu imaawa,
Fulaan dangliurla haa geeja,
Budasgenu qirig qoogonna,
Imaa budasgenu qirigwa.

十个山羊一个兵,
漫山遍野是灯笼,
别看我们兵马少,
山羊就是攻城的兵。

Ten goats were arranged in one team,
All over, lanterns covered the hills.
Despite our soldiers and horses being few,
Goats have become our soldiers.

Qagraaji sajiligu madungewa,
Qirigsge ghaljuuraagu madungewa,
Qirig da immla duuraadiija,
Dalii rdemxigu madungewa.

号炮一声连一声,
祁家延西急攻城,
祁家兵马真英勇,
喊杀阵阵若山洪。

The continuous sound of cannon fire,
The marshal of the Qi family urgently attacked the city wall,
The soldiers were fighting heroically,
The continuous sound of shouting and killing was like a torrential flood.

Looyangnu saigusge ayaadiija,
Tamainge qirig anjiiguna?
Tolghuinaa teeraanu tudaadiija,
Looyang bazarnu ken golana.

洛阳的贼寇慌了神,
哪来这么多马和兵?
呼爹喊娘紧逃命,
管他守城不守城。

The rebels inside Luoyang City were in a panic,
Where did so many soldiers come from?
They ran for their lives,
And Luoyang City was abandoned.

Looyangnu saigusge sajiraaxja,
Urogu nukoda ulidun gua,
Qiijanu Yanxii ni jarilig bauja,
Juraaji alaldu bii suidaarla.

洛阳的贼寇丧了胆，
四散奔跳没处钻，
祁家延西传将令，
追杀贼寇不停缓。

Luoyang City's defenses collapsed,
The rebels fled in disorder,
The marshal of the Qi family gave the order:
Continue chasing and killing the rebels.

Smunu smudaa buraalghaja,
Numunu tidaanu tasilija,
Uldinu qabjaanu furaalghaja,
Jiidaanu shdughoonu hghulaadiija.

雕翎利箭射完了，
牛角长弓拉断了，
褶花大刀倦刃了，
马耳长矛刺折了。

Those eagle-feather-plumed arrows were shot until they were finished,
Those ox-horn bows were used until broken,
Those swords were used until the blades became blunt,
Those horse-ear-shaped spears were used until broken.

Saigunu sgil ni fuuwaadiija,
Anjiida shge ghalnu taidiija,
Looyang bazarnu ghal hujija,
Qiijanu qirigsge hambulina.

洛阳的贼寇事做绝，
七处八处放了火，
洛阳城里到处着，
祁家兵赶紧去救火。

The rebels inside Luoyang City were utterly devoid of conscience
And set fire to everything,
The fire spread everywhere inside of Luoyang City.
The Qi family's soldiers put the fire out quickly.

Looyang bazar deereljinna,
Xoomaa ndughong dundaduna,
Ghal da kii ghuila furooldina,
Ngureewaa funeesidu furaadiija.

洛阳城里四角城，
雪马宝殿在当中，
大风阵阵火势猛，
雪马宝殿化灰烬。

Luoyang was a four-cornered city,
The Snow Horse Hall was located at its center,
Heavy wind blew the fierce fire,
The Snow Horse Hall was burnt to ashes.

Qiijanu Yanxii ni jarilig bauja,
Qirignu aghasge sunusi joo,
Sawaala ndughongge pusilghaya,
Looyangnu kunsgenu furonglam joo.

祁家延西传将令，
兵将哥哥们听分明，
兵器盖一座雪马殿，
保佑洛阳的好百姓。

The marshal of the Qi family gave the order:
All soldiers please listen carefully,
Rebuild the burnt hall with all your weapons,
Protect all the common people inside Luoyang City.

Ndughongnu muxi ni uldiwa,
Ndughongnu huino ni jiidaawa,
Ndughongnu dire ni smuwa,
Lamu sangnaa turo ni shdenleya.

褶花大刀前面竖，
马耳瓜矛子是后山柱，
宝弓雕箭顶上铺，
骡子天王里面塑。

Swords were used as pillars for the front of the hall,
Horse-ear-shaped spears were used as pillars for the back of the hall,
Treasure bows and eagle-plumed arrows were put on the roof of the hall,
Lamusang's statue was enshrined inside the hall.

Qiijanu Yanxii ni Qiizunbiinna,
Murgen da baatirdii Qiizunbiinna,
Qirig da morinaa hairlana,
Hara turuudunu ixida hairlana.

祁家延西祁总兵,
有勇有谋出奇兵,
爱惜兵马痛百姓,
不折一卒把贼寇平。

The marshal of the Qi family, Marshal Qi,
Was wise and brave, and was victorious in battle.
He loved his soldiers, horses, and common people,
And defeated the rebels without losing a single soldier.

Qiijanu Yanxi ni jarilig bauja,
Qirignu aghasge sunusi joo,
Looyangnu kirig tegxiraaja,
Qirig mori Xiiniinnaa hariya joo.

祁家延西传将令,
兵将哥哥们听分明,
洛阳的战事已得平,
速速撤兵回西宁。

The marshal of the Qi family gave the order:
All soldiers please listen carefully,
The Luoyang City rebellion has been suppressed,
Withdraw the troops to Xining quickly.

Kugo tingerdu shdarlanii joo,
Ulon purghaandu shdarlanii joo,
Tingere da purghaans furongla joo,
Budangula debxjirge hariya joo.

虔诚祷告苍天啊,
虔诚祷告诸佛啊,
请保佑您的子民们,
平平安安回家门。

Piously pray to Great Heaven,
Piously pray to all the deities,
Please protect your people,
Return home safely.

Qiijanu Yanxii ni Qiizunbiinna,
Soni ni juudinge juudilesa,
Lamu sang juudindu szonglana,
Harigu moor dire simjongla.

祁家延西祁总兵,
晚夕里作了一个梦,
骠子天王显神通,
回家的路上要小心。

The marshal of the Qi family, Marshal Qi,
Had a dream that evening:
Lamusang told him,
Please take care on the way home.

Qighaannu mosisansa qiiwaadii,
Haranu mosisansa qiiwaadii,
Xiranu mosisansa qiiwaadii,
Dii debxjirge haraanu kuraadim.

避过白人白马白旗号,
避过黑人黑马黑旗号,
避过黄人黄马黄旗号,
才能平安老家里到。

As long as you avoid white-clad robbers with white horses and white flags,
As long as you avoid black-clad robbers with black horses and black flags,
As long as you avoid yellow-clad robbers with yellow horses and yellow flags,
Then you will safely be able to return home.

Qiijanu Yanxii ni jarilig bauja,
Qanzun da Baazun sunusi joo,
Qirig da morisge hariya joo,
Harigu moor dire simjongla joo.

祁家延西传将令,
千总把总听分明,
炮响三声起大营,
回家路上要小心。

The marshal of the Qi family gave the order:
Every commanding officer, please listen carefully,
Please start after the cannon has resounded thrice,
Take care on the way home.

Urgon talaasa dawaadulaa,
Qighaan mosisannu xjuraadiija,
Qirig da moorisge niusangula,
Qighaan mosisansa qiiwaadiija.

走过宽广的草原时，
遇上了白人白马白旗号，
祁家兵马躲藏着，
避过了白人白马白旗号。

As they were passing through a broad grassland,
They encountered white-clad robbers with white horses and white flags.
The Qi family's soldiers and horses went into hiding
And successfully avoided the white-clad robbers with white horses and white flags.

Shge muroonsa dawaadulaa,
Hara mosisannu xjuradiija,
Qiizunbiin smugeer jariliglaanu,
Hara mosisansa qiiwaadiija.

渡过湍急的河流时，
遇上了黑人黑马黑旗号，
祁总兵密令使巧计，
避过了黑人黑马黑旗号。

As they were crossing a turbulent river,
They encountered black-clad robbers with black horses and black flags.
Marshal Qi was a clever man,
And successfully avoided the black-clad robbers with black horses and black flags.

Shge ghulsa dawaadulaa,
Xira mosisannu xjuraadiija,
Qirig da morisge hargaanu,
Xira mosisansa qiiwaadiija.

穿过深深的山沟时，
遇上了黄人黄马黄旗号，
祁家兵马巧转绕，
避过了黄人黄马黄旗号。

As they were passing through a deep ravine,
They encountered yellow-clad robbers with yellow horses and yellow flags.
Marshal Qi bypassed them,
And successfully avoided the yellow-clad robbers with yellow horses and yellow flags.

Qiijanu Yanxii ni qiizunbiinna,
Nasindu gharisan qiizunbiinna,
Qirignaa duraanu haaraa kurija,
Kunsge beesiji zeelelduna.

祁家延西祁总兵，
年事已高的祁总兵，
领兵马平安回西宁，
众百姓踊跃出城迎。

The marshal of the Qi family, Marshal Qi,
Elderly Marshal Qi,
Safely returned to Xining City with his soldiers and horses.
All the people enthusiastically came out of the city and greeted them.

Turongdar zeelejin Caizunbiinna,
Jongdu mori ghariji zeelena,
Rjaalaji harisan baatiriwa,
Morila zeelejin baatiriwa.

首程迎接的柴总兵，
用成百的马队来迎接，
凯旋而归的众勇士，
应该用马队来迎接。

First, they were received by Commanding Officer Chai,
Who greeted them with hundreds of cavalrymen,
Because brave soldiers returning in triumph
Should be received with cavalry.

Ghuidar ni zeelejin kuduguna,
Jongdu hunila zeelena,
Rjaalaji harisan murgenwa,
Hunila zeelejin murgenwa.

二程引接的是家人，
用成百的肥羊来迎接，
胜利而归的众智者，
应该用肥羊来迎接。

Secondly, they were received by his family,
Who greeted them with hundreds of fat sheep,
Because wise men returning in triumph
Should be received with fat sheep.

Ghuraanda udendunaa kuraadiija,
Xongnu longhula zeelena,
Rjaalaji harisan didewa,
Duraasila zeelejin didewa.

三程跃马到府门，
用成双的酒瓶来迎接，
平安而归的祁老爷，
应该用美酒来迎接。

Thirdly, they arrived in front of the mansion,
And were greeted with two bottles of liquor,
Because a senior man returning safely
Should be received with liquor.

Shgeqi mulaaqin ghariji ireenu,
Ghoor suusa suuderleji zeelena,
Xineedu nimpusi hamduwa,
Suuderleji udendu urolduna.

大妇小妾出府门，
搀扶祁总兵进家门，
笑逐颜开述衷肠，
日夜思念心不稳。

All his wives came out to receive him:
They supported Marshal Qi as he entered their front gate,
Smiles crept across their faces, telling each other
How much they had missed him.

Mulaaqin turosan kuu bulaiwa,
Yantongnu funenu jalghaadiija,
Qiizunbiin beesaanu hghui taija,
Bulaina teerisa sgil geeja.

小妾养下的小男童，
祁家总兵留了根，
祁总兵高兴实高兴，
怀抱小儿乐融融。

His concubine had given birth to a baby boy:
Marshal Qi had his chimney smoking,[35]
Marshal Qi was extremely happy,
And happily embraced his baby boy.

---

35   Implying that his family line would continue, and smoke would continue to come
     from the family's chimney.

Qiijanu Yanxii ni Qiizunbiinna,
Nasindu gharisan baatirwa,
Looyangnu biixindu uliji,
Gharisan nqugonu buraalghaja.

祁家延西祁总兵，
不惜年迈赴战阵，
为了洛阳的好百姓，
巧计把洛阳的战事平。

The marshal of the Qi family, Marshal Qi,
Made an expedition while advanced in age:
For the sake of Luoyang's common people
He successfully suppressed the rebels there.

Qiijanu Yanxii ni Qiizunbiinna,
Nasindu gharisan murgenwa,
Looyangnu biixindu uliji,
Gharisan kirignu tebxiraalghaja.

祁家延西祁总兵，
不顾一切赴战阵，
为了洛阳的好百姓，
大智大勇把贼寇平。

The marshal of the Qi family, Marshal Qi,
Disregarding everything, went to battle
For the sake of Luoyang's common people,
And with his wisdom and bravery suppressed the rebels.

Qiijanu Yanxii ni Qiizunbiinna,
Baatir da murgen nzomlaja,
Daunaa daulaji shdorlaya joo,
Jong menhen fondu ni shdorlaya joo.

祁家延西祁总兵，
智勇双全的祁总兵，
老了的时节争奇功，
千世万代都赞颂。

The marshal of the Qi family, Marshal Qi,
Was a wise and brave man,
Who gained merit in his later years.
Praise him for thousands of years.

3. Laarimbu and Qiimunso

The story of Laarimbu (a young man) and Qiimunso (a young woman) is a tragic love story that was traditionally transmitted orally among Mongghul people from one generation to the next. It is unclear when and where it originated. The original language is Mongghul.

The song tells the story of Laarimbu, a poor shepherd from the mountain. Qiimunso, the female protagonist, is also a shepherd, but from a wealthy family from the plains. They fall in love after meeting while herding. Their relationship is opposed by Qiimunso's brother, because of Laarimbu's impoverished background.

Qiimunso's brother kills Laarimbu, and Qiimunso, overcome with grief, throws herself on her lover's funerary pyre. Ever belligerent, the brother separates Laarimbu and Qiimunso's ashes, and buries them on opposite banks of a rushing river. However, two mimosa trees grow where the ashes are buried, and eventually their branches intertwine above the river. When the brother sees this, he chops down the two trees and burns them in his oven. But as the smoke rises up from the chimney, a pair of mandarin ducks fly out of the chimney. The two mandarin ducks attack the brother, pecking out his eyes and blinding him. The two mandarin ducks then freely and happily fly away together.

Laarimbu and Qiimunso was sung by a man and a woman, or two men, or two women, in Mongghul. It was usually sung outside of the home and village, at the local love song meetings which are held annually in the Seven Valleys, in the mountains when herding animals, or in the fields when people were working. Since around the year 2000, Mongghul young people started to sing the song in their homes during drinking parties if the family had no old people.

© 2017 Li Dechun (李得春, Limusishiden) and Gerald Roche, CC BY 4.0
https://doi.org/10.11647/OBP.0124.03

The song has a slow, sorrowful melody. People usually do not sing it in its entirety, but select certain sections.

Alternative versions of the same narrative can be found in Limusishiden and Stuart (1995), Limusishiden and Stuart (2011), and Aaguqog (2012).

Laarimbu Da Qiimunso

拉仁布与琪门索

Laaimbu and Qiimunso

 Listen to an audio recording of the song at
https://archive.org/details/LaarimbuDaQiimunsoVersion1

Ghulnu awu Laarimbu,
Tangnu ijee Qiimunso,
Nukorqi awu Laarimbu,
Sgildii ijee Qiimunso.

沟里的阿吾拉仁布，
滩里的依姐琪门索，
当雇工的阿吾拉仁布，
有心肠的依姐琪门索。

Brother Laarimbu was from the valley,
Sister Qiimunso was from the plain,
Brother Laarimbu was a servant,
Sister Qiimunso was kindhearted.

Nukordu sausan Laarimbu,
Lisge warijin baatirwa,
Jongdu huninaa tauwaanu,
Undur uladu gharina.

雇工的阿吾拉仁布,
勇敢勤劳的拉仁布,
赶着成百的羊群,
高高的山上去放牧。

Brother Laarimbu was a servant,
And a hard-working man.
He drove hundreds of sheep
To graze on the high mountain.

Bayaan ijee Qiimunso,
Lisge warijin uranwa,
Jongdu aasinaa tauwaanu,
Tebxin tangdu dulaana.

富家的依姐琪门索,
简朴勤快的琪门索,
赶着成百的牛群,
宽阔的滩里去放牧。

Qiimunso was wealthy,
And a diligent girl.
She drove hundreds of oxen
To graze on the plain.

Huniqi awu Laarimbu,
Aasinqi ijee Qiimunso,
Aasi huni neelena,
Udurnu biiri hamduwa.

放羊的阿吾拉仁布,
放牛的依姐琪门索,
牛羊欢奔来合群,
琪门索拉仁布心连心。

Brother Laarimbu was herding sheep,
Sister Qiimunso was herding oxen;
The oxen mixed with the sheep,
So Laarimbu and Qiimunso were often together.

Shdenu rimbanu xuudirewa,
Usi ujuurdu baujiiwa,
Ghulnu awu Laarimbu,
Huninaa tauwaa yaunii joo.

清晨的露水亮晶晶,
闪闪亮亮在草丛,
沟里的阿吾拉仁布,
赶着羊群往前行。

In the morning, when dew
Was on the grass,
Brother Laarimbu from the valley
Drove his flock of sheep straight ahead.

Fulaan nara gharina,
Ula tolghuindu xirlaja,
Tangnu ijee Qiimunso,
Aasinaa tauji gharghanii joo.

火红的太阳在起升,
满山满川都映红,
滩里的依姐琪门索,
赶着牛群出了门。

The red sun rose,
The sunlight dyed the mountain peaks red.
Sister Qiimunso from the plain
Drove her herd of oxen out of her homestead.

Aasi usinu sanana,
Laarimbu ndaa sanana,
Huni sogsogsa aldan gua,
Awu munu sgilduwa.

牛儿留恋绿草嫩,
拉仁布把我牵在心,
羊儿紧跟不离群,
阿吾是我心中的人。

The oxen are reluctant to leave the green grass;
Laarimbu touches my heart.
The sheep do not like to scatter, but always stay together;
Brother is in my heart.

Huni tangnu durlana,
Awu ijeenu durlana,
Sajaghai xjoosire hailana,
Ghuilanu sgilsa halongwa.

羊儿深情往滩中，
阿吾的心中情多深，
喜鹊盘窝在树顶，
相亲相爱多热情。

Sheep love the plain,
Brother loves Sister,
Magpies are calling from the treetops,
Brother's and Sister's hearts are warm.

Undur xjoosinu xjuur gomnii,
Ijee munu sgildu wai,
Xjoosi kiisa lii ayim joo,
Labxi huraasa lii ayim joo.

大树扎根深又深，
伊姐永在我心中，
树杆粗大不惧风，
叶茂不怕大雨淋。

A big tree's roots grow deep,
Sister is in my heart,
Trees without fear of wind,
Leaves without fear of rain.

Huni aasi idelduna,
Buda ghuila durlana,
Laarimbu uladu dulaana,
Qiimunso huinosa daghaana.

牛羊贪恋草青青，
阿吾和依姐情意深，
拉仁布上山放羊群，
琪门索赶牛随后跟。

The oxen and sheep eat grass,
Brother and Sister love each other,
When Laarimbu went to graze on the mountains
Qiimunso followed him, driving her oxen.

Tebxin tangdu bausamba,
Muroon szuda arinna,
Undur uladu gharsamba,
Narghai usi joolonna.

来到平展的草滩中，
蜿蜒的河水清又清，
来到高耸的深山中，
起伏的草丛软又嫩。

Down on the verdant plain
The river water is clean;
Up on the high mountain
The grass is tender.

Laarimbu muxi yausamba,
Qiimunso huinosa daghaana,
Nige jur ngusge nesina,
Ghajardu baugunaa sanaa gua.

拉仁布放羊前面行，
琪门索赶牛随后跟，
鸽子飞翔在空中，
自由自在多称心。

Laarimbu walked ahead,
Qiimunso followed behind him,
A pair of pigeons flew in the sky,
Freely and joyfully.

Undur uladu gharaanu,
Tebxin tangdu ujesa,
Aasi musi ulonna,
Sogsog sogsog idelduna.

从那高高的高山顶，
手搭凉蓬望川中，
黄牛犏牛数不清，
又成伙来又成群。

Climbing up to the high mountain,
Looking at the plain,
A large number of oxen and yaks are there,
Eating grass in herds.

Undur ulasa bauwaanu,
Tebxin tangdu ujesa,
Tangdu aasi ulonna,
Kennu aasinqi dulaana?

走下高高的高山顶,
看那宽阔的平川中,
平川中牛儿数不清,
不知谁家的牧牛人?

Coming down from the high mountain,
Looking at the verdant plain,
A large number of oxen are grazing there,
Who is the cowherd?

Tangnu aasi ulonna,
Qiimunso aasinu dulaana,
Undur ulasa ken nauna?
Ulanu huninu ken dulaana?

平川中的牛儿多又多,
牧牛的是我琪门索,
从那高山上谁望着?
山上的羊群谁放着?

A large number of oxen are on the plain,
The cowherd is Qiimunso,
Who is looking at the plain?
Who is herding the sheep on the high mountain?

Undur ulasa bu ujenii,
Ulanu huninu bu dulaanii,
Nire munu Laarimbu wai,
Qi yama gaanu iren gui?

从高山顶上我在望,
山上的羊群我在放,
我的名字叫拉仁布,
依姐你为啥不回望?

I am looking down from the high mountain,
I am herding the sheep on the mountain,
My name is Laarimbu.
Why don't you come up here?

Aaja nemqongnu uje shdan gua,
Buda ghoornu haajalghana,
Aaja bayaandu ulina,
Buda ghoornu sgelghan gua.

哥哥看不起穷雇工,
把我二人两下里分,
哥哥想的是富裕人,
我俩人会面万不能。

My brother dislikes poor servants,
He wants to separate us;
My brother likes rich men,
We two cannot come together.

Ghulnu awu Laarimbu,
Aasi da huninu tauwaanu,
Shge ghulnu turo ni,
Aasi da huninu dulaana.

沟里的阿吾拉仁布,
赶上母牛和母羊,
到那深深的山沟里,
去放牧母牛和母羊。

Brother Laarimbu from the valley,
Driving oxen and sheep,
Reached the big valley,
And grazed oxen and sheep.

Tangnu ijee Qiimunso,
Buruu da hurghanu tauwaanu,
Tebxin tangnu dire ni,
Buruu da hurghanu dulaana.

滩里的伊姐琪门索,
赶上牛犊和羊羔,
到那宽阔的平川上,
去放牧牛犊和羊羔。

Sister Qiimunso from the plain
Drove calves and lambs
On the verdant grassland
And grazed the calves and lambs.

Mori daahanaa sanana,
Aasi buruunaa sanana,
Huni hurghanaa sanana,
Awu ijeenaa sanana.

母马把马驹多思恋,
母牛把牛犊多思恋,
母羊把羊羔多思恋,
阿吾把伊姐多思恋。

A horse loves her colt,
A cow loves her calf,
A ewe loves her lamb,
Brother loves Sister.

Jongdu morinaa tauwaanu,
Jongdu daahala neeleya,
Jongdu aasina tauwaanu,
Jongdu buruula neeleya.

赶上成百的马群啊,
和那马驹成群,
赶上成百的牛群啊,
和那牛犊合成群。

Hundreds of horses are driven
And mixed with hundreds of colts,
Hundreds of oxen are driven
And mixed with hundreds of calves.

Jongdu huninaa tauwaanu,
Jongdu hurghala neeleya,
Huni aasinaa tauwaanu,
Buda ghuila hamdulaya.

赶上成百的羊群啊,
和那羊羔合成群,
我俩的牛羊和成群,
阿吾和伊姐来相逢。

Hundreds of sheep are driven
And mixed with hundreds of lambs.
Drive our oxen and sheep together,
Brother and Sister meet together.

Ula da tangnu hghua shdana,
Buda ghoornu hghua adam,
Hurgha uladuji haulina,
Narghai usidu ulina.

高山平川能分开，
我俩的心在一块，
羊儿超着山上跑，
为了吃那嫩青草。

Mountains and plains can be separated,
But we two cannot be separated.
Lambs run to the mountains
In order to eat tender grass.

Buruu bulagdu haulina,
Arin szudu ulina,
Urgon tangdu pusaanu,
Undur uladu ujenii.

牛儿向那山泉奔，
为了饮那泉水清，
伊姐伫立在平川上，
深情望着高山顶。

A calf runs to a spring
In order to get clean water;
Sister stands on the plain,
Looking toward the high mountain.

Muni awu Laarimbu,
Qimu sgegu durlani,
Awu huninaa tauwaa ire,
Hurgha aamala neeleya.

我的阿吾拉仁布，
伊姐真想见到你，
赶着羊群下山来，
羊羔要吃母羊的奶。

My brother, Laarimbu,
Sister really misses you,
Drive your sheep down from the mountain,
Mix lambs with ewes.

Aama hurghanaa hghalan gua,
Hurgha da aama haajan gua,
Ghulnu awu Laarimbu,
Mamunaa tauwaa bauji ire.

母羊把羊羔抛不掉，
羊羔和母羊分不开，
沟里的阿吾拉仁布，
赶着母羊下山来。

Ewes cannot part from their lambs,
Lambs and ewes will always be together.
Brother Laarimbu from the valley,
Drive your ewes down from the mountain.

Buruu aasinu tauwaanu,
Ghuila neeleji dulaaya,
Aama da buruu beesina,
Haajagu taada qirwal gua.

赶着母牛和牛犊，
我俩一块去放牧，
母牛和牛犊喜相处，
分离的心境真难受。

Drive your calves and oxen,
We two will graze together;
Ewes and calves like to be together,
It is sad for them to be separated.

Ijee sgilnaa hamburaa,
Awu taada kuriya,
Ula tangda hulo gua,
Daunge daulasa mudena.

滩上的伊姐请放心，
阿吾马上就下山岭，
高山平川不太远，
唱一首山歌吐心声。

Sister, please rest assured,
Your brother will soon come down from the mountains.
Mountains and plains are not far apart,
We get to know each other by singing songs.

Undur uladu gharaanu,
Urgon tangdu ujenii,
Sgilnu daunaa daulaji,
Qimii nige szaghanii.

攀岩登石爬上山，
辽阔平川在眼前，
放开喉咙放心声，
伊姐你能否听得见。

Climb up on the high mountain,
Look at the verdant plain,
Sing a heartfelt song,
Greetings to you.

Shge huninu tauwaanu,
Urgon tangdu ireya,
Hurgha aamala neeleya,
Buda ghuila hamdulaya.

赶着母羊快下山，
羊羔盼妈在平滩，
母羊羊羔合一处，
咱俩一同来放牧。

Drive sheep
To the vast grassland,
Lambs mix with ewes,
We two meet together.

Shge aasinu tauwaanu,
Tebxin tangdu ireya,
Buruu aamala neeleya,
Buda ghuila hamdulaya.

赶着母牛快下山，
牛犊等妈在平川，
母牛牛犊合一处，
咱俩一同来放牧。

Drive oxen
To the plain,
Calves mix with cows,
We two meet together.

Shge morinaa tauwaanu,
Dooro tangdu ireya,
Daaha aamala neeleya,
Buda ghuila hamdulaya.

赶着母马快下山,
马驹侯马在下川,
母马马驹合一处,
咱俩一同来放牧。

Drive horses
To the plain,
Colts mix with mares,
We two meet together.

Hurgha uladu gharisa,
Shge huni zeelena,
Buruu uladu gharisa,
Musi unee zeelena.

羊羔向着山上跑,
母羊急忙迎向前,
牛犊向着山上跑,
母牛急忙迎向前。

Lambs climb up the mountain,
They are greeted by ewes,
Calves climb up the mountain,
They are greeted by cows.

Daaha uladu gharisa,
Gurma mori zeelena,
Ijee uladu kurisa,
Awu qimii zeelenii.

马驹向着山上跑,
母马急忙迎向前,
伊姐向着山上来,
阿吾深情迎向前。

Colts climb up the mountain,
They are greeted by mares,
Sister climbs up the mountain,
She is greeted by Brother.

Ghulnu awu Laarimbu,
Qi munu daunu sunusi joo,
Tangnu ijee Qiimunso,
Qimu sgiji sananii joo.

沟里的阿吾拉仁布，
请你仔细听我唱，
滩里的伊琪门索，
时刻等待把你想。

Brother Laarimbu from the valley,
Please listen to my songs.
Sister Qiimunso from the plain,
I really miss you.

Awu huninaa tauji ire,
Ijee muxiji zeelenii,
Hghuaji dulaajin huniwa,
Hurgha aamala neeleya.

阿吾赶羊快下山，
伊姐疾步迎向前，
分群放牧的羊群，
急切盼望来相见。

Brother, please come, driving your sheep,
Sister will come out to receive you.
The sheep are grazing divided into groups,
They like to mix and eat grass together.

Awu aasina tauji ire,
Ijee qimu zeelenii,
Hghuaji dulaaji aasiwa,
Buruu aamala neeleya.

阿吾赶牛快下山，
伊姐疾步迎向前，
分开放牧的牛群，
急切盼望来相见。

Brother, please come, driving your oxen,
Sister will come out to receive you.
The oxen are grazing divided into groups,
They like to mix and eat grass together.

Awu morinaa tauji ire,
Ijee qimu zeelenii,
Hghuaji dulaajin moriwa,
Daaha aamala neeleya.

阿吾赶马快下山，
伊姐疾步迎向前，
分别放牧的马群，
急切盼望来相见。

Brother, please come driving your horses,
Sister will come out to receive you,
The horses are grazing, divided into groups,
They like to mingle and eat grass together.

Ghulnu awu Laarimbu,
Tangnu ijee Qiimunso,
Hunimaa aasinu neeleya,
Buda ghuila hamdulaya.

沟里的阿吾拉仁布，
滩里的伊姐琪门索，
赶着牛羊来合群，
我俩相见多高兴。

Brother Laarimbu from the valley,
Sister Qiimunso from the plain,
Let's drive our oxen and sheep together,
So we two can be together.

Buda ghuilanu dundogdu,
Huni da hurgha hamdulana,
Undur ulasa bauwaanu,
Urgon tangdu hamdulana.

为了我俩的爱情，
母羊和羊羔喜相逢，
从那陡峭的山岗上，
来到平川喜相逢。

For the sake of our love,
Ewes and lambs will mix,
Coming down from the high mountain,
Meet together on the vast plain.

Buda ghuilanu dundogdu,
Aasi da buruu hamdulana,
Undur ulasa bauwaanu,
Urgon tangdu hamdulana.

为了我俩的爱情，
母牛和牛犊喜相逢，
从那高高的山岭上，
来到平川喜相逢。

For the sake of our love,
Cows and calves will mix,
Coming down from the high mountain,
Meet together on the vast plain.

Buda ghuilanu dundogdu,
Mori da daaha hamdulana,
Undur ulasa bauwaanu,
Urgon tangdu hamdulana.

为了我俩的爱情，
母马和马驹喜相逢，
从那深深的山谷中，
来到平川喜相逢。

For the sake of our love,
Mares and colts will mix,
Coming down from the high mountain,
Meet together on the vast plain.

Ula tangda neeleja joo,
Huni aasi neeleja joo,
Buda ghuila sgeja joo,
Sgil turosa beesija joo.

山岗平川紧相连，
牛羊合群真喜欢，
阿吾和依姐见了面，
既高兴来又喜欢。

Mountains and plains are connected together,
Sheep and oxen are mixed,
Brother and Sister meet together,
They are excited.

Ghoornu gharsa warijii joo,
Nudu haajan ugui joo,
Ugo hghundu unaajii joo,
Nudu nimpusi nguroonii joo.

双手紧握暖人心，
目不转睛传深情，
千言万语在心中，
止不住眼泪往下滚。

They hold each other's hands,
They stare into each other's eyes with love,
They have a great many words to say,
Their tears are flowing.

Nige nigenaa szaghana,
Beesaa laghu ulin gua,
Ngusge tingerdu nesina,
Buda ghuilanu shdorlana.

你问长来我问短，
高兴的心里棉软软，
一对鸽子蓝天旋，
也把我俩来赞颂。

They talk wholeheartedly,
They feel excited,
A pair of pigeons is flying in the sky,
Seeming to praise them.

Buda ghuila hamdulasa,
Huni aasi neelem joo,
Buda ghuila hamdulasa,
Huni aasi beesim joo.

你我欢聚在一起，
牛羊各自成群伙，
你我如愿相依偎，
牛羊高兴也称快。

When we are together,
Sheep and oxen are mixed,
When we are together,
Sheep and oxen are happy.

Undur ula undurwa,
Nda ghoornu haajalgha adana,
Urgon tangda urgonna,
Nda ghoornu sajili adana.

山峦虽然高高耸,
难把我俩来割分,
平川辽阔广又宽,
难把我俩来拆散。

High mountains
Cannot separate us,
The vast plains
Cannot separate us.

Nige nigenaa nauwaanu,
Sgilnu daunaa daulaya,
Buda ghuilanu dautu dau,
Ula tangdu dongghudina.

含情对望喜眉梢,
把心里的话编成歌,
我俩的歌声多美妙,
在山谷平川中缭绕。

We gaze at each other,
Sing our heartfelt songs,
Our songs are so splendid,
And resound across the mountains and plains.

Huni idejin usiwa,
Narghai usi funurduwa,
Buda ghuila durilaanu,
Undur uladu ghariya.

河岸青草嫩又长,
羊儿吃草脆又香,
手拉手儿多欢畅,
唱着歌儿把山上。

Sheep eat tender grass,
The tender grass is sweet,
We two, hand in hand,
Climb up the high mountain.

Aasi uqujin szuwa,
Arin szuda ndatinna,
Buda ghuila durildaanu,
Undur uladu ghariya.

平川的河水清又清，
黄牛犏牛饮不尽，
咱俩一同肩并肩，
朝着山顶来攀登。

The water that the oxen drink
Is clear and sweet,
We two, hand in hand,
Climb up the high mountain.

Undur ula unduriwa,
Tensa ayigu xangan gua,
Ghoornu gharlanaa durisa,
Sgil teda neelena.

高山耸立插入云，
山高崖陡难攀登，
咱俩手儿紧相牵，
两颗心儿紧相印。

The high mountain is tall,
We do not fear to climb it,
We two, hand in hand,
Our two hearts are always together.

Ula kijeen baimaalwa,
Tensa ayigu dundog gua,
Halghu daghaaji gharisa,
Sgil turosa beesina.

山峰陡峭又险峻，
我俩不怕不担心，
手拉手儿脚相跟，
我俩心里喜盈盈。

The mountain's slope is steep,
We do not fear it,
We climb it step by step,
We are happy in our hearts.

Nara szargu gharaanu,
Nughoon xugonu xuliya,
Geril rogdu gharaanu,
Qighaan nkambanu doglaya.

攀上阳山山坡上,
折上绿色柏树枝,
登上阴山山坡上,
摘上白色嵁巴花。

Climb up the sunny side of the mountain,
Break off green cypress twigs,
Climb up the shady side of the mountain,
Gather lily bulbs.

Ulanu tolghuindu gharaanu,
Shge szangnu gharghaya,
Shge tingernu ughua giya,
Ulon purghaannu ughua giya.

来到高高的山顶上,
煨上冲天的大桑烟,
祈求苍天来保佑,
祈求众佛来保佑。

Climb further up the mountain,
Burn a large incense offering,
Beseech Great Heaven,
Pray to the all deities.

Kugo tingere ijindu sau,
Hara ghajar warwadu sau,
Buda ghuilanu dundogwa,
Nige sasiinu dundogwa.

苍天为我来做主,
大地为我来做媒,
成就我俩好姻缘,
白头偕老相依偎。

Great Heaven is our master,
Earth is our matchmaker,
If our love can be realized
We will love each other forever.

Tebxin tangdu bauwaanu,
Qighaan gurnaa pusilghuya,
Qighaan gurnu turo ni,
Kudu tenaa saulduya.

来到平坦草滩上,
搭起白色的毡帐,
白色毡帐就是家,
安下小家把福享。

Coming down to the plain,
We pitch our white felt tent.
Inside the white felt tent
We make our lives.

Ghuran tarnu joowaanu,
Tarnu zoohu jirgeleya,
Jas tughoonaa nireenu,
Sundii qaanu xjolghaya.

抬来三块大石头,
垒起石头的炉灶,
架起黄铜的锣锅,
锣锅里把奶茶熬。

Moving three big stones,
We set up a stove,
A brass pot supported by the three stones,
Boil milk tea in the brass pot.

Sundii qaanaa xjolghoonu,
Kugo tingerdu nqorlaya,
Sundii qaanaa xjolghoonu,
Ulon purghaandu nqorlaya.

熬上浓香的奶茶,
先敬无上的苍天,
熬上醇香的奶茶,
再敬至尊的神佛。

When the milk tea has boiled,
Asperse it to Great Heaven,
When the milk tea has boiled,
Asperse it to the all deities.

Kugo tingerdu nqorlasa,
Kugo tingere furonglam joo,
Ulon purghaandu nqorlasa,
Ulon purghaan furonglam joo.

奶茶敬献给苍天,
苍天就会保佑我,
奶茶敬献给神佛,
神佛就会保佑我。

Asperse it to Great Heaven,
Great Heaven will protect us,
Asperse it to all the deities,
All the deities will protect us.

Tebxin tangda nughoonna,
Undur usida joolonna,
Halong paisa xjirbuuwa,
Qighaan xjangsa joolonna.

广阔平滩绿油油,
高高牧草软绵绵,
温暖惬意似火炕,
松软舒适如毛毡。

The plain is green,
The high grass is tender,
The grass is warmer than a heated platform on the plain,
The grass is softer than felt.

Sala xjoosi shgewa,
Nughoon labxi pangleja,
Sarin dooro sauldusa,
Qighaan gursa xjirbuuwa.

高高大树枝杈多,
绿叶茂盛似把伞,
树荫底下共乘凉,
比那毡包更舒坦。

Big trees with many twigs,
With many green leaves,
We enjoy the cool under the green trees,
It is more comfortable than sitting inside a felt tent.

Deeran udignaa duikaanu,
Sundii qaanaa uqulduya,
Deeren udignaa duikaanu,
Ndatin tangxaa tailduya.

四个膝盖相对着，
把醇香的奶茶喝着，
四只眼睛相对着，
把心里的话儿说着。

Four knees pressed together,
Drinking tasty milk tea,
Four eyes gazing together,
Speaking from our hearts.

Udur soni uguiji,
Buda ghuila hamduwa,
Udur soni dawaanii,
Sgilnu ugo buraan gui.

不分白天和黑夜，
我俩永远不分离，
白天黑夜轮流过，
心里话儿用不完。

Not only in the daytime but also at night
We two are together,
As days and nights go by,
We two are together, speaking heartfelt words.

Dinloor daahunaa tailiya,
Qighaan laxjangnaa tailiya,
Haahaa buboowaa nanaaya,
Maha buyenaa neeleya.

脱下登洛与达乎，
脱下白色的长袍，
紧紧搂抱在一起，
两个肉身子连一起。

Qiimanso: I'll take off my headdress,
Laarimbu: And I'll take off my robe,
We'll embrace each other tightly,
And our bodies will mix together.

Qasi madu marawa,
Menhua madu keelewa,
Maha buye neelesa,
Yasi szunsa sajiraana.

像雪一样的肌肤，
像棉花一样的身子，
两个身子紧相连，
浑身筋骨都松散。

Snow-white skin
And cotton-soft belly,
Two bodies entwined,
All muscles and bones seemed to loosen.

Buda ghuilanu marawa,
Mara hamdu neeleja,
Buda ghuilanu sgilwa,
Sgil hamdu neeleja.

我俩的身子肉身子，
俩身子连在一块了，
我俩的心是不二心，
两个心合在一块了。

Our two bodies
Are linked together,
Our two hearts
Are joined together.

Gurnu turogu nqoqire,
Gigeen lamarnu dileya,
Gurnu ghadagu szangqire,
Shge szangnu gharghaya.

毡帐的供桌上，
点上圣洁的佛灯，
毡帐外的桑台上，
煨上芳香的桑烟。

On the table inside the felt tent
Holy butter lamps are offered,
On the altar outside the felt tent
Fragrant incense is offered.

Kugo tingerdu murguya,
Ghuraan tolghuinu murguya,
Ulon purghaandu murguya,
Ghuraan tolghuinu murguya.

我俩头顶苍天在，
恭恭敬敬拜三拜，
我俩头顶诸佛在，
恭恭敬敬拜三拜。

Bow down to Great Heaven,
Bow down three times,
Bow down to all the deities,
Bow down three times.

Tingerla amadagha ideya,
Purghaanla amadagha ideya,
Buyenaa zongda bii haajaya,
Sgilnaa zongda bii furaaya.

对着苍天来起誓，
对着诸佛来发愿，
两个身子永不离，
两颗真心到永远。

We swear to Heaven,
We swear to all the deities,
Our two bodies will never be separated,
Our two hearts will be together forever.

Ghulnu awu Laarimbu,
Tangnu ijee Qiimunso,
Sgil batidu neeleja,
Haajagu log ni nige gua.

沟里的阿吾拉仁布，
滩里的伊姐琪门索，
两颗心儿连一起，
要让分离万不能。

Brother Laarimbu from the valley,
Sister Qiimunso from the plain,
Our hearts have already melted together,
We can never separate.

Tebxin tangda urgonna,
Dauti dauda duurija,
Xongnu nerwaa nesina,
Jongnu xauda daulana.

平坦草滩宽又广,
动听歌声在飘荡,
一对鸳鸯在飞翔,
百灵鸟儿在歌唱。

The plain is broad,
It is full of loud songs,
A pair of mandarin ducks is flying,
Larks are singing too.

Jorotu morinu nurire,
Haldan imel hgilena,
Baatir awu Laarimbu,
Qijig ijeenu hgilena.

骏马奔驰在草原上,
马背上要配金鞍杖,
勇士般阿吾拉仁布,
配上鲜花似琪门索。

The gallant horse's back
Requires a golden saddle,
Brave Brother Laarimbu
Requires a flower-like sister.

Borboljin xaunu mangliire,
Nuruu foodi hgilena,
Qijig ijee Qiimunso,
Baatir awunu hgilena.

孛尔孛勒金鸟儿啊,
额上要配上宝羽毛,
鲜花似的琪门索啊,
对儿要配上拉仁布。

A hoopoe's crown
Requires a treasure plume,
Flower-like Qiimunso
Requires a brave man.

Sgilnu daunaa daulaldusa,
Undur tingerdu nesina,
Murii sgildii aajawa,
Sgil turosa furaana.

心中的歌儿放声唱，
在蓝天白云间回响，
坏心的哥哥听见了，
气愤的黑血堵胸膛。

They sang heartfelt songs,
And the sound lingered in the air.
Qiimunso's wicked older brother heard,
And was infuriated.

Aaja seerdu ulina,
Kunnu sgilnu muden gua,
Shge hadadu ulina,
Kunnu sgildu ulin gua.

坏心的哥哥爱钱财，
他不知人们的真爱，
为了大宗的金礼彩，
正直的人品他不爱。

Elder brother is greedy
And doesn't care about true love:
In order to get huge betrothal gifts
He ignores true love.

Sgildii kunda ghuilawa,
Nudu nausaar haajalghana,
Murii sgildii ndaqarwa,
Laarimbudu mau giguna.

明智妹妹有心上人，
眼看把二人要拆散，
恶毒的人有恶心肠，
要把拉仁布致害残。

Elder brother knows his sister has a true lover:
He wants to separate them.
This vicious man has a wicked heart:
He will murder Laarimbu.

Hara soninu dunda ni,
Nige deelnu mosija,
Laarimbunu gurdu uroo xjaanu,
Nige qudughu shdughuja.

漆黑的深夜黑如洞,
哥哥着女装来行凶,
摸进拉仁布的帐篷,
狠狠的一刀扎的深。

Deep in the night
He disguises himself in female attire,
He goes into Laarimbu's tent,
And stabs Laarimbu.

Munu awu Laarimbu,
Qimu yaan busi tughuna?
Buda ghuilanu dundogdu,
Qimu jublong ujelghaja.

可怜的阿吾拉仁布,
给你按的是什么罪?
只因我俩相爱的深,
竟让你受到此连累。

Laarimbu, my Brother,
What crime have you committed?
Only because we fell in love
Were you exposed to this terrible fate.

Munu awu Laarimbu,
Qimu anjii norlaja?
Qinu sgilnu Qiimunso,
Qimu ujelange irewa.

我的阿吾拉仁布,
你的伤痛在哪里?
你心上的琪门索,
心急如焚来看你。

Laarimbu, my Brother,
Where are you hurt?
Qiimunso, your lover,
Is coming to see you.

Munu awu Laarimbu,
Qimu jublong ujelghaja,
Munu jirgendu udina,
Munu sgildu udina.

我的阿吾拉仁布，
为我受尽人间苦，
伤疼痛在我心头，
痛得不忍回首顾。

Laarimbu, my Brother,
You are suffering because of me.
My heart is full of pain,
I'm in so much pain that I don't want to live.

Munu awu Laarimbu,
Qinu niurnunge joolghaya,
Xongnu nudunu nimpusilanaa,
Qinu niurnunge nghuaya.

我的阿吾拉仁布，
终能见了你一面，
双眼的眼泪止不住，
滚烫的泪水为你流。

Laarimbu, my Brother,
Eventually I see your dear face,
And with tears from my two eyes
I wash your face.

Munu awu Laarimbu,
Qimu werdunaa teeriya,
Munu halong jirgelanaa,
Qinu buyenu halalghaya.

我的阿吾拉仁布，
把你紧搂在怀里，
用我的热血热恋心，
把你的冰身来温暖。

Laarimbu, my Brother,
I clasp you in my bosom—
Use my hot heart
To warm your icy body.

Munu awu Laarimbu,
Qimu anjii norlaja?
Tangnu ijee Qiimunso,
Qimu ujela irewa.

我的阿吾拉仁布,
你的伤痛在哪里?
滩里的依姐琪门索,
心如刀绞来看你。

Laarimbu, my Brother,
Where were you stabbed?
Qiimunso from the plain
Has come to see you.

Munu awu Laarimbu,
Qimu lanjag ujelghawa,
Munu hghunsa udina,
Qinu anjii ni udina?

我的阿吾拉仁布,
让你受此万分疼,
我的心里真难受,
你的疼痛在哪里?

Laarimbu, my Brother,
You are suffering from your wound,
My heart is broken:
Where do you feel pain?

Norlansan kundun kungonnaa?
Qi ndaa nige kile joo,
Simjonglaji xulaaya,
Qinu sgilaa irelghaya.

伤势是重还是轻?
请你对我讲实情,
小心谨慎来侍奉,
舒适减痛称你心。

Is the wound severe or mild?
Please tell me truthfully,
I will look after you,
I will take good care of you.

Munu ijee Qiimunso,
Qinu niurnunge sgewa,
Fulaan niurnunge sgesa,
Munu sgilsa halongwa.

我的伊姐琪门索，
如今我俩又相见，
只要见到你的面，
我的心里暖烘烘。

Qiimunso, my Sister,
I see you again—
When I see your dear face again
My heart is warm and at peace.

Munu ijee Qiimunso,
Qinu yoronu sunurdawa,
Joolon yoronu sunurdasa,
Munu sgilsa xjirbuuwa.

我的伊姐琪门索，
你夜莺般的声音，
使我耳边多棉软，
使我心里暖融融。

Qiimunso, my Sister,
I heard your moan,
When I heard your moan,
I felt at peace.

Munu ijee Qiimunso,
Qinu werdunge ntiraawa,
Halong werdunge ntiraasa,
Munu sgil haniwa.

我的伊姐琪门索，
躺在你的怀抱里，
使我身子暖烘烘，
使我心里得满意。

Qiimunso, my Sister,
I lie in your arms—
After lying in your arms,
My spiritual wound is healed.

Munu ijee Qiimunso,
Sgilnu ugo jangiraana,
Ugo hghundu unaawaanu,
Guleji ghargha adani.

我的伊姐琪门索，
心里的话儿千千万，
实难启口把话讲，
真心话心里堵得慌。

Qiimunso, my Sister,
I have thousands of heartfelt words for you,
But they have fallen into the depths of my heart,
It is hard to say them now.

Munu ijee Qiimunso,
Qinu sgilnu mudewa,
Nimpusi kuinaa huraawaanu,
Sgilnaa uudu tailduya.

我的伊姐琪门索，
你的真心我知道，
擦干眼泪莫悲伤，
放宽心思把日子熬。

Qiimunso, my Sister,
I understand your heart,
Please wipe away your tears and don't feel sad,
Open your heart.

Munu ijee Qiimunso,
Malang shdeji sgelduya,
Undendu tergenge geejiisa,
Munu amun gharijii.

我的伊姐琪门索，
我俩明早再相见，
假如门前停着车，
便是我命已归天。

Qiimunso, my Sister,
Come tomorrow morning.
If you see a wooden cart in front of the gate
It means I have already died.

Munu ijee Qiimunso,
Malang sheleji sgelduya,
Yantongsa fune gharisa,
Munu amun ghariji gui.

我的伊姐琪门索，
我俩明早再相见，
假如烟囱冒青烟，
说明我还在阳间。

Qiimunso, my Sister,
Come tomorrow morning.
If you see smoke rising from the chimney
It means I'm still alive.

Harangghu marangghu pusaanu,
Kuko tingerdu ujesa,
Hara ulong haawaanu,
Gigeen bauji iren gua.

东方未白忙起身，
抬头仰望苍天空，
漆黑乌云遮漫天，
一片黑暗天不明。

She rises before it is light,
Looks up at the sky,
The sky is covered with black clouds,
It is difficult to see the light.

Munu awu Laarimbu,
Qinu halong yantongsa,
Kugo fune gharin gua?
Munu awu buraadiija.

我的阿吾拉仁布，
在你高高的烟囱里，
一片清冷不冒烟?
剜心挖苦多凄凉。

Laarimbu, my Brother,
From your chimney
Has no smoke risen up?
My Brother, you must have gone.

Anjii xjiji iregunii,
Anji pusiji saugunii,
Munu awu Laarimbu,
Kugo tingere anjiiwa?

何去何往难自主，
坐立不安难定神，
我的阿吾拉仁布，
苍天究竟在哪里？

I don't know where I should go,
I don't know where I should stand,
Laarimbu, my Brother,
Where is the gray sky?

Munu awu Laarimbu,
Qimu mau gisan aaja wai,
Tenu sgil ni muriiwa,
Munu sgildu szaliu wai.

我的阿吾拉仁布，
害死你的是我哥，
他的心狠手又毒，
我的心里最清楚。

Laarimbu, my Brother,
My elder brother killed you.
He is a black thorn,
I know him well.

Amdagha ideji kilewa,
Lii haajam giji kilewa,
Niudur ghoornu haajalghasa,
Nige foor dire sauldiya.

我俩曾经发誓愿，
今生今世永不分，
如今生死两相离，
愿咱长眠在同坟。

We two have sworn
To be together forever in our lives.
Today we are separated,
But we will be together in the same tomb.

Nensa muxigu udurdu,
Buda ghuila hamdulasa,
Halong suudu sauwaanu,
Sgilnu ugonaa gulenii.

以往甜蜜日子里，
我俩相遇在一起，
亲亲蜜蜜相依偎，
相互表达心话语。

Before our sweetest days
We were together,
Loving closely,
Speaking heartfelt words to each other.

Niudurgunge udurdu,
Munu awu Laarimbu,
Zandan moodinu zhiglaji,
Tendu jirgenge uliwa.

今天悲凄日子里，
我的阿吾拉仁布，
堆起檀香木柴堆，
你在木柴中心里。

Today, on this mournful day,
Laarimbu, my Brother,
Among the sandalwood,
You are placed in the sandalwood.

Nensa muxigu udurdu,
Buda ghuila hamdulasa,
Halong qireedu nauwaanu,
Naadiji xineeji sauldunii.

以往甜蜜日子里，
我俩相遇在一起，
相互凝视传情谊，
戏耍欢乐笑眯眯。

Before our sweetest days
We were together,
We soulfully gazed at each other,
Teasing each other joyfully.

Niudurgunge udurdu,
Munu awu Laarimbu,
Omog xaaxinu madunge,
Hara ghajardu xingeewa.

今天悲凄日子里，
我的阿吾拉仁布，
像那细细的流沙，
与大地融合为一体。

Today, this mournful day,
Laarimbu, my Brother,
You drift like fine sand,
Fused together with the earth.

Hara ghajarnu dire ni,
Qighaan tabnu turo ni,
Munu awu Laarimbu,
Tendu jirge uliwa.

在这灰昏天地的上面，
在这白色火化炉的里面，
我的阿吾拉仁布，
已成为火化炉的中心。

On the gray earth,
Inside the white cremation oven,
Laarimbu, my Brother,
Has been put at the center of the oven.

Qi toosi madu xindireem joo,
Qi hghuambar madu ngureem joo,
Qi qaalsi madu hualam joo,
Qi lamar madu nzhiblam joo.

愿你像酥油一样溶化，
愿你像佛灯一样燃烧，
愿你像黄裱一样化去，
愿你像佛灯一样熄灭。

I hope you will melt like butter,
I hope you will burn like a butter lamp,
I hope you will burn like paper,
I hope you will go out like a butter lamp.

Jongge moodinu shdaadisa,
Qi yama gaanu ngureen gui?
Jongge toosinu szurisa,
Qi yama gaanu ngureen gui?

烧去百捆的木柴,
你为什么不燃烧?
倒入百斤的酥油,
你为什么不燃烧?

Having burned hundreds of bundles of wood,
Why haven't you burned yet?
Having poured hundreds of kilograms of butter in the oven,
Why haven't you burned yet?

Munu awu Laarimbu,
Qi yaannu sgil tidawa?
Munu awu Laarimbu,
Qi kennu sgil tidawa?

我的阿吾拉仁布,
你在扯心什么呢?
我的阿吾拉仁布,
你在扯心谁人呢?

Laarimbu, my Brother,
What makes you reluctant to leave?
Laarimbu, my Brother,
From whom can you not bear to part?

Qinu sgilnu bu mudem,
Buda ghuiladu ugonge wai,
Munu awu lii ngureesa,
Hairan ijeenaa sgija.

你的心事我直销,
我俩有约已在先,
我的阿吾拉仁布,
心上的人儿在扯牵。

I understand your heart,
We have made a promise:
Laarimbu, my Brother,
You are waiting for your lovely Sister.

Ghulnu awu Laarimbu,
Tangnu ijee Qiimunso,
Xeele adagu yama gui?
Joosan malghanaa xeeleya.

沟里的阿吾拉仁布，
滩里的伊姐琪门索，
我舍不得的没什么？
头上的帽子舍给你。

Brother Laarimbu from the valley,
Sister Qiimunso from the plain,
You cannot leave me, what should I do?
I offer my hat to you.

Ghulnu awu Laarimbu,
Tangnu ijee Qiimunso,
Xeele adagu yama gui?
Mengu suugenaa xeeleya.

沟里的阿吾拉仁布，
滩里的伊姐琪门索，
我舍不得的没什么？
银子的耳坠舍给你。

Brother Laarimbu from the valley,
Sister Qiimunso from the plain,
You cannot leave me, what should I do?
I offer my silver earrings to you.

Ghulnu awu Laarimbu,
Tangnu ijee Qiimunso,
Xeele adagu yama gui?
Tirge pusinaa xeeleya.

沟里的阿吾拉仁布，
滩里的伊姐琪门索，
我舍不得的没什么？
绸缎腰带舍给你。

Brother Laarimbu from the valley,
Sister Qiimunso from the plain,
You cannot leave me, what should I do?
I offer my silk and satin sash to you.

Ghulnu awu Laarimbu,
Tangnu ijee Qiimunso,
Xeele adagu yama gui?
Ghudusi qaragnaa xeeleya.

沟里的阿吾拉仁布，
滩里的伊姐琪门索，
我舍不得的没什么？
古都斯腰鞋舍给你。

Brother Laarimbu from the valley,
Sister Qiimunso from the plain,
You cannot leave me, what should I do?
I offer my embroidered shoes to you.

Ghulnu awu Laarimbu,
Tangnu ijee Qiimunso,
Xeele adagu yama gui?
Mosisan simbeenaa xeeleya.

沟里的阿吾拉仁布，
滩里的伊姐琪门索，
我舍不得的没什么？
身上的长袍舍给你。

Brother Laarimbu from the valley,
Sister Qiimunso from the plain,
You cannot leave me, what should I do?
I offer my robe to you.

Ghulnu awu Laarimbu,
Tangnu ijee Qiimunso,
Xeele adagu yama gui?
Maha buyenaa xeeleya.

沟里的阿吾拉仁布，
滩里的伊姐琪门索，
我舍不得的没什么？
我把肉身子舍给你。

Brother Laarimbu from the valley,
Sister Qiimunso from the plain,
You cannot leave me, what should I do?
I offer my mortal body to you.

Ghulnu awu Laarimbu,
Tangnu ijee Qiimunso,
Buda ghuila hamdulaya,
Shge ghaldu hamdulaya.

沟里的阿吾拉仁布，
滩里的伊姐琪门索，
我俩人生死在一起，
在熊熊大火中来相会。

Brother Laarimbu from the valley,
Sister Qiimunso from the plain,
We will be together,
We meet among blazing flames.

Ghulnu awu Laarimbu,
Tangnu ijee Qiimunso,
Ghuraan udur ngureeja,
Ghuraan soni ngureeja.

沟里的阿吾拉仁布，
滩里的伊姐琪门索，
熊熊大火中燃三天，
熊熊大火中烧三天。

Brother Laarimbu from the valley,
Sister Qiimunso from the plain—
The two burned for three days,
The two burned for three nights.

Ghulnu awu Laarimbu,
Tangnu ijee Qiimunso,
Tingernu ulong fuleeja,
Ghajarnu xuruu fuleeja.

沟里的阿吾拉仁布，
滩里的伊姐琪门索，
天上的云彩烧红了，
地下的黄土烧焦了。

Brother Laarimbu from the valley,
Sister Qiimunso from the plain—
The clouds in the sky are burnt red,
The soil on Earth is burnt to blisters.

Kuko tingere kuilana,
Hara ghaja ulaana,
Laarimbu da Qiimunso,
Kugo taaxjadu furaawa.

苍天哀伤泪潜然，
大地抽泣声悲切，
拉仁布与琪门索，
化为青青的灰烬。

Tears trickle down sadly from the gray sky,
The earth sobs mournfully,
Laarimbu and Qiimunso
Turn to gray ashes.

Murii sgildii aajawa,
Funeesinu ghoor giji hghuwa,
Shge muroonla giilaanu,
Muroonnu ghoor rogdu bulaawa.

富人哥哥心歹毒，
强把骨灰葬两处，
埋在大河的两岸上，
用滔滔大河两相分。

The rich brother is vicious:
He separates their ashes,
And buries them on opposite sides of the river.
The surging river separated them again.

Yasi bulaasan ghajarsa,
Xjoosi ghoyur oosija,
Xjoosi ralag oosaanu,
Muroon dunda hamdulaja.

埋葬骨灰的泥土中，
长出一对合欢树，
枝条伸向河当中，
你盘我缠紧又紧。

At the site where the ashes were buried,
Grew two mimosa trees,
The branches grew
Until they twined together above the middle of the river.

Ndaqar sgildii aajawa,
Xjoosi ghuilanu qabjija,
Moodi tenu awaa xjaanu,
Zoohu turo shdaawaadija.

黑心的哥哥看到它，
把两棵大树齐根挖，
木头枝桠抬回家，
放到灶中当柴架。

The evil-hearted brother found them
And cut them down,
He carried the wood back home,
And burned it in his oven.

Yantong funenu daghaaji,
Goorjilagunge ireedija,
Nige jurnu xongnerwaa,
Nesaa gharaa ireedija.

随着烟囱冒青烟，
奇怪发生在猛然间，
一对美丽的鸳鸯鸟，
从烟囱之中直飞天。

As the smoke rose up from the chimney,
A miracle occurred:
A pair of mandarin ducks
Flew out of the chimney.

Xongnerwaa nesaa ireenu,
Ndaqar aajanu nghaalana,
Nudunii qugua sughulija,
Sgilnu qinji hanija.

鸳鸯双双飞过来，
直扑黑心的哥哥，
啄瞎罪恶的双眼睛，
罪有应得解心狠。

The two mandarin ducks
Pounce on the vicious brother
And peck his eyes until he is blinded.
He is rightly punished for his crimes.

Kugo tingere arilja,
Urgon talaare gigeenna,
Xongnerwaa nige jur nesina,
Luri uudu nesina.

乌云消散天湛蓝，
辽阔草原真灿烂，
一对鸳鸯在飞翔，
在浩瀚天空中飞翔。

The sky turns blue,
The vast grassland is splendid,
A pair of mandarin ducks is flying
In the immensity of the sky.

Ghulnu awu Laarimbu,
Tangnu ijee Qiimunso,
Nige jur xongnerwa nesina,
Urgondu nesisa duraalawa.

沟里的阿吾拉仁布，
滩里的伊姐琪门索，
一对鸳鸯在飞翔，
自由自在多欢畅。

Brother Laarimbu from the valley,
Sister Qiimunso from the plain,
A pair of mandarin ducks is flying,
Free, and thoroughly delighted.

4. The Song of the Dildima Bird

If asked to provide a translation for '*dildima* bird' into Chinese, some Mongghuls will say *yuanyang*, the term for the mandarin duck, but others cannot give a Chinese name for it. Instead, they describe it as a small bird that has a cockscomb on its head and a body covered in red, white and black feathers that is seen in the Seven Valleys in summer.

In the past, Mongghul women had a low position in their husband's home. Once a woman married, she lived with his family, including his parents, brothers, sisters, and, if the brothers were married, their wives and children. Only if the family became too large, and the household split, did she finally live in her 'own' home. In such cases, the old household usually belonged to the husband's youngest brother, who continued living with his parents. Only when the woman moved into her newly built house, and out of her husband's parents' house, was she free from her mother-in-law's surveillance and control.

While a woman still lived with her husband's extended family, her daily schedule was regulated by her mother-in-law, who might ask her, for example, to go cut livestock fodder; to fetch water from a spring or river; to cook for the family, even stipulating what should be cooked, and how; to carry manure from the stable out of the household compound; to work in the fields; and to do all the chores around the house. If the mother-in-law was happy with her daughter-in-law's performance, she would allow her to visit her parents often and to stay with them longer, but if not, such 'privileges' were withheld. The mother-in-law also decided to buy clothes for her yearly, and if the mother-in-law was unhappy or mistreated her, she would not be allowed to get new clothes, or would receive less than usual.

The following folktale exemplifies the stereotypical relationship between a Monggghul woman and her mother-in-law (Limusishiden and Stuart 2011:174-76).

The Qeo Family Girl

Told by Changminjii (Mongghul)

There was a mother whose daughter married and then went to live with her husband's family in a distant village. The mother missed her daughter very much after she left, and finally asked her youngest son to bring her daughter back home as soon as possible for a visit.

The youngest son went to the mother-in-law's home with a white horse and a piece of white felt draped over the back of the horse. The youngest son said to his sister's mother-in-law, 'I've come to bring my sister to visit my mother. Please let my sister visit my home.'

The mother-in-law replied, 'She cannot go home to visit her mother because the piles of manure in our twelve *mu* of fields have not been leveled. Once they are leveled, she will have time to visit.' The youngest son disappointedly returned home.

Some days later, the youngest son visited the mother-in-law's home again and said, 'Today, I have come on a white horse with a piece of white felt across its back to take my sister home. My mother desperately wants to see her, and she promises to let her return to your home as soon as possible. Please let her come visit.'

The mother-in-law said, 'Yes, she has finished leveling manure on the twelve *mu* of fields, but we did not dig the lumps of earth from the twelve *mu* of fields. She can go visit when she finishes digging all of them.'

In low spirits, the youngest son returned home.

One month later, the youngest son came again and said to the mother-in-law, 'Today I come again with a while horse and a piece of white felt draped over the horse's back to take my sister home. I beg you to please allow my sister to visit my home and see my mother. We will ensure she returns soon.'

The mother-in-law said, 'She cannot go today for she has not burned the lumps of soil on the twelve *mu* of land. We are going to use the burned lumps of dirt as fertilizer on our twelve *mu* of land. If we don't burn them, we'll have no food to eat next year. Once she finishes burning them, she can visit your home.'

The youngest son returned home again.

A month later, the youngest son came again, bringing the white horse with a piece of white felt draped over its back. He said to the mother-in-law, 'I have come to take my sister.'

The mother-in-law said, 'She has not finished leveling the burned piles of dirt. She can go visit her mother once she finishes this work.'

The youngest brother was filled with indignation but could only, again, return home without his sister.

Another month passed, and the youngest brother came again, leading the white horse with a piece of white felt draped over its back. He said again that he had come to take his sister home.

The mother-in-law said, 'She has not finished spreading the crushed earth over the twelve *mu* of land. Once she finishes this, I will let her visit your home.'

Without any success, the youngest brother returned home again.

Some days later, the youngest brother came again and said, 'She has spread the burned earth on the fields, so may she come visit her mother now?'

The mother-in-law said, 'We did not finish planting rapeseed on the twelve *mu* of land. Once that is done, I will let her visit her parents' home.'

The youngest brother sorrowfully returned home once again.

The daughter-in-law went to the fields, and in a short time she easily scattered rapeseed on the twelve *mu* of fields. The sown seed then sprouted.

Later the youngest brother came to take his sister, leading his white horse.

The mother-in-law said, 'She cannot visit her parents' home now, for she has not harvested the rapeseed from the twelve *mu* of fields. Once she does that, I will allow her to visit.'

The youngest brother despairingly returned home as before.

The Qeo family girl went to the fields to harvest the rapeseed, crying sadly. Magpies and pigeons noticed this, flew close to her, and said, 'You need not cry, we have come to help you now.' They very soon helped her collect all the seed, and then they flew away.

Then the youngest brother came to take his sister to see her mother, again bringing the white horse with a piece of white felt draped over its back. This time, the mother-in-law agreed that she could visit but stipulated, 'It's all right, you can go home, but you have to return tomorrow. And you have to come back with three pairs of shoes sewn for each member of our family during the time you are at your parents' home.' The Qeo family girl had to promise that she would do this.

When she reached her parents' home, she immediately started sewing shoes. The time flew by so fast that she wished she could tie the sun with a thread to hold it in the sky. After a day and a night, she finally finished making three pairs of shoes for each of the members of her mother-in-law's home. The next day, she delayed a little before she reached her mother-in-law's home.

This angered the mother-in-law, who ferociously scolded her, and the father-in-law and her husband's younger brother beat her. Finally, her husband's younger brother's wife beat her to death with a broom.

Later, the Qeo family girl's husband returned home accompanied by a large mounted retinue, for he was returning home in triumph after passing the examination to become a Number One Scholar. When he rode near the rear of his parents' home, a bird flew very near him. He then wondered if disaster had befallen his wife.

The retinue reached the front gate, but no one dismounted. The young man's father came to receive him, but he did not dismount. Instead, he said, 'Please ask the Qeo family girl to come receive me. Only she can make me dismount at once.'

Then his mother came to receive him. Her son said, 'I do not want to dismount unless the Qeo family girl receives me.'

His younger brother came to receive him, and he told him the same thing.

Then his younger brother's wife came to receive him, and he told her the same thing.

Finally, his younger sister came to receive him and said, 'Old brother, Old brother, now your younger sister has come to receive you, so please dismount.'

The Qeo family girl's husband said, 'Ah, I won't dismount if you come to receive me. I want only the Qeo family girl to receive me. Once she receives me, I will dismount immediately.'

His younger sister said, 'Old Brother, Old Brother, how can we let the Qeo family girl come here? Mother scolded her, father and elder brother beat her, and finally sister-in-law beat her to death soon after she returned from her parents' home. Then she was buried in the plow furrows in the field behind the house over there. Please go see.'

The young man then pulled his wife's corpse out from the plow furrows in the piles of earth in the field behind his home. He sorrowfully cremated the corpse and collected her ashes and bones in a small wooden box. He then turned his horse and slowly rode away.

In the twenty-first century the position of Mongghul women has improved, following social development, modernization, and globalization. After finishing nine years of compulsory education, some girls go on further studies and finally get official jobs. Others do not continue schooling, but go to Xining or other cities to find employment and start an urban life. Such socially and physically mobile young women typically prefer to find their own husbands, and so arranged marriage has mostly disappeared. Furthermore, it is increasingly common for young couples to set up their own home rather than living with their extended family. And, even in the rare cases where such residency patterns continue, the greater opportunities for mobility open to women today mean that the power of mothers-in-law to control their daughters-in-law has greatly decreased.

Before this change of women's fortunes, if a Mongghul woman was mistreated by her mother-in-law she would most likely think of the *The Song of the Dildima Bird*. This song was mostly sung by women whenever they felt sad in their husband's home. However, men also sang it when they were drinking together, an occasion when men displayed the breadth and flexibility of their musical repertoire. In this song, a daughter-in-law relates her woes to a *dildima* bird, and asks the bird to relate her story to her parents. She describes the difficult work she must do, complains of mistreatment by her mother-in-law, and describes how degraded her once beautiful wedding clothes have become since arriving in her parents-in-laws' home. In keeping with the melancholycontent of the song, the melody is slow and sad.

Dildima Xau

登登玛秀

The Song of the Dildima Bird

 Listen to an audio recording of the song at
https://archive.org/details/DildimaXau

Shdenu sghaudu ni, nige jur kungedu mulaa sulaa guiguna. Ghuilanaa
tingere ghajarnu ughua giji ghuirlasannu huino xjunge irejiguna. Xjun
ni shge ulaanu,awii amii ni hulo naamaidu ghadin gharghaadiijiiguna.
Ne xjunnu ghadin aama ni nganaa gula qiidag waiguna,xjun lii ujegu
jublongnu ujeenu buraajiiguna, nuduu nimpusinaa hghu turoji
qalginiiguna. Niguudurgedu,ne fii turo shdaaghu yerila xjiiguna, ne
juure hamnong ghajarsa nesiji iresan dildima xaungenu sgejiiguna.
Xaunu sgegu hamnong awii amiinaa ixida sanaadijiiguna, xaunu nausan
gula ulaan ulaan yama tigii jublong aadal ulaaniigunaa dailaji awii
amiidunaa ugonge kurgeelghaja. Te daulagu ni:

从前, 有对夫妻, 他俩无儿无女。后来他们拜天求地才得了一个女儿。女儿
长大后, 父母把她嫁到了很远很远的地方。她的婆婆非常恶毒, 使她受尽了
苦难, 委屈的泪水只能往肚子里咽。有一天, 他到林子里打柴, 看到了从娘
家那里飞来的登登玛鸟, 顿时, 思亲之情更加迫切, 禁不住失声大哭。她给
登登玛鸟唱诉在婆家受尽的苦难和心中无处诉说的委屈, 让登登玛鸟给她
的父母捎个口信, 盼望父母能来看望她一下。她唱到:

In the past there was a childless couple. They prayed to Buddha to have
a child, and finally they had a girl. When the girl had grown up, her
parents married her into a family that lived far away. Her mother-in-
law was a vicious woman who treated her badly, so the girl suffered

greatly and cried every day. One day, she went to collect firewood in a forest where she saw a bird that had flown from her parents' hometown. Seeing the bird, she missed her parents and her home deeply. She cried sadly and asked the bird to take a message to her parents. Then, she sang this song:

Dildima xau,
Zandan fiiregu dildima xau,
Hamnong rogdugu dildima xau,
Munu hamnong hudu hulawa,
Bu awii amiinaa sanani.

登登玛秀,
檀香林中的登登玛秀,
娘家飞来的登登玛秀,
遥远的地方有我的家,
至爱的双亲被我牵挂。

Dildima bird,
The *dildima* bird in the sandalwood,
The *dildima* bird flew here from my parents' hometown.
Their home is so far away,
I miss my parents very much.

Dildima xau,
Qi munu hamnong xjigu niu?
Qi munu hamnong xjisamba,
Qi munu awiidu kile joo,
Qi munu amiidu kile joo.

登登玛秀,
去我阿爸阿妈身边吗?
到我阿爸阿妈身边时,
给我的阿爸捎个口信,
给我的阿妈捎个口信。

Dildima bird,
Will you fly to my parents' home?
If you will fly there,
Please take a message to my father,
Please take a message to my mother.

Dildima xau,
Tigii hulodu kurgeeja,
Hara jublongnu ujenii,
Awii amiinaa sanaanu,
Munu nimpusi hoo xjija.

登登玛秀，
把我嫁到了遥远的婆家，
遥远的婆家我受苦受累，
远方的父母让我思念，
思念的泪水早已苦干。

Dildima bird,
I have been married off to a faraway place,
I have been treated very badly by my mother-in-law,
I have missed my parents,
And cried until I had no more tears to shed.

Dildima xau,
Tigii hulo ghajardu,
Ghadim tenunge gharaanu,
Awii amiinaa lii sgeni,
Sgilnu ugoge lii sunurdani.

登登玛秀，
在那样遥远地方，
遇了个蛮横的婆婆，
见不到慈祥的父母，
听不到父母的呼唤。

Dildima bird,
I am living far away,
I have a vicious mother-in-law,
I cannot see my mother,
And I cannot hear any words from my parents.

Dildima xau,
Ghadimdu aadal ulaasamba,
Sgoodal muxgha nailanii,
Durdundu shdaaghundu xjisamba,
Rgoosi hurinu tamdilina.

登登玛秀，
在婆婆家过日子时，
天天受婆母的打骂，
没日没夜逼我拾柴，
柴刺划破了我的手。

Dildima bird,
Every day in my mother-in-law's home,
Every day I am beaten and scolded,
Every day I am asked to collect firewood,
And black thorns hurt my hands.

Dildima xau,
Ghadimdu aadal ulaasamba,
Jublong shgedu dawaaxja,
Bu aasinu joodalnu joonii joo,
Bu mauxinuu idexinge idenii joo.

登登玛秀，
在婆婆家过日子时，
受尽了非人的待遇，
我干的是重活累活，
我吃的是猫食猪食。

Dildima bird,
I spend my life in my mother-in-law's home
Where I suffer inhuman treatment,
Do heavy work,
And eat food fit for a cat.

Dildima xau,
Bu ghadim gharigu qagduni,
Joosan niudaar xiniwa,
Xuri herge mologwa,
Ujegundu kidinge saihanna!

登登玛秀,
当我刚出家的时候,
戴的纽达尔是新的,
纽达尔珍珠圆圆的,
戴在头上多么好!

Dildima bird,
When I set out from my parents' home
The *niudaar*[1] headdress that I wore was brand new,
The coral beads on the headdress were round,
How beautiful it was to wear on my head!

Dildima xau,
Niudur malang kurisa,
Niudaar tenu logge gua,
Niudaar munu buraawaanu,
Gowii tendunge kurja joo.

登登玛秀,
现如今的日子里啊,
戴的纽达尔没样了,
纽达尔破得不像了,
仅剩纽达尔骨架了。

Dildima bird,
But now
My headdress is shapeless,
My headdress is shabby,
Only the frame of my headdress remains.

---

1   A traditional Mongghul woman's headdress; its use was forbidden under the reign
     of the Ma family warlords in about 1938.

Dildima xau,
Qi munu hamnong xjigula,
Qi munu awiidu kile joo,
Qi munu amiidu kile joo,
Ndaa nige ujela ire gi joo.

登登玛秀,
你回到我的娘家时,
给我的阿爸捎句话,
给我的阿妈捎句话,
让他们抽空来看我。

Dildima bird,
When you return to my parents' home
Please tell my father,
Please tell my mother,
Please ask them to come here and visit me.

Dildima xau,
Bu ghadim gharigu qagdu ni,
Niudaar sajog xiniwa,
Sajog tenu qijig maduwa,
Ujegundi kidinge saihanna!

登登玛秀,
当我刚出嫁的时候,
纽达尔穗子是新的,
穗子如花朵般鲜艳,
纽达尔穗子多好看!

Dildima bird,
When I set out from my parents' home
The tassels on my headdress were new,
So new, they were just like beautiful flowers,
How beautiful they were!

Dildima xau,
Niudur malang kurisa,
Sajog tenu logge gua,
Sajog munu buraawaanu,
Guduur tendunge kurijia joo.

登登玛秀，
现如今的日子里啊，
纽达尔穗子难看了，
纽达尔穗子损坏了，
穗子仅剩下穗球了。

Dildima bird,
But now
The tassels on my headdress are ugly,
The tassels on my headdress are broken,
Only the balls on the tassels are left.

Dildima xau,
Qi munu hamnong xjigula,
Qi munu awiidu kile joo,
Qi munu amiidu kile joo,
Ndaa nige ujela ire joo.

登登玛秀，
你回到我的娘家时，
给我的阿爸捎句话，
给我的阿妈捎句话，
让他们抽空来看我。

Dildima bird,
When you return to my parents' home
Please tell my father,
Please tell my mother,
Ask them to come here and visit me.

Dildima xau,
Bu ghadim gharigu qagdu ni,
Niudaar naayan xiniwa,
Naayan tenu pugiliiwa,
Ujegundu kidinge saihanna!

登登玛秀,
当我刚出嫁的时候,
纽达尔纳彦是新的,
纽达尔纳彦囫囵的,
纽达尔纳彦多好看!

Dildima bird,
When I set out from my parents' home
The inverted copper cups on my headdress were new,
The inverted copper cups on my headdress were complete,
How beautiful they were!

Dildima xau,
Niudur malang kurisa,
Naayan tenu logge gua,
Naayan munu sajiraawaanu,
Jamtog tendunge kurija joo.

登登玛秀,
现如今的日子里啊,
纽达尔那彦难看了,
纽达尔那彦损坏了,
那彦仅剩了半截了。

Dildima bird,
But now
The inverted copper cups on my headdress are ugly,
The inverted copper cups on my headdress are broken,
Only half the inverted copper cups on my headdress remain.

Dildima xau,
Qi munu hamnong xjigula,
Qi munu awiidu kile joo,
Qi munu amiidu kile joo,
Ndaa nige ujela ire joo.

登登玛秀，
你回到我的娘家时，
给我的阿爸捎句话，
给我的阿妈捎句话，
让他们抽空来看我。

Dildima bird,
When you return to my parents' home,
Please tell my father,
Please tell my mother,
Please ask them to come here and visit me.

Dildima xau,
Bu ghadim gharigu qagdu ni,
Joosan xangdi xiniwa,
Xangdi tenu pugiliiwa,
Ujegundu kidinge sahanna!

登登玛秀，
当我刚出嫁的时候，
头上的向斗是新的，
头上的向斗完整的，
戴在头上多么好看！

Dildima bird,
When I set out from my parents' home
The small bun on my headdress was new,
The small bun on my headdress was complete,
How beautiful it was!

Dildima xau,
Niudur malang kurisa,
Xangdi tenu logge gua,
Xangdi munu buraawaanu,
Nudu tendunge kurija joo.

登登玛秀,
现如今的日子里啊,
头上的向斗难看了,
头上的向斗损坏了,
向斗只剩下圆孔了。

Dildima bird,
But now
The small bun on my headdress is ugly,
The small bun on my headdress is broken,
Only the tips of the small bun on my headdress remain.

Dildima xau,
Qi munu hamnong xjigula,
Qi munu awiidu kile joo,
Qi munu amiidu kile joo,
Ndaa nige ujela ire joo.

登登玛秀,
你回到我的娘家时,
给我的阿爸捎句话,
给我的阿妈捎句话,
让他们抽空来看我。

Dildima bird,
When you return to my parents' home,
Please tell my father,
Please tell my mother,
Please ask them to come here and visit me.

Dildma xau,
Bu ghadim gharigu qagdu ni,
Xangdi huloosi xiniwa,
Huloosi teni batiwa,
Ujegundu kindinge saihanna!

登登玛秀,
当我刚出嫁的时候,
向斗的发髻是新的,
向斗的发髻是硬的,
硬的发髻多好看!

Dildima bird,
When I set out from my parents' home
The hair tie was new,
The hair tie was long,
How beautiful the long hair tie was!

Dildima xau,
Niudur malang kurisa,
Huloosi tenu logge gua,
Huloosi munu tasiraawaanu,
Huloosi tendunge kurija joo.

登登玛秀,
现如今的日子里啊,
向斗的发髻难看了,
向斗的发髻损坏了,
损坏到发髻旁边了。

Dildima bird,
But now
The hair tie is ugly,
The hair tie is damaged,
The hair tie is damaged right down to the base.

Dildima xau,
Qi munu hamnong xjigula,
Qi munu awiidu kile joo,
Qi munu amiidu kile joo,
Ndaa nige ujela ire joo.

登登玛秀，
你回到我的娘家时，
给我的阿爸捎句话，
给我的阿妈捎句话，
让他们抽空来看我。

Dildima bird,
When you return to my parents' home
Please tell my father,
Please tell my mother,
Please ask them to come here and visit me.

Dildima xau,
Bu ghadin gharigu qagdu ni,
Joosan nogdoo xiniwa,
Nogdoo tenu ilanwa,
Ujegundu kidinge saihanna!

登登玛秀，
当我刚出嫁的时候，
头上的发套是新的，
头上的发套蓝蓝的，
戴在头上多么好看！

Dildima bird,
When I set out from my parents' home
The strap that fastened my headdress was new,
The strap that fastened my headdress was blue,
How beautiful was the strap that fastened my headdress!

Dildima xau,
Niudur malang kurisa,
Nogdoo tenu logge gua,
Nogdoo munu buraawaanu,
Fuyaasar tendunge kurija joo.

登登玛秀,
现如今的日子里啊,
头上的发套难看了,
头上的发套损坏了,
发套损坏到系绳了。

Dildima bird,
But now
The strap on my headdress is ugly,
The strap on my headdress is damaged,
The strap is damaged right down to the base.

Dildima xau,
Qi munu hamnong xjigula,
Qi munu awiidu kile joo,
Qi munu amiidu kile joo,
Ndaa nige ujela ire joo.

登登玛秀,
你回到我的娘家时,
给我的阿爸捎句话,
给我的阿妈捎句话,
让他们抽空来看我。

Dildima bird,
When you return to my parents' home
Please tell my father,
Please tell my mother,
Please ask them to come here and visit me.

Dildima xau,
Bu ghadim ghargu qagdu ni,
Joosan suuge xiniwa,
Mengu suuge gergeljana,
Ujegundu kidinge saihanna!

登登玛秀,
当我刚出嫁的时候,
戴的耳坠儿是新的,
耳坠儿银光闪闪的,
在耳垂上多么好看!

Dildima bird,
When I set out from my parents' home,
The earrings I wore were new,
The earrings were shiny,
How beautiful they were!

Dildima xau,
Niudur malang kurisa,
Suuge tenu logge gua,
Suuge solosi buraawanu,
Suuge tolghuidu kurija joo.

登登玛秀,
现如今的日子里啊,
戴的耳环没样子了,
耳环的穗子损坏了,
耳坠仅剩下耳环了。

Dildima bird,
But now
The earrings are ugly,
Their tassels are broken,
And only the base of the earrings remains.

Dildima xau,
Qi munu hamnong xjigula,
Qi munu awiidu kile joo,
Qi munu amiidu kile joo,
Ndaa nige ujela ire joo.

登登玛秀,
你回到我的娘家时,
给我的阿爸捎句话,
给我的阿妈捎句话,
让他们抽空来看我。

Dildima bird,
When you return to my parents' home
Please tell my father,
Please tell my mother,
Please ask them to come here and visit me.

Dildima xau,
Bu ghadim gharigu qagdu ni,
Mosisan wangxir xiniwa,
Turghu wangxir gergeljana,
Ujegundu kidinge saihanna!

登登玛秀,
当我刚出嫁的时候,
穿的缎袍子是新的,
绸缎袍子亮晶晶的,
穿在身上多么好看!

Dildima bird,
When I set out from my parents' home
The satin robe I wore was new,
The satin robe I wore was shining,
How beautiful it was!

Dildima xau,
Niudur malang kurisa,
Wangxir tenu logge gua,
Wangxir munu tasiraanu,
Ghadarsa tudordu kurija joo.

登登玛秀,
现如今的日子里啊,
身上的袍子没样了,
穿的缎袍子烂完了,
从面子烂到里子了。

Dildima bird,
But now
The satin robe is ugly,
The satin robe is worn out,
The satin robe has worn down to the lining.

Dildima xau,
Qi munu hamnong xjigula,
Qi munu awiidu kile joo,
Qi munu amiidu kile joo,
Ndaa nige ujela ire joo.

登登玛秀,
你回到我的娘家时,
给我的阿爸捎句话,
给我的阿妈捎句话,
让他们抽空来看我。

Dildima bird,
When you return to my parents' home
Please tell my father,
Please tell my mother,
Please ask them to come here and visit me.

Dildima xau,
Bu ghadim gharigu qagdu ni,
Puseelesan pusee xiniwa,
Tolghuidii pusee alagwa,
Ujegundu kindinge saihanna!

登登玛秀,
当我刚出嫁的时候,
勒着的腰带是新的,
达博的腰带花花的,
勒在腰间多么好看!

Dildima bird,
When I set out from my parents' home
The embroidered sash I wore was new,
The embroidered sash was beautiful,
How beautiful it was!

Dildima xau,
Niudur malang kurisa,
Pusee tenu logge gua,
Pusee munu tasiraanu,
Tolghui tendunge kurija joo.

登登玛秀,
现如今的日子里啊,
勒的腰带没样子了,
达博的腰带烂完了,
一头烂到另一头了。

Dildima bird,
But now
The embroidered sash is ugly,
The embroidered sash is worn out,
The embroidered sash is worn out from one end to the other.

Dildima xau,
Qi munu hamnong xjigula,
Qi munu awiidu kile joo,
Qi munu amiidu kile joo,
Ndaa nige ujela ire joo.

登登玛秀,
你回到我的娘家时,
给我的阿爸捎句话,
给我的阿妈捎句话,
让他们抽空来看我。

Dildima bird,
When you return to my parents' home
Please tell my father,
Please tell my mother,
Please ask them to come here and visit me.

Dildima xau,
Bu gadim gharigu qagdu ni,
Mosisan hurmii xiniwa,
Buyere ghurge bau sauja,
Ujegundu kidinge saihanna!

登登玛秀,
当我刚出嫁的时候,
穿的红裙子是新的,
大红的裙子红彤彤,
穿在身上多么好看!

Dildima bird,
When I set out from my parents' home
The red skirt I wore was new,
The red skirt was colorful,
How beautiful it was!

Dildima xau,
Niudur malang kurisa,
Hurmii tenu logge gua,
Hurmii munu tasiraanu,
Jigha tendunge kurija joo.

登登玛秀，
现如今的日子里啊，
穿的裙子没样子了，
大红的裙子烂完了，
裙子仅剩下领子了。

Dildima bird,
But now
The red skirt is ugly,
The red skirt is worn out,
The red skirt isn worn out and only a small piece remains.

Dildima xau,
Qi munu hamnong xjigula,
Qi munu awiidu kile joo,
Qi munu amiidu kile joo,
Ndaa nige ujela ire joo.

登登玛秀，
你回到我的娘家时，
给我的阿爸捎句话，
给我的阿妈捎句话，
让他们抽空来看我。

Dildima bird,
When you return to my parents' home
Please tell my father,
Please tell my mother,
Please ask them to come here and visit me.

Dildima xau,
Bu ghadim gharigu qagdu ni,
Mosisan mulaa deel xiniwa,
Ilan teewan tusburwa,
Ujegundu kidinge saihanna!

登登玛秀,
当我刚出嫁的时候,
穿的黑裤子是新的,
蓝蓝的贴弯是直直的,
穿在身上多么好看!

Dildima bird,
When I set out from my parents' home
My pants were new,
The blue piece of cloth sewn at the knee was straight,
How beautiful it was!

Dildima xau,
Niudur malang kurisa,
Mulaa deel tenu logge gua,
Mulaa deel munu tasiraanu,
Udig taada kurija joo.

登登玛秀,
现如今的日子里啊,
穿的裤子没样子了,
裤子的贴弯烂完了,
烂到膝盖的跟前了。

Dildima bird,
But now
My pants are ugly,
My pants are worn out,
My pants are frayed almost up to the knee.

Dildima xau,
Qi munu hamnong xjigula,
Qi munu awiidu kile joo,
Qi munu amiidu kile joo,
Ndaa nige ujela ire joo.

登登玛秀,
你回到我的娘家时,
给我的阿爸捎句话,
给我的阿妈捎句话,
让他们抽空来看我。

Dildima bird,
When you return to my parents' home
Please tell my father,
Please tell my mother,
Please ask them to come here and visit me.

Dildima xau,
Bu ghadim gharigu qagdu ni,
Mosisan qarag xiniwa,
Qarag tenu alagwa,
Ujegundu kidinge saihanna!

登登玛秀,
当我刚出嫁的时候,
穿的花鞋子是新的,
脚上的鞋子花花的,
穿在脚上多么好看!

Dildima bird,
When I set out from my parents' home
My embroidered shoes were new,
My embroidered shoes were colorful,
How beautiful they were!

Dildima xau,
Niudur malang kurisa,
Qarag tenu logge gua,
Qarag munu tasiraanu,
Iwan taada kurija joo.

登登玛秀,
现如今的日子里啊,
穿的鞋子没样子了,
脚上的鞋子烂完了,
鞋子烂到叶弯处了。

Dildima bird,
But now
My embroidered shoes are ugly,
My embroidered shoes are worn out,
My embroidered shoes are worn down to the heels.

Dildima xau,
Qi munu hamnong xjigula,
Qi munu awiidu kile joo,
Qi munu amiidu kile joo,
Ndaa nige ujela ire joo.

登登玛秀,
你回到我的娘家时,
给我的阿爸捎句话,
给我的阿妈捎句话,
让他们抽空来看我。

Dildima bird,
When you return to my parents' home
Please tell my father,
Please tell my mother,
Please ask them to come here and visit me.

Dildima xau,
Ndaa ideji uqugunu ugui joo,
Ndaa baghaji sgoogunu ulonna joo,
Bu nenu xjigha adani joo,
Sgildu mauhan hghuiwa joo.

登登玛秀,
我没吃的也没喝的,
我即挨打来又受骂,
我再也忍耐不住了,
我的心里难过极了。

Dildima bird,
I have not been given enough food to eat,
I have frequently been beaten and scolded,
I cannot hold on for another second,
My heart is filled with pain.

Dildima xau,
Qi munu awiidu kile joo,
Qi munu amiidu kile joo,
Ndaa nige ujela ire gi joo,
Bu qimu bii mardaaya joo.

登登玛秀,
去给我的阿爸说一声,
去给我的阿妈说一声,
告诉他们来看看我,
我忘不了你的恩情。

Dildima bird,
Please tell my father,
Please tell my mother,
Please tell them to come here and visit me.
I will never forget your kindness.

5. The Song of the Calf

In this song, a calf complains to her mother that the grass they eat is short, tough, and bitter, and the water they drink is awful, so she has been unable to fill her stomach and has not grown taller. In addition, the calf feels sad that her mother often needs to pull a plough and that her master often beats her if she pulls too slowly. The calf therefore complains about their life and repeatedly asks her mother to escape with her into the mountains.

However, the calf's mother rejects her request to go up to the high mountains where the calf thinks the grass is tall, more tender and sweeter, and where she believes the spring water is pure. She says that although it sounds like an ideal place to live, there are also many ferocious wolves and tigers in the high mountains, and it is therefore not safe to live there.

Finally, the calf goes up to the mountains by herself. Her mother goes looking for her when she learns that her calf has escaped. When the cow finally finds her calf in the mountains, they encounter wolves. The cow fights with the wolves to protect her calf, and seeing this fight, the calf is frightened and flees back to their farm.

As a result, the wolves eat the cow, and the calf feels deep regret about what happened. Seven days later, she goes up to the mountains, where she finds her mother's bones, blood, and hair. The calf cremates her mother's bones, offers incense, and prays to all the deities to give her mother a good reincarnation. The calf then goes back to the farm, where she spends the rest of her life peacefully.

© 2017 Li Dechun (李得春, Limusishiden) and Gerald Roche, CC BY 4.0
https://doi.org/10.11647/OBP.0124.05

This folksong tells young children that they should listen to their parents' and grandparents' instructions, and not do whatever they like, or they will pay a terrible price.

In the past, Mongghul women sang *The Song of the Calf* to their babies when they were feeding them. A baby would pleasantly stare at her mother's face while drinking her breast milk, and the mother would smile, teasing her baby and singing *The Song of the Calf*. Sometimes two or three women sang together when they had gathered in a village lane or in a household. They would sing this song, or they might also chant, do embroidery, or tell folktales. Men also sang this song when they gathered to drink.

The song was sung slowly and quietly, without instrumental accompaniment, to a sad melody. It usually took about half an hour to sing it. And even though the song is divided into the different speaking roles of the calf and the cow, it was not sung antiphonally. Instead, singers sang both parts.

Since around the year 2000, Mongghul people no longer sing *The Song of the Calf*.

Buruunu Dau

布柔之歌

The Song of the Calf

 Listen to an audio recording of the song at
https://archive.org/details/BuruunuDau

Buruuyuu
Buruu tenu tughullaanu,
Aama tenu saajiiwa,
Kugo tenu arilghaja,
Buruu tenu hgalaaja,
Aama tenu hgalaaja,
Ghajar tenu fulija,
Xjau tela baghaja,
Buye tenu atighaja,
Guji tenu hgharaaja,
Buruu aamadunaa kileja,
Undur uladu ghariya?

布柔哟
母牛生下牛犊了,
母牛奶挤着喝了,
母牛的奶挤干了,
牛犊一天天瘦了,
母牛一天天瘦了,
母牛拉犁种田了,
脚步慢着挨打了,
打得全身疼痛了,

脖颈磨得裂开了,
牛犊央求母牛了,
央求母牛山上去?

Calf
A cow produced a calf,
The calf fed from her mother.
Her mother's milk went dry
And the calf got thinner and thinner,
And the cow got thinner and thinner too.
The cow pulled a plough and farmed;
She was beaten because she walked slowly,
She felt pain all over her body from being beaten,
The skin and flesh on her neck were torn from being drawn.
The calf begged her mother,
Can we go up into mountains?

Aamayuu
Tangnu usi bughunwa,
Tangnu usi hadongwa,
Tangnu usi haxinwa,
Tangnu tangghur pudagwa,
Keele munu qadin gua,
Buye munu oosi gua,
Tangnu aadal jublongwa.

阿妈哟
滩里牧草长得矮,
滩里牧草长得硬,
滩里牧草长得苦,
滩里池水浑又臭,
吃不饱来喝不足,
身子不长心不宽,
滩里生活真艰难。

Calf (to her mother)
The grass on the plains is short,
The grass on the plains is tough,
The grass on the plains is bitter,
And the water on the plains is awful.
I cannot fill my stomach,
I am not growing taller,
Life on the plains is difficult.

Aamayuu
Ulanu usiun durwa,
Ulanu usi joolonwa,
Ulanu usin datinwa,
Ulanu bulag arinwa,
Ulanu ghajar joolonwa,
Xjirbuu aadal ulaala yau.

阿妈哟
山里牧草长得高,
山里牧草长得嫩,
山里牧草长得甜,
山里泉水清又清,
山里睡觉软又软,
山里舒服过日子。

Calf (to her mother)
The grass in the mountains is tall,
The grass in the mountains is tender,
The grass in the mountains is sweet,
The water in the mountains is cleansing,
The soil in the mountains is soft to sleep on,
And life in the mountains is comfortable.

Buruuyuu
Ulanu usi undurwa,
Ulanu usi joolonwa,
Ulanu usin datinwa,
Ulanu bulang arinwa,
Ulanu kadam raariwa,
Ulanu bas raariwa,
Ulanu pugunag shdughuna,
Ulanu mparaa mantana,
Ulaanu aadal debxjir gua,
Ulanu xjigunu bii sana.

布柔哟
山里牧草长得高,
山里牧草长的嫩,
山里牧草长得甜,
山里泉水清又清,

山里狼比滩里害，
山里虎豹很迅猛，
山里牛虻要蛰身，
山里豹狗要扒肠，
山里日子多险凶，
千万不要上山去。

Cow (to her calf)
The grass in the mountains is tall,
The grass in the mountains is tender,
The grass in the mountains is sweet,
The water in the mountains is cleansing—
But the wolves in the mountains are ferocious,
And the tigers in the mountains are ferocious,
The gadflies in the mountains sting,
And the beasts in the mountains will eat us.
Life in the mountains is dangerous:
We mustn't climb up to the mountains.

Buruuyuu
Tangnu usi bughunwa,
Tangnu usi hadagwa,
Tangnu usi haxinwa,
Tangnu tangghur pudagwa,
Tangnu kadam raari gua,
Tangnu usinu ideya,
Tangnu szu uquya,
Tangdu losiji saulduya,
Tangdu kideeji saulduya,
Tangdu aadal ulaaya.

布柔哟
滩里牧草长得矮，
滩里牧草长得硬，
滩里牧草长得苦，
滩里池水臭又浑，
滩狼没有山狼害，
饿了吃把滩里草，
渴了喝口滩里水，
滩里饥饿日子推，

困了卧在滩里睡,
伴你滩里过生活。

Cow (to her calf)
The grass on the plains is short,
The grass on the plains is tough,
The grass on the plains is bitter,
The water on the plains is awful,
But the wolves on the plains are not ferocious.
It's better to graze on grass on the plains,
It's better to drink the water on the plains.
We'll make our lives on the plains even though we are hungry,
We'll make our lives on the plains even though the soil is hard,
We'll make our lives on the plains.

Buruuyuu
Buruu uladu yaodiija,
Aama huino daghaaya,
Ulanu kadam raariwa,
Ulanu bas raariwa,
Aama tela baghalduna,
Buruu tenu tudaaja,
Duluuu durulija,
Buruu aamana sanaja,
Nimpusi tenu urosija,
Buruu aamana yerija,
Aama tenu sarin gua,
Raari kadam idejiiwa,
Hara bas idejiiwa,
Buruu qisinu sgeja,
Sgee tenu ayija,
Buruu tenu ulaaja.

布柔哟
牛犊独自上了山,
母牛跟踪山上寻,
山里恶狼多厉害,
山里虎豹更凶猛,
母牛与它们搏斗,
牛犊怕得逃回滩,

七天的日日夜夜，
牛犊想念牛阿妈，
它的眼里泪水流，
牛犊上山找阿妈，
没见妈妈身和影，
凶恶山狼吃了妈，
黑虎吃了妈，
牛犊见了阿妈血，
害怕的目瞪口呆，
伤心的死去活来。

The calf went up to the mountains all alone.
The cow went to the mountains to look for her calf,
The wolves in the mountains were ferocious,
The tigers in the mountains were ferocious,
The cow struggled with them.
The calf was scared and fled to the plains again.
Seven days passed,
And the calf missed her mother greatly.
The calf's tears flowed down,
She went to the mountain to seek her mother again,
But she didn't find her mother.
Fierce wolves had eaten her mother,
Fierce tigers had eaten her mother,
And the calf found her mother's blood.
She was shocked,
And she cried.

Aamayuu
Qighaan qighaan yaahanna?
Fulaan fulaan yaahanna?
Nughoon nughoon yaahanna?
Xira xira yaahanna?
Hara hara yaahanna?

阿妈哟
白的白的是什么？
红的红的是什么？
绿的绿的是什么？
黄的黄的是什么？
黑的黑的是什么？

Calf (to her mother)
What are those white things?
What are those red things?
What are those green things?
What are those yellow things?
What are those black things?

Uneenu suneesi:
Buruuyuu
Qighaan qighaan aamanu yasiwa,
Fulaan fulaan aamanu qisiwa,
Nughoon nughoon aamanu suulziwa,
Xira xira aamanu fooguwa,
Hara hara aamanu nghuasiwa.

母牛灵魂唱:
布柔哟
白的白的是阿妈的骨,
红的红的是阿妈的血,
绿的绿的是阿妈的胆,
黄的黄的是阿妈的油,
黑的黑的是阿妈的毛。

Cow (her ghost sings to her calf)
Those white things are your mother's bones,
Those red things are pools of your mother's blood,
Those green things are patches of your mother's bile,
Those yellow things are pieces of your mother's fat,
Those black things are your mother's hairs.

Aamayuu
Undur uladu ghariya,
Aamanu maha buyenu,
Fulaan ghaldu awuya,
Aamanu hajinnu hariliya,
Geril rogdu gharaanu,
Kugo xugonu xuliya,
Nara sargu gharaanu,
Qighaan kambanu doglaya,
Njamba xjiindu bauwaanu,
Arin szunu wariya,

Ula tolghuindu ghariya,
Shge szangnu gharghaya,
Ulon purghaannu ughuagiya,
Aamadu molom jaalghaji,
Xambalangdu hargimjoo.

阿妈哟
上那高高的山头，
拾全阿妈的尸骨，
火花阿妈的尸骨，
报答阿妈的大恩，
爬到高山的阴坡，
折上绿绿的柏香，
跑到高山的阳坡，
摘上白白的毛香，
又到平坦的河滩，
滔上清清的河水，
到那高高的山顶，
为苍天众佛煨桑，
祈求苍天和众佛，
只愿阿妈的灵魂，
转生到那香巴拉。

Calf
I climbed up to the high mountain
And found my dead mother's skeleton,
I cremated my mother's bones.
In order to repay my mother's kindness
I climbed up the shady side of a high mountain
And broke off some green cypress twigs.
I climbed up the sunny side of a high mountain,
And gathered some *nkamba*[1] flowers.
I went to the plains,
And got clear water from a river,
I climbed up to the peak of a high mountain,
And lit a big pile of incense,
I made offerings to all the deities,
And prayed for my mother's soul
To be quickly reincarnated in Shambala.

---

1   A fragrant white flower that is often used to make incense in Mongghul areas.

Aamayuu
Qinu ugonu sunusiya,
Tangnu aadal ulaaya,
Jublong aadal ulaaya,
Debxjir aadal ulaaya.

阿妈哟
愿听阿妈的教导，
愿到滩里去生活，
愿过清苦的生活，
愿过平安的生活。

Calf (to her mother)
From now on I will listen to what you said,
I'll go down to make my life on the plains,
I'll live my life poorly,
But live my life peacefully.

6. The Crop-Planting Song

This folksong was collected in 1938 by the German missionary Dominik Schröder in Daquan Village, Dongshan Township, Huzhu Mongghul (Tu) Autonomous County. It was published in Germany in 1959, with a transcription of the lyrics in the International Phonetic Alphabet.[1]

Around 1994 Dr. Charles Kevin Stuart brought a copy of this manuscript from the USA and gave it to Limusishiden. In 1995 Dr. Stuart and Limusishiden went to Huzhu County to record a video entitled 'Teaching English In Mongghul'. Limusishiden then gave a copy of the manuscript to Lu Wenzhong, a Mongghul culture worker, translator of this song. Mr. Lu then transcribed this important folksong into Mongghul pinyin, and later published it along with others in Lu (2009).

This folksong begins with a popular Mongghul melody, *Tangdarihgiima*. Mongghul folksongs sung using the *Tangdarihgiima* melody are all sung in Mongghul, but their lyrics vary. Singers may even improvise their own lyrical content on the melodic template. At present no Mongghul can explain what *Tangdarihgiima* means. A Mongolian scholar[2] is said to have broken down the phrase as follows: *Tang* refers to 'plain', *darihgii* means 'like', and *ma* refers to 'household'. Therefore *Tandarihgiima* refers to the fact that Mongghul people live in houses on the plain, and this is thought to be in contrast with the Mongols who live in tents on the grasslands.

---

1   The teller's name was Ngombuxja. Schröder (1952-53) contains a translation of the lyrics into German.
2   We do not know who this Mongolian scholar was.

© 2017 Li Dechun (李得春, Limusishiden) and Gerald Roche, CC BY 4.0
https://doi.org/10.11647/OBP.0124.06

The opening sentences of all *Tangdarihgiima* folksongs are the same:

Tangdarihgiima—
We are the Mongghul khan's descendants,
We should sing special Mongghul songs,
We should keep our Mongghul customs.

The narrative that follows this opening refrain differs widely. In the case of the song transcribed here, it may be summarized as follows.

First, it explains the creation of the earth. In the beginning there was no night and no day, and no moon or sun. People lived in darkness and suffering with nothing to eat and nothing to wear. People reported their situation to the Buddha, and the Buddha then made the sun and moon. After they had been created, so that people would have something to eat the Buddha created highland barley, which he gave to them in a treasure bottle. Then, with the Buddha's help, the treasure bottle cracked open and highland barley sprouted out of it. Humans then learned how to plant highland barley. Finally, people succeeded in planting highland barley on the plain, using an ox. However, they still didn't know how to thresh the highland barley. Once again, the Buddha helped them, by introducing threshing. The song then concludes with words similar to those it opened with:

Mongghul khan's descendants,
Singing special Mongghul songs,
This is our Mongghul custom,
We joyfully make our lives,
Mongghul lives will be prosperous,
We keep our Mongghul customs,
And continue speaking our Mongghul language.

The song is mostly sung by pairs of men in unison, during drinking parties. Such parties are particularly common during the Spring Festival when relatives visit each other's homes. The song sounds slow and sorrowful, with a drawn-out melody. It is sung in Mongghul.

Mongghulnu Taraa Tarigu Dau

土族垦荒歌

The Crop-Planting Song

 Listen to an audio recording of the song at
https://archive.org/details/MongghulCropSong

Tangdarihgiima
Mongghul haannu kuu xjunwa,
Mongghul daunaange daulaya,
Mongghul kunnu darsuuwa.

唐德尔格玛
蒙古勒汗的子孙,
唱首蒙古勒的歌曲,
这是蒙古勒的习俗。

Tangdarihgiima—
We are the Mongghul khan's descendants,
We should sing special Mongghul songs,
We should keep our Mongghul customs.

Shde diinu udurdu ni,
Simqandu kun darilaja,
Nara sara ghariji gua,
Simqannu kundu harangghuwa,
Aadal ulaagu log ni gua,
Kundu mosigunu gua,
Kundu idegunu gua.

很久很久以前，
世上已有了人类，
太阳月亮未形成，
人们黑暗中生活，
人们的生活很苦，
没有遮体的衣裳，
没有充饥的食粮。

Long, long ago,
When the human world already existed,
There was no sun or moon,
People lived in darkness,
People lived in suffering,
People had no clothes to wear,
People had no food to eat.

Sangrji Zhuldandiidu xiilaya,
Sangrji Zhuldandii bauguna,
Taawun samba toorghu shdaasila,
Gurisan gurgenu pusilghawa,
Toorghu gurnu turo ni,
Haldannu chinge taisamba,
Haldannu chinu dire ni,
Wadima guduur duurija,
Wadima guduurnu dire ni,
Sangrji Zhuldandiinu uriya.

禀告卓勒丹迭佛尊，
卓勒丹迭佛尊要降临，
五色锦线织成缎，
扎起了绸缎帐篷，
绸缎帐篷的里面，
锻造了黄金宝座，

在那黄金宝座上,
铺满了莲花骨朵,
在那莲花骨朵上,
恭请卓勒丹迭佛。

This was reported to the Buddha.
The Buddha came down
With five sorts of thread,
A silk tent was woven,
And inside the silk tent
A golden throne was placed.
On the golden throne
Lotus flowers were placed.
On the lotus flowers
The Buddha was welcomed to sit.

Sangrji yaahan bauji irem?
Turong anjiisa bauji irem?
Ghuidar anjiisa bauji irem?
Ghuraandar anjiisa bauji irem?
Sangrji baugu log ghuraan wai,
Turong tingersa bauji irem,
Ghuidar jarim tingersa bauji irem,
Ghuraandar chi dire bausamba.

佛尊怎样降临的?
首次从哪里降临?
其次从哪里降临?
再次从哪里降临?
佛尊这样降临的,
首次从蓝天降临,
其次从半空降临,
再次从宝座降临。

How did the Buddha come down?
From where did the Buddha come down the first time?
From where did the Buddha come down the second time?
From where did the Buddha come down the third time?
The Buddha should come down like this.
First, he comes down from Blue Heaven,
Second, he comes down from mid-air,

Third, he comes down on the throne.

Sangrji anjiiji ujesamba?
Turong anjii ujesamba?
Ghuidar anjii ujesamba?
Ghuraandar anjii ujesamba?
Turong tenu ujesa,
Undur tingerdu ujesamba,
Nara sara qaglaji gua,
Ghuidar tenu ujesa,
Hulo ujuurdu ujesamba,
Hulo ujuurdu harangghuwa,
Ghuraandar tenu ujesa,
Hara ghajardu ujesamba,
Hara ghajar kuidenwa.

佛尊要朝哪里看?
首次要往哪里看?
其次要往哪里看?
再次要往哪里看?
首次佛尊看一看,
看那高高的天空,
太阳月亮未形成,
其次佛尊看一看,
看那无际的天边,
黑暗笼罩着天边,
再次佛尊看一看,
看那脚下的大地,
大地冷的像冰窟。

Where should the Buddha look?
Where should he look first?
Where should he look second?
Where should he look third?
First the Buddha should look
To the high heavens:
The sun and moon were not yet formed.
Second, he should look
To the endless horizon:
The universe was full of darkness.

Third, the Buddha should look
At the Earth:
The Earth was frozen.

Zhuldandii ncamdu sauguna,
Nige fon sauguda murgoom.
Ghuraan duloonge sausa ulim,
Hoosin ncamnu sausa loosowa,
Hoosin ncamnu hgablasa loosowa,
Omba halasinu zhiblaji gua,
Omba halasi anjiiwa?
Szaliu szaliunge kileji ughu.

卓勒丹迭要坐禅，
一年的禅不必做，
三个七天自圆满，
没备齐的禅难做，
所需东西难造办，
宝瓶壳子未造成，
宝瓶壳子在哪里？
详详细细说一说。

The Buddha will sit in meditation.
The Buddha doesn't need to meditate for a year:
Three weeks are enough.
He cannot meditate well if nothing is prepared well.
It is not easy to prepare the necessary things:
The treasure bottle hasn't been prepared,
Where is the treasure bottle?
Please tell in great detail.

Omba halasi tingerduwa,
Tingere tenu turo ni,
Ken tenu awuji irem?
Rigsum ngombu sang awuji irem.
Omba halasinu awaa ireja,
Zhiblagu taada loosowa,
Omba tenu turo ni,
Ghuraan samba rzii wai,
Yaahan tenu kilena?

Ndaanu daudu haril ire.

宝瓶壳子在苍天,
在那苍天的里面,
谁带来宝瓶壳子?
热松官布佛带来,
宝瓶壳子带来了,
制作甘露很困难,
那个甘露的里面,
要装三样的东西,
要装哪三样东西?
请回答我们的歌。

The treasure bottle is in Heaven,
Inside Heaven—
Who will bring it here?
Avalokiteśvara, Mañjuśrī and Vajrasattva will bring it.
The treasure bottle has been brought.
It is difficult to make sweet dew
Inside the treasure bottle
Which is required to encase three things.
Why do we mention it?
Please tell me in song.

Sangrji tenu szonglajii,
Ghuraan sambanu kilena,
Rjagar ghajarnu gurgum wai,
Uluyi ghajarnu szu wai,
Maaqu ghajarnu maarjo wai.
Zhiblajin sangrji ni kenwa?
Zhiblajin sangrji Zhuldandiiwa.
Nige duloon ncamdu sau,
Nige duloon ncam duurisa,
Omba tenu xjuurdu ni,
Yaahan tenu zhiblaja?
Omba tenu dundadu ni,
Yaahan tenu zhiblaja?
Omba tenu amandu ni,
Yaahan tenu zhiblaja?

佛旨指明了东西,

装的东西有三件，
要装印度的红花，
要装龙域的净水，
要装玛曲孔雀翎。
做甘露的佛是谁？
卓勒丹迭佛要做。
坐一个七天的禅，
七天的禅圆满了，
珍珠宝瓶的底部，
放些啥东西来做？
珍珠宝瓶的中部，
放些啥东西来做？
珍珠宝瓶的顶部，
放些啥东西来做？

Buddha pointed out the things.
There are three kinds of things,
First is safflower from India,
Water from Uluyi,[3]
And a peacock plume from the Yellow River.
Who will make holy water?
Buddha will make sweet dew.
Buddha sits in meditation for seven days.
After seven days sitting in meditation,
At the bottom of the treasure bottle,
What should we put?
Midway up the treasure bottle,
What should we put?
At the top of the treasure bottle,
What should we put?

Omba tenu xjuurdu ni,
Arin szunnu zhiblajii.
Omba tenu dundadu ni,
Gurgu tenu zhiblajii.
Omba tenu amandu ni,
Maarjo foodinu zhiblajii.
Omba tenu turo ni,

---

3   It is uncertain where this is.

Zhiblaa tenu duurijii.

珍珠宝瓶的底部，
盛了净泉水来做。
珍珠宝瓶的中部，
放了藏红花来做。
珍珠宝瓶的顶部，
插上孔雀翎来做。
珍珠宝瓶的里头，
所需东西齐全了。

At the bottom of the treasure bottle
Put clean water.
Midway up the treasure bottle
Put the safflower.
In the top of the treasure bottle
Thrust a peacock's plume.
Inside the treasure bottle
All the necessary things have already been prepared.

Sangrji Zhuldandii ncam sausa,
Fon saranu saugu murgoom,
Ghuraan duloonnu ncamge sau,
Solghui rogdu ni yaahanna?
Warang rogdu ni yaahanna?
Tolghuidu ni yaahanna?
Ndaanu daudu haril ire.

卓勒丹迭要坐禅，
长年累月做不了，
坐三个七天的禅，
佛尊左方看见啥？
佛尊右方看见啥？
佛尊头顶看见啥？
请回答我们的歌。

The Buddha sits in meditation.
He can't sit for a whole year.
He sits for three weeks.
What does the Buddha see on his left side?
What does the Buddha see on his right side?
What does the Buddha see on top of his head?

Please reply to our song.

Solghui rogdu ni ujesa,
Xira ndogge sgeni,
Yaahan tenu sgesamba?
Warang rogdu ni ujesa,
Qighaan ndogge sgeni,
Yaahan tenu sgesamba?
Tolghuindu ni ujesa,
Kugo ndogge sgeni,
Yaahan tenu sgesamba?
Ndaanu daudu haril ire.

看那佛尊的左方，
看见黄黄的东西，
黄黄的东西是啥？
看那佛尊的右方，
看见白白的东西，
白白的东西是啥？
看那佛尊的头顶，
看见青青的东西，
青青的东西是啥？
请回答我们的歌。

Look to the Buddha's left side,
You'll see something yellow.
What is the yellow thing?
Look to the Buddha's right side,
You'll see something white.
What is the white thing?
Look atop the Buddha's head,
You'll see something green.
What is the green thing?
Please reply to our song.

Sangrjinu solghui rogdu ni,
Xira nara gharijiiwa,
Tela xirange sgesamba.
Sangrjinu warang rogdu ni,
Qighaan sara gharijiiwa,

Tela qighaange sgesamba.
Sangrjinu tolghui dire ni,
Kugo foodi gharijiiwa,
Tela kugonge sgesamba.
Ombanu tolghuindu ujesa,
Yaahan tenu njonglaja?
Ndaanu daudu haril ire.

看那佛尊的左方，
太阳从东山升起，
那黄黄的是阳光。
看那佛尊的右方，
月亮悬挂在西方，
那白白的是月光。
看那佛尊的头顶，
星星闪烁在天上，
那青青的是星光。
看那甘露的头顶，
什么东西在闪耀？
请回答我们的歌。

Look to the Buddha's left side,
The sun is rising above the eastern mountain,
The yellow thing is the sunlight.
Look to the Buddha's right side,
The moon is hanging on the west side,
The white thing is the moonlight.
Look atop the Buddha's head,
The stars twinkle in the sky,
The green thing is the starlight.
Look at the treasure bottle's top,
What is twinkling?
Please reply to our song.

Xalji ombanu tolghuire,
Wadima tenu njonglaja,
Wadima tenu tolghuire,
Sala ghuraan gharijiiwa,
Dunda salanu ujesa?
Nara tenu njonglaja.

Solghui salanu ujesa?
Sara tenu njonglaja.
Warang salanu ujesa?
Foodi tenu njonglaja.

珍珠甘露的头顶，
一束莲花在闪耀，
那莲花的顶梢上，
生长了三个枝子，
看那中间的枝子？
阳光照在它身上。
看那左侧的枝子？
月光照在它身上。
看那右侧的枝子？
星光照在它身上。

At the top of the treasure bottle
A lotus is sparkling.
Atop the lotus
There are three twigs.
See the middle twig?
The sunlight is sparkling on it.
See the left twig?
The moonlight is sparkling on it.
See the right twig?
The starlight is sparkling on it.

Sangrji Zhuldandiinu saindu,
Nara sara foodi gharija,
Ghuraan tenu gireel ni,
Kugo tingerdu njonglaji gua,
Hara ghajardu njonglaja,
Kugo tingerdu njonglasa,
Looso looso loosowa,

有了卓勒丹迭佛，
有太阳月亮星星，
上面三个的光芒，
没有照到天空中，
照在茫茫大地上，
若要照到天空中，

困难多的无法说。

Under the Buddha
Are the sun, the moon, and stars.
A ray of light from each of the three
Has not yet shone over the sky,
And only shines over the earth.
If they shine over the sky
There will be many problems.

Nige duloon moxijiiwa,
Nara sara foodiwa,
Kugo tingerdu gharisa,
Xira nara halong gua,
Qighaan sara gigeen gua,
Kugo foodi rejiglaji gua,
Ndaanu daudu haril ire.

念了七天的佛经，
太阳月亮和星星，
升到湛蓝的天上，
黄黄的太阳不暖，
白白的月亮不亮，
青青的星星不闪，
请回答我们的歌。

People chanted Buddhist scriptures for seven days.
The sun, the moon, and the stars
Went up to the High Blue Heaven.
The yellow sun wasn't hot,
The white moon wasn't bright,
The green stars weren't bright.
Please reply to our song.

Nara sara foodi wai,
Ghuraan samba gireel gua,
Xira nara halong gua,
Qighaan sara gigeen gua,
Kugo foodi rejiglaji gua,
Sangrjinu ramii tebleji gua.

Omqunu undurdu nqurlaji,
Xira nara halong wai,
Qighaan sara gigeen wai,
Kugo foodi rejiglaji wai.

太阳月亮和星星，
三个身上没光芒，
黄黄的太阳不暖，
白白的月亮不亮，
青青的星星不闪，
没得到佛尊的光。
高空中祭奠甘露，
太阳才有了光芒，
月亮才有了明亮，
星星才有了闪耀。

The sun, the moon, and the stars—
The three had no rays of light,
The yellow sun wasn't hot,
The white moon wasn't bright,
The green stars weren't bright,
They had not yet received the Buddha's light.
After offering the sweet dew to the sky
The sun got its light,
The moon got its brightness,
The stars got their shimmer.

Sangrji Zhuldandiidu xiilaya,
Undur Rarabnu tolghuindu,
Nara yama giji gharijiiwa?
Sara yama giji gharijiiwa?
Foodi yama giji gharijiiwa?
Xiilajin sangrji kenwa?
Xogjatogba sang xiilaja.
Zhuldandiinu szong bauja,
Xagniinu undurdu shdarlaji,
Omqunu undurdu nqorlaji,
Nara sara da foodiwa,
Undur Rarabnu tolghuindu,
Nara Rarabnu sgorlajii,

Sara Rarabnu sgorlajii,
Foodi Rarabnu sgorlajii,
Hgarma foodi te nige,
Rarab tolghuindu gharija.

秉佛尊卓勒丹迭,
高高的须弥山上,
太阳怎样出来了?
月亮怎样出来了?
星星怎样出来了?
回秉佛陀叫什么?
释迦陀巴回禀了。
卓勒丹迭的佛旨,
空中撒青稞祈祷,
空中撒甘露祈祷,
太阳月亮和星星,
须弥山的蓝天里,
太阳围绕须弥山,
月亮围绕须弥山,
星星围绕须弥山,
那颗最亮的明星,
升起在须弥山顶。

People report to the Buddha
On the high Mount Sumeru:
How does the sun rise?
How does the moon rise?
How do the stars rise?
Who reported it to the Buddha?
Shakyamuni told the Buddha.
The Buddha's decree is:
Pray by casting highland barley,
Pray by sprinkling sweet dew.
The sun, the moon, and the stars
In the blue Heaven of Sumeru,
The sun circles Sumeru,
The moon circles Sumeru,
The stars circle Sumeru,
The brightest star,
Is rising up on the peak of Sumeru.

Rgulnu udurnu ujesa,
Nara sara foodi wai,
Rarab tolghuindu gharisa,
Nara sara undurwa.
Rgulnu udur kuidenwa,
Yaanla kuiden iresamba?
Nara Rarabnu undurduwa,
Rarab tolghui narinwa,
Nara hergigu ni undurwa,
Tela rgulnu udur kuidenwa,
Kuidennu log ni tigiinge,
Nara hgergigu ni undurwa,
Rgulnu udur ni hghurwa,
Hghurnu log ni tigiinge.

在那寒冷的冬天里，
太阳月亮和星星，
须弥山上升起了，
太阳和月亮很高。
冬天的日子很冷，
冬天为啥这么冷？
太阳在须弥山顶，
须弥山高而顶细，
太阳转的高又高，
日子变得冷又冷，
冬天怎样变冷了，
太阳转的高又高，
日子变得短又短，
日子这样变短了。

In the frozen winter
The sun, the moon, and the stars
Rise from Mount Sumeru.
The sun and moon are very high.
The days in winter are cold.
Why is winter so cold?
The sun is on the peak of Sumeru.
Sumeru is high and its peak is narrow.
The sun goes higher and higher,
And the days turn colder and colder:
This is why the days in winter are cold.

The sun goes higher and higher,
The days get shorter and shorter:
This is why the days are shorter.

Yarnu udurdu ujesa,
Yarnu udur shdurwa,
Yaahan dundogdu shdurwa?
Yarnu udur halongwa,
Yaahan dundogdu halongwa?
Ndaanu daudu haril ire.

那炎热的夏天里，
夏天日子长又长，
日子为啥这么长？
夏天天气热又热，
天气为啥这么热？
请回答我们的歌。

In the hot summer
The days get longer and longer.
Why do the days get longer?
The weather in summer is hot.
Why is the weather hot?
Please reply to our song.

Nara tenu ujesa,
Rarab dooro hergina,
Tela udur ni shdurwa,
Nara tenu hergisa,
Nara Rarabnu doorowa,
Hara ghajar halong wai,
Tela yarnu udur halong wai.

看那夏天的太阳，
绕须弥山的下部转，
日子这样变长了，
转的时间太长了，
转到须弥山下了，
广阔大地变热了，
夏天天气变热了。

The sun in summer
Goes to the lower part of Mount Sumeru:
This is why the days get longer,
As the sun turns
It is at the lower part of Sumeru.
The earth becomes hot.
This is why the days in summer are hot.

Hawurnu ghuraan saradu,
Kunnu gujeendu yaan idenii?
Yarnu ghuraan saradu,
Kunnu gujeendu yaan udenii?
Namurnu ghuraan saradu,
Kunnu gujeendu yaan idenii?
Rgulnu ghuraan saradu,
Kunnu gujeendu yaan idenii?

春天的三个月里,
人们吃些啥食物?
夏天的三个月里,
人们吃些啥食物?
秋天的三个月里,
人们吃些啥食物?
冬天的三个月里,
人们吃些啥食物?

During the three months of spring
What kinds of food do people have?
During the three months of summer
What kinds of food do people have?
During the three months of autumn
What kinds of food do people have?
During the three months of winter
What kinds of food do people have?

Hawurnu ghuraan saradu,
Kunnu tenu gujeendu,
Qijig tenu idenii,
Qijigdu qiko wai nuu gua?
Yarnu ghuraan saradu,

Kunnu tenu gujeendu,
Nughoon gurma sai idenii,
Gurma saindu qiko wai nuu gua?
Namurnu ghuraan saradu,
Kunnu tenu gujeendu,
Alima tenu idenii,
Alimadu qikoo wai nuu gua?
Rgulnu ghuraan saradu,
Kunnu tenu gujeendu,
Kugo malsi idenii,
Malsidu qiko wai nuu gua?

春天的三个月里,
人们为吃饱肚子,
吃春天开的花儿,
春花会不会受灾?
夏天的三个月里,
人们为吃饱肚子,
吃夏天的野苦菜,
野菜会不会受灾?
秋天的三个月里,
人们为吃饱肚子,
吃秋天结的果子,
果子会不会受灾?
冬天的三个月里,
人们为吃饱肚子,
吃冬天结的冰块,
冰块会不会受灾?

During the three months of spring
Humans in order to fill their stomach
Eat flowers.
Will the flowers be hit by natural disasters or not?
During the three months of summer
Humans in order to fill their stomach
Eat edible wild herbs.
Will the edible wild herbs be hit by natural disasters or not?
During the three months of autumn
Humans in order to fill their stomach
Eat fruit.
Will the fruit be hit by natural disasters or not?

During the three months of winter
Humans in order to fill their stomach
Eat ice.
Will the ice be hit by natural disasters or not?

Hawurnu ghuraan saradu,
Qjig tenu idenii,
Qijignu qikodu donge wai,
Kugo tingere burodisa,
Qijig tendu qiko wai.
Yarnu ghuraan saradu,
Gurma sai tenu idenii,
Gurma sainu qikodu donge wai,
Tingere tenu heesamba,
Gurma saidu qiko wai.
Namurnu ghuraan saradu,
Alima tenu idenii,
Alimanu qikodu donge wai,
Qighaan huraa urosamba,
Alima tendu qiko wai.
Rgulnu ghuraan saradu,
Malsi tenu idenii,
Malsinu qikodu donge wai,
Kii tenu tausamba,
Malsi tendu qiko wai.

春天的三个月里,
人吃春天开的花,
春花受灾有原因,
如遇阴天下大雨,
春花就受灾谢花。
夏天的三个月里,
人吃夏天的野菜,
野菜受灾有原因,
如遇干旱不下雨,
野菜受灾不生长。
秋天的三个月里,
人吃秋天的果子,
果子受灾有原因,
如遇天上下冰雹,

果树受灾不结果。
冬天的三个月里，
人吃冬天的冰块，
冰块受灾有原因，
如遇刮风太阳晒，
河水受灾不结冰。

During the three months of spring
Humans eat flowers.
Flowers will be hit by natural disasters.
If the flowers are hit by heavy rain
Then the flowers will wither.
During the three months of summer
Humans eat edible wild herbs.
The edible wild herbs will be hit by natural disasters.
If the edible wild herbs experience a drought
Then the edible wild herbs won't grow.
During the three months of autumn
Humans eat fruit.
The fruit will be hit by natural disasters.
If the fruit is hit by hailstones
Then there won't be any fruit.
During the three months of winter
Humans eat ice.
The ice will be hit by natural disaster.
If the ice is exposed to wind and sun
Then there will be no ice on the river.

Hawurnu ghuraan saradu,
Qijig tenu idenii,
Qijig tenu qikodu,
Danglagu log ni tigiinge,
Kugo tingere arilsa,
Qijig tendu qiko gui.
Yarnu ghuraan saradu,
Gurma sai tenu idenii,
Gurma sai tenu qikodu,
Danglagu log ni tigiinge,
Shge tingere lii heesa,
Gurma sai tendu qiko gui.

Namurnu ghuraan saradu,
Alima tenu idenii,
Alima tenu qikodu,
Danglagu log ni tigiinge,
Qighaan huraa lii bausa,
Alima tendu qiko gui.
Rgulnu ghuraan saradu,
Malsi tenu idenii,
Malsi tenu qikodu,
Danglagu log ni tigiinge,
Hara kii lii tausa,
Malsi tendu qiko gui.

春天的三个月里，
人吃春天开的花，
为了花不受灾害，
防护的办法这样，
湛蓝的天常无云，
春花常开不受灾。
夏天的三个月里，
人吃山上的野菜，
为了野菜不受灾，
防护的办法这样，
风调雨顺天不旱，
野菜常吃不受灾。
秋天的三个月里，
人吃秋天的果子，
为了果子不受灾，
防护的办法这样，
不下冰雹无霜冻，
果子常结不受灾。
冬天的三个月里，
人吃冬天冰块，
为了冰块不受灾，
防护的办法这样，
不刮大风不日晒，
冰块常冻不受灾。

During the three months of spring
Humans eat flowers.
In order to protect the flowers from natural disasters

There are methods.
There must be fine weather:
Then the flowers will not be hit by natural disasters.
During the three months of summer
Humans eat edible wild herbs.
In order to protect the edible wild herbs from natural disasters
There are methods.
There must be no drought:
Then the edible wild herbs will not be hit by natural disasters.
During the three months of autumn
Humans eat fruit.
In order to protect the fruit from natural disasters
There are methods.
There must be no hailstorms:
Then the fruit will not be hit by natural disasters.
During the three months of winter
Humans eat ice.
In order to protect the ice from natural disasters
There are methods.
There must be no wind:
Then the ice will not be hit by natural disasters.

Simqannu kunnu amun shgewa,
Simqandu xinaalgha gua,
Sangrji lanqagnu danglawa.
Aadal tenu ulaasa,
Deel tenu mosisa,
Keele tenu idesa,
Snagder tenu fuulaya,
Snagder tenu anjiiwa,
Sangrji tenu rgula xjija,
Sangrjinu nire ni yaahanna?
Ndaanu daudu haril ire.

世上人的命最大，
没有忧愁与烦恼，
全靠了佛尊的福。
人过个幸福日子，
身上穿件好衣服，
肚里吃上好饱饭，

黑土地上下宝瓶，
不知宝瓶在哪里，
要请佛陀取宝瓶，
佛陀名字叫什么？
请回答我们都歌。

People's lives are great,
Nothing troubles them—
This is all from the blessings of the Buddha.
To make a living,
Wear their clothes
And fill their stomachs
People will bury a treasure bottle.
But first they must find a treasure bottle.
A Buddha is needed to get the treasure bottle.
What is the Buddha's name?
Please reply to our song.

Snagder tenu zhiblaji gua,
Hara ghajarnu xjiinduna,
Sangrji tenu rgula xjija,
Nire tenu xogjatagbawa.
Sangrji tenu awuji kurisa,
Zhiblagu tenu hgurmuwa,
Snagder tenu zhonglaguna wai,
Yaahan tenu zhonglaguna?
Szin sambanu zhonglagunu wai,
Ndaanu daudu haril ire.

宝瓶里没装东西，
放在大地的中间，
有位佛陀取宝瓶，
佛陀是释迦陀巴。
宝瓶已取回来了，
装那宝瓶很困难，
装宝瓶需要东西，
装什么样的东西？
要装九样的东西，
请回答我们的歌。

Inside, the treasure bottle is empty.

It is put at the center of the world.
A Buddha goes to get the treasure bottle:
The Buddha is Shakyamuni.
The treasure bottle has been brought.
It is difficult to put anything inside it.
Something should be put inside it.
What should put inside it?
Nine things should be put inside it.
Please reply to our song.

Sangrji Zhuldandii ncamdu saum,
Nige duloonnu ncamdu saum,
Ncamdu sauji duurisa,
Szin sambanu rzii ni wai,
Szin sambadu donge wai.
Ghuisang ghajarnu haldan rogm,
Rjanag ghajarnu qijig rogm,
Amdo ghajarnu nkamba rgom,
Shdo Ghuisangnu lusman rgom,
Smar Rjanagnu shdaasi rgom,
Amdo ghajarnu xigo rgom,
Ghuisangnu xira xiruu rgom,
Rjanagnu hara xiruu rgom,
Amdonu qighaan xiruu rgom.
Szin samba rziinu szonglaji,
Moxijin sangrji kenna?
Zhiblajin sangrji kenna?
Rgujin sangrji kenna?
Ndaanu daudu haril ire.

卓勒丹迭佛坐禅，
坐一个七天的禅，
七天的禅圆满了，
宝瓶东西有九件，
九件东西要齐全。
西藏地方的黄金，
内地盛开的鲜花，
安多地方的艾草，
雪域地方的藏药，
北京出产的丝线，

安多地方的柏香,
西藏地方的黄土,
北京地方的黑土,
安多地方的白土。
九件东西齐全了,
装宝瓶的佛是谁?
诵经卷的佛是谁?
运宝瓶的佛是谁?
请回答我们的歌。

The Buddha sat in meditation
For seven days.
Then the seven days of sitting in meditation were finished.
Nine things must be put inside the treasure bottle—
Nine things are required:
Gold from Tibet is required,
Flowers from the inland areas are required,
Asiatic wormwood from Amdo is required,
Tibetan herbs from the snowland are required,
Silk thread produced in Beijing is required,
Cypress twigs are required,
Yellow soil from Tibet is required,
Black soil from Beijing is required,
White soil from Amdo is required.
The nine things are ready.
Which Buddha will put the nine things inside the treasure bottle?
Which Buddha will chant scriptures?
Who will transport the treasure bottle?
Please reply to our song.

Moxijin Rigsimgombu wai,
Zhiblajin sangrji Zhuldandii wai,
Rgujin sangrji Wosisang wai.
Snagder tenu fuulasa,
Anjii tenu fuulagunii?
Ghajar tenu lii mudeni,
Ndaanu daudu haril ire.

热松官布诵佛经,
卓勒丹迭装宝瓶,

觉光佛尊运宝瓶。
我们要是下宝瓶,
我们下哪个宝瓶?
下的地方不知道,
请回答我们的歌。

Avalokiteśvara, Mañjuśrī and Vajrasattva will chant Buddhist scriptures.
The Buddha will put the things inside the treasure bottle,
Kaśyapa Buddha will transport the treasure bottle,
We will bury the treasure bottle.
Where shall we bury the treasure bottle?
The place to bury the treasure bottle is unknown.
Please reply to our song.

Snagder tenu rguwaanu,
Undur tingeredu gharisa,
Fuulagu ghajar nige gua,
Nara sara yausamba,
Nenu dundogdu fuula adaguna.
Snagder tenu rguwaanu,
Jarim tingerdu gharisa,
Fuulagu ghajar nige gua,
Xuarig muarig nesisamba,
Nenu dundogdu fuula adaguna.
Snagder tenu rguwaanu,
Ghuisang ghajardu xjisamba,
Fuulagu ghajar nige gua,
Lamaa tenu yaulduna,
Nenu dundogdu fuula adaguna.
Snagder tenu rguwaanu,
Rjanag ghajardu xjisamba,
Fuulagu ghajar nige gua,
Huawu tenu yaulduna,
Nenu dundogdu fuula adaguna.
Snagder tenu rguwaanu,
Hara ghadaadu xjisamba,
Fuulagu ghajar nige gua,
Aardag tenu yaulduna,
Nenu dundogdu fuula adaguna.
Snagder tenu rguwaanu,

Dalii xjuurdu xjisamba,
Fuulagu ghajar nige gua,
Jaghasi tenu humbaasamba,
Nenu dundogdu fuula adaguna.
Snagder tenu rguwaanu,
Amdoo ghajardu xjisamba,
Fuulagu ghajar nige gua,
Kun da mori yaulduna,
Nenu dundogdu fuula adaguna.
Snagder tenu rguwaanu,
Rarabnu kijeendu xjisamba,
Fuulagu ghajar nige gua,
Ghalumu tenu yaulduna,
Nenu dundogdu fuula adaguna.
Snagder tenu rguwaanu,
Rarabnu szaardu xjisamba,
Fuulagu ghajar nige wai,
Solghui tenu ghuraan sgoorlawa,
Warang tenu ghuraan sgoorlawa,
Nuko tenu ghurdi manta,
Gomdu tenu mantasa,
Kidi kaa tenu mantagii?
Zhebjii tenu mantasa,
Kidi kaa tenu mantagii?
Ndaanu daudu haril ire.

背上了那个宝瓶,
到天上去下宝瓶,
没有空地下宝瓶,
太阳月亮在转动,
所以不能下宝瓶。
背上了那个宝瓶,
到半空中下宝瓶,
没有空地下宝瓶,
众多鸟类在飞动,
所以不能下宝瓶。
背上了那个宝瓶,
西藏圣地下宝瓶,
没有空地下宝瓶,
活佛僧人在走动,
所以不能下宝瓶。

背上了那个宝瓶，
中原内地下宝瓶，
没有空地下宝瓶，
帝王勇士在走动，
所以不能下宝瓶。
背上了那个宝瓶，
大山高岭下宝瓶，
没有空地下宝瓶，
飞禽野兽在走动，
所以不能下宝瓶。
背上了那个宝瓶，
大海深处下宝瓶，
没有空地下宝瓶，
鱼儿虾儿在游动，
所以不能下宝瓶。
背上了那个宝瓶，
安多地方下宝瓶，
没有空地下宝瓶，
人和牛马在走动，
所以不能下宝瓶。
背上了那个宝瓶，
须弥山坡下宝瓶，
没有空地下宝瓶，
天上仙女在走动，
所以不能下宝瓶。
背上了那个宝瓶，
须弥山根下宝瓶，
才有空地下宝瓶，
左转转了三个圈，
右转转了三个圈，
赶快挖下宝瓶坑，
宝瓶的坑挖多深，
要挖个几尺的坑?
挖四四方方的坑，
宽要挖几尺的坑?
请回答我们的歌。

Carrying the treasure bottle,
Go to high Heaven.
No place to bury the bottle was found.
The sun and moon are turning,

The treasure bottle cannot be buried there.
Carrying the treasure bottle,
Go to the sky.
No place to bury the bottle was found.
Lots of birds are flying,
The treasure bottle cannot be buried there.
Carrying the treasure bottle,
Go to Tibet.
No place to bury the bottle was found.
Monks are walking,
The treasure bottle cannot be buried there.
Carrying the treasure bottle,
Go to Beijing.
No place to bury the bottle was found.
Warriors are walking,
The treasure bottle cannot be buried there.
Carrying the treasure bottle,
Go to the high mountains.
No place to bury the bottle was found.
Beasts are walking.
The treasure bottle cannot be buried there.
Carrying the treasure bottle,
Go to the bottom of the ocean.
No place to bury the bottle was found.
Fish are walking,
The treasure bottle cannot be buried there.
Carrying the treasure bottle,
Go to Amdo.
No place to bury the bottle was found.
People and livestock are walking,
The treasure bottle cannot be buried there.
Carrying the treasure bottle,
Go to the slopes of Mount Sumeru.
No place to bury the bottle was found.
Fairy maidens are walking,
The treasure bottle cannot be buried there.
Carrying the treasure bottle,
Go to the foot of Mount Sumeru.
A place to bury the treasure bottle was found.
It was circled anticlockwise thrice,

It was circled clockwise thrice,
A pit was quickly dug.
The pit should be deep:
How deep should it be?
The pit should be wide:
How wide should it be?
Please reply to our song.

Gomdu tenu mantasa,
Nige kaanu mantagu rgo,
Zhebjin tenu mantasa,
Nige kaanu kaanu mantagu rgo.
Nuko tenu mantaya,
Snagder tenu fuulsa,
Furonglajin purghaan jirghoon wai,
Jirghoon tendu nire wai,
Purghaan tenu puxiiwa,
Jirghoon tarnu kilenii.
Snagder tenu xjuurdu ni,
Tar tenu taisamba,
Yaahan dundogdu taisamba?
Snagder tenu harghaadu ni,
Tar tenu taisamba,
Yaahan dundogdu taisamba?
Snagder tenu dire ni,
Tar tenu taisamba,
Yaahan dundogdu taisamba?
Ndaanu daudu haril ire.

下宝瓶的坑深度，
深里要挖到一尺，
下宝瓶的坑宽度，
宽里要挖到一尺。
挖的坑里下宝瓶，
下好的那个宝瓶，
保佑的神有六个，
六个神各有名字，
其实不是六个神，
说的是六块石头。
在那宝瓶的底部，

铺垫了一块石头，
这样做为了社么？
在那宝瓶的四周，
安放了四块石头，
这样做为了什么？
在那宝瓶的上方，
铺盖了一块石头，
这样做为了什么？
请回答我们的歌。

Dig the pit
To a depth of a third of a meter;
The pit's width
To a width of a third of a meter.
After digging the pit
Bury the treasure bottle.
Six deities will protect the treasure bottle.
The six deities have their own names,
But they aren't deities,
They are six stones.
Under the treasure bottle
Put a bedding stone.
Why is it done this way?
Around the treasure bottle
Put four stones.
Why is it done this way?
On top of the treasure bottle
Put a stone.
Why is it done this way?
Please reply to our song.

Tar tenu taisamba,
Snagder xjuurdu taisamba,
Taigu tendu donge wai,
Neeten rilan shgewa,
Snagder tenu norlamba,
Nenu dundogdu taisamba.
Tar deeren tenu taisa,
Snagder tenu harghaadu taisamba,
Taigu tendu donge wai?

Hurghui tenu ulonwa,
Snagder tenu norlamba,
Nenu dundogdu taisamba.
Tar tenu nigeniinu,
Snagder dire haasamba,
Haasan tendu donge wai,
Yarnu nogxjil nganaa wai,
Fulaan tog baugundu,
Nenu dundogdu haasamba.
Snagder deelge mosinii,
Yaahan deelnu mosinii?
Ndaanu daudu haril ire.

要铺垫一块石头，
铺垫在宝瓶底下，
铺垫石头有原因，
底下泥土很潮湿，
为了宝瓶不腐烂，
铺垫的原因这样。
要安放四块石头，
安放在宝瓶四方，
为了什么要安放？
底下的害虫很多，
为了宝瓶不受害，
安放的原因这样。
要铺盖一块石头，
铺盖在宝瓶上面，
铺垫石头有原因，
夏天的雷雨厉害，
为了宝瓶不雷击，
铺盖的原因这样。
宝瓶要穿件衣裳，
穿什么样的衣裳？
请回答我们的歌。

The bedding stone
Is put underneath the treasure bottle.
The reason why the stone is put there
Is because the soil is humid,
So to prevent the treasure bottle from decaying
The bedding stone is put underneath it.

Put four stones
Around the treasure bottle.
Why are four stones put there?
There are harmful insects in the soil,
So to prevent the treasure bottle from being damaged
Stones are put around it.
Put a stone
On top of the treasure bottle.
There is a reason for this,
Thunder in summer is severe,
So to prevent the treasure bottle being struck by a thunderbolt
A stone is put on top of it.
The treasure bottle needs to wear clothes.
What kind of clothes will it wear?
Please reply to our song.

Snagder tenu deel mosisa,
Xigo deelnu mosinii,
Mosijin tendu donge wai,
Luyi rjawu rjilenii,
Nenu dundogdu mosisamba.
Fuulajin sangrji kennii?
Moxijin sangrji kennii?
Warijin sangrji kennii?
Ndaanu daudu haril ire.

宝瓶所穿的衣裳,
是件绿柏香衣裳,
要穿衣裳有原因,
为了供奉土地爷,
穿衣的原因这样。
下宝瓶的佛是谁?
诵佛经的佛是谁?
祈福的佛陀是谁?
请回答我们的歌。

The clothes that will be worn by the treasure bottle
Are green clothes smelling of cypress twigs.
The reason why it wears these clothes
Is in order to delight the God of the Soil.

That's why it wears those clothes.
Which Buddha will bury the treasure bottle?
Which Buddha will chant Buddhist scriptures?
Which Buddha will pray for it?
Please reply to our song.

Fuulajin sangrji Zhuldandii wai,
Moxijin sangrji Xogxjatogba wai,
Warijin sangrji Wosirang wai.
Oorqiiji snagdernu fuulawa,
Shdeqi snagdernu ujesa,
Snagder tenu waina joo.
Durlaa snagdernu ujesa,
Snagder tenu waina joo.
Xiroo snagdernu ujesa,
Xiroodu snagder ugua joo.
Anjiigu hulghui hulghaja?
Anjiigu bulingii bulija?
Ndaanu daudu haril ire.

卓勒丹迭下宝瓶，
释迦佛陀诵佛经，
觉光佛尊来祈福。
天亮时下了宝瓶，
早上去看了宝瓶，
宝瓶在哪个地方。
中午去看了宝瓶，
宝瓶在哪个地方。
下午去看了宝瓶，
宝瓶不在原地方。
哪个小偷偷掉了？
哪个强盗抢掉了？
请回答我们的歌。

The Buddha buried the treasure bottle,
Shakyamuni chanted the Buddhist scriptures,
Kaśyapa Buddha prayed for it.
The treasure bottle is buried at daybreak.
Go look at the treasure bottle in the morning:
See the bottle at the place where it is buried.

Go look at the treasure bottle at noon:
See the bottle at the place where it is buried.
Go to look at the treasure bottle in the afternoon:
The bottle won't be found.
What thief has stolen it?
What robber has taken it away?
Please reply to our song.

Sangrji Zhuldandiidu xiilaya,
Shdedu ni snagder waina joo,
Durlaa ni snagder waina joo,
Xiroo ni snagder ugua joo.
Hulghui tenu hulghaji gua,
Bulingii tenu buliji gua,
Luyi rjawu tenu rjilejiiwa.
Kunnu nige nudundu,
Nige tenu lii sgem.
Luyi rjawu daglajii,
Kun tenu lii sgem,
Nige duloon ncamdu sausa,
Ncam tenu duurija,
Snagder tenu ujela xjisa,
Kunnu tenu nudundu ni,
Yaahan tenu sgenii?
Dagmu dagmudu kileji ughua.

禀佛尊卓勒丹迭,
宝瓶早上还在那,
宝瓶中午还在那,
宝瓶下午不在了。
小偷不会偷宝瓶,
强盗不敢抢宝瓶,
土地爷拿了宝瓶。
人虽有一双眼睛,
眼睛却不见宝瓶。
土地爷拿了宝瓶,
难怪人们看不见,
做一个七天的禅,
七天的禅圆满了,
又跑去看了宝瓶,

人们的一双眼睛，
看见了什么东西？
详详细细说一说。

Report to the Buddha:
The treasure bottle was in its place in the morning,
The treasure bottle was in its place at noon,
The treasure bottle wasn't there in the afternoon.
Thieves wouldn't have stolen it,
Robbers wouldn't have looted it:
The God of the Soil has taken it.
People have eyes
But they can't see the treasure bottle.
The God of the Soil has taken it,
That's why people can't see it.
Sit in mediation for seven days.
When the seven days of meditation are done,
Then go to look for the treasure bottle again.
People's pairs of eyes—
What will they see?
Please tell us in great detail.

Nige duloonnu udurdu ni,
Snagder tenu tolghui dire,
Kasga nige mur hgaraaja.
Yaahan dundogdu hgharaaja?
Sain shdagwa nuu mau shdagwa?
Sangrji Zhuldandiidu xiilaya,
Snagder tolghuindu ujesa,
Kasga tenu hgharaaja,
Hgharaasan tendu donge wai,
Mau shdag puxa sain shdagwa.
Hgharghaire dongxinge gharina,
Ayigu tenu murgoo joo.
Nige duloon ncamdu sau,
Ncamnu sauji duurisa,
Snagder tenu dire ni,
Juunu ujuur madu sgeni,
Huawu tenu sirin gua,
Huawunu smunu puxiiwa,

Ayiji tenu alani.
Sangrji Zhuldandiidu xiilasa,
Huawunu smunu puxiiwa,
Kun tenu ayigu murgoo joo,
Mau shdag puxa sain shdagwa,
Sbai naazi tenu gharinii,
Tenu log ni tigiinge wai.
Ghuraan duloon ncam sauwa,
Ncamnu sauji duurisa,
Snagder tenu dire ni,
Sala ghoorge gharijiiwa,
Sangrji Zhuldandiidu xiilaya,
Xiilajin sangrji kennii?
Ndaanu daudu haril ire.

一个七天的日子，
那宝瓶的身子上，
裂开了一道缝子。
为什么裂开缝子？
是吉兆还是凶兆？
禀卓勒丹迭佛尊，
看那宝瓶身子上，
裂开了一道缝子，
裂开缝子有征兆，
不是凶兆是吉兆。
裂缝上长了东西，
人们不必要惊慌。
坐一个七天的禅，
七天的禅圆满了，
那宝瓶的裂缝上，
见针尖细的东西，
未见武士的影子，
不是武士的箭头，
我们非常的害怕。
禀卓勒丹迭佛尊，
那不是武士的箭，
人们不必要惊慌，
不是凶兆是吉兆，
青稞发出苗芽了，
它的样子就这样。
坐三个七天的禅，

三七的禅圆满了，
看那宝瓶的上面，
长出两个枝杈了，
禀卓勒丹迭佛尊，
回禀的佛尊是谁？
请回答我们的歌。

After seven days
The treasure bottle's body
Had a crack in it.
Why did it crack?
Is that auspicious or inauspicious?
It was reported to the Buddha
That on the treasure bottle's body
A crack was found
As some sort of omen.
It isn't inauspicious, but auspicious.
Something is growing out of the crack,
But people needn't worry.
They should sit in meditation for seven days.
The seven-day meditation was finished.
In the crack of the treasure bottle
A narrow, needle-like thing was seen:
A warrior wasn't seen,
So it isn't an arrowhead.
They worried about it a great deal.
It was reported to the Buddha.
It's not a warrior's arrow,
People needn't be scared:
It isn't inauspicious, but auspicious.
Highland barley has sprouted,
It looks like this.
People should sit in meditation for three weeks,
The three-week meditation was finished.
See, from the treasure bottle's body
Two twigs are sprouting.
It was reported to the Buddha,
Who reported it?
Please reply to our song.

Xiilajin Rigsimgombu wai,
Sangrji Zhuldandii szonglaja,
Naazi tenu ujesa,
Sala ghoorge gharijiiwa,
Mau shdag puxa sain shdagwa.
Sbai labxi gharina,
Ayigu tenu murgoo joo.
Deeren duloondu ujesa,
Sbai kilenu oosijiiwa,
Yaahan dundogdu kileleja?
Kunnu sgildu ayiguna,
Ndaanu daudu haril ire.

热松官布回禀了，
卓勒丹迭降佛旨，
看那新长的芽子，
长出了两根枝杈，
不是凶兆是吉兆。
青稞长的两片叶，
人们不要受惊慌。
四个七天里去看，
看见青稞分叉了。
青稞为啥分叉了？
人们心里很恐慌，
请回答我们的歌。

Avalokiteśvara, Mañjuśrī and Vajrasattva reported it,
The Buddha ordered it.
Look, the sprouted highland barley
Has grown two leaves.
It isn't inauspicious, but auspicious.
Concerning the two leaves,
People needn't worry.
After four weeks of meditation,
See, the highland barley has more leaves.
Why does the highland barley have so many more leaves?
People are scared.
Please reply to our song.

Deeran duloondu ujesa,
Sbai kile oosijiiwa,
Ayigu tenu murgoo joo,
Tenu log ni tigiinge wai,
Sbai furee rjanglana.
Taawun duloondu ujesa,
Sbaidu tolghui gharina,
Raawa tenu ulonwa,
Tolghui tenu ulonwa,
Ayigu tenu ulonwa,
Amau munu azozoo!
Tigii nusoonu sgeji gua.

四个七天日子里,
青稞长的分叉了,
人们不必要惊慌,
青稞长势是这样,
全靠青稞的种子。
五个七天里去看,
青稞叶茎长了头,
头发长的那么多,
长出的头那么多,
人们多么害怕呀,
哎呀, 我的天哪!
这个怪物没见过。

Four weeks later,
The highland barley has more leaves.
People needn't worry:
It is growing according to the regular pattern,
All depending on the seeds.
Five weeks later,
The highland barley has its head
And a lot of hairs around its head;
There are more small pellets.
People needn't worry about it.
My god!
Never before has such a monster been seen.

Sangrji Zhuldandii xiilaya,
Sangrji Zhuldandii szong bauja,
Taawun duloondu ujesa,

Sbai tolghui gharijiiwa,
Sbai tenu rjanglaja,
Ayigu tenu murgoo joo.
Sbai tolghui suuraana,
Gooro tolghui puxiiwa,
Sbai koornu kilena,
Gooro raawa puxiiwa,
Sbai hagnu kilena,
Nensa ayiji yamagunii.
Jirghoon duloondu ujesa,
Sbai tenu ujesa,
Sbainu tolghui shgexja,
Kunsge ujesa ayina,
Yaahan dundogdu shgexja?
Ndaanu daudu haril ire.

快禀卓勒丹迭佛，
卓勒丹迭佛降佛旨，
五个七天里去看，
青稞叶茎长了头，
青稞长势很旺盛，
人们不必受惊慌。
青稞正在出穗头，
没有什么奇怪的，
要生青稞的颗粒，
那不是长出的发，
那是穗头长穗芒，
不要为这事害怕。
六个七天里去看，
看那青稞的生长，
青稞穗头长大了，
人们见了很害怕，
穗头为啥长大了？
请回答我们的歌。

People reported quickly to the Buddha,
And the Buddha sent a decree:
Go have a look after five weeks.
The highland barley had grown its head,
It was growing vigorously.
People weren't scared.
It has been coming into ear,

It is very normal,
It will grow seeds,
It isn't hair,
It is awns:
Don't be scared of it.
Go have a look after six more weeks,
See how the highland barley is growing,
Its head had already grown.
People are scared of this:
Why has its head grown?
Please reply to our song.

Sangrji Zhuldandiidu xiilaya,
Sangrji Zhuldandii szong bauja,
Tolghui tenu shgexjiiwa,
Tenu log ni tigiinge wai,
Xagge tenu baujiiwa,
Idegu tenu ghurdinna.
Duloon duloondu ujesa,
Labji tolghuinu hoojiiwa,
Ganzi tenu hadaajiiwa,
Sbai tenu qadijiiwa,
Idegu log ni nige gua.
Sangrji Zhuldandiidu xiilaya,
Yaahan tenu szonglani?
Ndaanu daudu haril ire.

禀卓勒丹迭佛尊，
卓勒丹迭佛降佛旨，
青稞穗头长大了，
它的长势是这样，
青稞穗头长籽了，
吃的时候快到了。
七个七天里去看，
青稞叶子变黄了，
青稞茎秆变硬了，
青稞早已成熟了，
没有吃的法子啊。
禀卓勒丹迭佛尊，
降什么好佛旨呢？
请回答我们的歌。

People reported to the Buddha,
The Buddha sent a decree:
The highland barley's head had grown,
It is normal and regular,
There are seeds on the head,
It will soon be time to eat it.
They went to have a look at it after seven weeks.
Its leaves had turned yellow,
Its stalk had hardened,
It had ripened.
It was not known how to eat it.
People reported to the Buddha,
What will he decree?
Please reply to our song.

Duloon duloondu ujesa,
Sbai tenu balijiiwa,
Idegu idexi kuriwa,
Tolghui tenu doglaji,
Shge tegla tegdaya,
Ghar ghoorla funguya,
Sbai koornu baulghaja,
Kugo tingerdu xanglaya.
Sbai tenu xanglasa,
Tolghui tenu murgoya,
Idegu log ni nige gua,
Sangrji Zhuldadiidu xiilaya,
Yaahan tenu szonglani,
Dagmu dagmu kileji ughu,
Ndaanu daudu haril ire.

七个七天里去看，
青稞真的成熟了，
人们食物就有了，
摘下沉甸甸的穗头，
拿上木棍来敲打，
伸出双手来揉搓，
脱下来的青稞粒，
供奉苍天和诸佛。
供奉那个青稞粒，

向苍天磕头谢拜,
吃那青稞难上难,
禀卓勒丹迭佛尊,
降什么好的佛旨,
详详细细说一说,
请回答我们的歌。

They went to have a look at it after seven weeks.
The highland barley had completely ripened.
People now have food to eat.
Pick up the heavy head,
Beat it with a stick
Or rub it with two hands.
Those threshed seeds,
Offer them to Heaven and all the deities.
Making the offering,
Thank Heaven—
But it was not known how to eat it.
A report was sent to the Buddha to ask,
And his decree was awaited.
Tell us in great detail,
Please reply to our song.

Sangrji Zhuldandii szonglaja,
Hara turuudu kunsgenu,
Gujee tenu duurigunaji,
Shbaawag koornu tailaaxja,
Sbai koornu tailaanu,
Anjii tenu xjiguna?
Ndaanu daudu haril ire.

佛尊的佛旨降了,
世上的平民百姓,
本来吃个饱肚子,
青蛙抬走了青稞,
青稞颗粒抬光了,
抬到哪个地方了?
请回答我们的歌。

The Buddha sent his decree:
All commoners in the world

Need to fill their stomachs.
But Frog has taken away the highland barley,
All the highland barley grain has been taken away.
Where has it been taken to?
Please reply to our song.

Sangrji Zhuldandiidu xiilaya,
Sangrji Zhuldandii szong bauja,
Shbaawag sbainu tailaanu,
Dalii xjuurdu xjisamba,
Szu ghaliudu kileji ughu,
Awula nige xji gi joo,
Awaa tenu iresamba,
Ghajar xjiindu geesamba,
Sajaghai koornu tailaa xjija.
Anjii tailaa xjijiiguna?
Hara ghadaanu tolghuindu,
Sajaghai tiree tailaaxja,
Yama giji awula xjim?
Awugu log ni nige gua!
Sangrji Zhuldandiidu xiilaya,
Xiilajin sangrji kenwa?
Dagmu dagmu kileji ughu,
Ndaanu daudu haril ire.

禀卓勒丹迭佛尊,
佛尊的佛旨降了,
青蛙抬走了青稞,
抬到大海底层了,
请求水鸭帮帮忙,
游到海底捞青稞,
青稞颗粒捞上了,
放到大地中间了,
不幸喜鹊叼走了。
喜鹊叼到哪去了?
那悬崖峭壁山顶,
喜鹊叼到山顶了,
什么办法拿回来?
拿回青稞难上难!
禀卓勒丹迭佛尊,

回禀的佛陀是谁？
详详细细说一说，
请回答我们的歌。

It was reported to the Buddha.
The Buddha sent his decree:
Frog has taken the highland barley grain
To the bottom of the ocean.
Ask ducks to help:
Ducks swim to the bottom of the ocean,
Take back the highland barley grain,
And put it at the center of the world.
Unfortunately, it was snatched away by Magpie.
Where has Magpie taken it to?
Magpie has put the grain on the peak of a mountain,
That's where the magpies took it,
How can it be got back?
It is so difficult!
It was reported to the Buddha,
Who will go to report to the Buddha?
Please tell me in great detail,
Please reply to our song.

Xiilajin njamyang rjawu wai,
Hara ghadaanu tolghuindu,
Sajaghai tenu bulaaja,
Kun sbainu yerisa,
Hara ghadaanu tolghuindu,
Yeriji tenu xjisamba,
Sajaghai tenu bulaaja.
Kun tenu maajija,
Yeraa tenu ulijiiwa,
Sbai tenu rguwaanu,
Ghadaasa hariji ireja,
Anjii tenu geeguna?
Ndaanu daudu haril ire.

嘉木养佛回禀了，
悬崖峭壁山顶上，
喜鹊藏埋了青稞，

人们要寻找青稞，
攀登悬崖峭壁上，
到山顶寻找青稞，
喜鹊把青稞埋了。
人们双手刨开土，
青稞颗粒找到了，
背上那个青稞粒，
下山回到了家里，
青稞储存在哪里？
请回答我们的歌。

Njamyang Buddha[4] replied:
On top of the mountain
Magpie buried the highland barley grain.
People looked for it,
Climbed up the mountain,
Looked for it on the mountain peak.
Magpie had buried it in the earth.
People dug in the soil with their hands
And found the grain.
They collected the grain
And came back.
Where did they keep it?
Please reply to our song.

Sangrji Zhuldandiidu xiilaya,
Yaahan tenu szonglani?
Udur nogxigu log wai nuu gua?
Sangrji Zhuldandiidu xiilasa,
Hara turuudusge sunusida,
Hara turuududu kileya,
Sangrji Zhuldandii szong bauja.
Undur tingeredu gharaanu,
Kugo liunu wariwa,
Haldan snaarjinu joolghaya,
Haldan denjaanu koliji,
Haldan njasinu taulaji,

---

4   'Jam dbyangs zhad pa, a living Buddha in Labrang Monastery in Xiahe Township, Gannan Tibetan Autonomous Prefecture, Gansu Province.

Kugo tingerenu fulisa,
Kadidii da kadadaa,
Nensa hadangnu yama gua,
Sbai tarigu ghajar gua.

稟卓勒丹迭佛尊,
降什么样的佛旨?
有无生活的希望?
稟卓勒丹迭佛尊,
稟佛尊的期间里,
庶民百姓请敬听,
佛尊的佛旨降了。
飞升湛蓝的天空,
捉了腾云的青龙,
扎了金造的鼻圈,
驾上金制的轭头,
套上金铸的犁铧,
蓝天上犁了两趟,
卡迭迭"后"卡嗒嗒,
坚硬的没办法犁,
天上无法种青稞。

It was reported to the Buddha.
What will his decree be?
Is there any hope for life?
It was reported to the Buddha.
While it was being reported,
Commoners please listen—
The Buddha's decree has been sent.
Fly up high into the sky,
Catch a dragon,
Put a golden nose ring on it,
Put a golden yoke on it,
Attach a golden plough,
Plough the sky twice
With the sound of *kadiedie* and *kadada*.
But it's too hard to plough,
There's no way to plough the sky.

Hara ghadaadu gharaanu,
Kugo njongnu waraanu,
Mengu snaarjinu joolghaya,

Mengu denjaanu koliji,
Mengu njasinu taulaji,
Hara ghadaanu fulisa,
Hariri da hararaa,
Nensa hadangnu yama gua,
Sbai tarigu ghajar gua.
Tebxin tangdu bauwaanu,
Shge tingernu yangjilaya,
Zhongja gigu log wai nuu gua?
Sangrji Zhuldandiidu xiilaya,
Yaahan tenu szongla ni?
Dagmu dagmu kileji ughu,
Ndaanu daudu haril ire.

登上雄伟的石山，
捉了凶猛的野牛，
扎了银造的鼻圈，
驾上银制的轭头，
套上银制的犁铧，
石山上犁了两趟，
哈热热"后"哈拉拉，
坚硬的没办法犁，
山顶无法种青稞。
下去平展的荒滩，
祈求苍天指个路，
有无种田的希望？
禀卓勒丹迭佛尊，
降什么样的佛旨？
详详细细说一下，
请回答我们的歌。

Climb up high on the mountain,
Catch a yak,
Put a silver nose ring on it,
Put a silver yoke on it,
Attach a silver plough,
Plough the mountain twice
With the sound of *harere* and *halala*.
It's too hard to plough:
There's no way to plough the mountain.
Come down on the level plain
And beg Heaven for help.

Don't you wish to plough crops?
It was reported to the Buddha.
What kind of decree did he send?
Please tell us in great detail,
Please reply to our song.

Tebxin tangdu bauwaanu,
Kuko ulaanu waraanu,
Xigo snaarjinu joolghaya,
Moodi halghanu kolaanu,
Timur njasinu taulaya,
Boodog deelgela huloowaanu,
Tebxin tangnu fuliya.
Moodi tegnu waraanu,
Tisma ramdanu taiwaanu,
Tebxin tangnu fuliya,
Fururuu da furaraa,
Nensa joolon joolon ni ndeewa,
Sbai tenu tariya,
Aadal ulaagu ghajarwa,
Sbai tenu tariwa,
Sbai tenu gharisa,
Sbai tenu qadisa,
Janqigu tenu log ni gua,
Ndaanu daudu haril ire.

到那平展的荒滩,
扑捉肥壮的黄牛,
扎上柏木的鼻圈,
驾上桦木的轭头,
套上铁铸的犁铧,
拴上牛毛的缰绳,
平坦上要开农田。
拿上赶黄牛的棍,
拽紧轭头的皮绳,
平滩上犁了两趟,
吠噜噜"后"发拉拉,
松软的地犁好了,
地上种了青稞,
找到了生活的地方,

地上种了青稞后,
青稞慢慢长高了,
青稞黄的饱满了,
没有打碾的法子,
请回答我们的歌。

Finally, people came down to the vast plain,
Caught an ox,
Put a cypress nose ring on it,
Put a cypress yoke on it,
Attached a metal plough,
Tied the rein made from ox-hair rope,
Ploughed the level plain.
They held a stick
And drew the rope
And ploughed the plain twice
With the sound of *fuluu* and *falala*.
The soft soil was ploughed.
Ploughing highland barley in the soil,
Earth was found,
After ploughing highland barley in the soil
The highland barley slowly grew,
And barley ripened into grain,
But it was not known how to thresh.
Please reply to our song.

Sangrji Zhuldandiidu xiilaya,
Yaahan tenu szonglani?
Sangrji Zhuldandii szonglana,
Hara turuudu sunusida,
Undur ghadaadu ghariji,
Tarnu loqinge szaldu joo.
Tebxin tangdu bauwanu,
Molog shdergenu szaldu joo.
Kugo ulaanu kolaanu,
Moodi denjaanu kolaanu,
Moodi bojanu hulooya,
Tarnu loqinu kolaanu,
Nghuasi deelgela hulooya,
Moodi tegnu waraanu,

Solghui warongnu hergiwa,
Xjirbuu aadal ndireewa,
Kunsgenu gujee qadiwa,
Kunsgenu lai ni shgediwa,
Sangrji sinkor haniwa.

禀卓勒丹迭佛尊，
降什么样的佛旨？
佛尊的佛旨到了，
庶民百姓请敬听，
到那雄伟石山根，
锻造石头的碌碡。
到那平坦的大地，
盘上圆圆的场院。
驾上一对老黄牛，
套上桦木的担架，
连上木头的拨枷，
拉上石头的碌碡，
拴上牛毛的缰绳，
拿上棍子赶黄牛，
场上左右地碾了，
快乐生活在这里，
人们的肚子饱了，
人们的命运转了，
佛尊愿望实现了。

It was reported to the Buddha.
What decree will the Buddha send?
His Buddhist decree has been sent.
All commoners please listen:
Please go to the foot of the high mountain,
Make a rolling thresher out of stone.
Then go back to the level plain,
Make a threshing ground.
Drive a pair of oxen,
Put yokes on them,
Draw the threshing stone attached by a *boja*.[5]
The threshing stone is drawn.

---

5   A wooden plank with two holes at its ends. One hole is attached to rods of iron at
     either end of the threshing stone. The other hole is tied to a rope so that it can be
     drawn by horses during threshing.

Tie the rein made of ox-hair rope,
Hold a stick to drive the oxen.
The threshing stone is rolling on the threshing ground,
People feel happy,
Their stomachs are full,
They have begun new lives.
The Buddha's wishes have become reality.

Mongghul haannu kuu xjunwa,
Mongghul daunaange daulaya,
Mongghulnu darsuu tingiinge wai,
Naadin xineen sauya joo,
Mongghulnu longshda darlam joo,
Mongghulnu darsuu darlam joo,
Mongghul ugonaa lii mardaaya.

蒙古勒汗的子孙，
唱起蒙古勒的歌曲，
这是蒙古勒的习俗，
欢乐和笑声永不消，
蒙古勒时运定兴旺，
蒙古勒习俗常流传，
蒙古勒语言永不忘。

Mongghul khan's descendants,
Singing special Mongghul songs,
This is our Mongghul custom—
We joyfully make our lives.
Mongghul lives will be prosperous—
We keep our Mongghul customs
And keep speaking our Mongghul language.

7. The Song of the Sheep

The Song of the Sheep (*Yangka Luu* [*g.yang dkar glu*] in Tibetan) was sung in Tibetan by Mongghul living in the Fulaan Nara area. Historically, Mongghul lived with Tibetans in this area. Before the 1950s, many Mongghul in Fulaan Nara spoke Tibetan, and marriage between Mongghul people and Tibetans was also common. In the same way that Mongghul people received Buddhism from Tibetans, so folksongs were once widely learned from local Tibetans and sung in Mongghul society. It is said that only a few extremely talented singers could sing *The Song of the Sheep*, however, and that they needed several days and nights to finish it. This song came from Tibetans, and so too did two other songs: *Szii* (Divination) and *Qarog* (Formation of the Earth). These are sung in Tibetan antiphonally, with questions and answers.

Folksong competitions were popular in the areas where Tibetans and Mongghul lived together. Historically, it is said that if someone could sing *The Song of the Sheep* they were regarded as an above average singer, and were deemed eligible to attend folksong competitions. It took several days and nights to sing *The Song of the Sheep* in full.

People thought it was shameful to be defeated by rivals during folksong matches. In the past, people learned folksongs in order to demonstrate their talents in public gatherings, such as weddings, drinking parties in the home, or village celebrations. Memorizing and singing folksongs was one way that Mongghul people showed their wisdom in Mongghul society, and that's why many young Mongghul people frequently went to study folksongs from singers in the past, in just the same way that young Mongghul people go to attend school today.

The Song of the Sheep is here translated into Mongghul, Chinese, and English from Tibetan.

Huninu Dau

霍尼之歌

The Song of the Sheep

 Listen to an audio recording of the song at
https://archive.org/details/HuninuDau

1. Shdochaa

1. 赞歌

1. Praising Song

Tingerdu njasi foodi gharigu rgo,
Njasi foodi lii gharisa,
Ngoyi foodi gharigu log ni gui.

天上先出的圈牛星,
圈牛星如果没出来,
其它星辰就无法出。

Venus must be in the sky:
Without it
No other stars can appear in the sky.

Hghuiqaa moxisa "Gaka" surigu rgo,
Hujin "Gaka"nu lii surisa,
Hghuiqaanu moxigu log ni gui.

要念佛经先学"尕卡",
三十个字母不会读,
佛经就无法念下去。

The Tibetan alphabet must be learned:
If you do not learn it
You cannot learn Buddhist scriptures.

Daulasa shdochaa mudegu rgo,
Shdochaa daulagunaa lii mudesa,
Shge dau daulagu log ni gui.

唱歌首先唱赞歌,
赞歌如果不会唱,
大传对歌无法唱。

Songs of praise must be learned:
If you do not learn them
You cannot sing important songs.

Deedu ghuldu aasi wai,
Qighaan toosila duurijii,
Lii idesada qadaadijia.

上沟里牧的是犏牛,
这是盛产酥油的象征,
是人有了足食的感觉。

Herding cattle in the valley's upper reaches,
Plenty of butter is produced.
Seeing the butter, people feel full even if they don't eat it.

Dunda ghuldu huni wai,
Qighaan nghuasila duurijii,
Lii mosisada halongjaja.

中沟里放的是绵羊,
这是堆满羊毛的象征,
使人有了暖和的感觉。

Herding sheep in the valley's middle reaches,
Plenty of wool is produced.
Seeing the wool, people feel warm even if they don't wear it.

Doodu ghuldu ghajar wai,
Qighaan sbaila duurijii,
Lii uqusada sogdoodijia.

下沟里种的是青稞,
这是酿制美酒的象征,
使人有了欲醉的感觉。

Planting highland barley in the valley's lower reaches,
Plenty of white highland barley seeds are produced.
Seeing the seeds, people feel drunk even if they don't drink barley liquor.

2. Duridal

2. 引子

2. Introduction

Deedu dunda doodu zoohowa,
Deedu zooho yaan kunna?
Dunda zooho yaan kunna?
Doodu zooho yaan kunna?

上中下部三锅灶,
上部锅灶谁人灶?
中部锅灶谁人灶?
下部锅灶谁人灶?

Three kitchen stoves are located in the upper, middle, and lower places.
Whose kitchen stove is the upper one?
Whose kitchen stove is the middle one?
Whose kitchen stove is the lower one?

Deedu dunda doodu zoohawa,
Deedu zooho Tewerna,
Shdileji naasannii qi kile?
Dunda zooho Qidarna,
Naasan da szursannii qi kilie?
Doodu zooho Mongghulna,
Szursan da shdilesannii qi kilie?

上中下部三锅灶,
上部灶贴瓦尔灶,
锻成还是砌成的?
中部灶齐达尔灶,
砌成还是铸成的?
下部灶蒙古勒灶,
铸成还是锻成的?

Three kitchen stoves are located in the upper, middle and lower places.
The upper kitchen stove belongs to the Tibetans.
Is it wrought iron or adobe brick?

The middle kitchen stove belongs to the Chinese.
Is it adobe brick or cast iron?
The lower kitchen stove belongs to the Mongghul.
Is it cast iron or wrought iron?

Deedu dunda doodu zoohowa,
Deedu zooho Tewerna,
Shdilesannu puxii naasannii.
Dunda zooho Qidarna,
Naasannu puxii szursannii.
Doodu zooho Mongghulna,
Szursannu puxii shdilesannii.

上中下部三锅灶，
上灶是贴瓦尔灶，
不是锻成是砌成。
中灶是齐达尔灶，
不是砌成是铸成。
下灶是蒙古勒灶，
不是铸成是锻成。

Three kitchen stoves are located in the upper, middle, and lower places.
The upper kitchen stove belongs to the Tibetans.
It is made of adobe bricks.
The middle kitchen stove belongs to the Chinese.
It is of cast iron.
The lower kitchen stove belongs to the Mongghul.
It is of wrought iron.

Deedu dunda doodu zoohowa,
Deedu zooho Tewerna,
Tughoore shdaasannu yaahanwa?
Dunda zooho Qidarna,
Tughoore qinaasannu yaahanwa?
Doodu zooho Mongghulna,
Tughoore xuusannu yaahanwa?

上中下部三锅灶，
上灶是贴瓦尔灶，
锅中熬的是什么？

中灶是齐达尔灶，
锅中炖的是什么？
下灶是蒙古勒灶，
锅中煮的是什么？

Three kitchen stoves are located in the upper, middle, and lower places.
The upper kitchen stove belongs to the Tibetans.
What is boiling inside their pot?
The middle kitchen stove belongs to the Chinese.
What is boiling inside their pot?
The lower kitchen stove belongs to the Mongghul.
What is boiling inside their pot?

Deedu dunda doodu zoohawa,
Deedu tughoore qaa shdaaja,
Turongnii kendu fuulana?
Dunda tughoore maha qinaaja,
Turongnii kend fuulana?
Doodu turong duraasi xuuja,
Turongnii kendu fuulana?

上中下部三锅灶，
上灶锅灶熬茯茶，
先舀头份敬给谁？
中部锅灶炖羊肉，
先割头份敬给谁？
下部锅灶煮美酒，
先接头份敬给谁？

Three kitchen stoves are located in the upper, middle, and lower places.
Black tea is boiling on the upper kitchen stove.
To whom is it first offered when it has boiled?
Mutton is cooking on the middle kitchen stove.
To whom is it first offered when it has boiled?
Delicious liquor is being distilled on the lower kitchen stove.
To whom is it first offered when it has boiled?

Deedu dunda doodu zoohowa,
Deedu tughoore qaa shdaja,

Turongnii purghaandu fuulana,
Alinge purghaandu fuulana?
Dunda tughoore maha qinaaja,
Turongnii purghaandu fuulana,
Alinge purghaandu fuulana?
Doodu tughoore duraasi xuuja,
Turongnii purghaandu fuulana,
Alinge purghaandu fuulana?

上中下部三锅灶,
上灶锅灶熬茯茶,
先舀头份敬神灵,
头份敬给何方神?
中部锅灶炖羊肉,
先割头份敬神灵,
头份敬给何方神?
下部锅灶煮美酒,
先接头份敬神灵,
头份敬给何方神?

Three kitchen stoves are located in the upper, middle, and lower places.
Black tea is boiling on the upper kitchen stove.
Offer it to the deities first.
Which deity should be first?
Mutton is cooking on the middle kitchen stove.
Offer it to the deities first,
Which deity should be first?
Delicious liquor is being distilled on the lower
Offer it to the deities first,
Which deity should be first?

Deedu dunda doodu zoohowa,
Deedu tughoore qaa shdaana,
Turongnii purghaandu fuulana,
Purghaan ganjangdu fuulan gua,
Shdalaqansangdu fuulana.
Dunda tughoore maha qinaana,
Turongnii purghaandu fuulana,
Purghaan ganjangdu fuulan gua,
Waringqansangdu fuulana.

Doodu tughoore duraasi xuuna,
Turongnii purghaandu fuulana,
Purghaan ganjangdu fuulan gua,
Xuulurqansangdu fuulana.

上中下部三锅灶,
上灶锅灶熬茯茶,
先舀头份敬神灵,
并非敬给所有神,
敬给什当拉欠神。
中部锅灶炖羊肉,
先割头份敬神灵,
并非敬给所有神,
敬给哇阿仁欠神。
下部锅灶煮美酒,
先接头份敬神灵,
并非敬给所有神,
敬给秀吾鲁尖神。

Three kitchen stoves are located in the upper, middle, and lower places.
Black tea is boiling on the upper kitchen stove.
Offer it to the deities first,
But not to all the deities:
Offer it to Shdalaqansang first.
Mutton is cooking on the middle kitchen stove.
Offer it to the deities first,
But not to all the deities:
Offer it to Waringqansang first.
Delicious liquor is being distilled on the lower kitchen stove.
Offer it to the deities first,
But not to all the deities:
Offer it to Xuulurqansang first.

Deedu dunda doodu zoohowa,
Deedu tughoore qaa shdaana,
Shdaasan qaanu kendu ughum?
Dunda tughoore maha qinaana,
Qinaasan mahanu kendu ughum?
Doodu tughoore duraasi xuuna,
Xuusan duraasi kendu ughum?

上中下部三锅灶,
上部锅灶熬茯茶,
所熬茯茶敬何人?
中部锅灶炖羊肉,
所炖羊肉敬何人?
下部锅灶煮美酒,
所煮美酒敬何人?

Three kitchen stoves are located in the upper, middle, and lower places.
Black tea is boiling on the upper kitchen stove.
To whom is the boiled tea offered?
Mutton is cooking on the middle kitchen stove,
To whom is the cooked mutton offered?
Delicious liquor is being distilled on the lower kitchen stove,
To whom is the distilled liquor offered?

Deedu dunda doodu zoohawa,
Deedu tughoore qaa shdaana,
Shdaasan qaanu njiwadu ughum,
Njiwadu ughoodisa xaaroo wai,
Ne xaaroonu kendu geem?
Duda tughoore maha qinaana,
Qinaasan mahanu njiwadu ughum,
Tughoore jangxjang yasi wai,
Ne yasinu kendu geem?
Doodu tughoore duraasi xuum,
Xuusan duraasinu njiwadu ughum,
Lailasan jangxjang rdomu wai,
Ne rdomnu kendu geem?

上中下部三锅灶,
上部锅灶熬茯茶,
所熬茯茶敬客人,
剩下熬的残茶叶,
留给谁的茶份子?
中部锅灶炖羊肉,
所剩羊肉敬客人,
剩下碎肉和骨头,
留给谁的肉份子?
下部锅灶煮美酒,

所剩美酒敬客人,
剩下煮的酒糟子,
留给谁的酒份子?

Three kitchen stoves are located in the upper, middle, and lower places.
Black tea is boiling on the upper kitchen stove.
Offer the boiled tea to the guests.
The tea dregs—
To whom will they be given?
Mutton is cooking on the middle kitchen stove.
Offer the cooked mutton to the guests.
The leftovers—
To whom will they be given?
Delicious liquor is being distilled on the lower kitchen stove.
Offer the distilled liquor to the guests.
The spent grain—
To whom will it be given?

Qaanu huinogu xaaroonu,
Ghuraan aaneedu geesanna,
Ghuraan aanee jauldaaxja,
Yaannu dundogdu jaulduna?
Lailasan jangxjang yasinu,
Ghuraan nohuidu geesanna,
Ghuraan nohui jauldaaxja,
Yaannu dundogdu jaulduna?
Lailasan duraasi rdomunu,
Ghuraan maujaadu geesana,
Ghuraan maujaa jauldaaxja,
Yaannu dundogdu jaulduna?

剩下熬的残茶叶,
留给三位老妪的,
三位老妪寻纠葛,
纠葛缘由从何起?
剩下碎肉和骨头,
留给三条老狗的,
三条老狗起争端,
争端缘由从何起?
剩下煮的酒糟子,

留给三头老猪的,
三头老猪起争端,
争端缘由从何起?

The tea dregs—
Give them to three old women.
The three old women have a conflict:
Why do they have a conflict?
The leftover cooked mutton—
Give it to three dogs.
The three dogs have a conflict:
Why do they have a conflict?
The spent grain from distilling liquor—
Give it to three sows.
The three sows have a conflict:
Why do they have a conflict?

Lailasan qaanu xaaroonu,
Ghuraan aaneedu geesanna,
Ghuraan aanee jauldusa,
Njeennaa ghuraanla njaglaji gua.
Lailasan jangxjang yasinu,
Ghuraan nohuidu geesanna,
Ghuraan nohui jauldusa,
Njeennaanu turosa njaglaji gua.
Lailasan duraasi rdomunu,
Ghuraan maujaadu geesanna,
Ghuraan maujaa jauldusa,
Maujaa njeennaanu yinganwa.

剩下熬的残茶叶,
留给三位老妪的,
三位老妪寻纠葛,
纠葛缘由自己起。
剩下碎肉和骨头,
留给三条老狗的,
三条老狗起争端,
争端来自狗内部。
剩下煮的酒糟子,
留给三头老猪的,
三头老猪起争端,

争端来自猪内部。

The tea dregs—
Give them to three old women.
The three old women have a conflict,
They have a conflict among themselves.
The leftover cooked mutton—
Give it to three dogs.
The three dogs have a conflict,
They have a conflict among themselves.
The spent grain from distilling liquor—
Give it to three sows.
The three sows have a conflict,
They have a conflict among themselves.

Xjarang oor qiigu sghaudu,
Pusisa raari aawange rgom,
Aawange waiwaa yama gi gui?
Aawange guiwaa yama gi gui?
Durnadu nara gharigu sghaudu,
Daudasa saini aanange rgom,
Aanange waisa yamahgiingewa?
Aanange guisa yamahgiingewa?
Xiroodu nara pagdagu sghaudu,
Qimsangdu saihan aaghadiunge rgom,
Aaghadiunge waisa yamahgiingewa?
Aaghadiunge guise yamahgiingewa?

东方破晓天亮时,
起床需要靠严父,
有父天亮时何样?
无父天亮时何样?
东方太阳升起时,
叫醒需要靠慈母,
有母日子是何样?
无母日子是何样?
日落西山黄昏时,
家中要有好兄弟,
有兄天黑是何样?
无兄天黑是何样?

As dawn breaks in the east,
As one is getting up, it would be good if one's father were there.
What would be good if one's father were there?
What would be bad if one's father weren't there?
As the sun rises in the east,
As one is waking up, it would be good if one's mother were there.
What would be good if one's mother were there?
What would be bad if one's mother weren't there?
As the sun is setting in the afternoon,
Brothers are needed in the family.
What would be good if there were brothers in the family?
What would be bad if there weren't any brothers in the family?

Xjarang oor qiigu sghaudu,
Pusisa raari aawange rgom,
Aawange guise dundog gui,
Aawange waisa dundog irem.
Durnadu nara gharigu sghaudu,
Daudasa saini aanange rgom,
Aanange guise hoosin wai,
Aanange waisa xjirbuu wai.
Sargu nara pagdagu sghaudu,
Qimsangdu saihan aghadiunge rgom,
Aghadiunge guise kordong wai,
Aghadiunge waisa kordong gui.

东方破晓天亮时,
起床需要靠严父,
无父天亮诸事空,
有父天亮诸事成。
东方太阳升起时,
叫醒需要靠慈母,
无母日子空落落,
有母日子万事兴。
日落西山黄昏时,
家中要有好兄弟,
无兄天黑诸事空,
有兄天黑诸事成。

As dawn breaks in the east,
As one is getting up, it would be good if one's father were there.

Everything would be empty if one's father weren't there,
Everything would be successful if one's father were there.
As the sun rises in the east,
As one is waking up, it would be good if one's mother were there.
Life would be meaningless if one's mother weren't there,
Life would be happy if one's mother were there.
As the sun is setting in the afternoon,
Brothers are in the family.
Nothing would be successful if the brothers weren't there,
Everything would be successful if the brothers were there.

Durnadu xjarang tidagu sghaudu,
Alag mparaa huxinaa nghaiwaanu,
Diulin diulindu anjii xjim?
Nara gharigu shdenu sghaudu,
Kugo kadam shdinaa rziiwaanu,
Yohong baihongdu anjii xjim?
Nara pagdagu uruinu sghaudu,
Hara kiree nudunaa bunkaanu,
Nesin nesindu anjii xjim?

东方破晓天亮时，
红斑豺狗咧着嘴，
一跳一跳去哪里？
太阳冉冉升起时，
灰色恶狼呲着牙，
一跃一跃去哪里？
日落西山黄昏时，
黑色乌鸦瞪着眼，
一飞一飞去哪里？

As dawn breaks in the east,
A red-spotted wild dog grins.
Where is he hopping off to?
As the sun rises,
A grey wolf bares his teeth.
Where is he leaping off to?
As the sun is setting in the afternoon,
A black crow's eyes glower.
Where is he flying off to?

Durnadu xjarang tidagu shaudu,
Alag mparaa huxinaa nghaiwaanu,
Diulin diulin deedu longdu xjim,
Te yaannu dundogdu longdu xjim?
Nara gharigu shdenu sghaudu,
Kugo kadam shdinaa rziiwanu,
Yohong baihong dunda longdu xjim,
Te yaannu dudongdu longdu xjim?
Nara pagdagu uruinu sghaudu,
Hara kiree nudunaa bunkaanu,
Nesin nesindu doodu longdu xjim,
Te yaannu dundogdu longdu xjim?

东方天亮破晓时,
红斑豺狗咧着嘴,
一跳一跳去上川,
它去上川为了啥?
太阳冉冉升起时,
灰色恶狼呲着牙,
一跃一跃去中川,
它去中川为了啥?
日落西山黄昏时,
黑色乌鸦瞪着眼,
一飞一飞去下川,
它去下川为了啥?

As dawn breaks in the east,
A red-spotted wild dog grins.
He is hopping off to the upper plain.
Why is he going to the upper plain?
As the sun rises,
A grey wolf bares his teeth.
He is leaping off to the middle plain.
Why is he going to the middle plain?
As the sun is setting in the afternoon,
A black crow's eyes glower.
He is flying off to the lower plain.
Why is he flying to the lower plain?

Durnadu xjarang tidagu sghaudu,
Alag mparaa huxinaa nghaiwaanu,
Diulin diulin deedu longdu xjim,

Tendu deedu longdu dundogge wai,
Idegundunaa ulaanu longdu xjim,
Tereexi aasi waigunu bu mudem,
Te yaannu ideguniiha bu lii mudem.
Nara gharigu shdenu sghaudu,
Kugo kadam shdinaa rziiwaanu,
Yohong baihong dunda longdu xjim,
Tendu dunda longdu dundogge wai,
Idegundunaa ulaanu longdu xjim,
Tireexi huni waigunu bu modem,
Te yaannu ideguniiha bu lii mudem.
Nara pagdagu uruinu sghaudu,
Hara kiree nudunaa bunkaanu,
Nesin nesin doodu longdu xjim,
Tendu doodu longdu dundogge wai,
Idegundunaa ulaanu longdu xjim,
Tireexi mori waigunu bu mudem,
Te yaannu ideguniiha bu lii mudem.

东方天亮破晓时，
红斑豺狗咧着嘴，
一跳一跳去上川，
它去上川有一事，
就为捕食去那里，
我知那里有牛群，
还吃什么你说说。
太阳冉冉升起时，
灰色恶狼呲着牙，
一跃一跃去中川，
它去中川有一事，
我知那里有羊群，
就为捕食去那里，
还吃什么你说说。
日落西山黄昏时，
黑色乌鸦瞪着眼，
一飞一飞去下川，
它去下川有一事，
就为啄食烂尸肉，
我知马群在那里，
还吃什么你说说。

As dawn breaks in the east,
A red-spotted wild dog grins.
He is hopping off to the upper plain.
He is going there
To hunt for something.
I know there are cattle in the upper plain,
But I don't know what he plans to eat.
As the sun rises,
A grey wolf bares his teeth.
He is leaping off to the middle plain.
He is going there
To hunt for something.
I know there are sheep in the middle plain,
But I don't know what he plans to eat.
As the sun is setting in the afternoon,
A black crow's eyes glower.
He is flying off to the lower plain.
He is flying there
To hunt for something.
I know there are horses in the lower plain,
But I don't know what he plans to eat.

Alag mparaa huxinaa nghaiwaanu,
Diulin diulin deedu longdu xjim,
Tendu deedu longdu dundog wai,
Aasinqinu aasi ni tiree wai,
Aasidu ulaanu longdu xjim,
Aasi jirgenu ideenu diuraaxjia,
Darang yaan idemha qi kile?
Kugo kadam shdinaa rziiwaanu,
Yohong baihong dunda longdu xjim,
Te dunda longdu dundog wai,
Asinqinu huni ni tiree wai,
Hunidu ulaanu longdu xjim,
Idejinnu mamunu sangraana,
Darang yaan idemha qi kile?
Hara kiree nudunaa bunkaanu,
Nesin nesindu longduxjim,
Te doodu longdu dundog wai,

Aasinqinu mori ni tiree wai,
Moridu ulaanu longdu xjim,
Idejinnu morinu nudu jirgena,
Darang yaan idemha qi kile?

红斑豺狗咧着嘴,
一跳一跳去上川,
它去上川有缘故,
牧人牛群在那里,
就为吃肉去上川,
饱食牛心心满足,
还吃什么你说说?
灰色恶狼呲着牙,
一跃一跃去中川,
它去中川有缘故,
牧人羊群在那里,
就为吃羊去中川,
专吃母羊跨子肉,
还吃什么你说说?
黑色乌鸦瞪着眼,
一飞一飞去下川,
它去下川有缘故,
牧人马群在那里,
就为此事去下川,
专吃马的肥眼仁,
还吃什么你说说?

A red-spotted wild dog grins.
He is hopping off to the upper plain.
He is going there for something:
A herdsman's cattle are grazing there,
He is going there to hunt cattle.
He is full from eating cattle's hearts.
What else will he eat?
A grey wolf bares his teeth.
He is leaping off to the middle plain.
He is going there for something:
A shepherd's sheep are grazing there,
He is going there to hunt sheep.
He is full from eating sheep's hip meat.
What else will he eat?

A black crow's eyes glower.
He is flying off to the lower plain.
He is going there for something:
A herdsman's horses are grazing there,
He is going there to hunt horses.
He is full from eating horses' eyes.
What else will he eat?

Alag mparaa huxinaa nghaiwaanu,
Diulin diulindu deedu longdu xjim,
Te longdu xjisa dundog wai,
Asinqinu aasi ni tiree wai,
Mahadu ulaanu longdu xjim,
Idejin ni aasinu jirgena,
Darang aasinu qisina.
Kugo kadam shdinaa rziiwaanu,
Yohong baihongdu dunda longdu xjim,
Te longdu xjisa dundog wai,
Asinqinu huni ni tiree wai,
Mahadu ulaanu longdu xjim,
Idejin ni mamunu sangraana,
Darang huninu nudu jirgena.
Hara kiree nudunaa bunkaanu,
Nesin nesindu doodu longdu xjim,
Te longdu xjisa dundog wai,
Asinqinu mori ni tiree wai,
Mahadu ulaanu longdu xjim,
Idejin ni morinu nudu jirgena,
Darang morinu qisina.

红斑豺狗咧着嘴，
一跳一跳去上川，
它去脑山有缘故，
牧人牛群在那里，
就为吃肉去那里，
专食牛的心脂肪，
还要吸食牛的血。
灰色恶狼呲着牙，
一跃一跃去中川，
它去中川有缘故，

牧人羊群在那里，
就为食肉去中川，
专食母羊跨子肉，
还食绵羊肥眼仁。
黑色乌鸦瞪着眼，
一飞一飞去下川，
它去下川有缘故，
牧人马群在那里，
就为食肉去下川，
专食马的肥眼仁，
还要吸食马鲜血。

A red-spotted wild dog grins.
He is jumping off to the upper plain.
He is going there for something:
A herdsman's cattle are grazing there.
He is going there to eat meat:
He eats cattle's hearts
And drinks cattle's blood.
A grey wolf bares his teeth.
He is leaping off to the middle plain.
He is going there for something:
A shepherd's sheep are grazing there,
He is going there to eat meat.
He eats ewes' hip meat
And eats sheep's eyes.
A black crow's eyes glower.
He is flying off to the lower plain.
He is flying there for something:
A herdsman's horses are grazing there,
He goes to there to eat meat.
He eats horses' eyes
And drinks horses' blood.

Jagha ghajarnu ula tangdu,
Shgebqi huri tigii ulange wai,
Ne uladu nire wai yiu gui?
Xjiin ghajarnu ula tangdu,
Mulaa moodi madu xjoosinge wai,
Ne xjoosidu nire wai yiu gui?

Dooro ghajardu szu raaldu,
Gireldu xal tigii noorge wai,
Ne noordu nire wai yiu gui?

上部地区群山中，
有座山像大拇指，
此山有无啥名称？
中部地区山林间，
有棵树如小木棍，
此树有无啥名称？
下部大雾弥漫处，
有个胡泊如明镜，
此湖有无啥名称？

In the upper area
There is a thumb-shaped mountain.
Does this mountain have a name?
In the middle area
There is a small tree.
Does this small tree have a name?
In the lower area with many rivers
There is a mirror-bright lake
Does this lake have a name?

Jagha ghajarnu ula tangdu,
Shgebqi huri tigii ulange wai,
Ne uladu nire jubda wai,
Lurjaa lumbu daudana,
Lumbu malgha jooja giji kilena,
Malgha jooja nuu jooji gua?
Xjiin ghajarnu ula tangdu,
Mulaa moodi madu xjoosinge wai,
Ne xjoosidu nire jubda wai,
Fulaan singe daudana,
Singe deel mosija giji kilena,
Deel mosija nuu mosiji gua?
Dooro ghajarnu szu raaldu,
Gireldu xal tigii noorge wai,
Ne noordu nire jubda wai,
Kugo noor giji daudana,
Munaan pudee sauja giji kilena,
Munaan pudeeja nuu pudeeji gua?

上部地区群山中，
有座山像大拇指，
此山当然有山名，
山名叫做须弥山，
人言须弥饰头盔，
到底有盔没有盔？
中部地区山林间，
有棵树如小木棍，
此树当然有树名，
树名叫做红跃狮，
人言此树披铠甲，
到底披甲不披甲？
下部大雾弥漫处，
有个胡泊如明镜，
此湖当然有湖名，
湖名叫库库诺尔，
人言湖被云雾罩，
到底有雾没有雾？

In the upper area
There is a thumb-shaped mountain.
The mountain truly has a name:
Its name is Mount Sumeru.
It is said that Mount Sumeru wears a helmet—
Does it wear a helmet on Earth or not?
In the middle area
There is a small tree.
The tree truly has a name:
Its name is Red Lion.
It is said that Red Lion wears armour—
Does it wear armour or not?
In the lower area with many rivers
There is a mirror-bright lake on the shady side.
The lake truly has a name:
Its name is Qinghai Lake.
It is said that Qinghai Lake is covered with mist—
Is it covered with mist or not?

Jagha ghajarnu ula tangdu,
Shgebqi huri tigii ulange wai,
Ne uladu nire jubda wai,

Lurjaa lumbu daudana,
Malgha guigu puxii malgha wai,
Qi kile ne malgha yaangewa?
Xjiin ghajarnu ula tangdu,
Mulaa moodi madu xjoosinge wai,
Ne xjoosidu nire jubda wai,
Fulaan singe daudana,
Deel guigunu puxii deelda wai,
Qi kile ne deel yaangewa?
Dooro ghajarnu szu raaldu,
Gireldu xal tigii noorge wai,
Ne noordu nire jubda wai,
Kugo noor giji daudana,
Munaan guigunu puxii munaan wai,
Qi kile ne munaan yaangewa?

上部地区群山中,
有座山像大拇指,
此山当然有山名,
山名叫做须弥山,
并非无盔确有盔,
你说此盔是何物?
中部地区山林间,
有棵树如小木棍,
此树当然有树名,
树名叫做红跃狮,
并非无甲确有甲,
你说此甲为何物?
下部大雾弥漫处,
有个胡泊如明镜,
此湖当然有湖名,
湖名叫库库诺尔,
并非无雾确有雾,
你说那雾是何物?

In the upper area
There is a thumb-shaped mountain.
The mountain truly has a name:
Its name is Mount Sumeru.
Mount Sumeru truly wears a helmet.
What helmet is it?

In the middle area
There is a small tree.
The tree truly has a name:
Its name is Red Lion.
Red Lion truly wears armour.
What armour is it?
In the lower area with many rivers
There is a mirror-bright lake on the shady side.
The lake truly has a name:
Its name is Qinghai Lake.
Qinghai Lake is truly covered with mist.
What mist is it?

Lurjaa lumbu malgha jooja,
Malgha guigunu puxii malgha wai,
Qighaan ulong malghana,
Jigi uladu xaaxi ulon,
Sunurda uu guiha mudeji gui.
Fulaan singe deel mosija,
Deel guigunu puxii deelda wai,
Kuiden kii deel niwa,
Jigi xjoosire shdur hghur ulon,
Sunurda uu guiha mudeji gui.
Kugo noorre munaan pudeeja,
Munaan guigunu puxii munaan wai,
Sal kii tausa munaan pudeena,
Jigi noorre pudag mudagge,
Sunurda uu guiha bu mudeji gui.

须弥山峰饰头盔，
并非无盔确有盔，
白云缭绕便是盔，
可惜山上飞沙多，
是否曾经听说过？
红跃狮树披铠甲，
并非无甲确有甲，
严寒袭来成披甲，
可惜树中多长短，
是否曾经听说过？
库库诺尔被雾罩，

并非无雾确有雾，
凉风吹拂雾缭绕，
可惜湖水多浑浊，
是否曾经听说过？

Mount Sumeru wears a helmet—
It is a helmet
Of white clouds coiling up the mountain.
Blown sand is common on the mountain:
Have you heard of this or not?
The Red Lion tree wears armour—
It is armour
Of cold wind.
Some trees are tall and some are short:
Have you heard of this or not?
Qinghai Lake is covered with mist—
It is mist
Formed by the blowing of cool breeze.
The water in the lake is muddy:
Have you heard of this or not?

Lurjaa lumbu malgha jooja,
Lurjaa lumbu ndog qugurdena.
Fulaan singe deel mosija,
Fulaan singe ndog qugurdena.
Kugo noorre munaan pudeeja,
Kugo noorre ndog qugurdena.

须弥山峰饰头盔，
须弥山呈四种色。
红跃狮树披铠甲，
红跃狮树呈四色。
库库诺尔被云罩，
库库诺尔呈四色。

Mount Sumeru wears a helmet,
Mount Sumeru radiates brilliant light.
The Red Lion tree wears armour,
The Red Lion tree radiates brilliant light.
Qinghai Lake is covered with mist,
Qinghai Lake radiates brilliant light.

Deedu ghajarnu jaghadu,
Szer ula dong ula xuri ula,
Ulasge szer ulanu hargija,
Szer ula yama giji harigija?
Dunda ghajarnu ula tangdu,
Szer bag dong bag xuri bag,
Bagsge szer bagnu hargija,
Szer bag yama giji hargija?
Doodu ghajarnu ulong dooro,
Szer noor dong noor xuri noor,
Noorsge szer noornu hargija,
Szer nor yama giji hargija?

上部地区最上方,
金山螺山碧玉山,
山山围绕大金山,
说说金山咱围绕?
中部地区山林间,
金树螺树碧玉树,
树树围绕大金树,
说说金树咱围绕?
下部地区云雾下,
金海螺海碧玉海,
海海围绕大金海,
说说金海咋围绕?

In the heights of the upper area
Are the Gold Mountain, Conch Mountain, and Jade Mountain.
The Gold Mountain is encircled by the others.
How is the Gold Mountain encircled?
In the forested place of the middle area
Are the gold tree, conch tree, and jade tree.
The gold tree is encircled by the others—
How is the gold tree encircled?
Under the clouds in the lower area
Are the Gold Sea, Conch Sea, and Jade Sea.
The Gold Sea is encircled by the others—
How is the Gold Sea encircled?

Szer ula dong ula xuri ula,
Ulasge szer ulanu hargija,
Szer ula dong ulanu hargija,
Dong ula xuri ulanu hargija,
Xuri ula szer ulanu hargija,
Nige nigenaa hargija.
Szer bag dong bag xuri bag,
Bagsge szer bagnu hargija,
Szer bag dong bagnu hargija,
Dong bag xuri bagnu hargija,
Xuri bag szer bagnu hargija,
Nige nigenaa hargija.
Szer noor dong noor xuri noor,
Noorsge szer noornu hargija,
Szer noor dong noornu hargija,
Dong noor xuri noornu hargija,
Xuri noor szer noornu harigija,
Nige nigenaa hargija.

金山螺山和玉山，
山山围绕大金山，
金山围绕白螺山，
螺山围绕碧玉山，
玉山围绕大金山，
三山相互围绕着。
金树螺树和玉树，
树树围绕大金树，
金树围绕白螺树，
螺树围绕碧玉树，
玉树围绕大金树，
三树相互围绕着。
金海螺海和玉海，
海海围绕大金海，
金海围绕白螺海，
螺海围绕碧玉海，
玉海围绕大金海，
三海相互围绕着。

Gold Mountain, Conch Mountain, and Jade Mountain—
Gold Mountain is encircled by the others,
Gold Mountain is encircled by Conch Mountain,

Conch Mountain is encircled by Jade Mountain,
Jade Mountain is encircled by Gold Mountain,
They are encircled by themselves.
The gold tree, conch tree, and jade tree—
The gold tree is encircled by the others,
The gold tree is encircled by the conch tree,
The conch tree is encircled by the jade tree,
The jade tree is encircled by the gold tree,
They are encircled by themselves.
Gold Sea, Conch Sea, and Jade Sea,
Gold Sea is encircled by the others,
Gold Sea is encircled by Conch Sea,
Conch Sea is encircled by Jade Sea,
Jade Sea is encircled by Gold Sea,
They are encircled by themselves.

Lurjaa lumbunu dundaxi,
Szer ula dong ula xuri ula,
Szer ula tolghuindu yaan ncoglam?
Dong ula tolghuindu yaan ncoglam?
Xuri ula tolghuindu yaan ncoglam?
Szer bag dong bag xuri bag,
Szer bag tolghuinsa yaan dawaam?
Dong bag tolghuinsa yaan dawaam?
Xuri bag tolghuinsa yaan dawaam?
Szer noor dong noor xuri noor,
Szer noor jaghasa yaan yaunii?
Dong noor jaghasa yaan yaunii?
Xuri noor jaghasa yaan yaunii?

须弥山的正中央,
金山螺山碧玉山,
金山顶上聚什么?
螺山顶上聚什么?
玉山顶上聚什么?
金树螺树碧玉树,
金树上面过什么?
螺树上面过什么?
玉树上面过什么?
金海螺海碧玉海,

金海上面走什么?
螺海上面走什么?
玉海上面走什么?

In the middle of the slopes of Mount Sumeru
Are Gold Mountain, Conch Mountain, and Jade Mountain.
What gathers atop Gold Mountain?
What gathers atop Conch Mountain?
What gathers atop Jade Mountain?
The gold tree, conch tree, and jade tree,
What passes over the top of the gold tree?
What passes over the top of the conch tree?
What passes over the top of the jade tree?
Gold Sea, Conch Sea, and Jade Sea,
What walks on the Gold Sea?
What walks on the Conch Sea?
What walks on the Jade Sea?

Szer ula dong ula xuri ula,
Szer ula tolghuindu nara baum,
Dong ula tolghuindu sara baum,
Xuri ula tolghuindu foodi baum.
Szer bag dong bag xuri bag,
Szer bag tolghuinsa nara dawaam,
Dong bag tolghuinsa sara dawaam,
Xuri bag tolghuinsa foodi dawaam.
Szer noor dong noor xuri noor,
Szer noor jaghasa nara yaum,
Dong noor jaghasa sara yaum,
Xuri noor jaghasa foodi yaum.

金山螺山和玉山,
金山顶上聚太阳,
螺山顶上聚月亮,
玉山顶上聚星星。
金树螺树碧玉树,
金树上面过太阳,
螺树上面过月亮,
玉树上面过星星。
金海螺海和玉海,

金海上面太阳走，
螺海上面月亮走，
玉海上面星星走。

Gold Mountain, Conch Mountain, and Jade Mountain—
The sunlight is gathered atop Gold Mountain,
The moonlight is gathered atop Conch Mountain,
The starlight is gathered atop Jade Mountain.
The gold tree, conch tree, and jade tree—
The sunlight passes over the top of the gold tree,
The moonlight passes over the top of the conch tree,
The starlight passes over the top of the jade tree.
The Gold Sea, Conch Sea, and Jade Sea—
The sunlight walks on the Gold Sea,
The moonlight walks on the Conch Sea,
The starlight walks on the Jade Sea.

Deedu szer noor xirange,
Yama gaanu xirange?
Dunda dong noor qighaange,
Yama gaanu qighaange?
Doodu xuri noor ilange,
Yama gaanu ilange?

上部金海是黄色，
不知为啥是黄色？
中部螺海是白色，
不知为啥是白色？
下部玉海是蓝色，
不知为啥是蓝色？

The upper area of the Gold Sea is yellow—
Why is it yellow?
The middle area of the Conch Sea is white—
Why is it white?
The lower area of the Jade Sea is blue—
Why is it blue?

Deedu szer noor xirange,
Xira haldan noorre wai,

Tela gaanu xirange.
Dunda dong noor qighaange,
Qighaan dongma noorre wai,
Tela gaanu qighaange.
Doodu xuri noor ilange,
Ilan xuri noorre wai,
Tela gaanu ilange.

上部金海是黄色,
黄金宝藏在海中,
因此海水呈黄色。
中部螺海是白色,
白螺藏在大海中,
因此海水呈白色。
下部玉海是蓝色,
碧玉宝藏在海中,
因此海水呈蓝色。

The upper area of the Gold Sea is yellow
Because gold is stored in the sea,
Hence the sea appears yellow.
The middle area of the Conch Sea is white
Because white conches are stored in the sea,
Hence the sea appears white.
The lower area of the Jade Sea is blue
Because jade is stored in the sea,
Hence the sea appears blue.

Deedu szer noornu jaghadu ni,
Jagha szer noor xirange,
Szer noor qireedu yaan gharina?
Deedu dong noornu xjiindu ni,
Dunda dong noor qighaange,
Dong noor qireedu yaan gharina?
Deedu xuri noornu dooro ni,
Dooro xuri noor ilange,
Ilan noor qireedu yaan gharina?

上部金海之上方,
上方金海呈黄色,
金海岸边要出啥?
上部螺海之中方,

中方螺海呈白色，
螺海岸边要出啥？
上部玉海之下方，
下方螺海呈蓝色，
蓝色海边要出啥？

At the top of the Gold Sea in the upper area
The Gold Sea appears yellow.
What will appear on the shores of the Gold Sea?
At the center of the Conch Sea in the upper area
The Conch Sea appears white.
What will appear on the shores of the Conch Sea?
In the lower part of the Jade Sea in the upper area
The Jade Sea appears blue.
What will appear on the shores of the Jade Sea?

Deedu szer noornu jaghadu,
Jagha szer noor xirange,
Noor qireesa haldan gharina.
Deedu dong noornu dundaxi,
Dunda dong noor qighaange,
Noor qireesa dong gharina.
Deedu xuri noornu dooro ni,
Dooro xuri noor qighaange,
Noor qireesa xuri gharina.

上部金海之上方，
上方金海呈黄色，
金海岸边出黄金。
上部螺海之中方，
中方螺海呈白色，
螺海岸边出白螺。
上部玉海之下方，
下方玉海呈蓝色，
玉海岸边出碧玉。

At the top of the Gold Sea in the upper area
The Gold Sea appears yellow:
Gold appears on the shores of the Gold Sea.
At the center of the Conch Sea in the upper area
The Conch Sea appears white:
White conches appear on the shores of the Conch Sea.

In the lower part of the Jade Sea in the upper area
The Jade Sea appears blue:
Jade appears on the shores of the Jade Sea.

Deedu dunda doodu noor,
Noorre dahu wai yuu gui?
Noorre harliqi wai yuu gui?
Noorre kauladal wai yuu gui?

上中下方三个海,
三海是否有主人?
三海是否有舵手?
三海是否有依托?

The three seas—upper, middle, and lower—
Do the three seas have an owner?
Do the three seas have a helmsman?
Do the three seas have a supporter?

Deedu dunda doodu noor,
Noorre dahu jubda wai,
Dahu lunwang purghaan wai.
Noorre harliqi noor wai,
Harliqida lunwang purghaan wai.
Noorre kauladal noor wai,
Kauladal lunwang purghaan wai.

上中下方三个海,
大海当然有主人,
主人就是龙王爷。
大海当然有舵手,
舵手也是龙王爷。
大海当然有依托,
依托也是龙王爷。

The three seas—upper, middle and lower—
The three seas have an owner,
The owner is the Dragon King.
The three seas have a helmsman,
The helmsman is the Dragon King.
The three seas have a supporter,
The supporter is the Dragon King.

3. Huninu Iredal

3. 形成

3. How the Sheep Took Shape

Szer noor qireegu huni wai,
Tingernu puxii szasannii,
Szasan purghaan alinge wai?
Dong noor qireegu huni wai,
Tingernu puxii szasannii,
Szasan purghaan alinge wai?
Xuri noor qireegu huni wai,
Tingernu puxii szasannii,
Szasan purghaan alinge wai?

金海岸边那福羊，
不是天生而造出，
造羊神佛是哪位？
螺海岸边那福羊，
不是天生而造出，
造羊神佛是哪位？
玉海岸边那福羊，
不是天生而造出，
造羊神佛是哪位？

A sheep on the shore of the Gold Sea
Is not from Heaven, but was created.
Which Buddha created it?
A sheep on the shore of the Conch Sea
Is not from Heaven, but was created.
Which Buddha created it?
A sheep on the shore of the Jade Sea
Is not from Heaven, but was created.
Which Buddha created it?

Gharghasan purghaan waijinna,
Nigedar jaghaagu shge tingerwa,
Ghoordar baudaldii purghaawa,
Ghuraandar iredal shdombawa,
Ghuraanla ghuraan huini gharghajii.

造羊神佛自然有,
一是上界自在天,
二是不空成就佛,
三是宝生如来佛,
三圣共造三只羊。

These are the Buddhas who created the sheep:
The first is Sovereign Great Heaven,
The second is Amoghasiddi,
The third is Gautama Buddha.
These three have created three sheep.

Szer noor huninu yaanla szajii?
Dong noor huninu yaanla szajii?
Xuri noor huninu yaanla szajii?

金海羊由什么造?
螺海羊由什么造?
玉海羊由什么造?

What is the sheep in the Gold Sea made of?
What is the sheep in the Conch Sea made of?
What is the sheep in the Jade Sea made of?

Szer noor huninu szerla szasannii,
Hunidu qisi wai yuu gui?
Dong noor huninu dongle szasannii,
Hunidu qisi wai yuu gui?
Xuri noor huninu xurila szsannii,
Hunidu qisi wai yuu gui?

金海羊由金子造,
请问羊身有无血?
螺海羊由白螺造,
请问羊身有无血?
玉海羊由碧玉造,
请问羊身有无血?

The sheep in the Gold Sea is made of gold.
Does the sheep have blood or not?
The sheep in the Conch Sea is made of white conch.

Does the sheep have blood or not?
The sheep in the Jade Sea is made of jade.
Does the sheep have blood or not?

Szer noor huninu szerla szasannii,
Qisi wainu puxii qisi gui,
Yama gaanu qisi gua?
Dong noor huninu dongle szasannii,
Qisi wainu puxii qisi gui,
Yama gaanu qisi gua?
Xuri noor huninu xurila szasannii,
Qisi wainu puxii qisi gui,
Yama gaanu qisi gua?

金海羊由金子造,
并非有血而无血,
请问为何没有血?
螺海羊由白螺造,
并非有血而无血,
请问为何没有血?
玉海羊由碧玉造,
并非有血而无血,
请问为何没有血?

The sheep in the Gold Sea is made of gold.
The sheep has no blood in its body.
Why doesn't it have any blood in its body?
The sheep in the Conch Sea is made of white conch.
The sheep has no blood in its body.
Why doesn't it have any blood in its body?
The sheep in the Jade Sea is made of jade.
The sheep has no blood in its body.
Why doesn't it have any blood in its body?

Szer huninu szerla szasannii,
Qisi wainu puxii qisi gui,
Qisi guigure dundog wai,
Szerma simqannu niruuwa.
Dong huninu dongle szasannii,
Qisi wainu puxii qisi gui,

Qisi guigure dundog wai,
Qighaan dongnu nire shge wai.
Xuri huninu xurila szasannii,
Qisi wainu puxii qisi gui,
Qisi guigure dundog wai,
Xuridu rdemnu ghur nzomlajii.

金海羊由金子造，
并非有血而无血，
羊羔无血有缘由，
金子自然是珍宝。
螺海羊由白螺造，
并非有血而无血，
羊羔无血有缘由，
白螺美名传天下。
玉海羊由碧玉造，
并非有血而无血，
羊羔无血有缘由，
碧玉具有智慧光。

The sheep in the Gold Sea is made of gold.
The sheep has no blood in its body.
The reason it has no blood
Is because gold is treasured.
The sheep in the Conch Sea is made of white conch.
The sheep has no blood in its body.
The reason it has no blood
Is because white conch is well known.
The sheep in the Jade Sea is made of jade.
The sheep has no blood in its body.
The reason it has no blood
Is because jade is the light of wisdom.

Szernu huni kenniiwa?
Dongnu huni kenniiwa?
Xeurinu huni kenniiwa?

金海福羊谁的羊？
螺海福羊谁的羊？
玉海福羊谁的羊？

To whom does the sheep in the Gold Sea belong?

To whom does the sheep in the Conch Sea belong?
To whom does the sheep in the Jade Sea belong?

Szernu hunidu dahu wai,
Dahu ni shge tingerwai.
Dongnu hunidu dahu wai,
Dahu ni haanjeen purghaanwa.
Xuri hunidu dahu wai,
Dahu ni sangrji shdombawa.

金海福羊有主人，
主人上界自在天。
螺海福羊有主人，
主人不空成就佛。
玉海福羊由主人，
主人宝生如来佛。

The sheep in the Gold Sea has its owner:
The owner is Great Heaven.
The sheep in the Conch Sea has its owner:
The owner is Amoghasiddi.
The sheep in the Jade Sea has its owner:
The owner is Gautama Buddha.

Ghuraan longre ghuraan noor,
Ghuraan noorre ghuraan ula,
Deedu szer noorre szer ula wai,
Dunda dong noorre dong ula wai,
Doodu xuri noorre xuri ula wai,
Ghuraan noor gaglasa guledal wai.
Deedu noorre yaan guledal wai?
Dunda noorre yaan guledal wai?
Noor qireere yaan guledal wai?

三滩中间有三海，
三海里面有三山，
上方金海有金山，
中方螺海有螺山，
下方玉海有玉山，
三海形成三传说。

上方大海有什么？
中方大海有什么？
大海岸边有什么？

There are three seas in three plains,
There are three mountains in the three seas.
Gold Mountain is in the upper Gold Sea,
Conch Mountain is in the middle Conch Sea,
Jade Mountain is in the lower Jade Sea.
There are sayings about how the three seas were formed.
What is said about the upper sea?
What is said about the middle sea?
What is said about the lower sea?

Deedu noorre sawal wai,
Sawaldu yaan yangsaa wai?
Dunda noorre tirge torghu wai,
Tirge torghudu yaan yangsaa wai?
Noor qireedu suuge wai,
Noor suugedu yaan yongsaa wai?

上方大海有水波，
形成水波有何用？
中方海上有绫罗，
有了绫罗有何用？
大海岸边有耳环，
形成耳环有何用？

There are ripples in the upper sea—
Why are the ripples useful?
There are bolts of silk in the middle sea—
Why are the bolts of silk useful?
There are earrings along the seashore—
Why are the earrings useful?

Deedu noorre szu sawal wai,
Sawal sawaljasa xira ndogge,
Noor mongliidu haldan chon szam,
Haldannu chonla anjii xjim?
Dunda noorre tirge torghu wai,

Torghu labxisa ilan ndogge,
Noornu qireedu xuri chon szam,
Xurinu chonla anjii xjim?
Doodu dong noorre suuge wai,
Dongnu joolghasa suugewa,
Noor qireedu dong chon szam,
Dongnu chonla anjii xjim?

上方海上有水波，
水波翻滚呈金色，
金色海边造金船，
制造金船去哪里？
中方玉海有绫罗，
绫罗飘绕呈蓝色，
玉海岸边造蓝船，
制造蓝船去哪里？
下方螺海有耳环，
海螺点缀如耳环，
螺海岸边造白船，
制造白船去哪里？

There are ripples in the upper sea:
The ripples undulate to reflect the golden luster.
A golden ship is built on the seashore:
Where will the golden ship go after being built?
There are bolts of silk in the middle sea:
The bolts of silk are blue.
A jade ship is built on the seashore:
Where will the jade ship go after being built?
There are earrings in the Conch Sea in the lower area:
The earrings are ornamented with conches.
A conch ship is built on the seashore:
Where will the conch ship go after being built?

Deedu noorre sawal wai,
Sawal sawaljasa xira ndogge,
Noor qireedu haldan chon szam,
Ne haldan huninu yerila xjim.
Dunda noorre tirge torghu wai,
Torghu labxisa ilan ndogge,

Noor qireedu xuri chon szam,
Ne xuri huninu yerila xjim.
Doodu noordu suuge wai,
Dongla joolghasa suugewa,
Noor qireedu dong chon szam,
Ne dongnu huninu yerila xjim.

上方海上有水波，
水波翻滚呈金色，
金色海边造金船，
金船去找金海羊。
中方玉海有绫罗，
绫罗飘绕呈蓝色，
玉海岸边造蓝船，
蓝船去找玉海羊。
下方螺海有耳环，
海螺点缀如耳环，
螺海岸边造白船，
白船去找螺海羊。

There are ripples in the upper sea:
The ripples undulate to reflect golden luster.
A golden ship is built on the seashore:
The golden ship will go to look for golden sheep.
There are bolts of silk in the middle sea:
The bolts of silk are blue.
A jade ship is built on the seashore:
The jade ship will go to look for jade sheep.
There are earrings in the lower sea:
The earrings are ornamented with conches.
A conch ship is built on the seashore:
The conch ship will go to look for conch sheep.

Dangmaa simqandu huni gui,
Huninu iredalniinu kileji ughu.
Deedu hunidu suneesi wai,
Muxisaagu suneesinii keleji ughu.
Dunda hunidu suneesi wai,
Muxisaagu suneesinii kileji ughu.
Doodu hunidu suneesi wai,
Muxisaagu suneesinii kileji ughu.

当初世间并无羊，
说说羊的形成史。
上方福羊古有魂，
说出羊的自古魂。
中方福羊古有魂，
说出羊的自古魂。
下方福羊古有魂，
说出羊的自古魂。

In the old times there were no sheep in this world.
Tell us how sheep were produced.
Sheep in the upper area have their own spirit.
Tell us about their spirit.
Sheep in the middle area have their own spirit.
Tell us about their spirit.
Sheep in the lower area have their own spirit.
Tell us about their spirit.

Dangmaa simqandu huni gui,
Huninu iredalniinu kileya.
Deedu hunidu suneesi wai,
Ne ghuisang qiinu suneesiwa.
Dunda hunidu suneesi wai,
Ne dunda dorjinu suneesiwa.
Doodu hunidu suneesi wai,
Ne doodu nqimnu suneesiwa.

当初世间并无羊，
说说羊的形成史。
上方福羊古有魂，
那是西藏佛教魂。
中方福羊古有魂，
那是中方金刚魂。
下方福羊古有魂，
那是下方王法魂。

In the old times there were no sheep in this world.
Tell us how sheep were produced.
Sheep in the upper area have their own spirit:
It is the spirit of Tibetan Buddhism.
Sheep in the middle area have their own spirit:

It is the spirit of Buddha's warrior attendant.
Sheep in the lower area have their own spirit:
It is the spirit of the law of the land.

Huninu iredal taawun wai,
Qisi ni anjiisa iresanna?
Yasi ni anjiisa iresanna?
Maha ni anjiisa iresanna?
Aur ni anjiisa iresanna?
Nghuasi ni anjiisa iresanna?

羊的形成有五种,
羊的血从哪里来?
羊的骨骼哪里来?
羊的肉从哪里来?
羊的气息哪里来?
养的毛从哪里来?

Five things make up sheep.
Where is sheep blood from?
Where are sheep bones from?
Where is sheep meat from?
Where is sheep flavor from?
Where is sheep wool from?

Qisi ni szuresa iresanna,
Szuresa ireenu urosina,
Qisi guise yama gim?
Yasi ni tarresa iresanna,
Tarresa ireenu hadongwa,
Yasi guise yama gim?
Aur ni kiiresa iresanna,
Kiiresa ireenu awuna,
Aurge guise yama gim?
Maha ni xiruusa iresanna,
Xiruusa ireenu joolonwa,
Maha guise yama gim?
Nghuasi ni usisa iresanna,
Usisa ireenu narinna,
Nghuasi guise yama gim?

羊血自那水中来，
来自水中成血流，
羊若无血会怎样？
骨骼自那石头来，
来自石头成坚骨，
羊无骨骼会怎样？
气息自那风中来，
来自风中才成气，
羊无气息会怎样？
羊肉自那土中来，
来自泥土才成肉，
羊若无肉会怎样？
羊毛自那草中来，
来自青草才成毛，
羊若无毛会怎样？

Sheep blood comes from water,
Comes from water and becomes the bloodstream.
What would it be if it had no blood?
The sheep's skeleton comes from stone,
Comes from stone and solidifies.
What would it be if it had no skeleton?
The sheep's flavor comes from the wind,
Comes from wind and becomes air.
What would it be if it had no flavor?
Sheep meat comes from soil,
Comes from soil and becomes meat.
What would it be if it had no meat?
Sheep wool comes from grass,
Comes from grass and becomes wool.
What would it be if it had no wool?

Qisi guise shdaasi qui,
Yasi guise xjau iaalam,
Maha guise oosigu harlam,
Aur guise guji hghur,
Nghuasi guise janjandu wai.

羊若无血心脉散，
羊若无骨胸腔瘪，

羊若无肉肝肺黑,
羊若无气颈椎短,
羊若无毛毛端尖。

It would have no vessels if it had no blood,
It would have no thoracic cavity if it had no skeleton,
Its lungs would be blackened if it had no meat,
Its neck would be shortened if it had no flavor,
It would be naked if it had no wool.

Undur shdongwasa iresan huniwa,
Nendu qisi wai yuu gui?
Jigmezhashgangnu lanhan huniwa,
Nendu yasi wai yuu gui?
Ncamdu saugui gijin huniwa,
Nendu maha wai yuu gui?
Shge tangnu ilan huniwa,
Qi kile aur wai yuu gui?
Wuqang ula szaarnu huniwa,
Qi kile nghuasi wai yuu gui?

高高虚空成的羊,
请问有血没有血?
久迈扎岗懒惰羊,
请问有骨没有骨?
修定空性等持羊,
请问有肉没有肉?
草滩上的蓝色羊,
你说有气没有气?
吾羌杂日山中羊,
你说有毛没有毛?

A sheep from a high vacant space,
Does it have blood or not?
A sheep from Jigmezhashgang,[1]
Does it have a skeleton or not?
A sheep who likes to sit in meditation,
Does it have meat or not?
A sheep from the great plain,

---

1   Unknown place.

Does it have flavor or not?
A sheep from the foot of Wuqang[2] Mountain,
Does it have wool or not?

Undur shdongwasa iresan huniwa,
Qisi waigunu puxii qisi gui,
Qisi gui ghuraan aghaniinu qi kile.
Jigmezhashgangnu lanhan huniwa,
Yasi waigunu puxii yasi gui,
Yasi gui ghuraan aghaniinu qi kile.
Ncamdu saugui gijin huniwa,
Maha waigunu puxii maha gui,
Maha gui ghuraan aghaniinu qi kile.
Shge tangnu ilan huniwa,
Aur waigunu puxii aur gui,
Aur gui ghuraan aghaniinu qi kile.
Wuqang ula szaarnu huniwa,
Nghuasi waigunu puxii nghuasi gui,
Nghuasi gui ghuraan aghaniinu qi kile.

高高虚空成的羊，
并非有血实无血，
说出无血三兄羊。
久迈杂岗懒惰羊，
并非有骨实无骨，
说说无骨三兄羊。
修定空性等持羊，
并非有肉实无肉，
说出无肉三兄羊。
草滩上的蓝色羊，
并非有气实无气，
说说无气三兄羊。
无羌杂日山中羊，
并非有毛实无毛，
说说无毛三兄羊。

The sheep from the high vacant space,
It has no blood.

---

2   Unknown place.

Please tell us who its three brothers are.
The sheep from Jigmezhashgang,
It has no skeleton.
Please tell us who its three brothers are.
The sheep that likes to sit in meditation,
It has no meat.
Please tell us who its three brothers are.
The sheep from the great plain,
It has no flavor.
Please tell us who its three brothers are.
The sheep from the foot of Wuqang Mountain,
It has no wool.
Please tell us who its three brothers are.

Qisi gui ghuraan aghadiu,
Wer qimusi da shdi ghuraan.
Yasi gui ghuraan aghadiu,
Nudu suu da nghuasi nukowa.
Maha gui ghuraan aghadiu,
Wer qimusi da shdi ghuraan.
Aur gui ghuraan aghadiu,
Wer qimusi da shdi ghuraan.
Shdaasi gui ghuraan aghadiu,
Wer qimusi da shdi ghuraan.

无血羊羔三兄弟,
羊角指甲和牙齿。
无骨羊羔三兄弟,
眼窝腋窝汗毛孔。
无肉羊羔三兄弟,
羊角指甲和牙齿。
无气羊羔三兄弟,
羊角指甲和牙齿。
无脉羊羔三兄弟,
羊角指甲和牙齿。

It has no blood, but it has three brothers:
They are horn, nails and teeth.
It has no skeleton, but it has three brothers:
They are eye sockets, armpits, and sweat pores.

It has no meat, but it has three brothers:
They are horn, nails and teeth.
It has no flavor, but it has three brothers:
They are horn, nails and teeth.
It has no pulse, but it has three brothers:
They are horn, nails and teeth.

Shge noornu nudunsa,
Shge huni ghariji irem,
Nireniinu yaan daudana?
Sarhaan noornu nudunsa,
Sarhaan huni ghariji irem,
Nireniinu yaan daudana?
Mulaa noornu nudunsa,
Mulaa huni ghariji irem,
Nireniinu yaan daudana?

从那大海的口岸，
生出来的是大羊，
大羊名字叫什么？
从那中海的口岸，
生出来的是中羊，
中羊名字叫什么？
从那小海的口岸，
生出来的是小羊，
小羊名字叫什么？

From the eye of a big ocean
A big sheep comes out.
What is the big sheep's name?
From the eye of a medium-sized ocean
A medium-sized sheep comes out.
What is the medium-sized sheep's name?
From the eye of a small ocean
A small sheep comes out.
What is the small sheep's name?

Shge hunidu nire wai,
Xira ndogdii qongqan huniwa.
Sarhaan hunidu nire wai,

Ilan ndogdii xuri huniwa.
Mulaa hunidu nire wai,
Qighaan ndogdii dong huniwa.

大羊当然有名字，
金色凤凰点头羊。
中羊当然有名字，
碧玉蓝色出海羊。
小羊当然有名字，
白色海螺亲属羊。

The big sheep has a name:
It is Golden Phoenix Sheep.
The medium-sized sheep has a name:
It is Blue Jade Sheep.
The small sheep has a name:
It is White Conch Sheep.

Xira ndogdii qongqan huniwa,
Bur buye xirange fulaannu gui,
Fulaan waisamba qisi yuu,
Fulaan qigire oosi juu?
Hawar dire ni oosijii?
Ilan ndogdii xuri huniwa,
Bur buye ilange qighaannu gui,
Qighaan waisamba yaannii hong?
Warang rogdu oosijii?
Solghui rogdu oosijii?
Qighaan ndogdii dongnu huniwa,
Bur buye qighaan niu hara wai?
Qighaan haranu waisamba,
Huninu dooro ni oosi juu?
Huninu jaghaadu oosijii?

金色凤凰点头羊，
身黄如金无红斑，
若有是红还是血，
那斑长在耳朵上？
还是长在鼻子上？
碧玉蓝色出海羊，
身蓝如玉无白斑，

若有那是什么点?
那斑长在羊右边?
还是长在羊左边?
白如海螺亲属羊,
有斑是黑还是白?
若有白色或黑色的斑,
那斑长在羊下方?
还是长在羊上方?

The Golden Phoenix Sheep
Has only yellow on its body, but no red.
It might be blood if there are some red spots on its body.
Is there a red spot on its ear?
Or just on its nose?
The Blue Jade Sheep
Has only blue on its body, but no white.
If there was white on its body, what would it be?
Does it grow on the right side of its body?
Or does it grow on the left side of its body?
The White Conch Sheep—
Does it have any black or white on its body?
If there are some white or black spots on its body
Are they on the sheep's lower body?
Or are they on the sheep's upper body?

Haldan madu alagnu wai,
Fulaannu waisamba qisiwa,
Qigirenu oosoji gui,
Hawar dire ni oosijii.
Xuri madu alagnu wai,
Alagnu waisada dong qighaanwa,
Warang rogdu oosiji gui,
Solghui rogdu oosijii.
Dongnu madu alagnu wai,
Alagnu waisada shdi qighaanwa,
Jagha rogdu oosiji gui,
Dooro rogdu oosijii.

身黄如金似有斑,
若有红斑是血斑,

不是长在耳朵上，
而是长在鼻子上。
蓝如碧玉似有斑，
有斑便是白螺斑，
不是长在羊右边，
而是长在羊左边。
白如海螺似有斑，
有斑便是白齿斑，
不是长在羊上方，
而是长在羊下方。

There could be a spot on its golden body.
The spot should be blood if it is red.
It couldn't be on the ears,
But could be on the nose.
There could be a spot on its blue jade body.
The spot should be a white conch spot.
It shouldn't be on the right side of its body
But should be on the left side of its body.
There could be a spot on its white conch body.
It should be a white spot.
It shouldn't be on the sheep's upper body,
It shouldn't be on the sheep's lower body.

Dong hurgha ghuraan aghadiuwa,
Te ghuraanlanu bu kileya,
Saidaar yaujin shge huniwa,
Siri saidaar anjii xjim?
Baidaji yaujin sar huniwa,
Nqaadan boodan anjii xjim?
Qighaan hurgha mulaana,
Qighaan hurgha anjii xjim?

白螺羊羔三兄弟，
把他三个我说说，
蹒跚而走是大羊，
踉踉跄跄去哪里？
摇晃而走是二羊，
东倒西歪去哪里？
白螺羊羔是小羊，
白螺羊羔去哪里？

The conch lamb has three brothers.
I would like to say something about those three.
The first sheep is one that walks lamely:
Where is the first sheep going with such a stumbling walk?
The second sheep walks shakily.
Where is the second sheep going with such an unsteady walk?
The white lamb is the youngest one.
Where is the white lamb going?

Saidaar yaojin shge huniwa,
Siri saidaar uladu xjim.
Baidaji yaujin sar huniwa,
Nqaadan boodandu ula szaardu xjim.
Qighaan mulaa hurghawa,
Qighaan hurgha szu qireedu xjim.

步履蹒跚大羊走,
踉踉跄跄去山岗。
摇摇晃晃二羊走,
东倒西歪去脑山。
小羊即是白螺羊,
白螺羊羔去水边。

The first sheep walks lamely
And is going to the high mountain with its stumbling walk.
The second sheep walks shakily
And is going to the hills with its unsteady walk.
The youngest white lamb
Is going to the riverbank to drink water.

Shge huni saidaar uladu xjim,
Purghaan liu wai yuu bas wai?
Sar huni nqaadaji ula szaardu xjim,
Purghaan liu wai yuu bas wai?
Qighaan hurgha szu qireedu xjim,
Purghaan liu wai yuu bas wai?

大羊蹒跚到山岗,
是神是龙还是虎?
二羊踉跄去脑山,
是神是龙还是虎?

白螺羊羔去水边,
是神是龙还是虎?

The first sheep walks lamely to the high mountain.
Is it a deity, a dragon, or a tiger?
The second sheep walks shakily to the foot of a hill.
Is it a deity, a dragon, or a tiger?
The white lamb is going to the river.
Is it a deity, a dragon, or a tiger?

Shge huni saidaar uladu xjim,
Shge tingere purghaannu huni wai.
Sar huni nqaadaji ula szaardu xjim,
Shdongwa liu rjawunu huni wai.
Qighaan hurgha szu qireedu xjim,
Naiman liu rjawunu huni wai.

大羊蹒跚上山岗,
是那自在天神羊。
二羊踉跄去脑山,
是那空性龙王羊。
白螺小羊去水边,
是那八大龙王羊。

The first sheep walks lamely to the high mountain
Because it is Heaven's sheep.
The second sheep walks shakily to the foot of a hill
Because it is the Sunyata Dragon King's sheep.
The white lamb goes to the river
Because it is the sheep of the eight Dragon Kings.

Bagtaa mpeelesa iredal wai,
Tenu jalghaadal yaahanwa?
Huni qaglasa iredal wai,
Huninu jalghaadal yaahanwa?
Mughui suuraasa iredal wai,
Mughuinu jalghaadal yaahanwa?

圣人发展有世系,
圣人传承啥来历?
绵羊形成有世系,

绵羊血统啥来历?
毒蛇匍匐有世系,
毒蛇爬行啥来历?

There is a lineage for a sage's development.
Who transmits the sage's lineage?
There is a lineage for a sheep's formation.
Who transmits the sheep's lineage?
There is a lineage for slithering snakes.
Who transmits the snake's lineage?

Bagtaa mpeelesa iredal wai,
Fulaan jaghasi jalghaanii.
Huni qaglasa iredal wai,
Xira jaghasi jalghaanii.
Mughui suuraasa iredal wai,
Muroon szula jalgaanii.

圣人发展有世系,
红面巨鲜所传承。
绵羊形成有世系,
海底金鱼所传承。
毒蛇匍匐有世系,
大江混水所传承。

There is a lineage for a sage's development:
Red fish transmit it.
There is a lineage for a sheep's formation:
Golden fish transmit it.
There is a lineage for slithering snakes:
River water transmits it.

Huni dong noorsa gharisa,
Dong noor amandu purge ulon,
Naiman shge liu jaghaduna,
Naiman sar liu xjiinduna,
Naiman mulaa liu doorona,
Yama giji noor amandu irem?

绵羊想从螺海出,
螺海口岸困难多,

八大龙王护上面,
八中龙王护中间,
八小龙王护下面,
怎么到达螺海口?

As the sheep emerges from the Conch Sea
Many challenges await on the shore of the Conch Sea:
Eight big dragons guard the upper shore,
Eight medium-sized dragons guard the middle shore,
Eight small dragons guard the lower shore.
How will the sheep come out of the Conch Sea?

Naiman shge liu jaghaduna,
Naiman sar liu xjiinduna,
Naiman mulaa liu doorana,
Noor snambaadu halong qireela,
Gharsa ni sain sman awaanu,
Laarzinu noorre sajisa,
Liu rjawu zambuunaa gharghaja,
Naiman shge liu tudaawaaxjia,
Naiman sar liu tudaawaaxjia,
Naiman mula liu tudaawaaxjia,
Noor ghudiligu qagdu ni,
Qighaan hurgha qaglaadija.

八大龙王护上面,
八中龙王护中间,
八小龙王护下面,
面对海医装笑脸,
从他手中买良药,
麝香投入大海中,
为此龙君发神威,
八大龙王弃而逃,
八中龙王弃而逃,
八小龙王弃而逃,
大海上下摇摆时,
白色螺羊出生了。

Eight big dragons guard the upper shore,
Eight medium-sized dragons guard the middle shore,
Eight small dragons guard the lower shore.

Greet the sea doctor with a smiling face:
Medicine was bought from his hands,
The medicinal musk was sprinkled into the sea,
So that the Dragon King was angered and demonstrated his courage and
    might.
Then eight big dragons escaped,
Eight medium-sized dragons escaped,
Eight small dragons escaped.
As the sea was shaking,
A small white lamb was formed.

Huni dong noorsa gharisa,
Njeenaadu ghuraan purge wai,
Ghuraan purgeniinu qi kile.
Yosgordu szin timur ula wai,
Szin timur ulanu kileji ughu.
Xjiindu szin ghal ula wai,
Szin ghal ulanu kileji ughu.
Turo ni haldan tulgha wai,
Haldan tulghanu kileji ughu.

绵羊想从螺海出，
身有三难不让出，
请你说出哪三难。
外环抱有九铁山，
请你说说九铁山。
中环抱有九火山，
说说中间九火山。
内有金顶耸入天，
说说金顶矗立法。

If the sheep emerges from the Conch Sea
There will be three obstacles.
Tell us what the three obstacles are.
Outside there are nine iron mountains.
Tell us about them in detail.
In the middle there are nine mountains of fire.
Tell us about them in detail.
Inside there are nine golden pillars.
Tell us about them in detail.

Ghadagu timur ula szin puxii,
Noorregu szin timur ulawa.
Xjiindugu ghal ula szin puxii,
Ghadaxi ghal ulala hgorlaja.
Haldannu tulghuda ghudlwa,
Liu furongnu ger tolghuiwa.

不是外部九铁山，
而是海中九铁山。
不是中间九火山，
而是火山在环抱。
不是金顶独矗立，
而是龙宫金屋顶。

It is not the nine iron mountains on the outside
But the nine iron mountains of the sea.
It is not the nine mountains of fire in the middle
But it is encircled by mountains of fire.
It is not the golden pillars
But it is the pillars of the Dragon King's palace.

Huni dong noorsa gharija,
Tolghuira ramda wai yuu gui?
Hawarre sinaaxja wai yuu gui?
Huinonu taujin wai yuu gui?

羊从螺海口岸出，
羊头有无牵羊绳？
鼻中有无牵鼻绳？
后面有无赶羊人？

As the sheep emerges from the Conch Sea,
Is there a vein on its head?
Is there a ring in its nose?
Is there a shepherd?

Kudilijin ramda jubda wai,
Shamnu nudu ni ramdawa,
Shge jaghasi sinaaxjawa,
Noor huninu taujinwa,
Huni isge noor nudundu kurija.

牵羊笼头当然有,
水獭眼睛牵鼻绳,
巨鲜便是牵头绳,
大海就是赶羊者,
绵羊才到螺海口。

There is a vein on its head:
It is made from otter's eyes.
A big fish is its vein,
The sea is its shepherd,
The sheep has arrived at the eye of the sea.

Shge noorsa shge huni gharim,
Yaanla sarlajin shdur guji?
Sar noorsa sar huni gharim,
Yaanla sarlajin mailagu log?
Mulaa noorsa hurgha gharim,
Yaanla sarlajin deeren ghar kol?

大海口岸出大羊,
脖颈长的像什么?
中海口岸出中羊,
它的叫声像什么?
小海口岸出小羊,
四肢细小像什么?

The big sheep emerges from a big sea.
What does its neck look like?
The medium-sized sheep emerges from a medium-sized sea.
What is its baa like?
The lamb emerges from a small sea.
What do its four limbs look like?

Shge noorsa shge huni gharim,
Guji shdurdu dundog wai,
Shdur gujidu alag bughuwa,
Alag bughu huninu yaahanwa?
Sar noorsa sar huni gharim,
Hger ni shgedu dundog wai,
Mailajin hger ni xira huniwa,

Xira huni huninu yaahanwa?
Mulaa noorsa mulaa huni gharim,
Narin ghar koldu dundog wai,
Narin ghar kol ni huniwa,
Kugo huni huninu yaahanwa?

大海口岸出大羊,
脖颈长的有原因,
脖颈长像梅花鹿,
梅花鹿是羊的啥?
中海口岸出中羊,
失口叫唤有原因,
它的叫声像黄羊,
那黄羊是羊的啥?
小海口岸出小羊,
四肢细小有原因,
四肢细小像青羊,
蹩脚羊是羊的啥?

The big sheep emerges from a big sea.
There is a reason why its neck is long:
Its neck is similar to that of a spotted deer.
What connection is there between a big sheep and a spotted deer?
The medium-sized sheep emerges from a medium-sized sea,
There is reason why its baa is loud:
Its baa is similar to that of a Mongolian gazelle.
What connection is there between a medium-sized sheep and a Mongolian
    gazelle?
The lamb emerges from a small sea.
There is a reason why its four limbs are thin:
Its four limbs are similar to those of a blue sheep.
What connection is there between a small sheep and a blue sheep?

Shge noorsa shge huni gharim,
Shdur guji ni alg bughuwa,
Alag bughu huninu aabana.
Sar noorsa sar huni gharim,
Mailagu hger ni xira huniwa,
Xira huni huninu aamana.
Mulaa noorsa mulaa huni gharim,

Narin ghar kol ni kugo huniwa,
Kugo huni huninu aghana.

大海口岸出大羊,
脖颈长像梅花鹿,
梅花鹿是羊父辈。
中海口岸出中羊,
失口叫声像黄羊,
黄羊是那羊母亲。
小海口岸出小羊,
四肢细小像青羊,
蹩脚羊是羊兄长。

The big sheep emerges from a big sea,
Its neck is similar to that of a spotted deer.
The spotted deer is the sheep's grandfather's ancestor.
The medium-sized sheep emerges from a medium-sized sea,
Its baa is similar to that of a Mongolian gazelle.
The Mongolian gazelle is the sheep's mother's ancestor.
The lamb emerges from a small sea,
Its four limbs are similar to those of a blue sheep.
The blue sheep is the sheep's brother.

Shge noorsa shge huni gharim,
Huni gharisa anjii xjim?
Sar noorsa sar huni gharim,
Huni gharisa anjii xjim?
Mulaa noorsa mulaa huni gharim,
Huni gharisa anjii xjim?

大海口岸出大羊,
大羊出去到哪里?
中海口岸出中羊,
中羊出去到哪里?
小海口岸出小羊,
小羊出去到哪里?

The big sheep emerges from a big sea.
Where will it go when it emerges from the sea?
The medium-sized sheep emerges from a medium-sized sea.
Where will it go when it emerges from the sea?
The lamb emerges from a small sea.
Where will it go when it emerges from the sea?

Shge noorsa shge huni gharim,
Nudunsa gharaa jaghadu yaum,
Jaghagu ula udenu ghuraan udaa neem,
Yama gaanu ghuraan udaa neem?
Sar noorsa sar huni gharim,
Nudunsa gharaa dundaji yaum,
Dunda dong udenu ghuraan udaa neem,
Yama gaanu ghuraan udaa neem?
Mulaa noorsa mulaa huni gharim,
Nudunsa gharaa dooroji yaum,
Dooro noor udenu ghuraan udaa neem,
Yama gaanu ghuraan udaa neem?

大海口岸出大羊,
出了口岸往上走,
上面山门开三次,
门开三次为什么?
中海口岸出中羊,
出了口岸往中走,
中间螺门开三次,
门开三次为什么?
小海口岸出小羊,
出了口岸往下走,
下方海门开三次,
门开三次为什么?

The big sheep emerges from a big sea.
It walks up after coming out of the big sea.
A high monastery gate is opened thrice.
Why is the gate opened thrice?
The medium-sized sheep emerges from a medium-sized sea.
It walks in the middle after coming out of the medium-sized sea.
A middle conch gate is opened thrice.
Why is the gate opened thrice?
The lamb emerges from a small sea.
It walks down after coming out of the small sea.
A lower sea gate is opened thrice.
Why is the gate opened thrice?

Shge noorsa shge huni gharim,

Nudunsa gharaa jaghadu yaum,
Jaghagu ula udenu ghuraan udaa neem,
Ghuraan udaa neesa dundog wai,
Huni ncoglagu ghajar wai.
Sar noorsa sar huni gharim,
Nudunsa gharisa dundaji yaum,
Dundagu dong udenu ghuraan udaa neem,
Ghuraan udaa neesa dundog wai,
Huni ncoglagu ghajar wai.
Mulaa noorsa mulaa huni gharim,
Gharaa ireenu dooroji yaum,
Doorogu noor udenu ghuraan udaa neem,
Ghuraan udaa neesa dundog wai,
Huni ncoglagu ghajar wai.

大海口岸出大羊,
出了口岸往上走,
上方山门开三次,
三次开门有原因,
山上是那聚羊处。
中海口岸出中羊,
出了口岸往中走,
中方螺门开三次,
三次开门有原因,
螺海是那聚羊处。
小海口岸出小羊,
出了口岸往下走,
下方海门开三次,
三次开门有原因,
小海是那聚羊处。

The big sheep emerges from a big sea.
It walks up after coming out of the big sea.
A high monastery gate is opened thrice.
There is a reason why it is opened thrice:
Because it is a place for sheep to gather.
The medium-sized sheep emerges from a medium-sized sea.
It walks in the middle after coming out of the medium-sized sea.
A middle conch gate is opened thrice.
There is a reason why it is opened thrice:
Because it is a place for sheep to gather.

The lamb emerges from a small sea.
It walks down after coming out of the small sea.
A lower sea gate is opened thrice.
There is a reason why it is opened thrice:
Because it is a place for sheep to gather.

Huni qaglagu log ghuraan wai,
Ghuraan sambanu kileji ughu:
Turong yama giji qaglaja?
Ghuidar yama giji qaglaja?
Huino yama giji qaglaja?

羊的形成有三种,
说说三种形成法:
第一次它咋生成?
第二次它咋生成?
第三次它咋生成?

There are three ways in which sheep are formed.
The three are:
First, how are they formed?
Secondly, how are they formed?
Third, how are they formed?

Qaglagu log ghuraan wai,
Ghuraan samba ni ne shdaar wai:
Qighaan hunidu qaglaadim,
Pujag madu qaglaadim,
Shgebxi huri tigii qaglaadim.

羊的形成有三种,
三种形成是这样:
一次所成白绵羊,
二次所成如豆子,
三次所成如拇指。

There are three ways in which sheep are formed.
The three are:
They are formed as white sheep,
They are formed in the shape of a bean,
They are formed in the shape of a thumb.

Muxi hghu guigu xjiilog wai,
Tenu shghai yasi ni yama tigiinge?
Tenu xjiin yasi ni yama tigiinge?
Tenu suul yasi ni yama tigiinge?

没有内脏先有形,
它的腿骨什么样?
它的中骨什么样?
它的尾骨什么样?

In the beginning it took shape without innards.
What do its leg bones look like?
What do its middle bones[3] look like?
What do its tail bones look like?

Muxi shghai yasinu kileya,
Rzannaa nembesan ulama tigiinge,
Shghai yasi ni anjii oosija?
Ghuidar xjiin yasinu kileya,
Singe moorogu tigiinge,
Xjiin yasi anjii oosija?
Huino suul yasinu kileya,
Tingerdu nesijin rgo tigiinge,
Suul yasi anjii oosija?

先说羊的大腿骨,
如同上师披大氅,
腿骨长在啥地方?
再说绵羊那中骨,
如同雄狮在怒吼,
中骨长在啥地方?
又说绵羊尾椎骨,
如同老鹰天上飞,
尾骨长在啥地方?

First, let's discuss the sheep's leg bones,
Like a high-ranking monk wearing his robe,
Where do the leg bones grow?
Secondly, let's discuss the sheep's middle bones,

---

3   It is unclear what 'middle bones' refers to.

Like a lion's roar,
Where do the middle bones grow?
Next, let's discuss the sheep's tail bones,
Like an eagle flying in the sky,
Where do the sheep's tail bones grow?

Turong shghai yasinu kileya,
Rzannaa nembesan ulamawa,
Huninu ghoor rogdu oosija,
Yama gaa tiree oosija?
Ghuidar xjiin yasinu kileya,
Moorojin singe tigiinge,
Huninu ghoor rogdu oosija,
Yama gaa tiree oosija?
Huino suul yasinu kileya,
Tingerdu nesijin rgo madu,
Huninu nuri huino oosija,
Yama gaa tiree oosija?

先说羊的大腿骨，
如同上师披大氅，
生在绵羊左右边，
生在那里为什么？
再说绵羊那中骨，
如同雄狮在怒吼，
生在绵羊左右边，
生在那里为什么？
又说绵羊尾椎骨，
如同老鹰天上飞，
生在绵羊背后边，
生在那里为什么？

First, let's discuss the sheep's leg bones,
Like a high-ranking monk wearing his robe.
They grow on the right and left sides of the sheep.
Why do the leg bones grow there?
Secondly, let's discuss the sheep's middle bones,
Like a lion's roar.
They grow on the right and left sides of the sheep.
Why do the middle bones grow there?

Next, let's discuss the sheep's tail bones,
Like an eagle flying in the sky.
They grow on the sheep's back,
Why do the tail bones grow there?

Turong shghai yasinu kileya,
Rzannaa nembesan ulamawa,
Huninu ghoor rogdu oosijii,
Tireexi oosisa dundogge wai,
Bur buyenu mudegundu oosijii.
Ghuidar xjiin yasinu kileya,
Moorojin singe maduwa,
Huninu ghoor rogdu oosijii,
Tireexi oosisa dundogge wai,
Doorogu buyenu taniguna.
Huino suul yasinu kileya,
Tingerdu nesijin rgo maduwa,
Huninu nuri huino oosijii,
Tireexi oosisa dundogge wai,
Deeren ghar kolnu taniguna.

先说羊的大腿骨,
如同上师披大氅,
生在绵羊左右边,
生在左右有原因,
只为识别羊全身。
再说绵羊那中骨,
如同雄狮在怒吼,
生在绵羊左右边,
生在左右有原因,
只为识别羊下身。
又说绵羊尾椎骨,
如同老鹰天上飞,
长在绵羊背后面,
长在背后有原因,
只为识别羊四肢。

First, let's discuss the sheep's leg bones,
Like a high-ranking monk wearing his robe.
They grow on the right and left sides of the sheep.

There is a reason why they grow on the right and left sides of the sheep:
It is in order to identify the whole sheep's body.
Secondly, let's discuss the sheep's middle bones,
Like a lion's roar.
They grow on the right and left sides of the sheep.
There is a reason why they grow on the right and left sides of the sheep:
It is in order to identify the lower part of the sheep's body.
Next, we discuss the sheep's tail bones,
Like an eagle flying in the sky.
They grow on the back of the sheep.
There is a reason why they grow on the sheep's back:
It is in order to identify the sheep's limbs.

Halgha yasi yama tigiinge?
Guji yasi yama tigiige?
Qurghu yasi yama tigiinge?

肩胛生成什么样?
颈骨生成什么样?
锁骨生成什么样?

What do the sheep's scapulae look like?
What do the sheep's cervical vertebrae look like?
What do the sheep's collarbones look like?

Halgha yasi warma tarwa,
Huninu anji ni oosijii?
Guji yasi urgusan bulaiwa,
Huninu anjii ni oosijii?
Qurghu yasi huyii malghawa,
Huninu anjii ni oosijii?

肩胛生成如秤砣,
长在绵羊啥地方?
颈骨生成如背娃,
长在绵羊啥地方?
锁骨生成如头盔,
长在绵羊啥地方?

The sheep's scapulae look heavy.
Where do scapulae grow on the sheep's body?

The sheep's cervical vertebrae look like a baby being carried on someone's
   back.
Where do cervical vertebrae grow on the sheep's body?
The sheep's collarbones look like helmets.
Where do collarbones grow on a sheep's body?

Halgha yasi warma tar tigii,
Solghui warangdu oosijii,
Yama gaa tireexi oosijii?
Guji yasi urgusan bulaiwa,
Solghui warangdu oosijii,
Yama gaa tireexi oosijii?
Qurghu yasi huyii malghawa,
Solghui warangdu oosijii,
Yama gaa tireexi oosijii?

胛骨生成如秤砣,
长在绵羊左右边,
长在那里为什么?
颈骨生成如背娃,
长在绵羊左右边,
长在那里为什么?
锁骨生成如头盔,
长在绵羊左右边,
长在那里为什么?

The sheep's scapulae look heavy.
They grow on the left and right sides of the sheep.
Why do they grow there?
The sheep's cervical vertebrae grow like a baby being carried on someone's
   back.
They grow on the left and right sides of the sheep.
Why do they grow there?
The sheep's collarbones grow like helmets.
They grow on the left and right sides of the sheep.
Why do they grow there?

Halgha yasi warma tar tigii,
Solghui warangdu oosija,
Tireexi oosisa dundog wai,

Jagha buyenu taniguna.
Guji yasi urgusan bulai tigii,
Solghui warangdu oosijii,
Ghoor rogdu oosisa dundog wai,
Muxi huinonu taniguna.
Qurghu yasi huyii malghawa,
Solghui warangdu oosija,
Ghoor rogdu oosisa dundog wai,
Ghar da kolnu taniguna.

肩胛生成如秤砣，
长在绵羊左右边，
长在左右有原因，
只为识别羊上身。
颈骨生成如背娃，
长在绵羊左右边，
长在左右有原因，
只为识别羊前后。
锁骨生成如头盔，
长在绵羊左右边，
长在左右有原因，
只为识别前后腿。

The sheep's scapulae look heavy.
They grow on the left and right sides of the sheep.
There is a reason why they grow there:
It is in order to identify the sheep's upper body.
The sheep's cervical vertebrae grow like a baby being carried on someone's
    back.
They grow on the left and right sides of the sheep.
There is a reason why they grow there:
It is in order to identify the sheep's front and back.
The sheep's collarbones grow like helmets.
They grow on the left and right sides of the sheep.
There is a reason why they grow there:
It is in order to recognize the sheep's legs.

Guji oosisan ni yamarwa?
Hoolo oosisan ni yamarwa?
Shdi oosisan ni yamarwa?

颈部生成什么样?
喉咙生成什么样?
牙根生成什么样?

How does the sheep's neck grow?
How does the sheep's throat grow?
How do the sheep's teeth grow?

Guji qoorden madu oosija,
Hoolo dong rimu madu oosija,
Shdi maha xil madu oosija.

颈部生成如金塔,
喉咙生成如螺阶,
牙根生成如肉路。

The sheep's neck grows like a pagoda,
The sheep's throat grows like the whorls of a conch shell,
The sheep's teeth grow like the lip of a conch shell.

Ghar kol oosisan ni yamarwa?
Hghu oosisan ni yamarwa?
Keele oosisan ni yamarwa?

四肢生成什么样?
上腔生成什么样?
下腔生成什么样?

How do its four limbs grow?
How does its thoracic cavity grow?
How does its abdominal cavity grow?

Ghar kol tulgha madu oosija,
Hghuma furong madu oosija,
Keele ndughong madu oosija.

四肢生成如木柱,
上腔生成如龙宫,
下腔生成如龙殿。

The sheep's four limbs grow like columns,
The sheep's thoracic cavity grows like a palace,
The sheep's abdominal cavity grows like a magnificent palace.

Nuri oosisan ni yamarwa?
Kugo oosisanni yamarw?
Suul oosisan ni yamarwa?

脊背生成什么样?
乳房生成什么样?
尾巴生成什么样?

How does the sheep's back grow?
How do the sheep's teats grow?
How does the sheep's tail grow?

Nuri kurgo madu oosija,
Kugo tulgha tar madu oosija,
Suul shdaasi madu oosija.

脊背生成如桥梁,
乳房生成如柱石,
尾巴生成似情线。

The sheep's back grows like a bridge,
The sheep's teats grow like a foundation stone,
The sheep's tail grows like a thread.

Tolghui oosisan ni yamarwa?
Wer oosisan ni yamarwa?
Nudu oosisan ni yamarwa?

羊头生成什么样?
羊角生成什么样?
羊眼生成什么样?

How does the sheep's head grow?
How do the sheep's horns grow?
How do the sheep's eyes grow?

Tolghui omba madu oosija,
Turogu szudu ni rdem nzomlaja,
Lagba szula ni nige wai.
Wer sulongghu madu oosija,
Wernii turosa niruu gharina,

Wer qisi turogu niruunii.
Nudu foodi madu oosija,
Nudu turo gergeljana,
Gireel madu qugurdena.

羊头生成如宝瓶，
瓶中之水有智慧，
大脑便是瓶中水。
羊角生成如彩虹，
羊角之中生宝藏，
角茸便是角中宝。
羊眼生成如明星，
明眼之中见光明，
光明闪烁如花朵。

The sheep's head grows like a treasure vase—
Wisdom is the water that fills the vase,
The brain is the water inside the vase.
The sheep's horns grow like a rainbow—
There are treasures inside the horns,
Antlers are the treasures in the horns.
The sheep's eyes grow like bright stars—
There is a bright light in the eyes,
The brightness flickers like a flower.

Qigi oosisan ni yamarwa?
Hawar oosisan ni yamarwa?
Huxi oosisan ni yamarwa?

羊耳生成什么样？
羊鼻生成什么样？
羊嘴生成什么样？

How do the sheep's ears grow?
How does the sheep's nose grow?
How does the sheep's mouth grow?

Qigi tawag madu oosija,
Qigidu yongsaa xjirna wai,
Yongsaanii nige kileji ughu.
Hawar buurag madu oosija,

Hawardu yongsaa xjirna wai,
Yongsaanii nige kileji ughu.
Huxi dong ama madu oosija,
Huxidu yongsaa xjirna wai,
Yongsaanii nige kileji ughu.

羊耳生成如金碟,
羊耳自然其功能,
耳之功能说说看。
羊鼻生成如胫号,
羊鼻自然其功能,
鼻之功能说说看。
羊嘴生成如螺门,
羊嘴自然其功能,
嘴之功能说说看。

The sheep's ears grow like a round wooden tray.
The ears have their own function—
Please tell us the function.
The sheep's nose grows like a thigh-bone trumpet.
The nose has its own function—
Please tell us the function.
The sheep's mouth grows like a conch gate.
The mouth has its own function—
Please tell us the function.

Qiginu yongsaa ne shdaarwa,
Hgernu sunusigu yongsaawa.
Hawarnu yongsaa ne shdaarwa,
Funurnu funisigu yongsaawa.
Huxinu yongsaa ne shdaarwa,
Usi idegu yongsaawa.

耳之功能是这样,
闻听声音耳之功。
鼻之功能是这样,
嗅闻气味鼻之功。
嘴之功能是这样,
揽吃青草嘴之功。

The function of the sheep's ears,
Is to listen to sound.

The function of the sheep's nose,
Is to smell odours.
The function of the sheep's mouth,
Is to eat grass.

Shdi yama tigiinge oosija?
Kile yama tigiinge oosija?
Ghus kile yama tigiinge oosija?

牙齿生成什么样？
舌头生成什么样？
小舌生成什么样？

How do the sheep's teeth grow?
How does the sheep's tongue grow?
How does the sheep's uvula grow?

Shdi ncowa madu oosija,
Shdidu yongsaa xjirna wai,
Shdinu yongsaanii kileji ughu.
Kile bos madu oosija,
Kiledu yongsaa xjirna wai,
Kilenu yongsaanii kileji ughu.
Ghus kile sasa madu oosija,
Ghus kiledu yongsaa xjirna wai,
Ghus kilenu yongsaanii kileji ughu.

牙齿生成似部落，
牙齿具有其功能，
牙齿之功说说看。
舌头生成似卧虎，
舌头具有其功能，
舌头之功说说看。
小舌就像小泥佛，
小舌生成有功能，
小舌之功说说看。

The sheep's teeth grow like a tribe.
Teeth have their own function—
Please tell us the function.
The sheep's tongue grows like a tiger.

The tongue has its own function—
Please tell us the function.
The sheep's uvula grows like a small clay Buddha.
The uvula has its own function—
Please tell us the function.

Shdidu yongsaa xjirna wai,
Usi ghajasa te yonglam.
Kiledu yongsaa xjirna wai,
Mailaji hailasa te yonglam.
Ghus kiledu yongsaa shge wai,
Ideji qalgisa te yonglam.

牙齿具有其功能,
啃嚼青草牙之功。
舌头具有其功能,
咩咩喊叫舌之功。
小舌生成有功能,
吞咽草料小舌功。

Teeth have their own function:
It is to chew grass.
The tongue has its own function:
It is to bleat sounds.
The uvula has its own function:
It is to swallow water and food.

Jirge yama tigiinge oosija?
Booro yama tigiinge oosija?
Siiraa yama tigiinge oosija?

心脏生成什么样?
肾脏生成什么样?
脂膜生成什么样?

How does the sheep's heart grow?
How do the sheep's kidneys grow?
How does the sheep's adipose tissue grow?

Jirge purghaan madu oosija,

Purghaan yama giji ncam sauja.
Booro lumbu madu oosija,
Lumbu yama giji suuderlana.
Siiraa tirge madu oosija,
Tirge yama giji hanhulana.

羊心生成如神佛，
说说神佛入定法。
羊肾生成像大臣，
说说二臣护持法。
脂膜生成如白绸，
说说白绸护卫法。

The sheep's heart grows like a Buddha.
Tell us how the Buddha makes law.
The sheep's kidneys grow like ministers.
Tell us how ministers defend and sustain the law.
The sheep's adipose tissue grows like silk.
Tell us how the silk gives protection.

Purghaan chirenaa tusdu sauja,
Lii ghudilaanu rdem muulam,
Ghoor lumbu hanhulanii,
Booro lii ghudilijin lumbuwa,
Siiraa simjongdu gidesidu ulim,
Qighaan goyilla nigewa.

神佛端坐宝座中，
心是不动悟道佛，
左右二臣来护持，
肾是不动二大臣，
脂膜小心护肠子，
犹如扯着白帘子。

Buddha sits steadly on his seat,
Dwelling on Buddhist scripture.
He is guarded by two ministers:
The kidneys are the unmoving ministers.
Adipose tissue protects the gut,
Just like a white curtain.

Oosigu yama tigiinge oosija?
Halge yama tigiinge oosija?
Diliu yama tigiinge oosija?

肺子生成什么样?
肝子生成什么样?
脾脏生成什么样?

How do the sheep's lungs grow?
How does the sheep's liver grow?
How does the sheep's spleen grow?

Oosigu langwuqeenu hurina,
Halge langwuqeenu shghaina,
Diliu langwuqeenu kilena.

羊肺生成如象指,
羊肝生成如象腿,
脾脏生成如象舌。

The sheep's lungs grow like toes on an elephant's foot,
The sheep's liver grows like an elephant's leg,
The sheep's spleen grows like an elephant's tongue.

Gujee yama tigiinge oosija?
Mulaa gujee yama tigiinge oosija?
Gidesi yama tigiinge oosija?

羊胃生成什么样?
小胃生成什么样?
肠子生成什么样?

How does the sheep's stomach grow?
How does the sheep's small stomach[4] grow?
How do a sheep's intestines grow?

Gujee langqan madu oosija,
Mula gujee langqong madu oosija,
Gidesi moglurge oosija.

---

4   It is unclear what the 'small stomach' refers to.

羊胃生成像大象,
小胃生成像小象,
肠子生成圆形状。

The sheep's stomach grows like an elephant,
The sheep's small stomach grows like a baby elephant,
The sheep's intestines grow like a cylinder.

Suulzi yama tigiinge oosija?
Dabsag yama tigiinge oosija?
Foogu yama tigiinge oosija?

胆囊生成什么样?
膀胱生成什么样?
胃脂生成什么样?

How does the sheep's gallbladder grow?
How does the sheep's bladder grow?
How does the sheep's fat grow?

Suulzi szer noor madu wai,
Dabsag szu puririi adu wai,
Foogu qighaan turghu madu wai.

胆囊生成如金湖,
膀胱生成似水轮,
胃脂生成像白绫。

The sheep's gallbladder grows like a golden lake,
The sheep's bladder grows like a waterwheel,
The sheep's fat grows like white silk.

Qighaan mamunu kilesa,
Ghada taawun ndogdii nghuasi wai,
Xjiindu taawun samba yasi wai,
Turo taawun samba maha wai,
Nige nige nirelaji ughu.

说起白色福母羊,
外面长有五色毛,
中间长有五种骨,

里面长有五种肉,
请你一一取个名。

The white ewe
Has five kinds of coloured wool on her outside,
Has five kinds of bone in the middle of her body,
Has five kinds of flesh inside her body.
Tell us their specific names.

Ghada taawun ndogdii nghuasi wai,
Qighaan hara da alag,
Nughoon kugo ne taawun,
Taawun ndogdii nghuasi wai.
Dunda taawun ndogdii yasi wai,
Huxi niur da tolghuida,
Hawar wernu yasi wai,
Ne taawun samba yasi wai.
Maha qisi taawun ni,
Jirge halge da oosgu,
Foogudu taawun sanadalwa,
Ne taawun samba maha wai.

外有羊毛五种色,
白色黑色和花色,
青色紫色共五种,
这就是那五色毛。
中有骨骼五种色,
嘴骨脸骨和头骨,
鼻骨角骨共五种,
这就是那五色骨。
内有血肉五种色,
心脏肝脏和肺脏,
脂肪自性共五种,
这就是那五色肉。

The sheep has five kinds of coloured wool on her outside:
White, black and multicolor,
Green and gray
Are the five colors of the wool.
The sheep has five kinds of bone in the middle of her body:
Jawbone, cheekbone and skull,
Nose bone and horn bone

Are the five kinds of bone.
The sheep has five kinds of flesh inside her body:
Heart, liver, two lungs
And fat
Are the five kinds of flesh.

Qighaan huninu kilesa,
Ghada harangghu ghuraan nuko wai,
Turo qisi gui ghuraan qighaan wai,
Qi nige nige kileji ughu.

说起白色福羊来,
外有无光暗三窟,
内有无血脂三白,
请你一一说出来。

The white ewe
Has three dark holes on the outside of her body,
Has three things without blood inside her body.
Please tell us about them one by one.

Nudu hawar suu nuko,
Ghur gui harangghu nukowa,
Xjau keele suuji fooguwa,
Qisi gui ghuraan qighaanwa.

眼窝鼻孔胳肢窝,
便是无光暗三窟,
胸脂腹脂和跨脂,
是那无血脂三白。

Eye sockets, nostrils, and armpits
Are the three dark holes.
Chest fat, abdominal fat, and hip fat
Are the three white things.

Huni tolghuire naiman zhaxii,
Naiman zhaxiinu kileji ughu?

羊头具备八吉祥,
说说各是那八个?

There are eight auspicious things in the sheep's head:
What are the eight auspicious things?

Ghoor wer sulongghu tigiinge,
Ghoor nudu qii nkorlo tigiinge,
Ghoor qigi mengu jaghasi tigiinge,
Ghoor hawar warang dong tigiinge,
Naiman zhaxii nzomlajii.

两角如同天上虹,
双目如同两法论,
两耳如同两金鱼,
两鼻如同右旋螺,
八种吉祥样样全。

Two horns like rainbows,
Two eyes like Dharma wheels,
Two ears like golden fish,
Two nostrils like right-spiralling conches
Are the eight auspicious things.

Tolghuire doloonla sarlanii,
Sarlajin doloonnu kileji ughu?

头有七处很相像,
说说分别哪七种?

Seven similar things are on its head.
What are they?

Ghoor roggu nudu sarlana,
Ghoor roggu qigi sarlana,
Ghoor hawar nuko sarlana,
Huxi sarlajin doloondarwa,
Doloon sarlajin kuriwa.

两眼两处最相像,
两耳两处最相像,
鼻孔两处最相像,
嘴唇相像第七处,
七处相像都齐全。

Two eyes are similar to each other,
Two ears are similar to each other,
Two nostrils are similar to each other,
The mouth and lips are similar.
These are the seven similar things.

Tolghuire naiman alag wer,
Ali naimanwa qi kile?

头有八只斑驳角,
说说各是哪八只?

Eight mottled horns—
What are they?

Jaghaduji ghoor wer wai,
Ghoor rogduji ghoor wer wai,
Doorondaaji ghoor wer wai,
Suulnu rogdu ghoor wer wai.

向上生有两只角,
左右生有两只角,
向下生有两只角,
尾部生有两只角。

Two horns are atop the sheep's body,
Two horns are on the two sides of the sheep's body,
Two horns are on the sheep's lower body,
Two horns are near the sheep's tail.

Tolghuire hujin imag wai,
Imagsgenu qi kile.
Tolghuire wer haran szin wai,
Haran szin wernu qi kile.
Tolghuire sanaa haran naiman wai,
Haran naiman sanaanu qi kile.

头上部落三十个,
说说部落有哪些。
头上有角十九只,
说说各是哪些角。

头上有情十八个，
说说有情是哪些。

Thirty tribes are on the sheep's head.
Tell us what they are.
Nineteen horns are on the sheep's head.
Tell us what they are.
Eighteen affections are on the sheep's head.
Tell us what they are.

Tolghuire imag hujin wai,
Hujin imag hujin shdi.
Tolghuire wer haran szin,
Wer diregu rmu haran szin.
Tolghuire sanaa haran naiman,
Haran naiman sanaa nuduwa.

头上部落三十个，
三十部落是牙齿。
头上有角十九只，
十九只角是角纹。
头上有情十八个，
十八有情是眼睛。

The thirty tribes on the sheep's head
Refer to the thirty teeth.
The nineteen horns on the sheep's head
Refer to the nineteen lines on the horns.
The eighteen affections on the sheep's head
Refer to the sheep's eyes.

Hunidu deeren buye wai,
Deeren buye ni aliwa?

羊有四身说不尽，
你说羊有哪四身？

The sheep has four bodies.
What are the four bodies?

Deeren buyenu kilesa,
Nigedar buye huxina,

Ghoordar buye nghuasina,
Ghuraandar buye hurghoosiwa,
Deerendar buye wer niwa.

要说福羊那四身,
四身之一是羊嘴,
四身之二是羊毛,
四身之三是羊粪,
四身之四是羊角。

The four bodies:
The first body is its mouth,
The second body is its wool,
The third body is its excreta,
The fourth body is its horns.

Hunidu ghuraan sala wai,
Aaba aama da kuu xjun,
Nige nige yaan daudam?

要说福羊有三支,
父亲母亲和儿子,
请问分别叫什么?

Sheep have three branches,
They are father, mother, and children.
What are their specific names?

Huninu aaba aama kuuniinu,
Aabanii lurja lumbu daudana,
Aamanii dabsi noor daudana,
Kuunii qighaan hurgha daudana.

要说福羊父母子,
父亲尊称须弥山,
母亲尊称白盐湖,
儿子叫做白螺羊。

Sheep's father, mother, and son:
The father is called Mount Sumeru,
The mother is called Salt Lake,
The son is called Conch Lamb.

Lurja lumbu malgha jooja,
Ne malghanu ken ughusanna?
Jarin buyere aasar wai,
Aasarnu yaan kun warisanna?
Kol dire hamnu mosija,
Hamnu yaan kun mosilghaja?

须弥山顶饰金冠，
请问金冠由谁赐？
须弥山腰三层楼，
请问楼层由谁造？
须弥山脚着皮靴，
请问皮靴由谁穿？

Mount Sumeru wears his hat.
Who gave him the hat?
A three-storey building was raised on the side of Mount Sumeru.
Who raised the building?
Mount Sumeru wears a pair of shoes.
Who helped him to wear the shoes?

Lumbu haldan malgha joo,
Nara ughusan malgha wai.
Jarin buyere aasar wai,
Zandan xjoosinu dongraawa.
Kol direnaa ham mosija,
Hara ghajarnu xiruuwa.

须弥山顶饰金冠，
金冠由那太阳赐。
须弥山腰三层楼，
那是檀香树成林。
须弥山脚着皮靴，
那是大地染尘泥。

Mount Sumeru wears his hat—
The sun gave him the hat.
A three-storey building was raised on the side of Mount Sumeru—
It is a sandalwood tree.
Mount Sumeru wears a pair of shoes—
They are the soil of the Earth.

Shge mulaa guinu deeren noor,
Aamani warang rogdu wai,
Nigedar qighaan shdennu noor,
Ne noornu yama giji kilena?
Ghoordar fulaan purghaan noor,
Ne noornu yama giji kilena?
Ghuraandar kugo liunu noor,
Ne noornu yama giji kilena?
Deerendar fulaan qisi noor,
Ne noornu yama giji kilena?

不大不小四圣湖,
座落母亲右身旁,
其一叫做白神湖,
请问此湖作何讲?
其二叫做红衹湖,
请问此湖作何讲?
其三叫做青龙湖,
请问此湖作何讲?
其四叫做红血湖,
请问此湖作何讲?

Four lakes neither big nor small
Are located on their mother's right side.
One is called White Sacred Lake.
What is it?
The second is called Red Cloth Lake.
What is it?
The third is called Blue Dragon Lake.
What is it?
The fourth is called Red Blood Lake.
What is it?

Aamanu deeren bagta noor,
Nigedar qighaan bagta noor,
Shge tingernu ngangjan noor.
Ghoordar fulaan bagta noor,
Labsi purghaannu ngangjan noor.
Ghuraandar kugo liunu noor,
Liu rjawunu ngangjan noor.

Deerendar fulaan qisi noor,
Hara qiirjaanu ngangjan noor.

要说母亲四圣湖,
其一叫做白神湖,
那是梵天当灵湖。
其二叫做红祇湖,
那是山神当灵湖。
其三叫做青龙湖,
那是龙王当灵湖。
其四叫做红血湖,
那是阎王当灵湖。

Mother's four sacred lakes:
The one called White Sacred Lake
Is Heaven's great lake.
The second, called Red Cloth Lake,
Is the mountain deity's great lake.
The third, called Blue Dragon Lake,
Is the Dragon King's great lake.
The fourth, called Red Blood Lake,
Is the King of Hell's great lake.

Noor nudundu haldannu bazaar wai,
Haldan bazardu haldannu qurghu wai,
Haldan qurghudu haldan yiuxi rogom,
Haldannu yiuxi anjii wai?

神湖口上打金城,
金城有门上金锁,
此锁只由金钥开,
请问金钥在哪里?

There is a golden city at the eye of the lake,
There is a golden lock on the golden city,
There is a golden key for the golden lock,
But where is the golden key?

Noor nudundu haldannu bazaar wai,
Haldan bazardu haldannu qurghu wai,
Yiuxi qongqannu gujire wai,
Qongqannu yeriji yiuxinu awu.

神湖口上打金城，
金门有门上金锁，
钥匙挂在凤凰头，
招来凤凰取钥匙。

There is a golden city at the eye of the lake,
There is a golden lock on the golden city,
The key is on the phoenix's neck—
Go look for the phoenix and get the key from it.

Noor nudundu haldannu bazaar wai,
Haldan bazardu haldannu qurghu wai,
Yiuxi qongqannu gujire wai,
Qongqan anjiiha kileji ughu?

神湖口上打金城，
金门有门上金锁，
钥匙挂在凤凰头，
请问凤凰在哪里？

There is a golden city at the eye of the lake,
There is a golden lock on the golden city,
The key is on the phoenix's neck—
But where is the phoenix?

Noor nudundu haldannu bazaar wai,
Yiuxi qongqannu gujire wai,
Qongqan lurja lumbure wai,
Yuxinu yama giji awugunii?

神湖口上打金城，
钥匙挂在凤凰头，
凤凰落在须弥顶，
请问金钥怎么取

There is a golden city at the eye of the lake,
There is a golden lock on the golden city.
The phoenix is on Mount Sumeru:
How can the key be got from the phoenix?

Deeren sara yernu sghaudu
Alag mughuinu waraanu,

Qongqannu duraa bau ireenu,
Yiuxinu awaanu udenu nee.

时在夏日四月里，
花花毒蛇当诱饵，
招引凤凰下须弥，
取得金钥开城门。

During the fourth month, in summer,
Hold a spotted snake,
Lure the phoenix to come down,
And get the key to open the gate.

Noor nudundu jas bazaar wai,
Bazar udendu jasnu qurghu wai,
Yiuxinu awuji udenu neesa,
Jasnu yiuxi anjii wai?

祇海口上打铜城，
铜城门上有铜锁，
要取钥匙开铜锁，
请问金钥在哪里？

There is a copper city at the eye of a lake,
There is a copper lock on the copper city.
Get a key and open the gate—
But where is the copper key?

Bazar udendu jas qurghu wai,
Jas yuuxi kireenu gujinre wai,
Kiree jaazoolangdu wai,
Yiuxinu yama giji awugunii?

祇海城门上铜锁，
钥匙挂在乌鸦脖，
乌鸦在那甲宗林，
请问钥匙怎么取？

There is a copper lock on the city.
The copper key is on a crow's neck,

The crow is in a place called Jaazoolang,[5]
How can the key be got?

Doloon saranu sghaudu,
Aasi mahanu waraanu,
Kireenu duriji bauwaa iree,
Yiuxinu awaanu udenu nee.

在那秋季七月里，
瘦瘦牛肉当诱饵，
招引老鸭下红崖，
取下钥匙开铜锁。

During the seventh month, in autumn,
Hold a piece of beef,
Lure the crow to come down,
And get the key to open the gate.

Noor nudundu dongnu bazaar wai,
Bazar udendu dongnu qurghu wai,
Yiuxinu awuji udenu neesa,
Yiuxi yaazinu gujire wai,
Yaazi ne sghaudu anjiiwa?

螺湖口上打螺城，
白螺城门白螺锁，
要取钥匙开螺锁，
钥匙却在黄鸭身，
请问黄鸭在哪里？

There is a conch city at the eye of a lake,
There is a conch lock on the city.
Get the key and open the gate.
The key is on a duck's neck,
But where is the duck?

Bazar udendu dong qurghu,
Yiuxi yaazinu gujire wai,

_____

5   Unknown place.

Yaazi noornu qireeduwa,
Te yiuxinu yama giji awugunii?

白螺城门白螺锁,
钥匙挂在鸭脖上,
我见黄鸭在湖边,
请问钥匙怎么取?

There is a conch lock on the city gate,
The key is on a duck's neck.
The duck is at the seaside:
How can the key be got from the duck?

Hawurnu turonggu saradu,
Joolon sghanu shdeewaanu,
Yaazinu duriji gharghaanu,
Yiuxinu awaanu udenu nee.

在那春季正月里,
嫩嫩芦苇当诱饵,
招引黄鸭上湖岸,
取下钥匙开城门。

During the first month, in spring,
Hold a tender reed,
Lure the duck to the shore,
And get the key to open the gate.

Ude qurghunu neewaaxja,
Ghuraan huni gharija.
Nige ni qighaan shden huniwa,
Shden huni tingerdu yaum.
Tingerdu xjirbuu aadal ulaam,
Ne hunidu nire ken fuyaajii?

三城三门三锁开,
三个海羊出三海。
其一是那白神羊,
白色神羊上天空。
青天在上授福乐,
此羊姓名由谁取?

The gate is unlocked,
Three sheep emerge.
One is a sacred white sheep.
The white sheep is going to Heaven.
It will have a happy life in Heaven.
Who will name the sheep?

Nige huni ni shdongwadu yaum,
Tingere furongdu xjiguna,
Nireniinu shdongwa fuyaaja,
"Haldan shden huni" daudasamba,
Haldan buyedu maha qisi gui.

其中一羊升天空,
那是去往梵天宫,
名由无上梵天取,
叫"金身飞天羊",
无血无肉是金身。

One sheep is going into empty space
In the heavenly palace.
The name is given by empty space:
The name is Golden Sacred Sheep,
But it has a golden body without flesh or blood.

Ghoordar fulaan huniwa,
Fulaan huni tar uladu xjim,
Baimaal ula hanhulanii,
Ne hunidu nire ken fuyaajii?

其二是那红祇羊,
红色祇羊上石山,
山势峻峨佑福乐,
此羊姓名由谁取?

The second is a red sheep.
The red sheep is going to a rocky mountain.
The steep mountain protects it.
Who will name the sheep?

Nige huni ni tar uladu xjim,
Ula purghaan taada xjiguna,
Nirenu ula purghaan fuyaaja,
"Xuri Ghurdin Huni" daudana,
Xuri buyedu maha qisi gui.

其中一羊上石山,
那是去往山神处,
名由山神"赞杰"取,
叫做"珊瑚善奔羊",
无血无肉珊瑚身。

One sheep is going to the rocky mountain.
The mountain deity is there.
The name is given by the mountain deity:
The name is Coral Running Sheep,
But it has a coral body without flesh or blood.

Ghuraandar qighaan dong huni,
Qighaan dong huni noorre wai,
Noornu qiree hanhulanii,
Ne hunidu nire ken fuyaajii?

其三那是白螺羊,
洁白螺羊留海中,
大海彼岸佑福乐,
此羊姓名由谁取?

The third is a white conch sheep.
The white conch sheep is in the sea,
The sea protects it.
Who will name the sheep?

Nige huni ni noorre saujii,
"Giril Liu Rjawu" furongdu xjim,
Nirenu Liu Rjawu fuyaaja,
"Qighaan Dong Mailajin" daudana,
Dong buyedu maha qisi gui.

其中一羊留海中,
去往"龙宫龙王"宫,

名由"东君龙王"取,
叫做"白螺善叫羊",
那羊螺身无血肉。

The sheep is in the sea,
It is going to the Dragon King's palace.
The name is given by the Dragon King:
The name is White Conch Baa,
But it has a conch body without flesh or blood.

Qisi noorregu qisi huniwa,
Noornu ghuraan hargaanu,
Noorregu szunu uqaanu,
Noorregu usinu ideenu,
Huxindunaa ghuraan ama mailaja,
Ne huninu nireni yaan daudana?

血海之中一血羊,
绕着血海转三圈,
饮得海中碧绿水,
吃得海中嫩嫩草,
口中咩咩叫三声,
那羊名称叫什么?

A blood sheep from a blood sea
Circled the blood sea thrice.
It drinks water from the sea,
Eats grass from the sea,
And baas thrice with its mouth.
What is the sheep's name?

"Usiqi Xjirbuu Huni" daudana,
"Sgildu Iregu Huni" daudana,
"Maha Buyedu Huni" daudana,
Jaghagu ghuraan samba nirewa,
Niredu hajir yamada gua,
Nige sarada dawaaji gui,
Ne huni anjiiha lii mudeni.

众叫"食草福禄羊",
有人叫做"心愿羊",

也叫"油草肉身羊",
如上得名有三种,
叫法虽多无差别,
未见此羊逾一月,
不知福羊在何处。

It is called Happy Grass Sheep,
It is called Hopeful Sheep,
It is called Human Body Sheep.
The given names are the above-mentioned three,
But the three names are not different.
For a month
We don't know where the sheep has gone.

4. Rjee Juraa

4. 寻迹

4. Searching

Qugu ujudur yerisa,
Ghurdin ghurdin jaghaduji yau,
Zandannu fiire kurisa,
Sergu xjoosi sergunu haa,
Geril xjoosi gerildu haa,
Zhuzhuan fiinu juuresa,
Nghuasinge sgeenu taalduna,
Bughu nghuasidu ulidhaja,
Laa nghuasidu ulighaja,
Huni nghuasidu ulighaja.

昨天前天寻福羊,
步履匆匆往上走,
到了茂密檀香林,
阳山树枝罩阴山,
阴山树枝遮阳山,
在那茂密树林里,
寻得一毛人生疑,
有人说那是鹿毛,
有人说那是麝香毛,
有人说那是福羊毛。

We searched for the sheep yesterday and the day before yesterday,
Walking quickly upwards,
We arrived at a sandalwood forest,
Trees covered the sunny side of the mountain,
Trees covered the shady side of the mountain,
In the dense forest.
We found a tuft of wool and inspected it.
Someone said it was wool from a deer,
Someone said it was wool from a musk deer,
Someone said it was wool from a sheep.

Zhuzhuan zandan fii dire,
Nghuasinu jubda taagunge wai,
Zandan fii dire bughu sauja,
Bughu nghuasu waisa goorji gua.
Zandan fii dire laa sauja,
Laa nghuasi waisa goorji gua.
Huni ndireexi jub jubnu gua,
Anjiiha darang lii mudeni.

茂密檀香树林中,
那毛确实令人疑,
檀香林是鹿的家,
有那鹿毛不奇怪。
檀香林是麝的家,
有那麝毛不奇怪。
福羊肯定不在林,
究竟在那仍不知。

In the dense sandalwood forest
Truly the wool was inspected.
Deer live in the sandalwood forest,
It is not strange at all to see the wool of a deer there.
Musk deer live in the sandalwood forest,
It is not strange at all to see the wool of a musk deer there.
Sheep don't live in the forest,
We don't know where the sheep is.

Yeraanu dunda moordu yau,
Xaaxi ghajardu kuraaxja,
Tingerdu xaaxila ntimlaaxja,
Giril sergudu xaaxiwa,
Giril da serguni juure ni,
Ghuraan kol rjeenu taalduna,
Bughunu kol rjeewa gina,
Laanu kol rjeewa gina,
Huninu kol rjeewa gina.

寻羊往那中路走,
却到无边大沙漠,
黄沙纷飞漫天日,
阴坡阳坡沙无定,
就在阴阳坡之间,

三个脚印令人疑,
有人说是鹿脚印,
有人说是麝脚印,
有人说是羊脚印。

We searched for the sheep, walking on the middle road,
Until arriving in a desert.
Dust and stones flew around in a storm
And covered the shady side of the mountain.
Between the shady and sunny sides of the mountain
We found three footprints, and inspected them.
Someone said they were a deer's footprints,
Someone said they were a musk deer's footprints,
Someone said they were a sheep's footprints.

Shge xaaxi ghajardu,
Ghuraan kol rjeenu muulasa.
Gigeen baugu qagdu ni,
Bughu tangnu xjiinduji xjim,
Kol rjee waisa goorji gua.
Nara gharigu sghaudu ni,
Xira huni tangnu xjiindu yaum,
Kol rjee waisada goorji gua.
Nara pagdagu sghaudu ni,
Laasge tangnu xjiindu yaum,
Laa kol rjee waisa goorji gua,
Huni guigunu bu tagjorlaya.

就在莽莽沙漠里,
三个脚印令人疑。
天亮东方发白时,
鹿群就在滩中行,
有那鹿印不奇怪。
红红太阳初升时,
黄羊就往滩中行,
黄羊脚印不奇怪。
日落西山黄昏时,
麝群往那滩中行,
有那麝印不奇怪,
福羊不在我肯定。

In the boundless desert
We checked the three footprints.
At daybreak,
If a deer goes to the center of the plain
Then it is nothing strange to see its footprints.
As the sun rises,
If a Mongolian gazelle goes to the center of the plain
Then it is nothing strange to see its footprints.
At sunset,
If a musk deer goes to the center of the plain
Then it is nothing strange to see its footprints.
I'm sure there is no sheep here.

Qugu ujudur yeraanu,
Naakoor qireedu kurisa,
Huninu kol rjee ni anjiiwa?
Fiire yeraanu kurisa,
Huninu nghuasi ni anjiiwa?
Yeraanu usi talaadu kurisa,
Hara hurghoosi anjiiwa?
Huni wai guinu lii mudeni?

昨天前天寻福羊,
寻羊寻到沼泽边,
福羊脚印在哪里?
寻羊寻到山林中,
福羊羊毛在哪里?
寻羊寻到草山中,
黑色粪粒在哪里?
不知福羊有没有?

A few days ago we looked for the sheep
In the swamp,
But where were the sheep's footprints?
We looked for the sheep in the forest,
But where was the sheep's wool?
We looked for the sheep in the grassland,
But where were the sheep's droppings?
Is there a sheep or not?

Usi deesisan ula dire,
Ghuraan hurghoosinu taaldna,
Bughu hurghoosiwa giji kilena,
Laa hurghoosiwa giji kilena,
Huni hurghoosiwa giji kilena,
Alinge nimbiiha bu lii medem.

芳菲如茵草山中，
三粒黑粪令人疑，
有人说那是鹿粪，
有人说那是麝粪，
有人说那是羊粪，
究竟是否我不定。

In the verdant grassland
People inspected three droppings.
Someone said they were deer droppings,
Someone said they were musk deer droppings,
Someone said they were sheep droppings.
I didn't know what on Earth they were.

Usi deesisan ula dire,
Ghuraan hurghoosinu muulasa,
Shdileji nara gharigu sghaudu,
Bughu idexi yerigu ghajarwa,
Bughu hurghoosi waisa ghoorji gua.
Ne laasge dawaajin ghajarwa,
Laa hurghoosi waisa ghoorji gua.
Huni ndireexi tagjor gua,
Anjii xjiwaha lii mudeni.

芳菲如茵草山中，
三粒黑令人疑，
东方朝日初升时，
那是鹿群觅食处，
有那鹿粪不奇怪。
那是麝群经过处，
寻得麝粪不奇怪，
福羊肯定不在此，
去往哪里仍不知。

In the verdant grassland
We inspected the three droppings.
At daybreak
It is the place where deer look for grass to eat,
So it would not be strange to see deer droppings.
It is the place where musk deers pass by,
So it would not be strange to see musk deer droppings.
The sheep is not here.
I don't know where the sheep is.

Jirghoon sara sgeji gua,
Huni jubda anjiiwa?
Kidi udur aamanaa sgeji gua,
Huni anjii uroo sauja?
Ideji gui hurin nige udur,
Ne kidi udur yaan ideja?

不见同伴有六月，
福羊究竟在哪里？
不见妈妈已几日，
福羊究竟在哪里？
不服水草廿一天，
这些日子吃什么？

We have not seen it for six months.
Where on Earth is the sheep?
It has not seen its mother for several days.
Where on Earth is the sheep?
It has not been fed for twenty-one days.
What has it been eating all this time?

Jirghoon sara aamanaa sgeji gua,
Jirghoon sara keelenduwa,
Sun kugoji gui kidi udur,
Kidi udurdu kii ngamlana,
Ideji gui hurin nige udur,
Sunla njeenaanaa tijeena.

不见母亲有六月，
六个月在胎中怀，
奶水不服已几天，

这几天里喝西风，
草料不服廿一天，
这些日子由奶养。

It has not seen its mother for six months,
It has been pregnant for six months,
It has not been milked for several days,
It has eaten nothing during these days,
It has not eaten for twenty-one days.
We should feed it some milk.

Huni noorre sauji gui,
Ghuisang ghajardu yauwaxja.
Ghuisang ulama kilena,
Usi idesa duko gui,
Nige udur jongge sunnurdana,
Sain ugo qigindu xingeeja,
Huninu alasa qimii ughuya,
Aldagu sanaanu kileji ughu.

福羊不在海里住，
却往西域"卫藏"走。
卫藏上师传话说，
食草有情无罪过，
一日听到一百遍，
教诫警言鸣耳中，
若要宰羊犒劳你，
说出解脱大功德。

The sheep didn't walk toward the sea
But toward Tibet.
The masters from Tibet said
The sheep is not guilty of eating grass.
This was heard one hundred times in a day.
We listened well.
The sound of the judgement resounded in people's ears,
As they told of great deeds.

Huni noorre sauji gui,
Ghuisang ghajardu yauwaaxja.
Ghuisang ulamanu ncog dire,

Jong menhannu lamadee wai,
Aasinqi ghajarnu kilesa,
Tireexi qiinu dasbalan gua.

福羊不在海里住，
却往西域"卫藏"走。
卫藏上师道场里，
僧人成百又上千，
若说放牧养畜处，
那里不闻佛法音。

The sheep didn't stay in the sea
But walked toward Tibet.
At a place in Tibet where an esteemed bodhisattva conducted rites
Hundreds and thousands of monks were gathered.
A shepherd said
People there don't believe in Buddhist scriptures.

Huni Ghuisang sauji gui,
Nqim ghajar Rjanagdu yauwaaxja.
Rjanag haanjeen kilegu ni,
Usi idesamba duko gui,
Nige udur jongge sunurdana,
Nqim sger qigindu xingeeja,
Huninu alasa qimii ughuya,
Nqim lognu qi nige kileji ughu.

福羊不在卫藏住，
却往法治汉地走。
汉地君王传旨说，
食草有情无罪过，
一日听到一百遍，
法判之声鸣耳中，
若要宰羊犒劳你，
说出法律怎么样。

The sheep didn't stay in Tibet
But walked to the lands of the law-abiding Han Chinese.
The Han Chinese Emperor said
The sheep is not guilty of eating grass.
This was heard one hundred times in a day.

The sound of judgement resounded in people's ears.
I will reward you if the sheep is slaughtered,
If you are able to tell us about the law.

Huni Ghuisang sauji gua,
Nqim lognu Rjanag ghajardu yauja.
Rjanag haanjeenu udendu,
Aasi huni dulaaldusa,
Nqim shdaar lii irejin anjii wai.

福羊不在卫藏住，
却往法治汉地走。
中土汉皇法门里，
若要放牧养牲畜，
哪有不尊王法处。

The sheep didn't stay in Tibet
But walked to the lands of the law-abiding Han Chinese.
In front of the gate of the Emperor's palace
Sheep and oxen were herded,
Which was prohibited by the law.

Huni Rjanag ghajardu sauji gua,
Tixi Yirmu tangdu xjija.
Ghajar tebxin tela gaa,
Ndireexi saugu durlaja.
Nige udurdu jong dawaam,
Xjirbuu aadalnu muulaja.
Huninu alasa qimii ughuya,
Muxi ghajarnii hghuaji ughu.

福羊不在汉地住，
却去西康耶摩滩。
只因地势很平坦，
很想落户在此间。
一日能有一百遍，
幸福感觉显心田。
若要宰羊犒劳你，
先请丈量划地方。

The sheep didn't stay in the land of the Han Chinese,
But walked to Yirmu[6] Plain in Xikang.
Since the earth there was level
The sheep wanted to live there.
Time passed slowly,
It wanted to live happily.
I will reward you if the sheep is slaughtered,
If you are able to make a place for the sheep to stay.

Huni qidar ghajardu sauji gua,
Yirmu tangdu xjaa sauja.
Qighaan huxidii mori aghadiu,
Muxisa ndireexi saulduja.
Huninu ndireexi bii saulgha,
Ghurdi ghurdi tauwaa ire.

福羊不在汉地住,
却去西康耶摩滩。
白唇野马俩兄弟,
早把此地占手中。
别把福羊留在那,
快快将它赶过来。

The sheep didn't stay in the land of the Han Chinese,
But went to live on Yirmu Plain.
Two white-lipped horse brothers
Had already occupied the area.
Please don't allow the sheep to stay here:
Quickly, drive the sheep away from there.

Huni Yirmu tang sauji gua,
Undur tingerduji yauwaaxja.
Kugo tingerdu qiree gua,
Purghaan bazar muxiwa.
Yiuxi ni hoosin shdongwaduwa,
Udeqi liunu ghaduwa.

---

6   Yirmu is said to have originally been a deity in Heaven, and later became the first
    ancestor of all humans.

Tireexi huninu jarin gua,
Jongnu fonge tujeeguna.

福羊不在西康住，
却往高高天上走。
天空瓦蓝广无边，
南云仙城挡前面。
钥匙不见在空中，
守门小龙在保管。
那里发誓不宰羊，
欲养福羊一百年。

The sheep didn't stay on Yirmu Plain
But went up to Heaven.
The blue sky was boundless,
An eternal city blocked the sheep.
The key to the city was not in the sky,
But in the hands of the gatekeeper, the Little Dragon King.
He won't slaughter the sheep,
But will raise it for a hundred years.

Huni Yirmu tang sauji gua,
Undur tingerduji yauwaaxja.
Kugo tingerdu qiree gua,
Purghaan bazar muxiwa.
Yiuxi ni hoosin shdongwaduwa,
Jarma purghaannu waraaduwa,
Purghaan bazarnu baghaa awuwa,
Kugo liunu ndanglalghaadiiwa,
Tingerdu baghaa log ni gua,
Huninu tireexi bii saulgha,
Ghurdi ghurdi tauwaa ire.

福羊不在西康住，
却往高高天上走。
天空瓦蓝广无边，
南云仙城挡前面。
钥匙不见在空中，
我已擒那护雹神，
攻破南云仙女城，
驯服南来那青龙，

搅得天空乱纷纷,
别把福羊留在那,
快快将它赶过来。

The sheep didn't stay on Yirmu Plain
But went up to Heaven.
The blue sky was boundless,
An eternal city blocked the sheep.
The key was in empty space.
Catch the hail-protecting deity
To break the city gate,
Tame the blue dragon
And stir up the sky.
Don't ask the sheep to stay there.
Quickly, drive the sheep away from there.

Shden huni ghadaadu yang xjina,
Tar bazaar muxi danglaaxja.
Qurghu ni hadong targewa,
Fulaan xira aasi sgija,
Huninu yama gisada lii alam,
Jong fon tujeeya giji kilena.

神羊又往石山去,
却见石城挡前面。
城门由那坚石锁,
红黄野牛守城门,
那里发誓不宰羊,
欲养福羊一百年。

The sheep went to a mountain.
A stone city blocked its road.
The lock was a hard stone.
Some red and yellow oxen guarded the gate.
They won't slaughter the sheep
But will raise it for 100 years.

Shden huni ghadaadu yang xjina,
Tar bazaar muxi danglaaxja.
Qurghu ni hadong targewa,

Bu kujidu kunla aghadiu giya,
Undur ghadaanu sajiliya,
Xira aasinu alaadiya,
Fulaan aasinu bii saulgha,
Ghurdi ghurdi tauwaa ire.

神羊又往石山去,
却见石城挡前面。
城门由那坚石锁,
我认力士做弟兄,
高高石山遂打烂,
射杀那头黄野牛,
赶跑那头红野牛,
快快将它赶过来。

The sheep went to a mountain.
A stone city blocked its road.
The lock was a hard stone.
Befriend some stong men
To smash the high mountain to pieces,
Slaughter the yellow oxen,
And drive the red oxen out.
Quickly, drive the sheep away from there.

Huni fii dire yang xjija,
Muxi zandannu bazaar danglaaxja.
Fulaan qurghula qughulaja,
Udeniinu alag bas sgija,
Tireexi huninu lii alam,
Jong fon tujeeya giji kilena.

福羊又往林中走,
檀木城堡挡前面。
城门由那红木锁,
斑斓猛虎守城门,
那里发誓不宰羊,
欲养福羊一百年。

The sheep went to a forest.
A sandalwood city blocked its road.
The city was locked by a sandalwood lock,
Mottled tigers guarded the gate.

They won't slaughter the sheep
But will raise it for a hundred years.

Huni fii dire yang xjija,
Muxi zandannu bazaar danglaja.
Fulaan qurghula qurghulaja,
Bu moqila aghadiu tanaanu,
Zandan xjoosinu qabjaanu,
Fulaan moodunu suudaadiya,
Huni tenu bii saulgha,
Ghurdi ghurdi tauwaa ire.

福羊又往林中去，
檀木城堡挡前面。
城门有那红木锁，
我认木匠做弟兄，
砍尽林中檀香树，
将那红木腋下挟，
别把福羊留在那，
快快将它赶过来。

The sheep went to a forest.
A sandalwood city blocked its road.
The city was locked by a sandalwood lock.
Befriend a carpenter
To cut down all the sandalwood trees
And put the red sandalwood trees in his armpits.
The sheep is not allowed to live there.
Quickly, drive the sheep away from there.

Huni tangdu xjisamba,
Muxi undur bazaar danglaja.
Tar dangghulla qurghulaja,
Qighaan huxidii mori ude sgija,
Tireexi huninu lii alam,
Jong fon tujeeya giji kilena.

福羊又往平摊去，
又一高城挡前面。
乱世沟壑城门锁，

白唇野马守城门，
那里发誓不宰羊，
欲养福羊一百年。

The sheep went to a plain.
A high city wall blocked its way.
The city was locked by locks of stone and clods.
White-lipped horses guarded the city gate.
They won't slaughter the sheep,
But will raise it for a hundred years.

Huni tangdu xjisamba,
Undur bazarnge danglaaxja,
Tar dangghulla qurghulaja,
Bu Qidar kunla aghadiu taniya,
Musi nige jurnu kolaanu,
Ghajardu kundunge fuliya,
Tebxin tangnu furauliya,
Tar da dangghul tebjiraa xjim,
Huni tenu bii saulgha,
Ghurdi ghurdi tauwaa ire.

福羊又往平摊去，
又一高城挡前面，
乱世沟壑城门锁，
我认汉人做弟兄，
架起一对大犏牛，
地心打造重铧犁，
在那平摊犁一遍，
乱世沟壑平展展，
别把福羊留在那，
快快将它赶过来。

The sheep went to a plain.
A high city wall blocked its way.
The city was locked by locks of stones and clods.
Befriend a Han Chinese
To prepare a pair of yaks,
Plow the ground,
Plow the plain,
And level the stones and clods.

The sheep is not allowed to live there.
Quickly, drive the sheep away from there.

Huni durnadu xjisamba,
Dorji pusaa huniqiwa,
Huninu lii alam giji kilena.

福羊又往东边去,
金刚菩萨是羊倌,
那里发誓不宰羊。

The sheep went in an easterly direction.
The Buddha's warrior attendant was the shepherd there.
He would not slaughter the sheep.

Huni durnadu xjisamba,
Dorji pusaa huniqiwa,
Tennu nige dasbalasa,
Guji shdaaji dasbalaya,
Sgilnu dasba kujidu wai,
Huninu tireexi bii saulgha,
Ghurdi ghurdi tauwa ire.

福羊又往东边去,
金刚菩萨是羊倌,
对他礼供须三遍,
金刚菩萨用香敬,
诚心敬仰福威尊,
别把福羊留在那,
快快将它赶过来。

The sheep went in an easterly direction.
The Buddha's warrior attendant was the shepherd there.
We should pay our respects to him,
Pay our respects to him with incense,
Pay our respects to him wholeheartedly.
Don't ask the sheep to live there.
Quickly, drive the sheep away from there.

Huni gerildu xjisamba,
Bayaan purghaan huniqiwa,

Huninu nige lii alaanu,
Mpeelelghaya giji kilena.

福羊又往南边去，
宝积如来是羊倌，
那里发誓不宰羊，
不为宰杀为繁衍。

The sheep went in a southerly direction.
The God of Wealth was the shepherd there.
He would not slaughter the sheep,
But would try to increase the number of sheep.

Huni gerildu xjisamba,
Bayaan purghaan huniqiwa,
Tenu nige dasbalasa,
Xininu xangleji dasbalaya,
Sgilnu dasba kujidu wai,
Huninu tireexi bii saulgha,
Ghurdi ghurdi tauwaa ire.

福羊又往南边去，
宝积如来是羊倌，
对他礼供须三遍，
献供谨施宝积佛，
诚心敬仰福威尊，
别把福羊留在那，
快快将它赶过来。

The sheep went in a southerly direction.
The God of Wealth was the shepherd there.
We should pay our respects to him,
Pay our respects to him by offering gifts,
Pay our respects to him wholeheartedly.
Don't ask the sheep to live there.
Quickly, drive the sheep away from there.

Huni urnadu xjisamba,
Sangrji shdamba huniqiwa,
Tireexi huninu lii alaanu,
Mpeelelghaya giji kilena.

福羊又往西边去,
大日如来是羊倌,
那里发誓不宰羊,
不为宰杀为繁衍。

The sheep went in a westerly direction.
Mahavaiocana was the shepherd there.
He would not slaughter the sheep,
But try to increase the number of sheep.

Huni urnadu xjisamba,
Sangrji shdamba huniqiwa,
Tennu nige dasbalasa,
Sgilnu dasba kijidu wai,
Huninu tireexi bii saulgha,
Ghurdi ghurdi tauwaa ire.

福羊又往西边去,
大日如来是羊倌,
对他礼供须三遍,
诚心敬仰慈心尊,
别把福羊留在那,
快快将它赶过来。

The sheep went in a westerly direction.
Mahavaiocana was the shepherd there.
We should pay our respects to him,
Pay our respects to him wholeheartedly.
Don't ask the sheep to stay,
Quickly, drive the sheep away from there.

Huni sargudu xjisamba,
Baudaldii purghaan huniqiwa,
Tireexi huninu lii alaanu,
Mpeelelghaya giji kilena.

福羊又往北边去,
不空成就是羊倌,
那里发誓不宰羊,
不为宰杀为繁衍。

The sheep went in a northerly direction.
Amoghasiddhi was the shepherd there.
He would not slaughter the sheep,
But try to increase the number of sheep.

Huni sargudu xjisamba,
Baudaldii purghaan huniqiwa,
Tennu nige dasbalasa,
Baudaldii purghaan ghal xangleya,
Sgilnu dasba kujidu wai,
Huninu tireexi bii saulgha,
Ghurdi ghurdi tauwa ire.

福羊又往北边去，
不空成就是羊倌，
对他礼供须三遍，
不空成就要火供，
诚心敬仰福威尊，
别把福羊留在那，
快快将它赶过来。

The sheep went in a northerly direction.
Amoghasiddhi was the shepherd there.
We should pay our respects to him,
Pay our respects to him by offering fire,
Pay our respects to him wholeheartedly.
Don't ask the sheep to live there,
Quickly, drive the sheep away from there.

Huni wawudu xjisamba,
Haran naiman ghulda wai,
Nige dau moorha janzi wai,
Nige tolghuire tar danglajii,
Darang fulaan moodila qigijii,
Huninu tausa purge shgewa.

福羊又往瓦吾去，
那有峡谷十八座，
道路险要就一条，
险道一块巨石堵，

还用红木塞石缝，
赶出福羊难又难。

The sheep went to Mount Wawu.
Eighteen valleys led to the mountain,
But one route was dangerous,
One boulder blocked the way,
And a red sandalwood tree blocked the way too.
There were great difficulties for the sheep to pass that way.

Huni wawudu xjisamba,
Haran naiman ghulda wai,
Nige dau moorha janzi wai,
Darang moodi da tarla danglajii,
Bu tarqila aghadiu tanaanu,
Tarnu ghoordu ulighaya,
Ghoor rogduji hghalaanu,
Fulaan moodinu qabjiya,
Tireesa gharisa qirwalwa.

福羊又往瓦吾去，
那有峡谷十八座，
道路险要就一条，
巨石红木堵险道，
我认石匠做弟兄，
将那巨石砸两瓣，
分别扔到路左右，
砍断红木别腰间，
出那险境真容易。

The sheep went to Mount Wawu.
Eighteen valleys led to the mountain,
But one route was dangerous,
A boulder and a red sandalwood tree blocked the way.
Befriend a stonemason
To cut the boulder in two
And push the boulder to the side of the road
And chop the red sandalwood to pieces.
It was easy to overcome these difficulties.

Wawu uledu yanzhang shgewa,
Wawu ula niurdu tar ulonna,
Wawu ula szaarnu naakoorwa,
Tireesa gharisa purgewa.

瓦吾山头烟瘴大，
瓦吾山腰石头多，
瓦吾山脚泥沼深，
出那险境难又难。

There was heavy mist on Mount Wawu.
There were many stones on the slopes.
There were swamps at the foot of Mount Wawu.
So it was difficult to ascend the mountain.

Wawu uladu yanzhang waisada,
Bu saarla aghadiu tanaanu,
Nesaa te rogdu dawaa xjim.
Wawu uladu tar waisada,
Bu mparaala aghadiu tanaanu,
Diulaa te rogdu dawaa xjim.
Wawu szaardu naakoorwa,
Bu shden xaula aghadiu tanaanu,
Nesaa te rogdu dawaa xjim,
Ne ghajarnu dawaasa qirwalwa.

瓦吾山头烟瘴大，
我认神鹰做弟兄，
一跃而飞到那边。
瓦吾山腰石头多，
我认红豺做弟兄，
一窜而过到那边。
瓦吾山脚泥沼深，
我认神鸟做弟兄，
一飞而过到那边，
出此险境真容易。

There was heavy mist on Mount Wawu.
Befriend a vulture
And fly to the other side of Mount Wawu.
There were many stones on the slopes.
Befriend a jackal

And leap to the other side of Mount Wawu.
There were swamps at the foot of Mount Wawu,
Take a holy bird as a sworn brother
And fly to the other side of Mount Wawu.
It was easy to get to the other side of Mount Wawu.

Wawu ulanu jaghadu,
Xau dawaa adajin szin zhog wai,
Mori yau adajin szin ula wai,
Nohui xighaa adajin szin rimaa wai,
Aasi dawaa adajin szin jarghai wai,
Tireesa dawaasa purgewa?

在那瓦吾上游里，
百鸟难逾九峭崖，
百马难走九高山，
百狗难越九危墙，
百牛难过九陡坡，
出那险境难又难?

On the upper reaches of Mount Wawu
There were nine precipitous rockfaces and sheer cliffs which birds could
    not fly over,
There were nine high mountains which horses could not pass over,
There were nine high walls which dogs could not pass over,
There were nine steep slopes which oxen could not pass over.
How could this dangerous area be traversed?

Wawu ulanu jaghadu,
Xau dawaa adajin szin zhog wai,
Xua qongqan tiree nesina.
Mori yau adajin szin ula wai,
Shden mori tiree ghar baghana.
Nohui xighaa adajin szin rimaa,
Fulaan mparaa tiree diulina.
Aasi dawaa adajin szin jarghai,
Shden aasi saidaar yaulduna,
Ne ghajarnu dawaasa qirwalwa.

在那瓦吾上游里，
百鸟难逾九峭崖，

自有凤凰展双翼。
百马难走九高山,
神马九匹蹄如飞。
百狗难越九危墙,
自有红豺任飞窜。
百牛难过九陡坡,
神牛九头行悠悠,
出此险境真容易。

On the upper reaches of Mount Wawu
There were nine precipitous rockfaces and sheer cliffs which birds could
    not fly over,
But a phoenix could fly over them.
There were nine high mountains which horses could not pass over,
But a sacred horse could gallop over them.
There were nine high walls which dogs could not pass over,
But jackals could jump over them.
There were nine steep slopes which oxen could not pass over,
But sacred oxen could walk over them—
So it was easy to traverse this area.

Wawu ulanu xjiindu ni,
Usi gui ghul szin wai,
Szu gui ghul szin wai,
Xjoosi gui ghul szin wai,
Ghal fune ghul szin wai,
Ndireesa gharisa purgewa?

在那瓦吾中游里,
无草山谷有九座,
无水山谷有九座,
无林山谷有九座,
火焰山谷有九座,
出那险境难又难?

Halfway up Mount Wawu
There were nine valleys without any grass,
There were nine valleys without any water,
There were nine valleys without any trees,
There were nine valleys with flaming mountains.
How could this dangerous area be traversed?

Wawu ulanu xjiindu ni,
Usi gui ghul szin waisada,
Bu direnaa usi warijii.
Szu gui ghul szin waisada,
Bu raalsa szunu uqua irewa.
Xjoosi gui ghul szin waisada,
Bu xauxalghanu hghulaa irewa.
Ghal fune ghul szin waisada,
Bu huraa daudasa qirwal wai,
Ne ghajarsa gharisa qirwalwa.

在那瓦吾中游里，
无草山谷虽九座，
我却随身带茅草。
无水山谷虽九座，
我在河边已饮饱。
无林山谷虽九座，
我将柳枝折在手。
火焰山谷虽九座，
我招雨水自然多，
出此险境真容易。

Halfway up Mount Wawu,
The nine valleys lacked grass
But I carried grass with me.
The nine valleys lacked water,
But I had already drunk water from the river.
The nine valleys lacked trees,
But I brought twigs with me.
There were nine valleys with flaming mountains,
But I easily made rain fall from the sky,
So it was easy to traverse this dangerous area.

Wawu baatir smuqiwa,
Wawu mori jorotuwa,
Wawu nohui udeqiwa,
Wawu anjiida ghul xongghuwa,
Nesgenu yama giji dawaagunii?

瓦吾勇士善射箭，
瓦吾马能走险道，

瓦吾狗是守门神，
瓦吾处处是深渊，
这些险境怎么办？

The warrior of Wawu was good at archery,
The horse of Wawu was good, quick and fierce,
The dog of Wawu was good at keeping guard.
Everywhere in Wawu there were abysses.
How could dangerous Wawu be traversed?

Wawunu baatir smuqi waisada,
Bu saihanlaa tendu kileya,
Kilee aghadiudu taniya.
Wawu mori raari waisada,
Ghuraan ramda fuyaawaanu,
Surghuawaadisa ndang hghui wai.
Wawu nohui raari waisada,
Bu timur xinjir wariji wai,
Tanaadisa njeenaanu wai.

瓦吾勇士虽善射，
我不凶狠讲和气，
说服之后如朋友。
瓦吾马儿虽性烈，
绊上三个绊马索，
驯服之后很温顺。
瓦吾守门狗虽凶，
我已备好铁嚼子，
亲近就如自家狗。

The warrior of Wawu was good at archery,
But I treated him politely
Until we finally become brothers.
The horse of Wawu was good, quick and fierce,
But it was hitched by three reins
Until finally it became tamed.
The dog of Wawu was good at keeping guard,
But I had an iron chain,
And tamed it until it finally became my friend.

Yaujinsge wawunu gulesa,
Bas ghulnu dawaagu rgom,
Kadam tangnu dawaagu rgom,
Muroon ghulnu dawaagu rgom,
Ilee ulanu dawaagu rgom,
Wawudu xjisa purgewa.

行人皆说去瓦吾，
须得经过老虎沟，
须得经过野狼川，
须得经过湍流谷，
须得经过魔鬼山，
要去瓦吾难又难。

Passersby at Mount Wawu all say:
People must pass through Tiger Valley to go to Mount Wawu,
People must cross Wolf Plain to go to Mount Wawu,
People must go through River Valley to go to Mount Wawu,
People must pass Ghost Mountain to go to Mount Wawu,
So it's difficult to go to Mount Wawu.

Bas ghulnu dawaasa,
Ndaa ghuraan baatir kuuda wai,
Ghuraan basnu jujile shdam.
Kadam tangnu dawaasa,
Bu hujin smu rgujii,
Ghuraan kadamnu duuyaana.
Muroon ghulnu dawaasa,
Jaghasi szudu madu qirwalwa.
Ilee ulanu dawaasa,
Ndaa tingere purghaan furonglam,
Maha idegu sghau kurija.

过那险恶老虎沟，
我有三子真勇士，
可给三虎颜色看。
过那险恶野狼川，
腰间备有三十箭，
可让三狼吃苦头。
过那险恶湍流谷，
如鱼得水轻松过。

过那险恶魔鬼山，
我有神彩可保佑，
现在该是吃肉时。

If you want to pass through Tiger Valley,
I have three warrior sons
Who can defeat the three tigers.
If you want to cross Wolf Plain,
I carry thirty arrows on my back
Which can shoot the three wolves dead.
If you want to go through River Valley,
You can go through it as a fish.
If you want to pass Ghost Mountain,
I will be protected by a heavenly deity.
Now it's time to start the song of eating mutton.

5. Huninu Jari

5. 宰杀

5. Slaughtering Sheep

Rgor tigii ziliu guise tannin gui,
Kii tigii maalii guise kuri adam,
Jar tigii ben guise wari adam,
Qimu huni maha idegu fayo gua.

无雕聪颖不认识，
无风快捷不到此，
无熊笨拙不能伏，
你还无缘吃羊肉。

You won't recognize the sheep unless you're as clever as an eagle,
You won't catch the sheep unless you're as quick as the wind,
You won't hold on to the sheep if you're as awkward as a bear,
So you can't eat the sheep's meat.

Huni jaghaduji yausamba,
Yang huni hanansa muxina,
Rgor tigee ziliuha mudena.
Huni saiguji yausamba,
Yang huni hanansa xjiinduna,
Kii tigii ghurdinha kurina.
Huni dooroji yausamba,
Yang huni hanansa huinona,
Jar tigii ben waisa waraadina.

羊群要往上面走，
福羊就在最前头，
聪颖如雕定知道。
羊群要往对面走，
福羊就在最中间，
快捷如风定能到。
羊群要往下面来，
福羊就在最后面，
笨拙如熊定能伏。

If the sheep walks uphill,
The sheep walks first in line:
You could see this if you were as clever as an eagle.
If the sheep walks straight ahead,
The sheep walks in the middle of the flock of sheep:
You could catch it if you ran as quickly as the wind.
If the sheep walks downhill,
The sheep walks last in the line:
You could catch the clumsy sheep.

Ghuraan maaneer nau shdana,
Qi kile yama giji nausamba.
Ghuraan dughulong juraa shdam,
Qi kile yama giji juraana.
Ghuraan ghar gui wari shdam,
Qi kile yama giji warina.

三个瞎子也能看，
你说他们怎么看。
三个瘫子也能赶，
他说你们怎么赶。
三个没手也能抓，
你说他们怎么抓。

Three blind men can catch sight of it—
Tell us how they see it.
Three lame men can catch up with it—
Tell us how they catch it.
Three men without hands can grasp it—
Tell us how they grasp it.

Ghuraan maaneer nau shdana,
Xiilaji sanaji szii bagha.
Ghuraan dughulong juraa shdam,
Qagraaji nguroji hgalana.
Ghuraan ghar gui wari shdam,
Toor barghal da deelge wai.

三个瞎子也能看，
靠卜靠算靠卦言。

三个瘸子也能赶，
靠喊滚石和抛石。
三个没手也能抓，
一网二扣三绳索。

Three blind men can catch sight of it
By practicing divination.
Three lame men can catch up with it
By shouting and throwing stones.
Three men without hands can grasp it
By using a trap.

Huninu jarijin ghuraan kun,
Qi kile tesge ken kenwa?
Huninu lii jarijin ghuraa kun,
Qi kile tesge ken kenwa?
Huninu banglajin ghuraan deelge wai,
Qi kile ali ghuraan deelgewa?
Huninu lii banglajin ghuraan deelge wai,
Qi kile ali ghuraan deelgewa?

还有三人说宰羊，
你说他们各是谁?
这有三人不宰羊，
你说他们各是谁?
这有三绳要绑羊，
你说各是那三条?
还有三绳不绑羊，
你说各是那三条?

Three men will slaughter the sheep.
Can you tell us who they are?
Three people won't slaughter the sheep.
Can you tell us who they are?
Three ropes will be used to tie up the sheep.
Can you tell us what they are?
Three ropes won't be used to tie up the sheep.
Can you tell us what they are?

Huninu jarijin ghuraan kun,
Qudughu xaaxi da jarijin kun,

Jarijin ghuraan kunna.
Huninu lii jarijin ghuraan kun,
Ulama lamaa da joomu,
Lii jarijin ghuraan kunna.
Huninu banglajin ghuraan delge,
Losi nghuasi da narin deelge,
Banglajin ghuraan deelgewa.
Lii banglajin ghuraan deelge,
Haldan mengu da dong deelge,
Lii banglajin ghuraan deelgewa.

这有三人说宰羊,
一刀二磨三宰把,
便是宰羊那三人。
这有三人不宰羊,
上师圣僧和修士,
便是不宰那三人。
这有绑羊绳三条,
麻绳粗毛细毛绳,
便是绑羊那三绳。
要说三绳不绑羊,
金绳银绳海螺绳,
就这三绳不绑羊。

Three men will slaughter the sheep:
One man with a knife, another with a whetstone, and another to kill the
   sheep,
These three men will slaughter the sheep.
Three people won't slaughter the sheep:
An esteemed bodhisattva, a monk, and a nun,
These three people won't slaughter the sheep.
Three ropes will be used to tie up the sheep—
A hemp rope, a wool rope, and a thin woolen string.
These three ropes will be used to tie up the sheep.
Three ropes won't be used to tie up the sheep—
A golden rope, a silver rope, and a conch rope.
These three ropes won't be used to tie up the sheep.

Daudasan dauqidu szaghaya,
Yang huni lii yaujin ghuraan moor,
Qi nige kileda szaraa giya.

请来歌手我问你，
福羊不走三种路，
请你说说再商量。

Ask the invited singers:
There are three roads the sheep won't walk on—
Please tell us what they are.

Yang huni lii yaujin ghuraan moor,
Nige ni hara bas ni moor,
Ghoor ni fulaa laanu moor,
Ghuraan ni hulghai yaujin moor,
Ne ghuraan moorni te lii yaum.

福羊不走三种路，
一是黑檀老虎路，
二是红崖麝香路，
三是道口强盗路，
以上三路它不走。

There are three roads the sheep won't walk on:
First is the black tiger's road,
Second is the red deer's road,
Third is the robber's road.
These are the three roads the sheep won't walk on.

Urisan dauqidu szaghaya,
Yang huni lii uqujin ghuraan szu,
Qi nige kileda szar giya.

请来歌手我问你，
福羊不吃三种水，
请你说说再商量。

Ask the invited singers"
There are three types of water the sheep doesn't drink—
Please tell us what they are.

Yang huni lii uqujin ghuraan szu,
Nige ni fulaan zhog niurnu szu,
Ghoor ni basnu kaqina,

Ghuraan ni saarnu nimpusina,
Ne ghuraan szunu te lii uqum.

福羊不喝三种水,
一是红崖山涧水,
二是猛虎那口水,
三是老鹰那泪水,
以上三种它不喝。

The sheep doesn't drink three types of water:
First is the water from a red cliff,
Second is a tiger's saliva,
Third is an eagle's tears.
These are the three the sheep doesn't drink.

Dauqidu dii nige szaghaya,
Yang huni lii idejin ghuraan usi wai,
Qi nige nige kileji ughu,
Qi huni idesa darang purgewa.

请来歌手再问你,
福羊不吃三种草,
你来分别说一说,
你要吃羊还困难。

Ask the singers again:
The sheep doesn't eat three sorts of grass—
Please tell us what they are,
Or it will be difficult for you to eat the sheep's flesh.

Yang huni lii idejin ghuraan usi wai,
Nige ni fulaan laa usiwa,
Ghoor ni saarnu foor usiwa,
Ghuraan ni ghuixji deesisan usiwa,
Ne ghuraan usinu te lii ide.

福羊不吃三种草,
一是红崖麝香草,
二是老鹰窝中草,
三是乞丐铺下草,
以上三草它不吃。

The sheep doesn't eat three sorts of grass:
First is grass from a red mountain,
Second is grass from an eagle's nest,
Third is grass from a straw mattress.
These are the three the sheep doesn't eat.

Daudasan dauqidu szaghaya,
Yang huni lii kideejin ghuraan ghajar wai,
Qi nige nige kileji ughu,
Kileji ughu shdasa szarlaya.

请来歌手我问你,
福羊不卧三处地,
请你分别说一说,
若能说出再商量。

Ask the invited singers:
There are three places where the sheep won't lie—
Please tell us what they are,
And we will discuss further if you can tell us.

Yang huni lii kideejin ghuraan ghajarwa,
Nige ni kiree aasi foor,
Ghoor ni fiinu bas foor,
Ghuraan ni ghulnu kadam foor,
Ne ghuraan ghajardu te lii kideem.

福羊不卧三处地,
一是石崖野牛窝,
二是林间老虎窝,
三是深山豺狼窝,
以上三处它不卧。

There are three places where the sheep won't lie:
First is the bison's cave on the cliff,
Second is the tiger's den in the forest,
Third is the wolf's den in the valley.
These are the three places where a sheep won't lie.

Daudasan dauqidu szaghaya,
Yang huni lii saujin ghuraan ghajar wai,

Qi nige nige kileji ughu,
Kile shdasa szarlya.

请来歌手我问你，
福羊不驻三样地，
请你分别说一说，
若能说出再商量。

Ask the invited singers:
There are three places where the sheep won't stay—
Please tell us what they are,
And we will discuss further if you can tell us.

Yang huni lii saujin ghuraan ghajarwa,
Nige ni ncam saugu ghajarwa,
Ghoor ni mori hauligu ghajarwa,
Ghuraan ni njiwanu uronduwa,
Ghuraan ghajardu te lii saum.

福羊不住三样地，
一是山中修仙处，
二是滩里跑马处，
三是在此宾朋处，
此上三地它不驻。

There are three places where the sheep won't stay:
First is the place where people sit in meditation on the mountain,
Second is the place where horses race on the plain,
Third is the place where important guests are permitted to sit.
These are the three where the sheep won't stay.

Daudasan dauqidu szaghaya,
Nghuasidu ghuraan xjadoo wai,
Qi nige nige kileji ughu,
Kile shdasamba szarlaya.

请来歌手我细问，
福羊毛料有三种，
请你分别说一说，
若能说出再商量。

Ask the invited singers:
The sheep produces three different types of woolen cloth—

Please tell us what they are,
And we will discuss further if you can tell us.

Nghuasinu ghuraan xjadoowa,
Nige ni Ghuisangnu fulaan nchogwa,
Ghoor ni Rjanagnu marnag boswa,
Ghuraan ni Mongghulnu qighaan murgewa,
Nghuasinu xjadoo ne ghuraanwa.

福羊毛料那三种,
一是红色藏氆氇,
二是褐色汉毛呢,
三是白色毛褐子,
福羊毛料这三种。

The sheep produces three different types of woolen cloth:
First is red pulu from Tibet,
Second is brown cloth from the land of the Han Chinese,
Third is the white woolen cloth of the Mongghul.
These are the three types of woolen cloth from sheep.

Dauqidu tuuxidu szaghaya,
Yang huni idejin ghuraan usi wai,
Qi nige nige nirenge fuyaa,
Nire fuyaa shdasa szarlaya.

请来歌手我细问,
福羊喜食有三草,
请你分别取其名,
若能取名再商量。

Ask the singers in detail:
The sheep eats three sorts of grass—
Please tell us what they are,
And we will discuss further if you can tell us.

Huni idejin ghuraan usiwa,
Nige ni ghadaanu sman usiwa,
Ghoor ni tangnu joolon usiwa,
Ghuraan ni fiinu ndatin usiwa,
Duraalajin usi ne ghuraanwa.

福羊喜食那三草，
一是崖顶那药草，
二是滩里那嫩草，
三是林间那香草，
福羊喜食这三草。

The sheep eats three sorts of grass:
First is the medicinal herb from the mountains,
Second is the tender grass from the plain,
Third is the sweet grass from the forest.
These are the three sorts of grass the sheep eats.

Hunire ghuraan xjoosi wai,
Xjoosire lii baujin ghuraan xau wai,
Qi nige nige kileji ughu.

那羊未栽有三树，
那树未落有三鸟，
请你分别说一说。

There are three trees on the sheep's body,
Three birds land on the trees—
Please tell us what they are.

Xjoosi nige ni gujinii,
Xjoosi nige ni jisgaanii,
Xjoosi nige ni hoolonii,
Lii bausan xau tolghuinii,
Lii bausan xau jirgenii,
Lii baosan xau gujeenii.

未栽一树是羊脖，
未栽一树是前颈，
未栽一树是咽喉，
未落一鸟是羊头，
未落一鸟是羊心，
未落一鸟是羊肚。

One of the trees is the sheep's neck,
One of the trees is the sheep's ligament,
One of the trees is the sheep's throat.
The place where no bird has landed is the sheep's head,

The place where no bird has landed is the sheep's heart,
The place where no bird has landed is the sheep's stomach.

Hunire baghaji gui bazaar ghuraan wai,
Bazarsge ali aliwa?
Qi nige nige kileji ire.

那羊未筑有三城，
那城分别是哪个？
请你一一来说说。

There are three self-arisen cities in the sheep's body,
What are they?
Please tell us about them one by one.

Tolghuire baghaji gui lagba wai,
Xjaure baghaji gui jirge wai,
Keelendu baghaji gui gidesi wai,
Baghaji gui bazar ghuraanla wai.

羊头未筑大脑城，
上身未筑心脏城，
下身未筑肠子城，
便是未筑羊三城。

The brain is the self-arisen city in the sheep's head,
The heart is the self-arisen city in the sheep's chest,
The intestines are the self-arisen city in the sheep's abdomen.
Those are the three self-arisen cities.

Hunire noor ghuraan wai,
Te noor ali aliwa?
Qi nige nige kileji ughu.

那羊未积有三海，
那海分别是哪个？
请你一一来说说。

There are three lakes in the sheep's body.
What are they?
Please tell us about them one by one.

Hunire ghuraan noorda wai,
Nige ni booro aur noor wai,
Yama gaa huxinsa aur gharina?
Ghoor ni helge qisi noor wai,
Yama gaa shdaasire qisi yauna?
Ghuraan ni gujee fog noor wai,
Yama gaa ghunjosila baasi baana?

那羊未积有三海，
一是肺子为气海，
嘴里出气为什么？
二是肝子为血海，
血通脉中为什么？
三是羊肚为粪海，
密处排粪为什么？

There are three lakes in the sheep's body.
First are the lungs, the lake of air.
Why does air come out of the mouth?
Second is the liver, the lake of blood.
Why does blood circulate inside the vessels?
Third is the stomach, the lake of faeces.
Why do faeces come out of the anus?

Nige ni oosigu aur noorwa,
Huxinsa aur yausa aur jalghaana.
Ghoor ni helge qisi noorwa,
Shdaasisa qisi yausa jim xiigina.
Ghuraan ni gujee fog noorwa,
Ghunjosila baasa xingeelghana.

一是肺子为气海，
嘴不出气咋呼吸。
二是肝子为血海，
血通脉中为吸收。
三是羊肚为粪海，
密处排粪为消化。

First are the lungs, the lake of air.
The air comes out of the mouth to aid breathing.
Second is the liver, the lake of blood.
The blood flows inside the vessels to aid circulation.

Third is the stomach, the lake of faeces.
The faeces come out of the anus to aid digestion.

Dauqi dide qi qangla,
Te yinjannu xjiinu ghajardu,
Nige menhan taawun jong huni wai,
Qi ne xjeegu guinu kun,
Bughu hurgha madu doorona,
Yang huninu waaraa lii tilgem,
Gooro kun sgesa mau kilem,
Hurghoosinu bii sajilgha,
Huni sgesa mau kilem,
Deeren ghar kolnu bii sgelgha,
Kadam sgesa mau kilem.

你这歌手听我说,
在往中阴界上面,
有那福羊一千五,
你这没羞没臊人,
却如鹿羔在下面,
抓住福羊勿防脱,
浪人若见真是羞,
勿让羊粪撒一地,
羊若看见真是羞,
勿教四肢示他人,
恶狼若见真是羞。

Dear singers, please listen:
In the middle of the nether world
There are fifteen hundred sheep.
You shameless men,
If you press the sheep
Under your body and don't release the dear lamb
You will be blamed by other people.
Don't scatter sheep's droppings everywhere
Or you will be blamed by other sheep.
Don't expose its limbs
Or you will be blamed by wolves.

Qi ne dauqi qi qangla,
Niruu tolghuisa doorondaa,
Halgha yesisa jaghandaa,
Kidihaange nghusi wai?
Gur madu xjausa doorondaa,
Narin suulsa haghandaa,
Kidihaange nghusi wai?

你这歌手听我说，
如意宝贝头下面，
如镜护胛骨上面，
数数羊毛有几根？
如帐胸腔往下面，
细细尾巴往上面，
数数羊毛有几根？

Singers, please listen:
From the head
To the upper scapula,
How many types of sheep wool are there?
From the tent-like thoracic cavity
To the upper tail,
How many types of sheep wool are there?

Qi ne dauqidu xjeegunu gua,
Niruu tolghuisa doorondaa,
Halgha yasisa jaghandaa,
Ulamanu qiigui ni tireewa.
Halgha yasisa doorondaa,
Gur madu xjausa jaghandaa,
Dide kunnu mosgu wai.
Gur madu xjausa doorondaa,
Narin suulsa jaghandaa,
Qirignu rgul deel ni wai.
Yang huninu banglasa,
Nige jong qighaan musinu,
Sinaaxji boodagnu yonglaadii.
Nige jong hara hainagnu,
Olo boodagnu yonglaadii.
Nige jong murge gur tenu,
Fuyaanin boodagnu yonglaadii.

你这歌手真没臊，
如意宝贝头下面，
如镜护胛骨上面，
有那上师百纳衣。
如镜护胛骨下面，
再往如帐胸上面，
有那百男盛装艳。
入账胸腔往下面，
细细尾巴往上面，
是那百役寒衣裹。
若说要绑那福羊，
有白镉牛一百头，
可用它们鼻圈绳。
有黑牦牛一百头，
可用它们肚带绳。
有褐账房一百顶，
可用这些账房绳。

You shameless singer:
From the head
To the upper scapula
Is for the bodhisattva's ragged robe.
From the scapula
To the top of the tent-like thoracic cavity
Is for men's clothes.
From the tent-like thoracic cavity
To the upper tail
Is for soldiers' winter robes.
If you are going to tie up the sheep,
A hundred white yaks' nose ropes
Are used to tie it up,
A hundred black yaks' bellybands
Are used to tie it up,
A hundred brown tent ropes,
Are used to it up.

6. Ndiilal

6. 圆满

6. Perfection

Tolghui ni maharegu mahawa,
Tolghuila yama giguna?
Guji ni maha nqoordenwa,
Gujila yama giguna?
Oosgu ni deeren ninewa,
Jirge rjawu madu xjiinduna,
Jirge oosgula yama giguna?

羊头是那肉中王,
拿上羊头干什么?
羊脖是那肉宝塔,
拿上羊脖干什么?
肺子好比四贵妃,
心如君王坐中央,
拿上心肺干什么?

The meat on the sheep's head is the king of all meats:
What are you going to do with it?
The meat on the sheep's neck is a stupa:
What are you going to do with it?
The lungs are like four women,
The heart is like a king, sitting in the center:
What are you going to do with the heart and the lungs?

Tolghui maharegu mahawa,
Ne mahala nuyoon daudana,
Tela gaanu tolghui gua.
Guji maha nqoordenwa,
Ne mahala gaaqan uriya,
Tela gaanu guji gua.
Oosgu deeren ninewa,
Jirge rjawu madu xjiinduna,
Ninesla kuu xjunnaa daudana,
Tela gaanu jirge oosgu gua.

羊头是那肉中王,
拿上肉王为大官,
没有羊头有此因。
羊脖是那肉宝塔,
拿上肉塔请贵人,
没有羊脖为此因。
肺子好比四贵妃,
心如君王坐中央,
拿上王妃请子女,
没有心肺为此因。

The meat on the sheep's head is the king of all meats:
The sheep's head is given as an invitation to officials,
So that's why there's no sheep's head.
The meat on the sheep's neck is a stupa:
The sheep's neck is given as an invitation to esteemed guests,
So that's why there's no sheep's neck.
The lungs are like four women,
The heart is like a king, sitting in the center:
The sheep's lungs and heart are given as an invitation to children,
So that's why there are no sheep's lungs or heart.

Xjau ni lamanqan mahawa,
Yama gaanu xjau ni gua?
Hoolo ni haldan shdaasiwa,
Yama gaanu hoolo ni gua?
Guji ni mengu shdaasiwa,
Yama gaanu guji ni gua?

肉中尖子是羊胸,
没有羊胸为什么?
肉中金线是羊喉,
没有羊喉为什么?
肉中银钱是前颈,
没有前颈为什么?

The chest meat is excellent meat,
Why isn't there any left?
The throat is a golden thread,
Why isn't there any left?
The neck is a silver thread,
Why isn't there any left?

Xjau ni lamanqan mahawa,
Xjaunu aagusge waraaxja,
Tela gaanu xjau ni gua.
Hoolo ni haldan shdaasiwa,
Hoolonu mauxi tailaaxja,
Tela gaanu hoolo ni gua.
Guji ni mengu shdaasiwa,
Gujinu nuhuidu ughoodija,
Tela gaanu guji ni gua.

肉中尖子是羊胸,
羊胸给了姑娘们,
不见尖子为此因。
肉中金线是羊喉,
羊喉给了猫儿们,
不见金线为此因。
肉中银线是前颈,
前颈给了守门狗,
不见银线为此因。

The chest meat is excellent meat;
The chest has been taken away by women,
So that's why there's none left.
The throat is a golden thread;
The throat has been taken away by the cat,
So that's why there's none left.
The neck is a silver thread;
The neck was given to the dog,
So that's why there's none left.

Halge ni maharegu lumbuwa,
Yama gaanu lumbu gua?
Gidesi maharegu xaniwa,
Yama gaanu xani gua?
Ghonsi ama maharegu mughuiwa,
Yama gaanu mughui gua?

肝子是那肉中臣,
没有肉臣为什么?
肠子是那肉庄员,
没有庄员为什么?

肛门是那肉毒蛇，
没有毒蛇为什么？

The liver is another key meat in the sheep:
Why isn't there any left?
The intestines act like a member of the sheep's clan:
Why aren't there any left?
The anus is like a snake among the meat:
Why isn't there any left?

Halge ni maharegu lumbuwa,
Lumbunu doorogu kundu ughudija,
Tela gaanu halge gua.
Gidesi maharegu xaniwa,
Xani ayildu ughudija,
Tela gaanu gidesi gua.
Ghonsi mughuila sarlana,
Ghonsinu nuhuidu ughudija,
Tela gaanu ghonsi gua.

肝子是那肉中臣，
肉臣给了下人们，
不见肝子为此因。
肠子是那肉庄员，
庄员给了乡亲们，
不见肠子为此因。
肛门如那肉毒蛇，
肛门给了守门狗，
不见肛门为此因。

The liver is another key meat in the sheep;
The liver has been distributed to our people,
That's why there's none left.
The intestines act like a member of the sheep's clan;
The intestines have been distributed to the villagers,
That's why there are none left.
The anus is like a snake among the meat;
The anus has been thrown to the dog,
That's why there's none left.

Tolghui qongqanla sarlana,
Tingerdu nesisa yamarwa?
Qigi xaula sarlana,
Xaudu jaar guise yamarwa?
Nudu nara sarawa,
Ghajardu bausa yamarwa?

头羊好比大鹏鸟,
大鹏傲空什么样?
羊耳好比俩小鸟,
小鸟无翅什么样?
羊眼如比日和月,
日月照地什么样?

The sheep's head is like a phoenix,
What would it be like if it flew into the sky?
The sheep's ears are like a bird,
What would it be like if it had no wings?
The sheep's eyes are like the sun and moon,
What would it be like if the sun and moon shone on the ground?

Tolghui qongqanla sarlana,
Tingerdu nesaa gharaa xjisa,
Ghajarnu mughuinu ideguna.
Qigi ghoor xaula sarlana,
Jaar ni oosaa kuraadisa,
Rgornu kuu xjun tagqorwa.
Nudu nara sarala sarlana,
Gireel ni gharaa iresamba,
Hara ghajardu szolge wai.

羊头好比大鹏鸟,
一旦展翅天上飞,
地上毒蛇当食物。
羊耳好比俩小鸟,
一旦羽翼丰满时,
定是雄鹰好子孙。
羊眼好比日和月,
一旦发出光芒时,
南赡部洲显庄严。

The sheep's head is like a phoenix:
If it flew in the sky
It would eat snakes on the ground.
The sheep's ears are like a bird:
If its wings grew
It would be the excellent offspring of an eagle.
The sheep's eyes are like the sun and moon:
If they had rays of light
It would be brighter in this world.

Hawar ni haldan dongle sarlana,
Dongnu puulesa yamarwa?
Yiruu ni ghadirla sarlana,
Ghadirnu janqisa yamarwa?
Shdi ni gakala sarlana,
Pujignu moxisa yamarwa?

羊鼻好比金角号，
吹这金号什么样？
下颌好比快镰刀，
打这快镰什么样？
牙齿如经三十字，
你说这字怎么讲？

The sheep's nose is like a golden trumpet:
How will it sound if it is blown?
The sheep's jaw is like a sickle:
What will it do if we sharpen it?
The sheep's teeth are like the thirty letters of the Tibetan alphabet:
How will they sound if we recite them?

Hawar ni haldan dongle sarlana,
Dongnu puulee dongghudisa,
Rgombanu sog dongle sarlana.
Yiruu ni ghadirla sarlana,
Huja ghadirnu janqaadisa,
Usi ghadisa qirwalw.
Shdi ni gakala sarlana,
Nenu tusaanii mudeedisa,
Sasii hguseedu ulama wai.

羊鼻好比金角号，
金角号筒吹响时，
就像寺院法会号。
下颌好比快镰刀，
一旦快镰打好时，
如割青苗很轻松。
牙齿如经三十字，
一旦得知其好处，
此生来世有上师。

The sheep's nose is like a golden trumpet;
If the trumpet were blown
It would sound like a Buddhist ceremony.
The sheep's jaw is like a sickle;
If it were sharpened
It would easily cut green grass.
The sheep's teeth are like the thirty letters of the Tibetan alphabet;
If one knew their benefit
One would be reincarnated as a bodhisattva.

Hajar huiqaala sarlana,
Ne huiqaadu yaan sain wai?
Kile darqagla sarlana,
Darqagnu iredalnu kileji ughu?
Huxi usiqi kaardawa,
Usi idejinnu kileji ughu?

上颌好比经卷螺，
你说这经啥好处？
舌头好比一红旗，
你说这旗做什么？
这嘴好比食草畜，
畜生食草为什么？

The sheep's face is like a Buddhist scripture:
What benefit does the scripture have?
The sheep's tongue is like a flag:
What benefit does the flag have?
The sheep's mouth is like a horse:
Why does the horse have grass?

Hajar huiqaala sarlana,
Qiinu guleji mudelghana,
Gaaqan baghaxidu szaghagunii.
Kile darqagla sarlana,
Ne darqagnu nige jiisa,
Shge tingernu hurmiinii.
Huxi usi idejin kaardawa,
Kaarda usi idela xjisamba,
Njeenaa njeenaanaa tujeenii.

上颌好比经卷撂,
是说佛法来路广,
正对恩师想请教。
舌头好比一红旗,
是说这旗一举起,
可做梵天下围裙。
这嘴好比食草畜,
是说畜生去食草,
只为自己养自己。

The sheep's face is like a Buddhist scripture
That lets people know of the scripture,
And summons a respected teacher to expound more Buddhist scriptures.
The sheep's tongue is like a flag
That when raised
Becomes the apron of great Heaven.
The sheep's mouth is like a horse
That goes to eat grass
Only to fill its stomach.

Nuri ni sbaila sarlana,
Sbainu iredalnu qi kile?
Xjau ni qighaan gurla sarlana,
Gurnu iredalnu qi kile?
Haibsi huyiila sarlana,
Huyiinu iredalnu qi kile?

羊腰好比长青稞,
你说青稞做什么?
胸椎好比白帐篷,
搭起白帐为什么?
肋骨好比白甲胄,

你说这又为什么?

The sheep's back is like a highland barley seed:
What benefit does the highland barley seed have?
The sheep's chest is like a white tent:
What benefit does the white tent have?
The sheep's ribs are like armour:
What benefit does the armour have?

Nuri sbaila sarlana,
Sbainu ghajardu tarisa,
Duraasi noor madu xuuji wai.
Xjau ni qighaan gurla sarlana,
Qighaan gurnu pusilghasa,
Njiwa baulghgu ghajar wai.
Haibsi huyiila sarlana,
Huyiinu buyerenaa mosaadisa,
Duuyaanu danglajin baatir wai.

羊腰好比长青稞,
是说青稞种地里,
可酿美酒盈如海。
胸椎好比白帐篷,
是说搭起白帐篷,
便是贵客落座处。
肋骨好比白甲胄,
是说甲胄穿身上,
便成御敌一勇士。

The sheep's back is like a highland barley seed;
If the highland barley seed is cultivated
An ocean of liquor can be distilled.
The sheep's chest is like a white tent;
If the white tent is pitched
Esteemed guests can be invited to come and sit.
The sheep's ribs are like armour;
If the armour is worn
One can become a hero.

Suul yasinu gulesa,
Saar nesigula sarlana,

Saar nesiji yaaguna?
Halgha yasinu gulesa,
Haldan mengula huloona,
Haldan mengula yaaguna?
Ghar yasinu gulesa,
Baatir tela hamdulalghana,
Duuyaanu alaji yaaguna?

尾椎好似鹰在飞，
往往理解成觅食，
鹰飞天空为什么？
一听说起肩胛骨，
往往理解成积财，
富人积财为什么？
一听说起前腿骨，
往往理解成勇士，
男儿杀敌为什么？

The sheep's caudal vertebrae
Are like flying eagles.
Why do eagles fly?
The sheep's scapulae
Are like people begging for money.
Why do people collect money?
The sheep's front leg bones
Are like warriors.
Why does one fight the enemy?

Suul yasinu gulena,
Tenu iredal ni tigiingewa,
Urgondu uliji nesina.
Halgha yesinu gulesa,
Haldan mengula huloona,
Xjirbuudu uliji huloona.
Ghar yesinu gulena,
Baatir tela hamdulalghana,
Debxjirdu uliji hamdulalghana.

尾椎好似鹰在飞，
鹰飞天空是这样，
鹰飞天空为自由。
一听说起肩胛骨，

往往理解成积财,
富人积财为幸福。
一听说起前腿骨,
往往理解成勇士,
男儿杀敌为安宁。

The sheep's caudal vertebrae
Are like flying eagles
In order to be free.
The sheep's scapulae
Are like people collecting money
In order to have a happy life.
The sheep's front leg bones
Are like warriors
Who fight their enemies for peace.

Udig demdergiinu nurdaghawa,
Demdergii nurdaghanu yaan gulena?
Shghai yasi warang dongle sarlana,
Dong hgernu qanglasa yaan gulena?

膝骨如那傻人拳,
傻人捏拳怎么讲?
腿骨好比右旋螺,
听闻螺声怎么讲?

The sheep's knees are like a foolish man's fists;
What do his fists mean?
The sheep's leg bones are like a conch;
What does a conch's sound mean?

Udig demdergiinu nurdaghawa,
Demdergii nurdaghanaa neekisa,
Yama hara jarla nigewa.
Shghai yasi warang dong madu,
Dong daunu nige qanglasa,
Hguseedu sain moornu neewaadijii.

膝骨如那傻人拳,
是说傻人捏拳头,
就像黑熊更蠢笨。
腿骨好比右旋螺,

是说听闻右螺声，
今生善道可开启。

The sheep's knees are like a foolish man's fists:
When a foolish man punches with his fists
He appears as awkward as a black bear.
The sheep's leg bones are like a conch:
When one hears the conch's sound
It means good fortune in this generation has begun.

Kol ni ghadasila sarlana,
Bayaan kun jong mori fuyaasa,
Yaandu nere fuyaana joo?
Tughui ni numu smuwa,
Qi kile yaandu tidana?
Sag ni bas qimsila sarlana,
Bas huloduji yausamba,
Yaandu ulaanu yausamba?

后腿如那拴马桩，
你说富人拴百马，
究竟那是为什么？
肘子好比白弓箭，
你说拉弓为什么？
关节好比老虎爪，
老虎去往偏远处，
究竟那是为什么？

The sheep's feet are like a hitching post
Where rich men tie their hundreds of horses.
Why do they tie them to the hitching post?
The sheep's elbows are like a bow and arrow.
Why do people draw the bow?
The sheep's joints are like a tiger's paw.
The tiger goes far away.
Why does the tiger go such a long distance?

Kol ni ghadasila sarlana,
Bayaan kun morinaa fuyaasamba,
Haldan mengu ngurooji irem.
Tughui ni numu smuwa,

Raari duuyaanu kujile shdam.
Sag ni bas qimsila sarlana,
Bas radagnu rjawuna.

后腿如那拴马桩,
富人一旦拴百马,
财源滚滚获利来。
肘子好比百弓箭,
凶猛敌手必征服。
关节好比老虎爪,
老虎是那百兽王。

The sheep's feet are like a hitching post.
If rich men tie their hundreds of horses
Profits will pour in from all sides.
The sheep's elbows are like a bow and arrow
That can defeat its great enemy.
The sheep's joints are like a tiger's paw.
The tiger is the king of all beasts.

Ayil kuxin qangla joo,
Dauqi ghuila yixida,
Saihange nige qanglaldu.
Huninu arang marangdu jarisa,
Dii da mughuila nige wai.
Huinogunaa ndangge baghasa,
Hunidu shmolomge jaalgaya.

我请庄员听一听,
尤其在座二歌手,
你们好好听一听。
无缘无故去宰羊,
就像毒蝎不见光。
只为来世得安乐,
谨向福羊做祈祷。

All tribal members please listen,
Particularly you two singers,
Listen carefully please.
If someone casually slaughters a sheep
Then their heart is as evil as a poisonous snake.
In order for your next life to be bright
Please bless the sheep.

About the Texts

The Ballad of Taipinggoor

Sghau: 1993 fon
> Ghajar: Buuzin Naaja
> Dauqi: Zhin Qonfu
> Huraaqin: Su Chinshuu
> Turuuleji furooliqin: Su Chinshuu, Qiixinyo

搜集时间：1993年
> 搜集地点：威远镇纳家村
> 讲唱者：郑全福
> 搜集者：苏成寿
> 整理翻译：苏成寿，祁兴月

Collected in: 1993
> From: Najia Village, Weiyuan
> Singer: Zheng Quangu
> Collector: Su Chengshou
> Translators: Su Chengshou and Qi Xinyue

The Ballad of Marshal Qi

Sghau: 1987 fon
> Ghajar: Xjir ghul Loxoo,
> Dauqi: Qau Wusher
> Turuuleqin: Qau Zhiliang
> Mongghulqileqin: Qau Zhiliang, Dun Wunshuu

搜集时间: 1987年
  搜集地点:东沟乡洛少村
  讲唱者: 乔五十二
  搜集整理:乔志良
  土文翻译:乔志良, 董文寿

Collected in: 1987
  From: Luxuu Village, Donggou Township
  Singer: Qau Wusher
  Collector: Qau Zhiliang
  Translators: Qau Zhiliang and Dun Wunshuu

Laarimbu and Qiimunso

Sghau: 1989 fon
  Ghajar: Xjir ghul Szangghul, Qarsi
  Dauqi: Yang Zhanliin, Su Rinqanso
  Turuuleqin: Qau Ziliang
  Qidarqileqin: Qau Ziliang

搜集时间: 1989年
  搜集地点:东沟乡年先村,卡子村
  唱述者: 杨占林, 苏仁欠素
  搜集整理:乔志良
  汉文翻译: 乔志良

Collected in: 1989
  From: Szangghul and Qarsi Villages in Dongou Township
  Singers: Yang Zhanliin and Su Rinqanso
  Collector: Qau Ziliang
  Translator: Qau Ziliang

The Song of the Dildima Bird

Sghou: 1998 fon
  Ghajar: Xjir ghul Qarsi
  Dauqi: SuRinqanso
  Turuuleqin: Dun Wunshuu
  Qidarqileqin: Dun Wunshuu

搜集时间：1998年
　　搜集地点：东沟乡卡子村
　　演唱者：苏仁欠索
　　搜集整理：董文寿
　　汉文翻译：董文寿

Collected in: 1998
　　From: Qarsi Village, Donggou Town
　　Singer: Su Rinqanso
　　Collector: Dung Wunshuu
　　Translator: Dung Wunshuu

The Song of the Calf

Sghau: 1983 fonnu 10 sara
　　Ghajar: Fulaannara Jighur
　　Dauqi: Lu Sangrjixja
　　Turuuleqin: Lu Wunzhun
　　Qidarqileqin: Lu Wunzhun

搜集时间：1983年10月
　　搜集地点：五十镇卓科村
　　唱述者：鲁桑吉什加
　　记录者：鲁文忠
　　汉文翻译：鲁文忠

Collected in: October 1983
　　From: Jighuar Village, Wushi Town
　　Singer: Lu Sangrjixja
　　Collector: Lu Wunzhun
　　Translator: Lu Wunzhun

The Crop-Planting Song

Sghau: 1938 fon
　　Ghajar: Narin ghul Shge Hhuniqi,
　　Dauqi: Ngombuxja
　　Juuriqin: [Dii lus] Si Laudii
　　Turuuleji Qidariqileqin: Lu Wunzhun

搜集时间:1938年
　搜集地点:东山乡大泉村
　讲述者:官布希加
　记录者:【德】斯劳德
　整理翻译:鲁文忠

Collected in: 1938
　From: Daquan Village, Dongshan Township
　Singer: Ngombuxja
　Collector: Dominik Schröder
　Translator: Lu Wenzhong

The Song of the Sheep

Sghau: 1993 fon — 1996 fon
　Ghajar: Ndarma Hghuarin, Xjir ghul Szang ghul
　Dauqi: Yii Nianbu, So Yiixiniru, Su Yimsirang
　Huraaqin: Qau Sinhua
　Turuuleji furooliqin: Qau Sinhua, Qau Sinju

搜集时间:1993年至1996年
　搜集地点:丹麻镇桦林村, 东沟乡年先村
　讲唱者: 伊娘布, 男, 土族, 66岁
　索依西尼柔, 男, 土族, 81岁 (已故)
　苏英四让, 男, 土族, 66岁
　搜集者: 乔生华
　整理翻译:乔生华, 乔生菊

Collected in: 1993–1996
　From: Hualin Village, Danma Township, and Nianxian Village,
Donggou Township
　Singers: Yi Niangbu, Suo Yixinirou and Su Yingsirang
　Collector: Qiao Shenghua
　Translators: Qiao Shenghua and Qiao Shengju

References

Aaguqog. 2012. Larinbog Qiminsuu. In Jugui, Limusishiden, Ha Mingzong and Kevin Stuart (eds). *Three Treasures-Huzhu Mongghul Folklore. Asian Highlands Perspectives* 16:146.

Anonymous. 1932. Tangbabu, Jiuwei Dong Qitusi Xiamin. 塘巴堡, 旧为东祁土司辖民. Tangba Fork, the people for the East Qi tusi in the Past. *Zuijin Zhi Qinghai*. 最近之青海. *Recently Qinghai*: 269.

Gesangben 格桑本. 1999. Baiya Gucheng. 白崖古城. The Baiya Citadel. Huzhuxian Ping'anxian Wenwuzhi 互助县平安县文物志. Huzhu County and Ping'an County Cultural Relics Record: 39.

Lai Weili 来维礼, Yang Fangke 杨方柯 Mo Zinu 莫自恕. 1977. Nianbo Shixi Tusi… 碾伯世袭土司… Nianbo Hereditary Tusi… Xiningfu Xuzhi. 西宁府续志. The Xining Prefecture Record Continuation: 157.

Limusishiden and Kevin Stuart. 1995. Larinbuda and Jiminsu: A Monguor Tragedy. *Asian Theatre Journal* 12.2:221–63.

Limusishiden and Kevin Stuart. 2011. Larinbu and Jiminsu. In Victor Mair and Mark Bender (eds). *Columbia Anthology of Chinese Folk and Popular Literature.* New York: Columbia University Press, 174–76.

Limusishiden, Ha Mingzhong, and Kevin Stuart. 2013. "Niidosang: A Huzhu Mongghul (Tu) Deity." *Studia Orientalia* 113:127–43.

Lu Wenzhong. 2009. *Mongghul Ulon Kun Dundagu Hghui Xulig* [Mongghul Long Narratives]. Huzhu Mongghul Autonomous County: Huzhu Mongghul Ethnic and Religious Office 互助土族自治县民族宗教事务局 (*Huzhu Tuzu zizhixian minzu zongjiao shiwuju*).

Qi Wenru 祁文汝. 2012. Tanmi (Qijia Yanxi) Jiqi Yuanfadi . 探秘(祁家延西)及其源发地. Exploring the *Ballad of Marshal Qi* and its Place of Origin. *Zhongguo Tuzu*. 中国土族. *China's Tu Nationality*. 55:66–69.

Schröder, D. 1952–1953. Zur Religion der Tujen des Sininggebietes (Kukunor) [On the Religion of the Monguor of the Xining Region (Koknor)]. *Anthropos* 47:1–79, 620–58, 822–70; 48:202–49. [Available in an English translation (1962) by Richard Neuse in the Human Relations Area Files AE9].

Stuart, Kevin and Limusishiden (eds). 1994. China's Monguor Minority: Ethnography and Folktales. *Sino-Platonic Papers* 59.

Yang Yingju 杨应琚. 1747. Jinhua Fuzongbing Qi Zhongzhimu. 金华副总兵祁仲豸墓… Jinhua Vice-commanding Officer, Qi Zhongzhi's Tomb. Xiningfu Xinzhi. Dili. Guji. 西宁府新志.地理.古迹. *The Xining Prefecture New Record: Geography and Relics*. 234.

Yang Yingju 杨应琚. 1747. Qi Zhongzhi Qi Bozhi Diye. 祁仲豸, 伯豸弟也… Qi Zhongzhi is Qi Bozhi's Younger Brother… Xiningfu Xinzhi. Zhengxian. Renwu. 西宁府新志.征献.人物. *The Xining Prefecture New Record: Achievements and Figures*: 704–05.

Selected Non-English Terms[1]

A

Amoghasiddhi
Ashiji 阿士记

B

Bagharisang
Baiya Gucheng 白崖古城
Baiya Village 白崖村
boja
Bulong 布隆

C

Chai 柴
Chai Guozhu 柴国柱
Chang 常
Chang *bazong* 常把总
Changshou 长寿
Chang Yuzhang 常煜章
Chang Zenghua 常增华
Chai Zongbing 柴总兵
Chenggao 承诰
Chongzhen 崇祯

---

1   Regular nouns are italicized in this list; proper nouns are not. Chinese or Tibetan equivalents are provided where possible.

D

Dacaizi 大菜子
Dacaizigou 大菜子沟
Danma Town 丹麻镇
Dili 地理
Dasi 大寺
Donggou 东沟(乡)
Donghe townships 东河乡
Dongshan Township 东山乡
Duanzhu 端竹
Duluun Lunkuang

E

Eerduosi 鄂尔多斯
Erxiangbu 二乡堡

F

falala
Fulaan Nara
fuluu
Fushun City 抚顺

G

g.yang dkar glu གཡང་དཀར་གླུ
Gannan 甘南
Ganzhou 甘州
Gaolan 皋兰
Geerdan 葛尔旦
Gesangben 格桑本
Gong 龚
Gongchang 巩昌
Gongta 公他
Guji 古迹
guoshi 国师

H

halala
Han Chinese 汉族
harere
Haliqi
Hebao 河保
Hebei 河北
Heihe 黑河
Hehuang 河湟
Hekouxiang 河口乡
Hexi 河西
HMNDX Szarbaten Da Qii Uilenu Ges 互助土族自治县民族宗教事务局
Hongshui 洪水
Hongyazigou 红崖子沟(乡)
Huangpu 黄埔
Huang Taiji 皇太极
Huangzhong 湟中
Huangyuan 湟源
hutukhtu
Huzhu County 互助县
Huzhuxian Ping'anxian Wenwuzhi 互助县平安县文物志

J

Jaazoolang
'Jam dbyangs zhad pa འཇམ་དབྱངས་ཞད་པ།
Jiaomu 角木
Jiaqing 嘉庆
Jieguanting 接官亭
Jigmezhashgang
Jijiawan 吉家湾
Jilin 吉林
Jin 金
Jingguantian 井观天
Jingxiangyang 晋襄阳
Jingxian 锦县
Jingyang 景阳
Jinhua 金华
Jingyongchang 晋永昌
Jinhua Fuzongbing Qi Zhongzhimu 金华副总兵祁仲豸墓.

K

kadada
kadiedie
Kangxi 康熙
Kegan 科干
Kuixin 魁星
Kundulu 坤都鲁

L

Laarimbu
Labrang བླ་བྲང་།
Lai Weili 来维礼
Lamusang
Lanzhou 兰州
Ledu 乐都
Li 李
Liangzhou 凉州
Liaodong 辽东
Liaoning 辽宁
Liaoyang 辽阳
Lingtao 临洮
Li Honglin 李洪林
Liluo 里落
Limusishiden
Liu 刘
Liu Qu 刘渠
Lixian 礼县
Li Yande 李延德
Longqing 隆庆
Longwei 龙尾
Luoyang 洛阳
Lǚyangyi 闾阳驿
Lu Wenzhong 鲁文忠

M

Mahavaiocana
Mingxizong 明熹宗
Mongghul (Tu 土族, Monguor)
Mo Zinu 莫自恕
Muzong 穆宗

N

Nanchuan 南川
Ngombuxja
Nianbo Shixi Tusi 碾伯世袭土司
niudaar
Niidosang
Njamyang
nkamba
Nurhaci 努尔哈赤

P

Pingliang 平凉
Pingyang 平阳
Puhe 蒲河

Q

Qarog
Qiaka 恰卡
Qianlong 乾隆
Qianjiu 千九
Qi Bozhi Diye 祁伯豸弟也
Qi Bing 祁炳
Qi Bingzhong 祁秉忠
Qi Guiyu 祁贵玉
Qi Guobing 祁国屏
Qi Huan 祁焕
Qi Lin 祁麟
Qi Huisi 祁惠思
Qijiafengwan 祁家坟湾
Qiija Yanxii 祁家延西
Qi Mingsi 祁民思
Qingshuibu 清水堡
Qinhuangdao City 秦皇岛市
Qinzhou 秦州
Qi *tusi,* Qi Bingzhong 祁土司, 祁秉忠
Qi Wenru 祁文汝
Qi Yinsi 祁银思
Qi Youren 祁有仁
Qi Zhongzhi 祁仲豸
Qi Zongbin 祁总兵
Qiimunso

S

Saeryou 萨尔游
Shaba 沙坝
Shanhaiguan 山海关
Shashatu 刹刹兔
Shdara Township 达拉乡
Shenyang 沈阳
Shoushan 寿山
Shunzhi 顺治
Songzhu Lamasery
Sun Degong 孙得功
Suzhou 肃州
Songduo 松多(乡)
Szii

T

Taizi 台子(乡)
Taipingeer 太平哥儿
Tangba 塘巴
Tangbabu, Jiuwei Dong Qitusi Xiamin 塘巴堡, 旧为东祁土司辖民
Tangdarihgiima
Tanmi (Marshal Qi) Jiqi Yuanfadi 探秘(祁家延西)及其源发地
Tongzhi 同治
Tianqi 天启
Tieling 铁岭
Tong 童

W

Wailuo 外落
Wang Fucheng 王铺臣
Wang Jinbao 王进宝
Wanli 万历
Wawu
Weiyuan Town 威远镇
Wen 文
Wu Sangui 吴三桂
Wushi Town 五十镇
Wuqang
Wutai Mountain

X

xanjiang 参将
Xiahe 夏河
Xiaosi 小寺
Xiaozhuang 小庄
Xiaoquzhang 小曲掌
Xie Lianji 解连吉
Xigu 西固
Xihe 西河
Xikang西康
Xining 西宁
Xincheng 新城
Xiningfu Xinzhi西宁府新志
Xiningfu Xuzhi 西宁府续志
Xiping 西平

Y

Yangka Luu
Yaomu 药木
Yatou 崖头
Yang Fangke 杨方柯
Yang Yingju 杨应琚
Yirmu
Yongan 永安
Yongchang 永昌
youjun 右军
yuanyang 鸳鸯

Z

Zhabaesseer
Zhangjia 张家
Zhangjiahewan 张家河湾
Zhangjiakou 张家口
Zhaofan 肇藩
Zhaoyan 肇衍
Zhengxian. Renwu征献.人物.
Zhenhai 镇海
Zhongguo Tuzu 中国土族
zhongjun 中军
Zhuanglang 庄浪
Zhumaluo 助马路
Zu Dashou 祖大寿
Zuijin Zhi Qinghai 最近之青海

This book need not end here…

At Open Book Publishers, we are changing the nature of the traditional academic book. The title you have just read will not be left on a library shelf, but will be accessed online by hundreds of readers each month across the globe. OBP publishes only the best academic work: each title passes through a rigorous peer-review process. We make all our books free to read online so that students, researchers and members of the public who can't afford a printed edition will have access to the same ideas.
This book and additional content is available at:
https://www.openbookpublishers.com/product/638

Customize

Personalize your copy of this book or design new books using OBP and third-party material. Take chapters or whole books from our published list and make a special edition, a new anthology or an illuminating coursepack. Each customized edition will be produced as a paperback and a downloadable PDF. Find out more at:
https://www.openbookpublishers.com/section/59/1

Donate

If you enjoyed this book, and feel that research like this should be available to all readers, regardless of their income, please think about donating to us. We do not operate for profit and all donations, as with all other revenue we generate, will be used to finance new Open Access publications.
https://www.openbookpublishers.com/section/13/1/support-us

Like Open Book Publishers

Follow @OpenBookPublish

BLOG   Read more at the OBP Blog

You may also be interested in:

Oral Literature in the Digital Age
Archiving Orality and Connecting with Communities

Edited by Mark Turin, Claire Wheeler and Eleanor Wilkinson

https://www.openbookpublishers.com/product/186

Frontier Encounters
Knowledge and Practice at the Russian, Chinese and Mongolian Border

Edited by Franck Billé, Grégory Delaplace and Caroline Humphrey

https://www.openbookpublishers.com/product/139

Stories from Quechan Oral Literature

Linguistic work by A.M. Halpern and Amy Miller

https://www.openbookpublishers.com/product/142

Xiipúktan (First of All)
Three Views of the Origins of the Quechan People

George Bryant (linguistic work by Amy Miller)

http://www.openbookpublishers.com/product/141

www.ingramcontent.com/pod-product-compliance
Lightning Source LLC
Chambersburg PA
CBHW070747030726
47504CB00003B/461